African Orchids

AFRICAN ORCHIDS
in the Wild
and in Cultivation

Isobyl and Eric la Croix

Timber Press
Portland, Oregon

All color photographs by Eric la Croix, unless otherwise stated.

Published in 1997 by
Timber Press, Inc.
The Haseltine Building
133 S.W. Second Avenue, Suite 450
Portland, Oregon 97204, U.S.A.

ISBN 0-88192-405-9

Printed in Hong Kong

Library of Congress Cataloging-in-Publication Data

La Croix, I. F.
    African orchids in the wild and in cultivation / Isobyl and Eric la Croix.
        p. cm.
    Includes bibliographical references (p.   ) and index.
    ISBN 0-88192-405-9
    1. Orchid culture.   2. Orchids–Africa, Sub-Saharan.   I. La Croix,
Eric.   II. Title.
    SB409.L22   1997
    635.9'344–dc21
                                                                    96-54603
                                                                        CIP

Contents

Color plates follow page 256.

Preface

This book has been written mainly because so many people have said that it is difficult to find information on African orchids. Some countries are covered by regional floras and other books, there are monographs on several genera, and there are numerous scientific papers and articles in orchid journals, but many of these are out of print and inaccessible. There is no one book to which a person can refer if, for example, an unfamiliar species is listed in a catalog, or if the name is familiar but the details of habitat are unknown.

Africa has fewer orchid species than do other tropical continents, with about 1550 species in 99 genera. The epiphytic orchids are rarely brightly colored, and few have large flowers, yet they have a beauty of their own, and more and more people are falling under their spell. The terrestrial orchids, on the other hand, include some of the most beautiful and vividly colored orchids in the world, yet these, apart from *Disa uniflora* and its relatives and hybrids, are rarely grown. All African orchids are increasing in popularity, as indeed are species orchids of all kinds.

We have tried to include all plants that we have seen in any nursery list or that we know are being grown, even if these orchids are not available commercially. There is always the hope that they will be propagated and become more widely available. The more people who grow a particular species, the more secure its future is likely to be. We have also included a few species that we are fairly sure are not at present in cultivation, but would be well worth growing, in the hope that they might be introduced in the future. Even so, it is certain that we must have omitted something.

Although this book is titled *African Orchids in the Wild and in Cultivation,* it deals only with Africa south of the Sahara. The terrestrial orchids of North Africa, in coun-

7

tries bordering the Mediterranean, are species with European affinities and do not have a place here. We have not included the orchids of Madagascar and other Indian Ocean islands, such as the Comoro and the Mascarene Islands (Mauritius and Réunion), as to do so would make this book of unmanageable length. While these islands share many genera with mainland Africa, they have relatively few species in common and there are also many endemic genera. We do include the islands off the west coast of Africa, such as São Tomé and Príncipe, Bioko (Fernando Po), and Pagalu (Annobón). To our knowledge, they have no endemic genera, and although they have a few endemic species, these are closely related to other species that occur on the mainland.

We have avoided the use of botanical terms as much as possible, but in some cases they are the shortest way of saying something. It is easy to say "sword-shaped" instead of "ensiform," for example, but much quicker to say "inflorescence secund" than "inflorescence with all the flowers on one side and facing the same way." Also, there is no convenient way to describe shapes of leaves and petals other than with terms such as "lanceolate" and "obovate." Any unfamiliar terms should be explained in the glossary and in the diagrams showing shapes.

Measurements are given first in metric, with the equivalent English unit of measure in parenthesis, with one exception: flower measurements given in millimeters are not converted as they are too small to be meaningful in the English system of measures.

Acknowledgments

We are grateful to all the people who took the time to read through our lists of species in cultivation and add to it where appropriate. Going back in time, we should like to thank all our friends who went with us into the bush, in a variety of countries, to look for orchids, especially our sons Neil and Tim.

More specifically, we want to thank Kath Fairhurst for help and advice with the chapter on propagation; Jaco Truter for telling us what is grown in South Africa and how he grows it; and Dr. Louis Vogelpoel for invaluable information on growing *Disa uniflora* and its hybrids, and Dr. Vogelpoel again and Mrs. Joyce Stewart for very kindly letting us use some of their photographs.

Illustrations of Orchid Flowers, Leaves, Petals, and Inflorescences

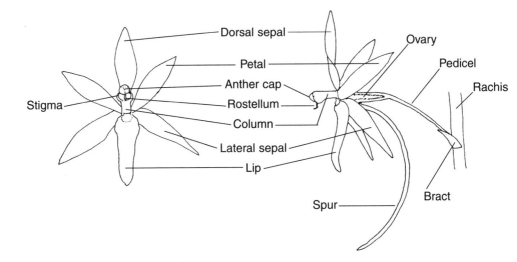

Figure 1-1. Parts of an orchid flower (*Aerangis* sp.).

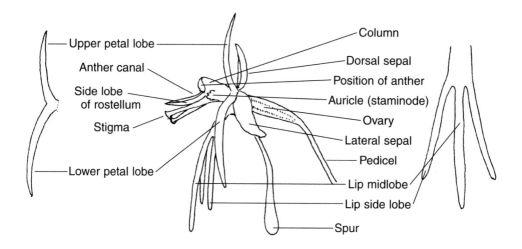

Figure 1-2. Parts of an orchid flower (*Habenaria* sp.).

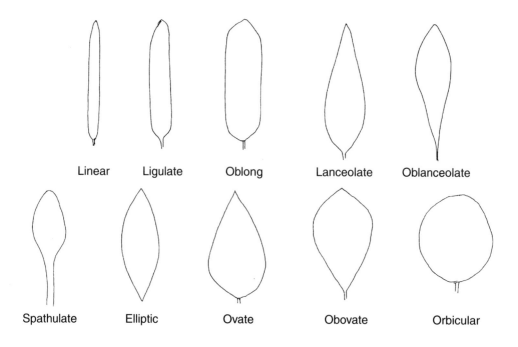

Figure 1-3. Shapes of orchid leaves and petals.

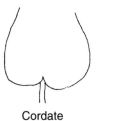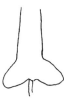

| Cordate | Sagittate | Hastate | Auriculate |

Figure 1-4. Shapes of orchid leaf and petal bases.

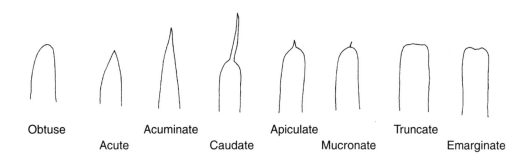

Obtuse   Acuminate   Apiculate   Truncate

      Acute   Caudate   Mucronate   Emarginate

Figure 1-5. Shapes of orchid leaf and petal apices.

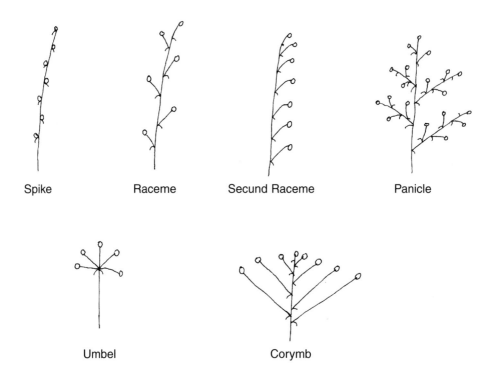

Figure 1-6. Types of orchid inflorescences.

Part 1

Chapter 1

Geography and Climate

Africa to the north and west of a line drawn from western Ethiopia to northern Angola is generally lower than the area to the south and east of that line; the former consists mainly of sedimentary basins and upland plains, 150–600 m (500–2000 ft.) above sea level and includes the catchment areas of several large rivers, the lower Nile, Senegal, Niger, Shari, and Zaire. There is very little land higher than 1000 m (3300 ft.), except for the Jos plateau in Nigeria, the Cameroon Highlands, and Jebel Marra in Sudan. Most of what White (1983) refers to as "High Africa," that is, the area to the south and east of the line, is more than 1000 m (3300 ft.) in altitude, except for Somalia, the Mozambique lowlands, and relatively narrow coastal strips and valleys elsewhere.

In "High Africa" the Rift Valley is the most striking feature. In fact, there are two fault lines. The eastern rift includes the Red Sea, the Gulf of Aden, and the Afar Depression; it splits the Ethiopian plateau and runs from Lake Turkana across the Kenya Highlands and through Tanzania. The western rift runs from the Upper Nile and Lake Edward through Lakes Kivu, Tanganyika, and Malawi to reach the coast near Beira. A branch extends to the west along the Luangwa Valley, the middle Zambezi to the southern edge of the Okovango swamps in Botswana.

Most of the lower ground in "High Africa" is hot and fairly arid, and orchids tend to grow at higher altitudes, while in "Low Africa," the lower areas are largely forested. In general, orchids originating in West Africa tend to like warmer conditions, with a higher humidity throughout the year, than those from the eastern side.

Over the past million years, climatic conditions have varied all over Africa. The pattern of change is not clear, but there is evidence that the climate in the past has been both warmer and colder, as well as wetter and drier than it is now. How much and in what way these changes have influenced the distribution of African orchids can only be a matter for conjecture.

Walter and Lieth (1960–1967) distinguished ten world climatic types, of which five occur in Africa. Each has many subdivisions, but the main five types in Africa are as follows: equatorial (humid or with two rainy seasons), tropical (summer rain), subtropical (hot and arid), Mediterranean (winter rain, dry summer, almost frost free), and mountain types. Epiphytic orchids occur in equatorial and tropical climates and to some extent in mountain climates. Terrestrial orchids could occur in all five of these types, although there would be few or none in the more extreme subtropical climatic types. For epiphytic orchids, the distribution of rainfall is almost as important as the absolute amount—an area with a high rainfall concentrated into six months of the year, with a six-month dry season, would not be very suitable. The rainfall in the drier season need not be very high; in fact, mist and low clouds are sufficient for many epiphytic orchids to survive. This is why there are nearly always more epiphytic orchids at higher altitudes (within limits, of course). The effect of mist and low clouds can be very local—the "weather" side of a hill will have more epiphytes than the rain-shadowed side, although the latter may well have more terrestrials.

A surprising feature is how high relative humidity tends to be in tropical Africa, even in the dry season. At Dimonika, Congo, which lies at an altitude of ca. 350 m (1150 ft.), the relative humidity in the dry season was actually slightly higher, at 89 percent, than in the rainy season, when it was 86 percent. This is because it is cloudy with some mist in the dry season and also cooler, and so the air cannot hold so much moisture (Plate 1). In Ghana and Nigeria, a dry wind from the Sahara, the harmattan, blows in January and February. It feels very dry; furniture becomes covered by a fine layer of dust which is replaced in as little as a couple of hours if it is wiped off. Yet in Ghana, the relative humidity at 3 p.m. Greenwich Mean Time has been measured at 53 percent. We feel quite pleased if our orchid house does not fall below that, yet few orchids can survive where the harmattan blows. Most terrestrial orchids have perennating organs such as tuberoids or pseudobulbs that enable them to survive a dry season, when in any case most are dormant, and so the distribution of rainfall is of less significance.

In the parts of West Africa where evergreen forest is the climax vegetation, the rainfall is lower than in most areas that support rainforest in other continents. It is usually between 1600 and 2000 mm (64–80 in.) per year, and hardly anywhere is the mean monthly rainfall more than 100 mm (4 in.). In the equatorial parts of the Zaire basin, there are one or two months when the rainfall is ca. 50 mm (2 in.) a month; farther from the Equator, and nearer the Atlantic coast, the length and severity of the dry season increases. In most of this area, there are two peaks in the rainfall pattern, separated by one fairly severe and one less severe dry period, but around the Bight of Biafra (or Bonny), where the rainfall is particularly high, there is one peak. In Guinea, the rainfall in places exceeds 4000 mm (160 in.) per year, but there is a four-month-long dry season. In Benin and Togo, what is known as the Dahomey Gap occurs, where the rainfall is less; this divides the rainforest into two blocks, a smaller one to the west and a much larger one to the east.

South of the equatorial zone, lying mainly to the east but including part of Angola as well as the whole of Zambia, Malawi, and Zimbabwe, and parts of Mozambique and

Transvaal in South Africa, there is much greater seasonal variation in temperature than in the area just discussed. There is one rainy season, from November till April. Over this area, the temperature depends much more on altitude than on latitude. In general, the rainfall is between 500 and 1400 mm (20–56 in.) per year, usually decreasing from north to south and increasing with altitude. This is sometimes spoken of as a summer rainfall area, but such words as summer and winter have little meaning there. Countries like Malawi, Zambia, and Zimbabwe have basically three seasons. The wet season runs pretty much from November to April; there are usually a few thunderstorms in October, but they are very local and many places get no rain. It is hot; the rain tends to fall in heavy showers so that part of each day is likely to be sunny. This is followed by a cool season from May to August. The weather is often very pleasant: warm and sunny in the day but cooler at night. In some places, though, particularly in Malawi and Mozambique, there are spells of cloudy and drizzly weather that last for several days and are not at all pleasant, although splendid for epiphytic orchids. The hot season runs from September to November, becoming hotter and more oppressive as the humidity increases with the approach of the rains.

In this part of Africa, the rains are much more erratic than on the western side; drought years occur, apparently with greater frequency, although there is a natural cycle. Lake Malawi has been known to have periodic fluctuations in its water level for a long time. When we arrived in Malawi in 1978, the level of the lake was low. Over the next few years, it gradually increased until by 1985, several of the lakeside hotels had to abandon chalets as the water was lapping at the doors. It was an odd sight to see the thatched umbrellas meant to shelter guests sitting on the shores, protruding from the water several yards from the edge. By the time we left, at the end of 1987, the waters had already receded more or less to their 1978 level. There is no doubt, though, that mist and cloud, and so presumably rainfall, are affected by vegetation. Blantyre, in Malawi, is surrounded by hills, some of which retained (or did when we lived there) their forest cover, while on others the trees had all been felled. It was very noticeable how, by evening, the forested hills would have a cap of cloud while the denuded hills had none. Many parts of this region have no rain for about six months of the year. In such areas, epiphytes are only found on the high ground where mist regularly occurs. Only *Ansellia africana, Acampe pachyglossa,* and sometimes *Aerangis verdickii* seem able to survive where these mists, or some dry season rains, do not occur.

To the north of this area, and to the east of the wet equatorial belt, in Kenya and Tanzania, the rainfall tends to be lower but has two peaks. Much of the area has less than 500 mm (20 in.) per year, although this increases with altitude. The "long rains" last from April till July and the "short rains" from late August into September. In Kenya, some orchids, both epiphytic and terrestrial, grow in the coastal belt; few are found inland until the Kenya Highlands and the foothills of Kilimanjaro are reached. In Tanzania, again there are orchids in the coastal strip, but there are other, more scattered areas of high ground inland, including Kilimanjaro and its foothills to the north and several ranges of mountains, such as the Usambaras, the Ulugurus, and the Ngurus, which are very rich with many endemic species. In the south are the southern Highlands and the Livingstone Mountains, again excellent orchid areas. There are also smaller areas such as the forest on the rim of the Ngorongoro crater which have some epiphytes. Many areas of Tanzania are still not well known and when a collecting trip visits these isolated ranges, some new species are usually discovered.

Along the coast, from southern Somalia to the mouth of the Limpopo River, there is a strip of land, mostly from 50 to 200 km (30–120 miles) wide which is mainly less than 200 m (660 ft.) above sea level, but there are a few hilly areas such as the Shimba Hills in Kenya (ca. 400 m, 1320 ft.) and the Pugu Hills and the East Usambara Mountains in Tanzania. The rainfall along this strip is 800–1200 mm (30–50 in.) per year; in the northern part, including the Kenya Coast, there are two rainy seasons; farther south there is only one. The East Usambara Mountains, which rise to 1250 m (4100 ft.), have a high annual rainfall of ca. 1950 mm (80 in.) and the area around Amani supports rainforest and is rich in orchids—the name is commemorated by *Angraecopsis amaniensis* and *Rangaeris amaniensis*. Lower areas have coastal scrub forest, which has a few epiphytic orchids—or did have, as little of this vegetation is now left.

South Africa has two main rainfall patterns. In the north and east, approximately east of longitude 25° east, rain falls in summer and the winters are cool and dry, with regular frosts at higher altitudes. In the southern and southwestern parts of the Cape Region, rain falls in winter, almost all between April and September, and the summers are hot and dry. Along the eastern part of the southern coast there is usually at least some rain all the year round, while in central and western South Africa, rainfall is low and erratic.

Western Cape, between 32° and 35° south and 18° and 25° east, has a completely different climate from anywhere else in Africa south of the Sahara. Physically, it is dominated by more or less parallel mountain ranges with an average altitude of 1000–1500 m (3300–5000 ft.), with some peaks over 2000 m (6600 ft.). The rainfall is mostly between 300 and 2500 mm (12–100 in.) per year, although in some parts of the mountains it can reach 5000 mm (200 in.). The western part receives 60–80 percent of its rain in winter, but from around Swellendam and to the east, the rainfall starts to become more evenly distributed throughout the year. In the winter rain area, the higher mountains have low cloud and mist in the summer. Snow falls on the higher mountains, but only lasts for any time on south-facing slopes. Frost occurs inland at high altitudes, but not on the coast. This region has a very rich flora with several endemic plant families and many endemic species, including orchids. All the orchids in the winter rainfall area are terrestrial.

We have not given much detail on temperature, as the records are rarely from places where orchids grow. In the hottest areas, if orchids occur, they will be found in the forests, where the temperature will be considerably lower. At the other extreme, orchids, both epiphytic and terrestrial, grow in places like the Nyika plateau in Malawi, where the grass is frequently white with frost in the dry season. This does not mean, however, that these orchids are frost hardy; the frost does not penetrate the ground, so the resting tubers of terrestrials are unaffected, and it does not enter the forests, so that the epiphytes, although they are exposed to low temperatures, would not experience frost. Temperature figures are often given as "mean maximum" and "mean minimum"; this, again, is of limited value as in most cases the extremes are more important than the average.

Chapter 2

Vegetation

Obviously in an area the size of Africa, it is possible here to give only the most general review of the types of vegetation that occur and their distribution. There have been many systems of classification over the years; in this volume we have followed mainly White (1983) in *The Vegetation of Africa*. How relevant much of this is now is open to question, as the natural vegetation, especially forest and woodland, is under threat all over the continent.

The influence of soil on vegetation is relatively unimportant, with a few exceptions. If the soil is very shallow, for example, it will not support tall woodland, or if it contains high amounts of heavy metals such as chrome, nickel and copper, only certain plants can grow in the "toxic" soil. In general, climate is the vital factor, although even there, the relationship is complex and in some places the past history is important.

White (1983) divided the vegetation of Africa into 16 types, not all of which are relevant to a book about orchids. There are eight main vegetation types: forest, woodland, bushland and thicket, shrubland, grassland, wooded grassland, desert, and Afroalpine vegetation. In addition there are three transitional zones, which White called scrub forest, transition woodland, and scrub woodland, and five more specialized groups: mangrove; herbaceous swamp and aquatic vegetation; saline and brackish swamp; bamboo; and anthropic landscape. The latter includes areas where the vegetation is no longer natural, such as farmland. Figure 2-1 is a map of the vegetation zones of sub-Saharan Africa, much simplified.

Figure 2-1. Vegetation zones of sub-Saharan Africa.

Forest

Forest can be defined as a continuous stand of trees with the canopy 10–50 m (33–165 ft.) high or more; the crowns of the trees overlap and interlock and are often laced with creepers (Plate 2). There are several layers of vegetation, including a shrub layer, and the ground layer is often sparse, with, in tropical forests, few grasses. Epiphytes, such as orchids and ferns, are characteristic of the wetter tropical and subtropical forests. Almost all African forests are evergreen or semi-evergreen, although deciduous forests can occur locally.

The term *rainforest* is used a great deal now; this is not really a precise term, but is quite appropriate for the most widespread type of tropical African forest on well-drained soils, with a canopy more than 30 m (100 ft.) tall, which occurs most widely in western and central Africa. In slightly drier areas, this type of forest can be semi-evergreen—some of the trees are deciduous for a short time, but seldom at the same time, so the canopy is never bare. In deciduous forest, most trees, both in the upper and lower canopy, lose their leaves at the same time and remain leafless for several weeks or even months. Riverine or riparian forest, as the name suggests, is found by streams and rivers and varies in depth from a single fringe of trees to blocks 50 m (165 ft.) wide (Plate 3).

As would be expected, forest is one of the most important habitats for epiphytic orchids. There is a noticeable difference between the forests of western and western central Africa and those on the eastern side of the continent. In western Africa, the trees tend to be taller and the orchids are almost confined to branches 20 m (66 ft.) or more above the ground, where large colonies often occur, particularly on the big, horizontal branches. It can be imagined how frustrating this is for anyone wanting to study the orchids. The tree trunks are straight and clean, and apart from having specialized climbing equipment, the only solution is to look for fallen or felled trees and branches—they have to be fairly recently down, as in the heat and humidity, orchids on the ground soon rot. In Congo, we found very few terrestrial orchids on the forest floor, where the light intensity was extremely low. We presumed that it was this low light intensity that prevented orchids from growing on the trunks of the trees, as is relatively common in eastern Africa. There, too, the edge of a forest, where there is rather more light, is often a productive place for orchids. In western Africa, the edge of every forest is smothered in a tangle of creepers; in fact, it is not easy to get inside the forest, although once through the creeper layer, it is easy to walk. In eastern Africa, some creepers and climbers grow at the forest edge, but we have never seen them so dense there, and the climbers are shorter, so that the outer branches often bear orchids. In western Africa, the creepers go right into and over the crowns of the trees.

As mentioned in the previous chapter, most of western Africa lies at a lower level than eastern Africa. On the eastern side, the trees tend to become shorter with increasing altitude and these higher altitude forests, below the true Afroalpine zone, can be very rich in orchids, which are much easier to see and identify. However, less forest remains on the eastern side, almost all is in forest reserves; population pressure is such that trees are felled either for fuel or to clear land for agriculture. This can have a very destructive effect, particularly when the land is sloping: after the first season's rain, all too often the soil ends up in the rivers and the land is no longer suitable for trees or crops. Western Africa tends to be less densely populated. There is more commercial logging there, but as yet, in most places, it does not seem to occur too extensively. There is little clear felling, and while selective logging does cause damage, it is relatively limited.

In South Africa, there are still some forested areas along the coast and on escarpments inland, to ca. 1800 m (6000 ft.).

Woodland

Woodland can be defined as an open stand of trees where the crowns form a canopy from 8 to 20 m (26–66 ft.) high and trees cover at least 40 percent of the surface area. The crowns of the trees often touch, but are not closely interlocked. While there are some evergreen species of tree, most are deciduous or semi-deciduous, although in areas of higher rainfall, they tend to be leafless at different times and not for very long. The ground flora is predominantly grassy. White (1983) remarked that vascular epiphytes (such as orchids) are often present, though relatively rare, except in secondary woodland occurring on forest sites. At first we disagreed with this remark because we have found many orchids in woodland; however, compared with forest orchids, woodland orchids tend to be scattered and localized. Secondary woodland is usually poor, unless it is of long standing.

For orchids in woodland, the amount and distribution of rainfall are of vital importance. The type of woodland that occurs in the higher rainfall areas of eastern Africa, "miombo" or *Brachystegia* woodland, is a very good habitat for terrestrial as well as epiphytic orchids (Plate 4). Many species of *Cynorkis, Eulophia, Habenaria,* and other genera can be found there. At higher altitudes, there tends to be mist in the dry season, which is of great importance for the epiphytes. In slightly drier areas, the woodland may look very similar, but epiphytes will be poorly represented, although terrestrials may be more plentiful, particularly on sloping, stony ground. The presence of the hanging lichen, *Usnea,* is a good indicator of high rainfall and humidity; if it is abundant, epiphytic orchids are likely to be present, although exceptions occur. Sometimes a patch of woodland looks ideal for orchids, but none grow there. Often this means that it is secondary woodland, but sometimes the reason is more obscure.

The deciduous woodland that is so widespread in hot, dry, low-lying areas in eastern and southern Africa, characterized by trees such as baobab (*Adansonia digitata*) and species of *Acacia, Combretum,* and *Terminalia,* has few orchids, although some, notably *Ansellia africana* and *Acampe pachyglossa,* may occur there. Terrestrials are also scarce.

Bushland and Thicket

Bushland is defined as an open stand of bushes between 3 and 7 m (9–20 ft.) high, with a canopy cover of 40 percent or more. Thicket is a closed stand of bushes and climbers, again usually ca. 3–7 m (9–20 ft.) tall. Usually this type of vegetation is associated with dry areas and has few epiphytes, although some species of *Microcoelia,* for example, *M. exilis* and *M. megalorrhiza,* grow in this sort of habitat. There are also likely to be few terrestrials, although some, such as *Eulophia petersii* and species of *Bonatea,* may occur.

Bushy plants occur most widely where the rainfall is from 250 to 500 mm (10–20 in.) per year, but only cover large areas where there are two rainy seasons, sporadic rainfall throughout the year, or very high humidity in the dry season. If the rainfall is entirely seasonal, grassland is more likely to be found.

On most mountains, there is a zone of bushland above the forest zone. White (1983) gave an interesting example of what he called "elphin thicket" from the Belinga Mountains in Gabon, at an altitude of 950 to 1000 m (3100–3300 ft.) and 400 km (250 miles) from the sea. There, in dense thicket 4–8 m (13–26 ft.) tall, epiphytic orchids, mosses, and lichens clothe the stems to ground level.

Shrubland

Shrubland is dominated by shrubs from 10 cm (4 in.) to 2 m (6 ft.) tall or more. It is found where taller woody plants cannot grow for some reason, such as low rainfall, summer drought, low temperatures, high winds, or shallow or salty soil. The most extensive area of shrubland in Africa is the Great Karroo, which, it is believed, has increased in size because of overgrazing by sheep, which encourages the growth of woody plants at the expense of grass. As far as we know, no orchids occur there.

Another important area, again in South Africa, is in the Cape, where the characteristic vegetation is known as fynbos; this seems to be the climax vegetation, and is now under great threat from development of various kinds. There are no epiphytic orchids here, but many endemic terrestrials grow in this habitat.

Grassland

Most grassland in Africa is secondary, often the result of fire. One tends to think of fire as being the result of human activity, and in most cases it is, but fires are also quite often started by lightning. The main reasons for human-induced fires, apart from carelessness, are to clear old, dead vegetation to encourage the growth of new grass for grazing, either for domestic stock or for herbivores in game reserves and national parks, and for hunting. In Malawi, we observed that many dry season fires are lit by small boys hunting mice. Unfortunately, after the hunt is over, the fires continue to burn and can cause considerable destruction.

While fire is obviously fatal to epiphytic orchids unless they are high up on trees, it can be beneficial to terrestrial orchids. It is well documented that several species of South African terrestrial orchids flower only after a fire, and many species (not only orchids) flower much more profusely after a fire. However, if the fires are too frequent, the long-term effect is likely to be harmful as seed and seedlings must be destroyed.

Sometimes grassland is a result of soil conditions—the most widespread is that which occurs on seasonally or permanently waterlogged soil. These areas are less frequent in western Africa and in the equatorial belt, but are common on the eastern side where rainfall is strongly seasonal. These wet areas, whether permanently or seasonally so, are often rich in terrestrial orchids, including many outstandingly beautiful tropical *Disa* and *Eulophia* species. Unfortunately orchids adapted to this type of habitat are among the most difficult to satisfy in cultivation. This applies, too, to orchids of montane grassland. Whether this is a natural climax, or has been fire-induced in the past, it has obviously been grassland for a very long time, judging by the wealth of orchid species, many of which grow nowhere else. Montane grassland seems to be mainly confined to eastern Africa; notable areas are the Nyika plateau in northern Malawi (Plate 5), the Kitulo plateau in southern Tanzania, the Mulanje plateaus in southern Malawi, parts of the Chimanimani Mountains in Zimbabwe, and parts of the Drakensberg Mountains in South Africa. Many smaller areas also occur (Plate 6).

In South Africa, highveld grassland seems to be the climax vegetation between 1220 and 2150 m (4000–7100 ft.) on much of the plateau extending west of the Drakensbergs to the Eastern Cape. The winters here are dry and frosty; the annual rainfall is 250–500 mm (10–20 in.), increasing towards the Drakensbergs in the east, almost all falling in summer.

Wooded Grassland

The name is self-explanatory. White (1983) said that woody plants should cover 10 to 40 percent of the surface, but there is, of course, a gradual transition to woodland, in one direction, and grassland in the other. This type of country is often referred to as "savanna," a term applicable to South American conditions that, strictly speaking, should not be used in Africa. Various types of wooded grassland occur in Africa, from the orchard bush of northern Ghana to the acacia "savanna" of East Africa, familiar from many natural history programs. Usually they occur in the wetter parts of essentially dry areas, such as the Sahel, and are of little significance as far as orchids are concerned. The Transvaal lowveld in South Africa is essentially grassland with scattered trees.

Desert

No orchids grow in Africa's deserts, of course, but it is worth pointing out how much of the African continent is covered by desert. Apart from the Sahara, the Kalahari and Namib deserts occupy very large areas, and parts of northern Kenya and Somalia are semi-desert, such vegetation as there is consisting of thornbush and thicket.

Afroalpine Vegetation

True Afroalpine vegetation is confined to the highest mountains of tropical Africa. This is where one finds giant rosette plants, mainly species of *Lobelia* and *Senecio,* and numerous cushion plants, and where night frosts are frequent. It is not known which orchid holds the altitude record, but we would make a guess at *Disa stairsii,* an East African terrestrial species that has been recorded at 4200 m (13,860 ft.).

Scrub Forest

Scrub forest, one of three transition zones described by White (1983), is intermediate between true forest and bushland and is usually 10–15 m (30–50 ft.) high. There are various types, but one of the most widespread, with fairly numerous trees of cactus-like *Euphorbia* species, occurs in lower-lying areas of tropical and subtropical Africa. In parts of South Africa, *Mystacidium capense* grows on these candelabra euphorbias, but otherwise there is little in the way of epiphytic orchids, although there may be some terrestrials. Because of the fragmented nature of this zone, it is not shown on the map.

Transition Woodland

As far as orchids go, transition woodland can be grouped with wetter types of woodland (see discussion above).

Scrub Woodland

Scrub woodland, the third transition zone described by White (1983), is dominated by stunted trees of typical woodland species, often only ca. 3 m (9 ft.) high. It can arise in various situations where conditions, for some reason, limit the development of normal trees. Often, the limiting factor is altitude; in this case the woodland can be rich in orchids, as long as it is not burnt, since the dwarf trees give little protection to epiphytic orchids. As in other forms of woodland, the presence of *Usnea* is a good indicator of the likely presence of epiphytic orchids. Some terrestrial orchids also grow in this habitat.

Anthropic Landscapes

Of White's five specialized vegetation zones, only anthropic landscapes have orchids. If some natural vegetation exists, as is still the case in most parts of tropical Africa, orchids can sometimes be found in these human-made landscapes. In African cities, one often sees epiphytic orchids growing on street trees: we have seen *Graphorkis lurida* in the center of Brazzaville, Congo; *Rangaeris amaniensis* in Nairobi, Kenya; and *Microcoelia exilis* in the middle of Blantyre, the commercial capital of Malawi. Provided there is a source of seed, epiphytic orchids will colonize many exotic trees; they grow well on jacaranda, for example, but do not become established on trees like gums with peeling bark, or on trees with very smooth bark such as frangipani (*Plumeria*). They will grow on the latter if mature plants are tied down firmly, but the bark is too smooth for seed to lodge on it. We have seen orchids on eucalyptus trees, but these were very large, old trees where the lower half of the trunk was covered with thick, corky bark that obviously did not peel. Many species grow well on cypress and on plantation trees such as coffee, cocoa, and citrus, and even tea if it is not pruned. The only place in Congo where we found the beautiful *Aerangis arachnopus* was on an old citrus tree in an abandoned garden.

Terrestrial orchids will also survive in plantations; we have seen big colonies of *Cynorkis* and *Disperis* species under pine and cypress. Even under eucalyptus, which is usually sterile, we have found several species of *Eulophia,* such as *E. speciosa* and *E. streptopetala,* and species of *Habenaria.* Often, in a fairly intensively cultivated landscape, small pockets of land are left uncultivated for one reason or another. Near one house where we lived in southern Malawi, was a small "dambo," that is, seasonally wet grassland that is often the source of a stream. It was surrounded by farmland and plantations. There we found 12 species of terrestrial orchid, including the rare, yellow-flowered *Habenaria villosa,* the first record for Malawi and only the second or third time that the species had ever been collected. Alas, after a couple of years with low rainfall, the dambo had dried out and was dug up for planting tomatoes, the day after we had found the habenaria. One tends to be pessimistic and think that these species are gone for ever, but tubers can persist in the ground, and possibly seed also, and if heavy rains return and the ground goes out of cultivation again, these species could well reappear.

Chapter 3

Countries of Sub-Saharan Africa

Some of the information given here will, inevitably, be out of date in some respects by the time it appears in print. The population figures mostly refer to 1991; it is safe to assume that they will now be a great deal higher. In a few cases, the figures given come from a census, but in most, they can only be estimates. Even capital cities change; many countries (not only in Africa) have the capital near one end, and there has been a trend towards moving them into a more central position. The names of several countries have also changed in the past 20 or 30 years, but older names are given as synonyms, as it were, because many people still remember the geography they learned at school better than the current situation. There is little point in commenting here on political stability as that can change, in either direction, in a very short time. Population figures are based on UN estimates made in 1991, unless otherwise stated.

The orchids of many African countries are poorly known, and many are not covered by any flora. When a regional flora is undertaken, often the Orchidaceae seems to be one of the last families to be written up.

The *Flora of West Tropical Africa* covers Benin, Bioko, western Cameroon, Gambia, Ghana, Guinea, Ivory Coast, Liberia, Mali, Nigeria, Senegal, Sierra Leone, Togo. The volume including the Orchidaceae, by V. S. Summerhayes, was first published in 1936, and a revised edition was produced in 1968; the Orchidaceae are in volume 3, part 1.

The *Flora of East Tropical Africa* covers Kenya, Tanzania, and Uganda. The Orchidaceae are in three volumes; volume 1, by V. S. Summerhayes, appeared in 1968; volumes 2 and 3, by P. J. Cribb, appeared in 1984 and 1989, respectively.

The *Flore d'Afrique Centrale* covers Burundi, Rwanda, and Zaire. There are two volumes of Orchidaceae, both by D. Geerinck, which appeared in 1984 and 1992, respectively.

The *Flora Zambesiaca* covers Botswana, the Caprivi Strip, Malawi, Mozambique, Zambia, Zimbabwe. The Orchidaceae will be covered in two parts; part 1, by I. F. la Croix & P. J. Cribb, appeared in 1995; part 2 is in preparation.

The Orchidaceae of the *Flora of Ethiopia,* by P. J. Cribb, is in press, and a flora of South Africa is in preparation.

Figure 3-1 is a map of Africa. Figure 3-2 identifies the continent's major rivers and lakes.

Figure 3-1. Map of Africa.

Angola
Capital: Luanda
Area: 1,246,700 sq. km (481,225 sq. mi.)
Population: 10,303,000
     A narrow coastal strip lies below 200 m (660 ft.) in altitude, but most of the country lies over 1000 m (3300 ft.). The Luanda Plateau rises to 2620 m (8650 ft.) in Serra Moca. The orchids are little known and are likely to be numerous, but are not covered by any flora; they have been little collected in modern times because of the long-running civil war.

Figure 3-2. Rivers and lakes of Africa.

Benin (Dahomey)
Capital: Porto Novo
Area: 122,620 sq. km (43,470 sq. mi.)
Population: 4,889,000
    Along with Togo and southeastern Ghana, this country falls into the drier area known as the "Dahomey Gap." The altitude is less than 200 m towards the coast, with most of the interior lying between 200 and 500 m (660–1650 ft.). Few orchids are recorded. This is one of the most heavily populated areas in West Africa.

Botswana (Bechuanaland)
Capital: Gaborone
Area: 581,730 sq. km (224,607 sq. mi.)
Population: 1,348,000
    Most of the country lies between 200 and 500 m (660–1650 ft.); the Okovango basin is a vast wetland area. There are few terrestrial species and even fewer epiphytes.

Burkina Faso (Upper Volta)
Capital: Ouagadougou
Area: 274,122 sq. km (105,811 sq. mi.)
Population: 9,242,000
    Most of the country is semi-desert, lying at an altitude of 200 to 500 m (660–1650 ft.). Epiphytic orchids are likely to be present only in the riverine fringes of the various branches of the Volta River. Terrestrial orchids are also likely to be few.

Burundi
Capital: Bujumbura
Area: 27,835 sq. km (10,745 sq. mi.)
Population: 5,620,000
    This very densely populated country is characterized by mountainous terrain over 1000 m (3300 ft.) with peaks rising to 2000 and 3000 m (6600 and 9900 ft.). Like neighboring Rwanda, it is affected by civil war.

Cameroon
Capital: Yaoundé
Area: 475,500 sq. km (183,545 sq. mi.)
Population: 12,239,000
    The rainfall is heavy, particularly around the coast, with a main rainy season from August to December and small rains in March. The country is mountainous, with only a coastal strip below 200 m (660 ft.); much of the southern half of the country lies between 500 and 1000 m (1650–3300 ft.). The Massif de l'Adoumaoua in the north rises to 2460 m (8100 ft.); parts of it are well forested, although much is grassland. The country is rich in orchids, but still not well known. Recent intensive collecting on Mount Cameroon, which, although it lies near the coast, rises to 4095 m (13,500 ft.), has resulted in the discovery of several new species, as well as new records.

Central African Republic (Central African Empire; Oubangi–Char)
Capital: Bangui
Area: 622,984 sq. km (240,535 sq. mi.)
Population: 3,127,000
   The rainfall varies from ca. 2000 mm (80 in.) per year in the southeast to 800 mm (30 in.) in the extreme north, and the vegetation ranges from lowland equatorial forest to sub-Sahel. In 1958, forest was estimated to cover about 5 percent of the land surface; it is likely to be considerably less now. Most of the country lies between 500 and 1000 m (1650–3300 ft.), but it rises well above this in the Massif des Bongos in the north; there is more high ground in the west, near the Cameroon border. The orchid flora of the forests seems to be rich and is still not completely known. Cribb and Fay (1987) listed about 130 species, more or less equally divided between terrestrial and epiphytic.

Chad
Capital: N'Djamena
Area: 1,284,000 sq. km (495,625 sq. mi.)
Population: 5,819,000
   Most of the land lies between 200 and 500 m (660–1650 ft.), but it rises to ca. 1000 m (3300 ft.) in the interior; however, this is desert. If any orchids occur in Chad, they are likely to be in the extreme south, near the border with Cameroon and Central African Republic.

Congo (French Congo)
Capital: Brazzaville
Area: 342,000 sq. km (132,010 sq. mi.)
Population: 2,346,000
   Congo is lightly populated by African standards. The coastal strip lies below 200 m (660 ft.); inland there is an area between 200 and 500 m (660–1650 ft.), which occasionally rises higher. In the north, the land lies again mainly between 200 and 500 m (660–1650) with large areas of marsh. Access is difficult to most parts of the country outside Brazzaville. In the south, a large block of forest, the Mayombe (Plate 1), lies more or less parallel to the Atlantic coast and extends for 170 km (100 mi.) from Gabon through Congo into Bas-Zaire. The total area is estimated at ca. 17,000 sq. km (6,640 sq. mi.) with ca. 11,000 sq. km (4300 sq. mi.) lying in Congo. The highest point of the Mayombe is 730 m (2400 ft.) near the Cabinda border. This area is rich in epiphytic orchids, which are little known. There is no literature available.

Djibouti (French Somaliland)
Capital: Djibouti
Area: 22,000 sq. km (8,494 sq. mi.)
Population: 520,000
   Much of the country is semi-desert and the climate is harsh. We know of no orchids that grow here.

Equatorial Guinea (Río Muni; Spanish Guinea)
Capital: Malabo
Area: 28,050 sq. km (10,825 sq. mi.)
Population: 356,000
    This country consists of a mainland section (Río Muni) and the islands of Bioko (Fernando Po; Macias Nguema) and Pagalu (Annobón). The coastal strip lies below 200 m (660 ft.), but inland the land rises to 1200 m (4000 ft.). Bioko is mountainous, rising to 3807 m (12,560 ft.), and apparently rich in orchids. There are many old collections, but nothing recent as far as we know. The tiny island of Pagalu also has some interesting species; its flora is included in Exell (1944).

Eritrea
Capital: Asmara
Area: 93,679 sq. km (36,170 sq. mi.)
Population: 3,500,000
    This country became independent from Ethiopia in 1993. A narrow, low-lying coastal strip rises to highlands in the center and north, 2000 to 3000 m (6600–9900 ft.) in altitude, which are an extension of the Ethiopian highlands. It is here that most orchids occurred, but almost all the trees were felled by the Ethiopian army, and it must be doubtful if any are left.

Ethiopia (Abyssinia)
Capital: Addis Ababa
Area: 1,128,221 sq. km (435,608 sq. mi.)
Population: 49,883,000
    A mountainous country, with almost all land over 1000 m (3300 ft.) in altitude, and much of it well above that. There are several peaks over 4000 m (13,200 ft.) with Ras Dashan reaching 4623 m (15,250 ft.). About 150 orchids in 45 genera are known. The Orchidaceae of *Flora of Ethiopia,* by P. J. Cribb, is in press.

Gabon
Capital: Libreville
Area: 267,665 sq. km (103,320 sq. mi.)
Population: 1,212,000
    Much of the country lies below 200 m (660 ft.), but inland reaches 1000 m (3300 ft.). There is still much forest, which is rich in orchids, but they are still not well known nor are they as yet covered by any flora. Any intensive collecting seems to produce new species.

Gambia
Capital: Banjul
Area: 11,295 sq. km (4,360 sq. mi.)
Population: 884,000
    A fifth of the total area is taken up by the Gambia River. All the land lies below 200 m (660 ft.), and the climate is typical of the Sahel, with a dry season between

October and May and rain in July and August, giving 800–1000 mm (32–40 in.) annually. There are few orchids.

Ghana (Gold Coast)
Capital: Accra
Area: 238,305 sq. km (91,985 sq. mi.)
Population: 15,509,000
    Most of the country lies below 200 m (660 ft.), but parts are from 200 to 500 m (660–1650 ft.). The rainfall varies considerably over short distances; it is highest in the southwest, where it is more than 1750 mm (70 in.) per year, but even here a 4- to 5-month-long dry season is characterized by less than 100 mm (4 in.) of rain per month. The coastal strip has several terrestrial orchids, and Ashanti, in the center of the country, was once well forested, with many epiphytes; we have heard, though, that much of the forest has now gone (Plate 2). The northern region has a long dry season; there are a few terrestrials and some epiphytes by the rivers.

Guinea (French Guinea)
Capital: Conakry
Area: 245,855 sq. km (94,900 sq. mi.)
Population: 5,931,000
    The rainfall in places exceeds 4000 mm (160 in.) per year, but there is a four-month-long dry season. Most of the country lies between 200 and 500 m (660–1650 ft.), with some between 500 and 1000 m (1650–3300 ft.). Mount Nimba, in the southeastern corner near the borders with Liberia and Ivory Coast, reaches 1768 m (5800 ft.); a number of orchid collections come from here. Mount Kavendou, in the center of the country, reaches 1425 m (4700 ft.).

Guinea-Bissau (Portuguese Guinea)
Capital: Bissau
Area: 36,125 sq. km (13,945 sq. mi.)
Population: 984,000
    Apparently few orchids grow here, but little is known. All the land lies below 200 m (660 ft.).

Ivory Coast
Capital: Abidjan
Area: 322,465 sq. km (124,470 sq. mi.)
Population: 12,464,000
    About 210 species in 45 genera are known from Ivory Coast (Cribb and Perez-Vera 1975). Most of the southern half of the county lies below 200 m (660 ft.) and is (or was) mostly forested, but much of the interior lies from 200 to 500 m (660–1650 ft.), with a high point of 1116 m (3700 ft.) towards the west. Mount Boutourou in the northwest is 560 m (1850 ft.) high. Wooded grassland occurs in the center and east, with grassland in the north.

Kenya

Capital: Nairobi
Area: 582,645 sq. km (224,900 sq. mi.)
Population: 25,905,000

At one time (and perhaps it still has) Kenya had the highest rate of population growth in the world. The coastal strip lies below 200 m (660 ft.); much of the interior lies above 1500 m, with the highest point, Mount Kenya in the Aberdare Mountains, reaching 5200 m (17,160 ft.). Part of Mount Elgon also lies within Kenya, although the peak is just inside Uganda. The orchids are well known and are covered in the *Flora of Tropical East Africa* (Cribb 1984, 1989; Summerhayes 1968b) and also in Piers (1965) and Stewart (1996), where 280 species in 50 genera are described. Some orchids occur in the coastal strip (or did occur, as there has been a great deal of development connected with tourism along the coast), but most are found in the highlands, where there is still some forest and forest remnants.

Lesotho (Basutoland)

Capital: Maseru
Area: 30,345 sq. km (11,715 sq. mi.)
Population: 1,826,000

Much of the land of this mountainous country lies more than 2000 m (6600 ft.) above sea level, rising to 3482 m (11,500 ft.) in the Drakensberg Mountains near the South African border.

Liberia

Capital: Monrovia
Area: 111,370 sq. km (42,990 sq. mi.)
Population: 2,705,000

The annual rainfall can be over 3000 mm (120 in.), but falls in a single season. The coastal area lies below 200 m (660 ft.); the interior lies between 200 and 500 m (660–1650 ft.), with a small area in the northwest reaching 1000 m (3300 ft.).

Malawi (Nyasaland; British Central Africa)

Capital: Lilongwe
Area: 118,484 sq. km (45,767 sq. mi.)
Population: 8,556,000

This small country, with altitude ranging from 60 to 3000 m (200–9900 ft.), contains a great variety of habitat. Most of the country lies more than 1000 m (3300 ft.) above sea level; Lake Malawi, which is part of the Great Rift Valley, lies at 474 m (1500 ft.) and occupies about 30 percent of the total area. There are several areas of high ground; the highest point is in the Mulanje massif in the south, which reaches 3002 m (ca. 10,000 ft.) and has 11 peaks over 2500 m (8250 ft.) and a number of plateaus at ca. 1800 m (6000 ft.). Mount Dedza in the central region reaches 2198 m (7250 ft.), and the Nyika plateau in the north (Plate 5) is one of the great orchid areas of Africa, lying between 1900 and 2500 m (6300–8250 ft.). The rainfall is always seasonal, lasting from November to early April; the amount varies throughout the country, with the areas of higher altitude having more "out-of-season" rain, as well as frequent mists. Only 5 percent of Malawi has an annual rainfall of less than 750 mm (30 in.), so most of the country has a climate suitable for orchids. Nevertheless, Malawi is densely populated, and forest and woodland are under much pressure. More than 400 species of orchid in 59 genera are known. About one-third of these species are epiphytic. Apart from the *Flora Zambesiaca* (la Croix and Cribb 1995, and in press), three other books deal with orchids in Malawi, one by B. Morris (1970) and two by I. F. la Croix et al. (1983, 1992).

Mali (French Sudan)
Capital: Bamako
Area: 1,240,140 sq. km (478,695 sq. mi.)
Population: 9,507,000
This arid, semi-desert country lies primarily between 200 and 500 m (660–1650 ft.); Mount Mina in the south reaches 762 m (2500 ft.). Epiphytic orchids are only likely to occur near the border with Ivory Coast, and there are probably few terrestrials.

Mozambique (Portuguese East Africa)
Capital: Maputo
Area: 801,590 sq. km (309,495 sq. mi.)
Population: 16,084,000
A relatively wide coastal strip lies below 200 m (660 ft.); the highest ground is on the west side, in the Livingstone Mountains, which run down from Tanzania, and the Chimanimani Mountains, which form part of the border with Zimbabwe. Mozambique is not well collected and there are undoubtedly more species than those included in the *Flora Zambesiaca*.

Namibia (South West Africa)
Capital: Windhoek
Area: 824,295 sq. km (318,180 sq. mi.)
Population: 1,837,000
Much of the country is desert and there are likely to be few, if any, orchids. The average rainfall over 70 percent of the country is less than 400 mm (16 in.) a year.

Niger
Capital: Niamey
Area: 1,267,000 sq. km (489,191 sq. mi.)
Population: 7,984,000
Most of the country lies between 200 and 500 m (660–1650 ft.), but rises much higher inland, reaching 2000 m (6600 ft.); this, however, is on the fringe of the Sahara. Almost the entire country is covered by grassland or desert, apart from a small area along the Niger Valley. Few orchids are recorded.

Nigeria
Capital: Abuja (declared the federal capital in 1991, replacing Lagos)
Area: 923,850 sq. km (356,605 sq. mi.)
Population: 112,163,000

Mangrove forest occurs along the coast and, north of it, tropical rainforest and palms. Farther north, open woodland and grassland occur, and in the extreme north, semi-desert. The Jos plateau, more or less in the middle of the country, is one of the few areas of West Africa with land over 1000 m (3300 ft.); it has a high point of 1698 m (5600 ft.). In the east, near the Cameroon border, the Gotel Mountains rise to 1510 m (5000 ft.), while the Mambilla Plateau lies mainly between 1200 and 1300 m (4000–4300 ft.). A checklist of Nigerian orchids by C. Z. Tang and P. J. Cribb in Segerbäck (1983) lists more than 280 species in 27 epiphytic genera and 20 terrestrial genera, but more species undoubtedly occur; there are likely to be more than 300.

Rwanda
Capital: Kigali
Area: 26,330 sq. km (10,165 sq. mi.)
Population: 7,491,000

This was the most densely populated country in Africa, although it is mountainous, lying almost entirely over 1000 m (3300 ft.), with several peaks over 2000 m (6600 ft.) and 3000 m (9900 ft.). A good area of forest had been included in the Mountain Gorilla Reserve, but much of this has probably been felled by refugees in the recent civil war.

São Tomé e Príncipe
Capital: São Tomé
Area: 1001 sq. km (391 sq. mi.)
Population (1992): 120,000

Although these islands are small, there is still forest left and orchids are plentiful. São Tomé Peak reaches 2024 m (6700 ft.). The island of Príncipe is lower than the island of São Tomé, the highest point there being Príncipe Peak, at 948 m (3100 ft.). There is a surprising variation in rainfall given the small area. On São Tomé island rainfall varies from 6000 mm (240 in.) per year in the mountains to only 200 mm (8 in.) per year in northeast. About 70 species of orchid are listed in Exell (1944), but there are undoubtedly more. Several species are endemic.

Senegal
Capital: Dakar
Area: 196,122 sq. km (75,750 sq. mi.)
Population: 7,533,000

This dry country has few orchids. Almost all the land lies below 200 m (660 ft.).

Sierra Leone
Capital: Freetown
Area: 72,325 sq. km (27,920 sq. mi.)
Population: 4,260,000

The annual rainfall can exceed 3000 mm (120 in.), but falls in a single season. Most of the country lies below 200 m (660 ft.), rising to 200–500 m (660–1650 ft.) in the northwest, with the Lomia Mountains, on the border with Guinea, reaching ca. 1000 m (3300 ft.).

Somalia
Capital: Mogadishu
Area: 637,654 sq. km (246,201 sq. mi.)
Population: 7,691,000

Most of the land is desert and semi-desert and lies below 200 m (660 ft.). Some areas inland lie between 500 and 1000 m (1650–3300 ft.). Few, if any, orchids are likely to occur.

South Africa
Capital: Pretoria (administrative) and Cape Town (legislative)
Area: 1,221,031 sq. km (471,445 sq. mi.)
Population (1993 estimate): 40,716,000

South Africa is now divided into nine provinces. The old Cape Province is split into Northern Cape, Western Cape (which includes the Cape peninsula and Cape Town), and Eastern Cape (including Transkei); what had been Transvaal now consists of Northern Province, North West Province, Gauteng (which includes Johannesburg and Pretoria), and Mpumalanga (the old Eastern Transvaal). The Orange Free State has become Free State, and Natal is known as KwaZulu-Natal. This large country has very varied habitats, but many of these are under pressure from developments of all kinds. Much of the interior is desert or semi-desert, but the Western Cape in particular is very rich in terrestrial orchids, many of which are endemic. Mpumalanga is still forested in parts and has both terrestrial and epiphytic orchids. The coastal forests of KwaZulu-Natal, once another rich area, are much depleted with only small pockets left. Inland, the Drakensberg Mountains rise to over 3000 m (9900 ft.), their highest point being just over the border in Lesotho. Most of South Africa has rainfall in the summer, but most of the Western Cape has winter rain, and a strip along the coast towards the east having some rain all year round. South Africa has about 450 orchid species, about 50 of which are epiphytic, in 54 genera, and new species and records still turn up. Between half and three-quarters of the species are thought to be endemic. Stewart et al. (1982) covered all the orchids known at that time.

Sudan
Capital: Khartoum
Area: 2,505,815 sq. km (967,245 sq. mi.)
Population: 25,941,000

This is the largest country in Africa, just beating Zaire, but much of the land is desert or semi-desert. Only the extreme southern region (where a long-running civil war is in progress) is suitable for orchids. The altitude rises to 3187 m (10,500 ft.) near the Uganda border.

Swaziland
Capital: Mbabane
Area: 17,365 sq. km (6,705 sq. mi.)
Population: 817,000

Much of the country is hot and dry, but the mountainous area around Pigg's Peak in the northwest, where the land rises to 1862 m (6150 ft.), has a few remnants of natural forest among extensive pine plantations. These have some epiphytic orchids and nearby there are areas of montane grassland with terrestrials (Plate 6). A few species, both epiphytic and terrestrial, occur in the hills around Mbabane and in the Lebombo Mountains (there, reaching 625 m (2050 ft.)), which form part of the eastern boundary with Mozambique. Swaziland has 90 to 100 orchid species in about 27 genera (Kemp 1983).

Tanzania (Tanganyika, with Zanzibar and Pemba Islands; German East Africa)
Capital: Dar es Salaam
Area: 945,087 sq. km (364,900 sq. mi.)
Population: 28,359,000

As in Kenya, a narrow coastal strip lies below 200 m (660 ft.), but inland, much lies over 1500 m (5000 ft.). Tanzania includes the highest mountain in Africa, Kilimanjaro, which rises to 5965 m (19,700 ft.). Mount Meru reaches 4565 m (15,060 ft.). Much of the interior is relatively dry, but orchids are found on several isolated mountain ranges, such as the Usambaras, the Ulugurus, and the Ngurus; these ranges have numerous endemics, and any intensive collecting seems to produce new species and new records. The Livingstone Mountains, running down the east side of Lake Malawi and into Mozambique, are another little-known area. In the orchid-rich southern highlands, Mount Rungwe rises to 2959 m (9760 ft.). After Zaire, Tanzania probably has the greatest number of orchid species in Africa. These are covered in the *Flora of Tropical East Africa* (Cribb 1984, 1989; Summerhayes 1968b).

Togo
Capital: Lomé
Area: 56,785 sq. km (21,920 sq. mi.)
Population: 3,643,000

This is part of the "Dahomey Gap," an area where the lower rainfall more characteristic of the interior reaches the coast. Rather than the forest found to the west and to the east, the natural vegetation is a mosaic of dryish evergreen forest and grassland. Most lies below 200 m (660 ft.), but inland it reaches 200–500 m (660–1650 ft.) with a high point of 786 m (2600 ft.). Relatively few orchids are recorded from this country.

Uganda
Capital: Kampala
Area: 236,580 sq. km (91,320 sq. mi.)
Population: 19,517,000

Much of the country is intensively cultivated, but there is still forest in various reserves. Uganda lies mostly between 1000 and 1500 m (3300–5000 ft.). Apart from the Ruwenzori in the west, which runs along the border with Zaire, there is another mountainous area in the east, on the Kenya border, rising to Mount Elgon, 4321 m (14,260 ft.). The orchid flora, which is rich and relatively well known, is included in the *Flora of Tropical East Africa* (Cribb 1984, 1989; Summerhayes 1968b).

Zaire (Belgian Congo)
Capita: Kinshasha
Area: 2,345,410 sq. km (905,330 sq. km.)
Population: 36,672,000

Most of this vast country, still with much forest, lies between 200 and 1000 m (660–3300 ft.). In the east there are several mountain ranges. The Ruwenzori range, known as the "Mountains of the Moon," on the Uganda border, rises to 5119 m (16,900 ft.). Farther south, Mount Karisimbi, near the Rwanda border, rises to 4507 m (14,900 ft.). Most of these mountains lie within national parks; their lower slopes had been well forested, but much of this has been cut by refugees from the civil war in Rwanda. The orchids of Zaire have been covered in two volumes (Geerinck 1984, 1992), but there are still undoubtedly more to be found, as any intensive collecting seems to turn up new species.

Zambia (Northern Rhodesia)
Capital: Lusaka
Area: 752,615 sq. km (290,510 sq. mi.)
Population: 8,780,000

Much of the country lies between 1000 and 1500 m (3300–5000 ft.), with the Luangwa and Zambezi Valleys lower, to 500 m (1650 ft.). There is not much forest, but large expanses of woodland. The Mwinilunga area in the northwest corner has several species of orchids more typical of western Africa. About 370 species of orchid are known in 50 genera. These are covered in the *Flora Zambesiaca* (la Croix and Cribb 1995, and in press) and in Williamson (1977), the latter with many color illustrations.

Zimbabwe (Southern Rhodesia)
Capital: Harare
Area: 390,310 sq. km (150,660 sq. mi.)
Population: 10,019,000

Much of the country is dry and subject to fairly frequent droughts, but the mountains of the eastern highlands, which rise to 2595 m (8560 ft.), are particularly rich in orchids. Most of the central part of the country lies over 1000 m (3300 ft.), and this area has many more terrestrial species than epiphytic. About 350 species are known in 54 genera; about one-quarter of these species are epiphytic. Orchids of Zimbabwe are covered in the *Flora Zambesiaca* (la Croix and Cribb 1995, and in press); the epiphytic orchids of Zimbabwe are also covered in Ball (1978).

Chapter 4

Classification

The Orchidaceae is generally thought to be the largest family of flowering plant, the only possible rival being the Compositae (Asteraceae). There are probably at least 20,000 species, three-quarters of which are epiphytic, in more than 700 genera, but estimates vary greatly. Over the years, there have been many attempts to classify the family, and there will doubtless be more. A good classification should reflect relationships, and ideas about relationships tend to change as more information becomes available.

Earlier classifications took into account only morphological features, that is, what the plants looked like. Today, other factors, such as anatomy, chemical composition, and genetic analysis, are considered. None of this, however, is of any great concern to the grower of orchids. In this volume, we have followed Dressler's 1993 classification, an update of his 1981 arrangement, but not the last word. Dressler (1993) recognized five subfamilies in the Orchidaceae: the Apostasioideae, Cypripedioideae, Spiranthoideae, Orchidoideae, and Epidendroideae. The first two subfamilies are not represented in Africa, nor are there many of the Spiranthoideae; most African orchids belong to the Epidendroideae or to the Orchidoideae. Table 4.1 lists only the genera that are represented in Africa; those that are described in this volume are printed in bold type.

What concerns growers of orchids much more than the system of classification is the frequent name changes that take place. Complaints about this are not confined to orchid growers: all gardeners blame botanists for substituting unfamiliar names for ones that are well known, but orchid growers are probably more affected than most as there is rarely any common name that can be used as an alternative. There are good reasons for these name changes; they are not, as many horticulturists seem to believe, made deliberately by botanists to spite them. The most common reason is to fulfill the law of priority, which states that the earliest name validly published after 1753, when Linnaeus published *Species Plantarum,* takes precedence. Sometimes the earliest name has simply been overlooked. More often, a widespread species was described by different botanists in different parts of its range and may have become quite well known under more than one of these names. In such a case, the earliest name is the one by which the species should be known.

Frequently, two apparently different plants have been described as two species, but further collections have shown that there is such a range of intermediates that no dividing line can be drawn. This is more or less the situation with *Ansellia.* In the early days of orchid collecting in Africa, most angraecoid orchids were described as species of *Angraecum, Listrostachys,* or *Mystacidium.* With greater knowledge, a number of different genera have been created. The reverse can also occur: *Megaclinium* and *Cirrhopetalum,* originally described as genera in their own right, are now included in *Bulbophyllum,* although some people believe that *Cirrhopetalum* should be retained.

Another reason for changing a name is because it has already been used. This is probably more common at specific than at generic level. It should be possible to check names in advance, but in practice, mistakes can easily occur. The tiny orchid *Angraecopsis parva* illustrates two types of change. It was originally described by Phillip Cribb in 1977 as *Holmesia parva.* It transpired that there was already a genus of alga by the same name, and the plant became *Microholmesia parva* (Cribb) Cribb, the name being published in Mabberley (1987). Then, while Dr. Cribb was working on the Orchidaceae for the *Flora of Tropical East Africa,* more material became available, and the species is now known as *Angraecopsis parva* (Cribb) Cribb. A name given in parenthesis is that of the first person to apply the specific name.

The plant we know as *Aerangis kotschyana* was first described in 1864 by H. G. Reichenbach as *Angraecum kotschyanum.* In 1918, Schlechter decided that it was better placed in the genus *Aerangis,* and so it is now known as *Aerangis kotschyana* (Reichenbach f.) Schlechter. Changes of this kind occur much less often now, but can still happen. The genus *Cribbia* was created by the German botanist Senghas in 1986 for the plant that V. S. Summerhayes had described in 1936 as *Rangaeris brachyceras;* Summerhayes recognized that it differed in some ways from other species in the genus and in his revision of *Rangaeris* in 1949, he placed *R. brachyceras* in a section of its own; Senghas subsequently decided that these differences warranted recognition at generic level, and so that plant became *Cribbia brachyceras* (Summerhayes) Senghas.

When a new species is described, there must be a "type specimen," the actual plant on which the description of the species is based. The plant may not necessarily be typical of the species as a whole. For example, *Disa uniflora* is not usually one-flowered, but presumably the type specimen was. Some of the older type specimens are not very good, and it is not always easy to interpret them. The type specimen of *Bulbophyllum oreonastes* was collected on Mount Cameroon, and the species was described by H. G. Reichenbach in 1881. For many years, plants of an orange-flowered *Bulbophyllum* from East Africa and Malawi were known by this name, but J. J. Vermeulen, while preparing his monograph on African species of *Bulbophyllum,* discovered that they really belong to *Bulbophyllum fuscum,* in its variety *melinostachyum. Bulbophyllum oreonastes* is a valid species, but much more widely distributed in West Africa.

Of the 99 orchid genera currently recognized in mainland Africa, 60 are found only there; 12 are found only in Africa and the Indian Ocean Islands; 16 occur in Africa, Madagascar, and Asia (this includes *Aerangis,* in which one of the African species, *A. hologlottis,* also occurs in a few localities in Sri Lanka); 10 are distributed worldwide; and 1 (*Oeceoclades*) is found in Africa and America.

Table 4.1. Orchid genera with African species. Boldfaced genera are discussed in detail in this volume.

	Total no. of species	No. of African species
Subfamily Spiranthoideae Dressler		
Tribe Cranichideae Endlicher		
Subtribe Goodyerinae Klotzsch		
Cheirostylis Blume	ca. 22	3
Hetaeria Blume	ca. 20	5
Platylepis Lindley	ca. 10	1
Zeuxine Lindley	ca. 76	4
Subtribe Manniellinae		
Manniella Reichenbach f.	1	1
Tribe Diceratosteleae Dressler		
Diceratostele Summerhayes	1	1
Tribe Tropidieae Dressler		
Corymborkis Thouars	ca. 6	2
Subfamily Orchidoideae		
Tribe Diseae Dressler		
Subtribe Coryciinae Bentham		
Ceratandra Lindley	3	3
Corycium Swartz	14	14
Disperis Swartz	ca. 75	50
Evotella Kurzweil, Linder & Chesselet	1	1
Pterygodium Swartz	15	15
Subtribe Disinae Bentham		
Brownleea Lindley	6	6
Disa Bergius	ca. 145	ca. 142
Herschelianthe Rauschert	16	16

(continued)

Table 4.1 continued.

	Total no. of species	No. of African species
Monadenia Lindley	16	16
Schizodium Lindley	6	6
Subtribe Huttonaeinae Schlechter		
Huttonaea Harvey	5	5
Subtribe Satyriinae Schlechter		
Pachites Lindley	2	2
Satyridium Lindley	1	1
Satyrium Swartz	ca. 100	ca. 90
Tribe Orchideae		
Subtribe Orchidinae		
Bartholina R. Brown	2	2
Brachycorythis Lindley	ca. 33	ca. 20
Dracomonticola Linder & Kurzweil	1	1
Thulinia Cribb	1	1
Holothrix Lindley	ca. 55	ca. 55
Neobolusia Schlechter	3	3
Schwartzkopffia Kränzlin	2	2
Schizochilus Sonder	10	10
Subtribe Habenariinae Bentham		
Habenaria Willdenow	ca. 600	ca. 200
Bonatea Willdenow	ca. 12	ca. 12
Centrostigma Schlechter	3	3
Cynorkis Thouars	ca. 125	ca. 17
Oligophyton Linder & Williamson	1	1
Platycoryne Reichenbach f.	17	17
Roeperocharis Reichenbach f.	5	5
Stenoglottis Lindley	5	5
Subfamily Epidendroideae Lindley		
Tribe Arethuseae Lindley		
Subtribe Bletiinae Bentham		
Ancistrochilus Rolfe	2	2
Calanthe R. Brown	ca. 200	1
Phaius Loureiro	ca. 50	2
Tribe Cymbidieae Pfitzer		
Subtribe Eulophiinae Bentham		
Eulophia R. Brown	ca. 250	ca. 160
Oeceoclades Lindley	ca. 30	ca. 12
Pteroglossaspis Reichenbach f.	3	3

	Total no. of species	No. of African species
Subtribe Cyrtopodiinae Bentham		
Acrolophia Pfitzer	9	9
Ansellia Lindley	1	1
Graphorkis Thouars	5	1
Tribe Dendrobieae Endlicher		
Subtribe Bulbophyllinae Schlechter		
Bulbophyllum Thouars	ca. 1000	ca. 70
Chaseella Summerhayes	1	1
Genyorchis Schlechter	6	6
Tribe Epidendreae		
Subtribe Polystachiinae Pfitzer		
Polystachya Hooker	ca. 200	ca. 180
Neobenthamia Rolfe	1	1
Tribe Gastrodicac Lindley		
Subtribe Gastrodiinae Lindley		
Auxopus Schlechter	3	2
Didymoplexis Griffith	ca. 20	2
Subtribe Epipogiinae Schlechter		
Epipogium R. Brown	2	1
Tribe Malaxideae Lindley		
Liparis L. C. Richard	ca. 250	ca. 20
Malaxis Swartz	ca. 300	7
Oberonia Lindley	ca. 100	1
Orestias Ridley	3	3
Tribe Neottieae Lindley		
Subtribe Limodorinae Bentham		
Epipactis Zinn	25	3
Tribe Nervilieae Dressler		
Nervilia Gaudichaud	60	13
Tribe Podochileae Pfitzer		
Subtribe Eriinae Bentham		
Stolzia Schlechter	ca. 15	ca. 15
Tribe Vandeae Lindley		
Subtribe Aeridinae Pfitzer		
Acampe Lindley	ca. 10	1
Taeniophyllum Blume	ca. 120	1
Subtribe Angraecinae Summerhayes		
Aeranthes Lindley	ca. 30	2
Angraecum Bory	ca. 200	ca. 40
		(continued)

Table 4.1 continued.

	Total no. of species	No. of African species
Calyptrochilum Kränzlin	2	2
Jumellea Schlechter	ca. 45	2
Ossiculum Cribb & van der Laan	1	1
Subtribe Aerangidinae Summerhayes		
Aerangis Reichenbach f.	ca. 50	ca. 30
Ancistrorhynchus Finet	14	14
Angraecopsis Kränzlin	16	16
Bolusiella Schlechter	4	4
Cardiochilos Cribb	1	1
Chamaeangis Schlechter	7	7
Chauliodon Summerhayes	1	1
Cribbia Senghas	4	4
Cyrtorchis Schlechter	16	16
Diaphananthe Schlechter	ca. 50	ca. 50
Dinklageella Mansfeld	2	2
Distylodon Summerhayes	1	1
Eggelingia Summerhayes	3	3
Eurychone Schlechter	2	2
Listrostachys Reichenbach f.	1	1
Margelliantha Cribb	ca. 5	ca. 5
Microcoelia Lindley	27	20
Mystacidium Lindley	ca. 9	ca. 9
Nephrangis Summerhayes	1	1
Plectrelminthus Rafinesque	1	1
Podangis Schlechter	1	1
Rangaeris Summerhayes	6	6
Rhaesteria Summerhayes	1	1
Solenangis Schlechter	6	5
Sphyrarhynchus Mansfeld	1	1
Summerhayesia Cribb	3	3
Taeniorrhiza Summerhayes	1	1
Triceratorhynchus Summerhayes	1	1
Tridactyle Schlechter	ca. 40	ca. 40
Ypsilopus Summerhayes	5	5
Tribe Vanilleae Blume		
Subtribe Vanillinae Lindley		
Vanilla Swartz	ca. 100	9

Chapter 5

Cultivation

Most people who grow African orchids are already experienced orchid growers, and so there is no need here to go into the more fundamental details of orchid culture, such as water quality, different heating systems, and methods of shading, as there are many books that cover these subjects. African orchids are like others in their basic requirements.

Epiphytes and Terrestrials

In the area covered by this book, there are more or less equal numbers of epiphytic and terrestrial genera. Epiphytes predominate near the equator, with the proportion of terrestrials rising as one goes south. In Kenya, epiphytic and terrestrial species are approximately equal in number, while in Malawi, there are twice as many terrestrial species as epiphytic, although there are only a few more terrestrial genera than epiphytic. In South Africa, there are more than ten times as many terrestrial species as epiphytic. Epiphytic orchids, however, are much more widely cultivated than terrestrial ones and so they occupy what might seem a disproportionate amount of this book.

While most orchid genera are either epiphytic or terrestrial, some, such as *Stenoglottis,* can grow in either way. Several predominately terrestrial genera have at least one epiphytic member, including *Brachycorythis* (*B. kalbreyeri*) and *Habenaria* (*H. procera*).

Temperature

Many people are put off the idea of growing African orchids, believing that these plants need much heat because Africa is a hot continent. In reality, few orchids grow in very hot places, and almost all will grow well in an intermediate house. Here, we shall use the standard classification of warm, intermediate, and cool (see Table 5.1).

Table 5.1. Ideal minimum and maximum temperatures for growing orchids.

Classification	Night minimum	Day maximum
Warm	18°C (65°F)	26°C (80°F)
Intermediate	13–15°C (55–60°F)	26°C (80°F)
Cool	10°C (50°F)	21°C (70°F)

If the temperature falls a couple of degrees below the minimum on the odd occasion, it is unlikely to do harm, but the cooler it is, the drier the plants should be kept. It is important that there should be a day lift of about 5°C (10°F), although a short spell without this should not be harmful. It can be difficult to get much day lift in a cold, dull spell in winter. Maximum temperature is often more difficult to control than minimum. Since most orchids suffer in temperatures over 35°C (95°F), it is best not to let it rise much over 30°C (90°F); at these high temperatures, high humidity is very important. Any greenhouse will have hot spots and cooler areas, and the grower soon gets to know where they are. There are few, if any, African species that cannot be made happy somewhere in an intermediate house.

In sub-Saharan Africa, altitude has much more of an effect on temperature than latitude. Some of the hottest places, such as the Karroo in South Africa, are not even in the tropics. Malawi is a long, narrow country, ca. 900 km (560 miles) from north to south, but the hottest part is in the south, farthest from the equator, where the altitude is only ca. 60 m (200 ft.) above sea level. From whatever part of Africa an orchid comes, the higher the altitude where it grows, the less heat it will require, so knowledge of the altitude is very useful.

Ventilation

Good ventilation and air movement seem to be particularly important for African orchids. Many species are prone to fungal leaf spotting and rot when they are in the confined situation of a greenhouse. In tropical and subtropical areas where they are grown in a shade house, usually with open sides, this is much less of a problem. We have found that an electric fan hung near the apex of the greenhouse has been a great help. Furthermore, our greenhouse has automatic vents, so in summer a great deal of fresh air enters. This does have the disadvantage that it is more difficult to keep the humidity high, but we think it is worth it.

Humidity and Watering

It is impossible to give hard-and-fast rules for watering, as there are so many variables involved, such as type of mixture, size of pot, position in greenhouse, temperature, and so forth. Almost everywhere in Africa, however, even in the equatorial forests, there is a dry season and a rainy season, varying in length from place to place, and everywhere, except in parts of South Africa, the dry season is also the cool season. In winter, all the plants should be kept decidedly cooler and drier. Usually, for epiphytes, weekly watering is sufficient. A plant that originates in the equatorial forests will require less of a dry rest than a woodland plant; it indicates the adaptability of orchids that some species, such as *Rangaeris muscicola,* can grow in both of these habitats. As a general rule, the thicker the roots of a plant, the more likely it is to be adapted to surviving a long, hard, dry season. That applies to monopodial orchids; sympodial orchids, such as species of *Bulbophyllum* and *Polystachya,* have pseudobulbs as a reserve, and most can withstand some drought.

It is vitally important that water should be at ambient temperature, rather than used straight from a hose pipe. Cold water causes black and yellow spots and blotching on leaves, which may lead to fungal infection and which may cause buds to drop. Sophisticated equipment is available to regulate water temperature, but not necessary. All that is needed is a tank in the greenhouse with a submersible pump (sold in garden centers for fountains in ornamental ponds) connected to a hose and watering lance. When watering is finished, the tank is refilled and left to stand until the following day. If in any doubt about the quality of the water available, rainwater should be used.

Atmospheric humidity can be measured either as absolute humidity or, more usually, as relative humidity. The latter is the more relevant as it determines what moisture is available. Warm air can absorb more moisture than cold, which is why relative humidity rises at night, even though no more moisture has entered the atmosphere. In a forested or wooded area, it is surprising how high the relative humidity is, even in the dry season. Often the relative humidity at night will be more than 90 percent throughout the year. In the greenhouse, we try to keep a relative humidity of at least 60 percent and to not let it fall below 40 percent. We have a nebulizer, used by asthma sufferers to create a humid atmosphere, that blows out a cold mist. Situated near a fan, the moist air will circulate. Frequent misting and damping down of the floor will also help. We find that plants of Spanish moss (*Tillandsia usneoides*) hanging up in the greenhouse are a good indicator of humidity. Where the plants grow vigorously, all is well; places where the plants just seem to survive need extra attention.

Terrestrial Orchids

A few forest-dwelling African orchids, such as *Calanthe sylvatica,* are evergreen, but most die back in the dry season, after flowering, and have some form of perennating organ, usually a tuber but sometimes fleshy roots or partly aerial pseudobulbs. Strictly speaking, the use of the term *tuber* here is not correct; by definition, a tuber originates from a stem, so orchid "tubers" should be called tuberoids; in some cases they are root-stem tuberoids. However, it does seem more convenient to continue using the word *tuber.*

Perhaps the most important factor in the cultivation of terrestrial orchids is getting the plant's natural rhythm right. After it has died back, the plant must be kept dry or very nearly so. It is a pity that tubers of terrestrial orchids cannot be lifted and kept cool and dry, like dahlias, but unfortunately they shrivel and die if given that treatment. Usually, orchids let you know when they are ready to grow again, as green shoots appear above the surface; once this happens, and the shoot has grown to ca. 2 cm (1 in.) high, careful watering can start. In the wild, many species of orchid start to flower with the coming of the rains, and we used to think that it was these first rains that triggered them off. This may be so in some cases, but in many others, such as *Herschelianthe baurii* and many of the early *Eulophia* species, the orchids consistently come into flower before the first rain. Most of these early species flower before the leaves develop.

If possible, terrestrial orchids should be kept apart from epiphytes, as they do not like too much water flying around. Water on the new growth will almost certainly start up a rot. Why this should be, we have never been able to understand, as in the wild these orchids are exposed to tropical storms without apparently suffering in any way. It can be difficult, using a watering lance or a can, to prevent water from falling on the leaves. When plants start to show growth, we use a small (1 pint, 600 ml) watering can generally used for indoor plants. It has a nozzle that fits on the end of the spout, which is directed downwards, so that it is easy both to control the can, as it is never heavy, and to make sure that the water goes straight on to the soil. It is also a good idea, if there are a number of terrestrials, to sort them out according to their natural habitat. Species from dry areas, such as *Eulophia petersii,* will require much less frequent watering than moisture-loving species, such as *Disa uniflora.* More details of water requirements are given with the individual genera and species descriptions in Part 2.

Composts

Again, it is impossible to lay down rules as every grower has a favorite mix. It is important to use the smallest size of pot into which the plant can be fitted, as compost that is not used by roots soon becomes stagnant and sour. We are becoming more and more convinced that for orchids in pots, whether epiphytic or terrestrial, the greatest single cause of death is soggy compost. With epiphytes, there is usually some warning if a plant is not doing well, as it looks generally unhappy, and it is often possible to rescue it. Terrestrials tend to be less forgiving and if the plant is dormant, nothing amiss may be noticed until it is too late. Successful growers of terrestrial orchids usually insist that they are no more difficult than epiphytes, but we think that, because these orchids are invisible for so much of the year, they are more difficult, until one acquires the knack.

It has long been known that orchids have an association with fungi in the soil, known as mycorrhiza. The fungus enters the cells in the orchid's roots and rhizomes, and plant and fungus live in what is sometimes a precarious balance, known as symbiosis. Fungi can break down organic debris such as leaf litter and fallen wood, and these nutrients are transferred to the orchid plant through the breakdown of fungal hyphae. In a symbiotic relationship, both partners are supposed to be able to derive benefit from the association, but in this case, it is rather difficult to see any gain for the fungus.

Epiphytic orchids seem to be able to survive perfectly well in cultivation without the necessary fungus being present, as do some terrestrial orchids, but for other terrestrial orchids, their survival without fungus is more problematical. In South Africa, a number of indigenous terrestrial orchids are grown successfully by some enthusiasts, but few of these are in cultivation elsewhere. The noted grower Louis Vogelpoel (1994b), writing about growing *Herschelianthe* species, commented how the most successful growers of this difficult genus use compost from the original site and do not repot. This would ensure the presence of the necessary fungus, but is certainly not practicable for growers outside the plant's country of origin. Elsewhere, articles on growing terrestrial orchids have recommended that when plants are repotted, about a third of the old soil is reused, for the same reason.

For both terrestrials and epiphytes, it is best to let the pot become practically dry before re-watering. What a terrestrial compost is made up of is much less important than that it is free-draining. For forest terrestrials, we use a mix that is approximately two parts fine bark (as used for seedlings), one part peat, one part perlite, and one part perlag or expanded clay granules, about the size of a fingernail. For terrestrials that grow in more open areas, we use only one part bark and, in addition, one part gritty loam and one part coarse sand. We are sure that there are many variations that work just as well.

When we lived in Africa, we used to find many terrestrial orchids growing in wet, heavy, clay soils, but they will not grow in this environment in cultivation, where even species that in the wild grow virtually in standing water, need good drainage. We suppose this is because they never grow in stagnant water, there is always movement, even if imperceptible, and, as a consequence, a steady supply of oxygen to the roots. When a deciduous terrestrial orchid shows signs of dying back, it should be dried off and kept dry until signs of new growth appear. We give the surface of the pot a light sprinkling of water perhaps once a month, otherwise the tubers shrivel.

Species of *Disa* need different treatment, which is described in Part 2.

Epiphytic Orchids

For epiphytes in pots, we use a simple bark mix, with medium-sized pieces of fir bark, plus perlite, perlag, and, if possible, charcoal. We like to put a few pieces of polystyrene at the bottom of the pot. Many people get excellent results with rockwool, but we have not been successful with that. We suspect that it is necessary to use entirely bark, or entirely rockwool, and not to have plants in both.

Many of the epiphytes we grow are mounted on bark, and for these it is even more important to keep the humidity high. It is usually possible to spray mounted plants without getting excess water on other pots. A small amount of moss helps to keep the plant moist while it is becoming established, but do not use too much. The plant must be tied on firmly; if the roots can wobble about, they will not adhere to the bark. We use cork or pine bark; we have tried blocks of tree fern, but never found that very successful, although some people like it. Many species grow happily either mounted or in a pot; others greatly prefer one or the other; this will be mentioned when the individual genera are described. We must say here that experiences vary: what does well on a mount in one person's greenhouse may do better in a pot in someone else's. We tend to grow long-spurred species, such as *Aerangis,* mounted where possible, as the inflorescences are presented much more attractively when the spurs can hang freely.

We used to allow ferns to grow in orchid pots, as they look attractive and so often orchids associate with them in the wild. However, we soon found out why ferns are so important in the ecology of a forest for breaking down dead tree trunks and branches. Very quickly, even quite coarse pieces of bark break down into powder; if the pot is heavily watered, it becomes a soggy, airless mass, but if it is lightly watered, all the moisture goes to the fern and the orchid roots dry out. It is best to pull out the ferns when they start to grow, as their roots can be difficult to disentangle from the orchid once they are large. Much the same applies to moss on the surface of a pot. If it is too dense, the mat absorbs the water and the compost below stays dry.

Feeding

African orchids behave like any other orchids, so growers should follow their normal regime. The only qualification we would make is that African orchids are perhaps more intolerant than most of heavy feeding. *Ansellia africana,* while in active growth, may be an exception.

Repotting

Terrestrial orchids should be repotted while they are dormant. This does not need to be done every year, provided the compost has remained open. Epiphytic orchids can be potted at most times, although obviously it is better not to do it when they are in flower. The best time is probably just as fresh root growth is starting, but if the compost has broken down, it should be done at once, whatever the time of year.

With sympodial orchids such as species of *Bulbophyllum* and *Polystachya,* it is always a temptation to divide them when repotting, either to have spare plants to exchange with fellow enthusiasts, or because the plant is getting too large for its pot. Some species of *Bulbophyllum* have a rambling habit of growth and are not easy to keep tidy. Obviously, a large plant can be divided. Sometimes they more or less divide themselves if old pseudobulbs die in the center of the plant, but it is a great mistake to divide a plant into too small portions, as some plants never recover from that. Three or four pseudobulbs are the absolute minimum. In general, the larger the plant, the better it does.

Light and Shade

Few people who have not seen orchids growing in the wild realize in what deep shade many species grow. We have seen plants growing low down on tree trunks in forest, where a light meter gave no reading at all. More species, however, grow higher up in the trees, usually on the larger branches, where it will not be quite so dark, but few forest or woodland species grow right up in the canopy. The species we have found growing in the darkest conditions are probably *Aerangis distincta* and *A. montana* in Malawi, and *Diaphananthe pellucida* in the Congo. Relatively few epiphytic orchids grow in exposed situations, although some can grow lithophytically; these will be used to more intense light. Many terrestrial orchids grow in the open, in bogs and grassland, although they may get some shade from long grass.

In North America, the amount of light recommended for an orchid is usually given in foot-candles. We have not known this term to be used in Europe, at least not in Britain, where terms such as heavy shade, light shade, bright light, and so on, tend to be used. Low light corresponds to ca. 1000 foot-candles, medium light to 1500–2000 foot-candles, and high light to 2500–3000 foot-candles.

All greenhouses will have one part more shaded than another. Our greenhouse runs from east to west, and so the staging running along the south side is much brighter than that on the north side, which is further shaded by plants hanging in the middle. Plants that require heavy shade are hung below the staging, thus making it possible to accommodate most preferences, although the shadier parts tend to become rather over-crowded. Species that grow in forest like fairly heavy shade, and woodland plants, rather less. A plant that is grown in too heavy shade will usually have dark green and luxuriant foliage, but may not flower, whereas one that is grown where it is too bright for its liking will flower well, but have small, yellowish leaves. It is often necessary to move plants about a bit to find the spot in the greenhouse that suits them best.

There is relatively little annual variation in day length in the tropics. On the equator, of course, there is a 12-hour day throughout the year. In Malawi, which lies between 9°22′ and 17°7′ south and 33° and 36° east, the longest day is about 13 hours, and the shortest, 11 hours. In South Africa, much of which lies outside the tropics, the differences are greater. Day length does not appear to have significance in triggering flowering in African orchids. Where we grow orchids in northern Scotland, there is as little as six hours of daylight in the middle of winter. We give additional lighting to bring the day length to a minimum of 11 hours. The 18-hour day we get in summer gives some compensation for slower winter growth.

When growing only one type of orchid, say cymbidiums, it is easy to provide exactly the right conditions. Almost everyone, though, has a mixed collection and so some compromise is inevitable. Fortunately, most orchids are surprisingly adaptable, and it is usually possible to grow a range of species together which, on the face of it, have rather different requirements, by making full use of the range of microclimates in every greenhouse. A widespread species that occurs in a variety of habitats will not be too fussy in the greenhouse, but conversely, it does not necessarily follow that because a species is rare in the wild and confined to one particular type of habitat, it will be difficult to grow. A good example of this is *Polystachya lawrenceana,* an attractive species with bronze flowers and a pink lip that is known from only very few localities in Malawi on Zomba plateau and even fewer on Mount Mulanje. In these places, it grows as a lithophyte on windswept rocks, conditions that might be considered impossible to reproduce. Indeed they are, but *P. lawrenceana* grows very happily for us and flowers regularly potted in bark mix. Why it should be so rare in the wild is a mystery; it is not, as so often is the case, because of destruction of its habitat.

In the descriptions of genera and species that follow, we have tried to give as much detail on the natural habitats of plants as possible, but while it is important to know the natural habitat of a plant, it is also essential to remember that conditions in a greenhouse or shade house cannot be the same as in the wild, and it is possible to try too hard to reproduce these conditions. We have already mentioned how terrestrial orchids often grow in a sticky clay soil, which would mean instant death if they were potted up in it. Also, in the tropics, rain often falls at night and the humidity is highest then, but this does not mean that orchids in a greenhouse should be watered in the evening. The usual recommendation that orchids should be watered in the morning to give the foliage time to dry before the temperature falls in the evening should be followed. Orchids in the wild are rarely packed so closely together as in a greenhouse, and even if they are, they are high on branches, with plenty of air movement around them. It is possible that mounted orchids, suspended in the greenhouse, would not suffer from an evening watering, but it is a recipe for disaster for orchids in pots.

We have written here mainly about growing orchids in a greenhouse, with some mention of shade houses. African orchids can be grown in other ways, but we do not have experience with these. We know people who grow African orchids very successfully in a case; this seems to suit the majority of epiphytic species very well. We also know people who grow African orchids on windowsills in their houses with good results. *Stenoglottis* species do well as house plants, but for epiphytes, obviously the most difficult thing is to keep the humidity sufficiently high. Misting frequently and standing pots on trays with clay granules that are kept moist seem to be effective. *Orchids as House Plants,* by Rebecca Northen (1975), is useful to anyone who grows orchids in this way. The main drawback of growing African orchids in a house is that, once the bug has bitten, there will not be enough windowsills to go round.

Chapter 6

Pests and Diseases

African orchids, like any other orchids, are attacked by a range of organisms from viruses, some of which are invisible under an optical microscope, to baboons. When in cultivation, orchids can be attacked by the organisms of the country where they are living, and by organisms brought in on orchids from yet another country. It is therefore more profitable to consider the range of pests and diseases which do, and probably may, infect them, rather than look exclusively for specifically African ailments.

Everyone knows that plants are examined at least for health before they can be brought into a country, and yet not everyone is as rigorous in examining plant material that has been bought within a country or, the more insidious, plants that are being kept for a short while for a friend. There is also the near certainty, in the normal vented glasshouse, of invasion by organisms in what some consider to be the quaintly named "aerial plankton," in other words, small insects, mites, bacteria, and fungal spores picked up by the wind or convection currents and carried, sometimes for vast distances, until they gently come to rest on your darling and then start to do it no good at all.

The threat to orchids from pests and disease is continual and there is simply no substitute for the eye of the owner in picking out affected plants. Early treatment is the ideal: it cuts risks and costs and plays an important part in delaying the onset of resistance to insecticides and fungicides. With early recognition of danger, it is sometimes possible to use very simple means of control, including detergent and water and the ubiquitous fingernail. Cleanliness is another invaluable aid.

Biological versus Chemical Control

On the universal principle expressed in the verse, "Big fleas have little fleas which on their backs do bite 'em, Little fleas have smaller fleas, and so *ad infinitum,*" any pest has a number of enemies, though some, admittedly, are difficult to find. These enemies include both predators, which eat the pests, and parasites, which feed upon the living prey usually inside but sometimes outside, most usually for as long as it takes to complete one stage of development. These processes are lumped together as biological control.

The most common parasites of orchid pests are the young or larvae of some small wasps, the larvae of some flies, and some nematodes or roundworms. Predators include coccinellids, ladybirds (both larvae and adult), the larvae of some flies, ground beetles (Carabidae), rove beetles (Staphylinidae), and some predaceous mites.

The advantages of using biological control are that only the pests are affected and there is no cross-contamination (the enemies are specific) and that the pests' enemies keep themselves going in most cases once there are sufficient numbers. The big disadvantage is that it is not in the interest of the parasite or predator to wipe out the pest and therefore themselves. You never get 100 percent control with biological control. While this does not matter in large-scale agricultural production, it does matter if you are trying to sell or show an orchid plant with damaged leaves.

Insecticidal control is not always straightforward; there are a number of considerations to be remembered. Correct identification of the pest or disease is the first essential. The second is the correct selection of the chemical to be applied. It is then a matter of technique, selecting the right dosage and method of application, and ensuring that the application is at the correct time. The first two considerations are fundamental, and if one is in any doubt, it is strongly advised to seek professional help from extension or advisory services. Use of the correct dosage, as given on the label, is not as elastic as one might think; using too low a dosage means that the more susceptible organisms are killed off, leaving the more tolerant. This is how pesticide resistance is caused, it is also the way in which resistant strains are developed in the laboratory. Use too much chemical, and chemically burnt plants may result.

Pesticides can be applied in a number of ways: foliar application, the commonest technique; root drenches for attacking organisms in a medium; and in dips or in a medium. Foliar applications should be applied to all visible parts of a plant, spraying to run-off.

Pest and disease controlling chemicals come in a number of preparations, the most common ones being emulsifiable concentrates and wettable powders. Emulsifiable concentrates require little agitation, seldom clog, adhere readily to plant cuticles, and last longer, but they are more likely to cause phytotoxicity. Wettable powders are the exact opposite to this. They require frequent agitation, clog and abrade more easily, are more easily removed from surfaces, and are less phytotoxic. There are other preparations, including granules, flowables, dusts, and water dispersible granules. Always read the label.

Integrated Pest Management

Integrated pest management is a combination of intensive management, biological control, and very careful selection of insecticides. As far as orchids are concerned it is very much in its infancy, but the concept has a lot to recommend it.

Arthropod Pests

Arthropods are animals with jointed limbs and a hard outside skeleton, such as insects, mites, and crustaceans. The first insects we shall look at are the most primitive. The young, called nymphs, are like the adults except that they do not have wings and are smaller.

The order Collembola or springtails, are small, white or cream, to 5 mm long, wingless, with a muscular appendage which they use in jumping. When they are noticed, they are usually in vast numbers. They normally feed on dead plant material, but can damage fine roots, such as those of *Bulbophyllum* species or any seedlings, in a medium. We suspect them of entering peat-based composts. They can be controlled by a malathion drench.

Cockroaches (family Blattidae, order Orthoptera) were a minor source of irritation when we had plants in an open shade house in Africa, but we did not need to take active measures. The situation could be different in the Pacific region.

Thrips (order Thysanura) are small or minute, slender-bodied insects 0.5–5 mm long with very narrow wings fringed by long hairs. They are mostly yellow, yellowish-brown, or black and are found on both flowers and foliage. Some have the habit, when disturbed, of drawing the abdomen up and then usually taking flight. They feed by rasping the tissues and sucking up the juices, causing the characteristic damage, a dense browning of tissue. This is very persistent and may not appear until the insects have gone. They may also carry bacterial, fungal, and viral diseases. The black thrip, *Thrips pisivora,* has an alternative common name of thunder flies, which indicates the sort of weather in which they are common. There are usually only a few generations in the year. The worldwide yellow or greenhouse thrip, *Heliothrips haemorrhoidalis,* has several generations and is active year round. Adults are ca. 2 mm long with a dark brown body and yellow antennae. The nymphs are white to yellow with red eyes. The eggs are laid singly in plant tissue and cause blisters. This species is much more cryptic than other thrips, so plants should be checked frequently—lower leaf surfaces are attacked first, then the upper. Damaged leaves are silvery, bleached and, later on, wilting. Control is simple: an organophosphorus insecticide such as diazinon or malathion.

Bugs (Order Hemiptera)

No other order of insects affects people so directly because of the vast amount of damage done to vegetation and the transmission of viruses. An important reason for their large impact is their extraordinarily rapid rate of reproduction. Bugs feed by means of piercing mouth parts. All the bugs described here are in the suborder Homoptera, which do not have thickened wings (like shield-bugs) and are generally soft-bodied.

Greenfly, Blackfly, Plant-lice (Family Aphididae)

Aphids are winged or wingless, soft-bodied green, yellow, brown, or black insects, living in colonies. They are 1–6 mm long, and have a pair of tubelike cornicles on the abdomen. The remarkable thing about aphids is that they are parthenogenetic; that is, they produce young, which are females, without mating. A female aphid can produce between 50 and 100 live young. Normally these are wingless, but when conditions become crowded, winged forms are produced, which fly to fresh plants and start up again. Outdoors, sexual forms of aphids may appear in the fall, and these mate to produce eggs which overwinter. Aphids concentrate on the growing points of plants and have to take in excess sap, which is rich in carbohydrates, to get enough protein to produce young. The excess sugars are secreted from the anus as "honeydew." Sooty molds develop on honeydew and reduce photosynthesis. Ants may seek out aphids for their honeydew and tend them like cows.

Aphids are very important carriers of viruses, although there are, so far, not many orchid viruses. Orchid genera attacked by aphids include *Eulophia, Eurychone, Habenaria, Polystachya,* and *Vanilla.* Worldwide, aphids include the cotton aphid, *Aphis gossypii,* which is 1.2 mm long and is found on buds, and *Macrosiphon luteum,* which occurs on leaves and stems.

Aphids are eaten by some common insects, such as adult and larval ladybirds (family Coccinellidae), and the larvae of hoverflies (family Syrphidae), which are green and rather sluglike. There is therefore a possibility of using some biological control on aphids. Many insecticides also will control them. If it is intended to use some biological control, systemic insecticides such as menazon, dimethoate, and dimeton-S-methyl, which quickly enter the plant, have advantages. Contact insecticides such as diazinon, malathion, and synthetic pyrethroids may also be used.

Scale Insects and Mealybugs (Family Coccoidea)

This is a superfamily of insects with a protective covering that obscures the shape and protects the female and later, nymphs. The systematics of the group are complicated. They all feed by the long proboscis and cause chlorotic areas on plants. Like aphids, they produce honeydew sought out by ants. The first instar nymph is mobile and crawls not only over the plant but can move on to a contiguous plant. As the eggs hatch over a period, insecticide applications should be repeated sufficiently to keep up the efficacy.

Armored Scales (Family Diaspididae)

Armored scales secrete a hardened, waxy shield that may be circular, pear-shaped, or elliptical, over the body but separate from it. The shield protects the insect against predators and repels water and therefore insecticides carried in water. Eggs are produced under the shield and are sheltered until the nymphs hatch and crawl out to colonize a new area. Because these bugs have a fairly slow uptake of sap and in many cases do not take up enough systemic insecticide to be lethal, emulsifiable agents are usually more effective in control. White oil, diazinon, malathion, and triazophos are often recommended. An effective small-scale control for armored scales and indeed all the bugs mentioned in this chapter is the application of methylated spirit (in United Kingdom) or rubbing alcohol (in the United States) with a swab or brush.

Boisduval scale (*Diaspis boisduvalii*) is a worldwide pest that has been recorded from most orchid genera. Although we have not seen it yet on African orchids, it may only be a matter of time. This scale is small, 1–2 mm in diameter, circular, off-white or yellow. Males are 1 mm long, with three ridges. The scales infest leaves, leaf axils, stems, rhizomes, roots, and pseudobulbs. In the United States, it is considered the most damaging of all scales.

Proteus scale (*Parlatoria proteus*) is usually found at leaf bases where they form dense colonies. The female is 1–2 mm long, elongate oval, and brown or green with lighter edges. The male has parallel sides and is less than 1 mm long.

Soft Scales (Family Coccidae)

These are universal pests found on all orchid genera. They do not have a detached body armor, but are covered with a soft wax that may vary in texture. They feed and reproduce in the same way as armored scales. Because they may be found on any plant in the greenhouse, including ferns, which commonly grow in orchid houses, a very careful watch has to be kept. Again white oil, dimethoate, diazinon, or malathion may be used to control these pests, as well as alcohol.

Brown soft scale (*Coccus hesperidus*) is usually found on the undersurface of a leaf near a vein. The female is oval, 1–5 mm long, and yellowish-green or brown in color, frequently with brown spots. It produces live young parthenogenetically; these live under the females for a while.

Hemispherical scale (*Saissetia coffeae*) is dome-shaped, deep brown, and ca. 3 mm long. The dome sometimes has a depressed H-shape on it. There are no males, and the female produces up to 2000 eggs. This pest is more easily seen than brown soft scale.

Mealybugs (Family Pseudococcidae)

Mealybugs protect themselves with white, waxy covering, which may be moved to see the pink or yellow unprotected female underneath. The female is 2–5 mm long and can move freely. The male is much smaller and unprotected. Damage is the same as with scales, but more severe, and mealybugs seek out the safer sites, such as leaf axils. Insecticides that control other members of the family Coccoidea are effective on mealybugs, as are smokes and aerosol generators.

A very effective predator of mealybugs on the market, *Cryptolaemus montrouzieri*, a ladybird or coccinellid, requires a fairly high, stable temperature, 21°C (69°F). The female produces up to 500 eggs, which hatch into predaceous larvae that closely resemble mealybugs in their early instars, but grow into something much bigger. Obviously, insecticides cannot be combined with this predator.

Planococcus citri, citrus mealybug, is up to 4 mm long and has stout, marginal filaments. Up to 500 eggs can be produced in fluffy white masses. As the life cycle can be completed in eight weeks, this species can increase its numbers at a distressing rate.

We now move on to the higher insects. In these, the young, called larvae, are totally different from the adult. Feeding can be totally different as well, as in butterflies and caterpillars, but not always, as in beetles and grubs.

Butterflies and Moths (Order Lepidoptera)

Caterpillars, the larvae of the Lepidoptera, develop from eggs laid on the host plant. Some small caterpillars feed on and in flowers, while others damage roots. Most are cryptic.

Spodoptera litura (family Noctuidae) is only an occasional pest of orchids, but is so well spread that it has to be mentioned. The caterpillar is dark green with rows of dark, triangular patches on each side. It grows to 4 cm (2 in.) long and eats anything it encounters.

Phytometra aurifera (family Noctuidae) is found all over Africa. It can feed on any part of the plant and is over 3 cm (1 in.) long.

Theretra orpheus (family Sphingidae) is a hawk moth we have encountered in Africa. As is true for almost all hawk moths, the caterpillar has a projecting dorsal horn towards the end of the abdomen. The moth lays its eggs singly on orchids (species of *Aerangis* and *Tridactyle* seem to be particularly preferred), and the caterpillar eats the actively growing tips of roots. When not feeding, the caterpillar lies appressed to the underside of roots where it is beautifully camouflaged. It destroys all the growing tips and then moves on. This species may be confined to Africa, but there may well be another species somewhere which could emulate it.

Beetles (Order Coleoptera)

Both adults and larvae have chewing mouth parts. The adults have hard, armored bodies, while the larvae, or grubs, have soft bodies. Adults can fly and run rapidly.

Black twig borer (*Xylosandrus compactus*) is found in Florida, where it attacks canes of *Dendrobium* species and pseudobulbs of other orchids; it could move on to African orchids. It introduces ambrosia fungus into its tunnels where its larvae develop.

Vine weevil (*Otiorhynchus sulcatus*) is a common pest in Europe. It is liable to attack anything. The adults are 1 cm (0.5 in.) long, a dull black with fine yellow speckles, and feed on leaf and petal edges. Up to 500 eggs may be laid in flower pots by females. The grubs are ca. 8 mm long, white with a brown head, and live below the surface, where they feed on roots and tubers. An insecticide such as Sybol (a mix of pirimiphos-methyl with synergized pyrethrin sold in the United Kingdom) works, but there is also a nematode worm, *Heterorhabditis* sp., which enters and parasitizes adults and larvae. The latter is sold in sponges.

Mites (Order Acarina)

Mites, a group of arthropods, have eight jointed legs, an outside skeleton that is soft in parts, and are not segmented. Spider mites, which are important pests in several areas, feed on sap that they suck after puncturing the surface of the plant with their mouth parts. They live mainly on the underside of leaves, which turn silvery, then brown, then fall off. True spider mites form webs that are more easily seen by the unaided eye.

Red spider mite, *Tetranychus urticae* (synonyms *T. telarius, T. bimaculatus*), is sometimes called the two-spotted spider mite. In temperate zones, when the day length is more than 12 hours, this mite is greenish in color with two dark spots on the upper surface of the body. At this stage the mite is very active on plants. When the day length falls below 12 hours in these zones, red forms appear. These may be active, but more usually move on to the framework of the orchid house and hibernate within webs. Nearer the equator, red forms are more common and more active. Females lay red eggs, which seem remarkably large in comparison with the parent, at a rate of about five per day and up to several hundred in a lifetime. The egg hatches to produce a six-legged larva, which is generally red, then goes on to become an eight-legged nymph and adult.

Every one of our African orchids has, at some time, been attacked by red spider mite. Leaves can be covered by them, but, in *Cyrtorchis* species the central funnel is more favored. Control can be approached in a number of ways. Cleaning the orchid house with dilute bleach in winter to get rid of over-wintering individuals will slow down reinvasion in the spring. On a small scale, washing affected leaves with soap and water can help. There is a school of thought that believes that high humidity keeps down numbers, yet one of the worst areas for mites we have had is just in front of a humidifier. If humidity is high enough to coat a mite with water, this clearly would interfere with its respiration, but orchids would not relish such dampness.

There is a very well established technique of using the predatory mite *Phytoseiulus persimilis* as biological control. The predatory mite, which is introduced when red spider mite numbers are rising, attacks all stages. It can be distinguished from red spider mites by its pear-shaped body, long legs, and greater activity. Any insecticide present will eliminate this predator as, like all predators, it is more active and has a more sensitive nervous system. It would therefore not combine with chemical control of other pests.

Chemical control of red spider mite is bedeviled by the ability of the mite to develop resistance to miticides. These must therefore be changed every few years. The eggs of the mite are immune to nearly every insecticide and so multiple applications must be made. Useful chemicals include mineral oils, dicofol, tedion, and dimethoate.

Tetranychus cinnabarinus is sometimes found with *T. urticae,* but is more active throughout the year. Apart from this, what has been written about the latter also applies to this species.

Woodlice (Order Isopoda)

Known as woodlice, slaters, or pillbugs, this group of arthropods is among the few members of the order Crustacea that can live on land. They gather under cover and are especially prevalent under epiphytes that are tied to slabs, where they eat the new roots. They can also be found under pots standing on a solid surface and sometimes in pots. Virtually any insecticide will kill them. We have found permethrin, methiocarb, and bendiocarb to be effective.

Slugs and Snails

The last remaining group of animals that attack orchids is the slugs and snails, phylum Mollusca, order Pulmonata. With their muscular body and slime-producing foot they can move freely over any surface and are little affected by most chemicals. They are traditionally animals of cool, moist areas with plenty of vegetation, so cleaning up plant residues helps. We have found them to be prodigious climbers, so damage that looks like slug damage—large holes eaten out of leaves and, very distressingly, flower buds about to open—even though it is above head height in the orchid house, could very well be that. Biological control is a great help with these pests: ducks outside the greenhouse, frogs and toads inside. A preparation of a nematode parasite on slugs is available; it is in granules that are scattered around. Metaldehyde pellets sprinkled on vulnerable plants should complete measures.

Diseases

There is probably no intrinsic reason why African orchids should be immune to fungal and bacterial disease. Lack of information is most likely due to scarcity in cultivation rather than innate resistance. African orchids must be vulnerable to more diseases than have been reported.

Rainfall in Africa is seasonal, giving wild epiphytic orchids a drying season. It is not natural for plants to be moist all year. Even during the rainy season, though rainfall may be heavy, it is seldom of long duration and so the surface of orchids dries out between showers. From this it is clear that keeping the surface of African orchids wet for long periods can be damaging. Another factor is temperature; rain falls in Africa during the hot season and so water sprayed on foliage should be of ambient temperature. Ignoring these precepts invariably leads to trouble.

Leaf spots caused by fungi occur from time to time in Africa. The worldwide disease of anthracnose, *Colletotrichum gloesporoides* (synonym *Gloesporeum cingulata / Glomerella cingulata*), starts as a light green, rounded discoloration on the leaf, turning through yellow to brown, with a clear demarcation between affected and healthy tissue. As with all plants, damage marks cannot be removed without removal of affected tissue. The only curative fungicides contain thiophanate-methyl, although mancozeb is a good protectant. This disease is more prevalent in plants that have been weakened in some way.

Several *Cercospora* leaf spot diseases attack orchids. The most relevant is *Cercospora angraeci,* which, as the name suggests, is found on *Angraecum* species. It starts as an irregularly shaped yellow spot on the undersurface of the leaf, darkening to a purplish color. The upper surface then shows necrosis. A related leaf spot disease reported on African orchids is *Cercospora epipactides.* It is distinguished by having the spotting on both leaf surfaces from an early stage and the eventual dropping out of diseased tissue.

Phyllostica leaf spot, *Phyllostica capitalensis,* is reported on some African orchids from Australia, the Pacific, the Caribbean, Central and South America, and the United States. It is more cosmetic than *Cercospora* diseases and not so severe. It starts as lesions on the pseudobulbs or leaves, which become oval, sunken and brown and then form tiny, black pycnidia in the center of the lesions. Prevention and cure of these diseases are as for anthracnose.

Rusts occur rarely on Africa orchids. The most widespread is *Sphenospora kevorkianii / Uredo nigropuncta,* which has the typical appearance of small, orange pustules on the leaf undersurface. These pustules then appear on the upper surface and, later on, a black center appears. It is best to isolate the plant, remove affected tissue, and protect against further infection by mancozeb.

Bacterial rots readily start if moisture is left on a plant for a long time. These belong most commonly to the genus *Erwinia.* Prevention of bacterial rots is a management problem. General bactericides including copper sulphate mixtures are of value as protectants, and n-alkyl dimethyl benzyl and ethyl benzyl ammonium chlorides, sold as physan, consan, or green shield, as a curative.

Viruses are among the smallest organisms that cause disease. They are all parasitic, living within the tissues of the host, and cannot exist freely. They are transmitted from plant to plant by one of four ways: (1) when blades contaminated with sap from diseased plants are used in plant propagation or for cutting flowers; (2) when transplants are placed in infected pots; (3) when water containing infected pustules is applied to plants; and (4) by the mouth-parts of infected aphids. The necessary steps for control are obvious. The only methods of control now in practice are sanitation, isolation, and destruction of affected plants. Genetic engineering is being developed, and it may be possible to have virus-resistant orchids in the future. Until then, one has to continue with the above measures against an uncommon pathogen. Viruses can be detected by bioassay, serological tests, and electron microscopy. Details of these methods are given in the American Orchid Society's (1995) *Handbook on Orchid Pests and Diseases.*

Flower blight (*Botrytis cinerea*) is likely to form on flower buds. It can be controlled by thiophanate-methyl, physan, iprodione, or vinclozolin.

Practical measures of control often differ from the ideal. In our orchid house in northwestern Scotland, we have suffered from continual invasion by red spider mites, whitefly, mealybugs, and aphids. Attempts at biological control of the first two with selective insecticidal control of the others were not totally successful, and the plants did not look as they should. We now apply a monthly cocktail of permethrin and dimethoate with a fungicide and a foliar feed. This seems to be extremely effective, but the insecticide regimes have to be changed from time to time.

Chapter 7

Propagation

Vegetative Propagation

Sympodial orchids, such as species of *Bulbophyllum* and *Polystachya,* produce new growths each year and eventually form large clumps or long chains. These are easily divided by cutting the woody rhizome between pseudobulbs with a sterile knife. Sometimes clumps more or less divide themselves if the oldest pseudobulbs in the center of a clump or chain die off. The best time to divide these plants is when the new growth is just starting, or immediately after flowering. There are rarely problems, unless the divisions are too small: three pseudobulbs should be the minimum, but at least twice that number is better. It is better still not to divide a plant at all unless it is much too big for its pot, or a division is wanted for some particular reason, or, as mentioned earlier, if the pseudobulbs in the center have died and the plant is already forming two groups.

Monopodial orchids do not lend themselves so readily to division. Some species form branches, and any well-rooted piece can be established on its own. A branch without roots rarely develops any, although inevitably there are exceptions. Side branches of *Angraecum distichum* can be struck like cuttings while the plant is in active growth; they are particularly successful when started in an inert material like perlite. The related species *A. bancoense* and *A. aporoides* probably behave in the same way.

Seed Propagation

Growing orchids from seed is a complex matter that has led to extensive literature. African orchids in general behave no differently from other orchids (but see *Disa* in Part 2). The first stage in propagation from seed is pollination of a plant.

Pollination

In the wild, orchids are almost all insect-pollinated. It has been estimated that most are pollinated by bees and wasps of various kinds, but it is rather surprising to learn that perhaps 25 percent of orchids are pollinated by flies (Christensen 1994). Orchids have some of the most sophisticated pollination mechanisms of any plants. Very often, a species can only be pollinated by one species of insect; the exact pollinator is still unknown for the majority of orchids. It is often possible to make a fairly good guess from the color and shape of the flower. For example, orchids with red or bright pink flowers are often pollinated by butterflies (Vogelpoel 1994a). White-flowered, night-scented orchids with long spurs, such as species of *Aerangis* and many species of *Angraecum,* are almost certainly pollinated by night-flying moths, usually hawk moths. Most growers with an interest in African and Madagascan orchids will know how Charles Darwin, when he first saw *A. sesquipedale* in flower, predicted that a moth with a proboscis long enough to reach into the 30-cm (12-in.) long spur must exist, although no such moth was known then.

With orchids grown in artificial conditions, growers have to pollinate plants themselves if they want seed. Even when we grew orchids in a shade house in Africa, sometimes not far from where a plant was originally collected, the flowers were rarely pollinated, suggesting that the pollinator does not range far from the place where the orchids grew in the wild. Fortunately, hand pollination is not too difficult, unless the flower in question is very small. Figures 1-1 and 1-2 show the position of the pollinia and the stigma. The anther cap should first be lifted up. Occasionally the pollinia come away inside it, in which case they will have to be fished out, but usually they remain in place and are easily lifted up with the tip of a cocktail stick (though we sometimes use the end of a stalk of grass). The viscidium usually adheres to the cocktail stick. The stigmatic surface should be shiny and sticky, and usually the pollinia adhere without trouble, although occasionally it is not so easy to get the viscidium off the cocktail stick. In general, flowers seem to be most receptive when they are about two days old. It is important that the humidity be fairly high.

If possible, orchids should be cross-pollinated. Often growers have only one plant of a species, but if they grow more than one plant, yet only one is in flower, it is easy to keep pollinia for future use. After the pollinia are removed from the flower as already described, they are put on a square of tissue paper, which should have the name of the plant clearly written on it. The tissue paper is then folded loosely, placed in a small tube or jar with an airtight lid, and stored in the refrigerator. Pollen will keep in this way for some months; for longer periods it is better to freeze it.

Some species seem to be self-sterile; others yield some seed if self-pollinated but rarely as much as if two different individuals are crossed, and the seed tends to be less vigorous. It is, however, always worth trying self-pollination if there is no alternative. Pollinia are easily sent by post, as long as they are in a rigid container so that they do not become squashed. Make a note of the date that a flower was pollinated.

For hybridization, it is even more important to keep proper records. The pods should be labelled on the plant, and notes kept on any crosses that are made with details of which is the seed parent and which the pollen parent. Before hybridizing, it is better to remove the pollinia from the flower that is going to be the seed parent to prevent accidental self-pollination. For intergeneric hybrids, it may be necessary to try several, or even many, times before a cross will "take."

Collecting Seed

Before seed is sown, it must first be collected. It is not always easy to tell when a capsule is ripe, or nearly so. Usually there is a change of color from green to yellowish or orange-brown, but in most species of *Aerangis* the capsule is always pinkish-brown and a color change can be difficult to see.

When a capsule looks ready, it should be picked, wrapped in tissue paper, and kept in a warm, dry place for a couple of days. By this time, if it is ready, it should have split so that all the seed can be tapped out and the capsule discarded. It is important that no pieces of capsule or other foreign body remain with the seed; being usually larger than the seed, they are often not properly sterilized by the weak bleach solution used on the seed and cause contamination after sowing. The seed should be packeted in folded pieces of tissue paper, which can then be put into small envelopes and labelled with name and date. If it is not going to be sown at once, seed should be stored in a refrigerator in a dry screw-top jar.

It is even more difficult to get the time right for green podding. In general, once a pod has stopped growing, it should be all right. Once the grower becomes familiar with how long the capsules of various species take to develop, it becomes easier.

The time that capsules of different species take to develop can vary from barely two months to more than a year. *Angraecum* species belonging to section *Perrierangraecum* are among the slowest. It is not uncommon to see a plant in flower with last year's capsule still bright green, and the one from the previous year just starting to turn brown. Even within one species, times vary, presumably depending on conditions. Our notes on times of pod collection list *Aerangis verdickii* twice, once with 8 months to a ripe capsule, and the other time with 11 months to a green pod. It is always worth keeping a note of dates. In general, small pods such as those of *Microcoelia* species take a shorter time to ripen than large ones such as *Ansellia africana*. Table 7.1 is drawn up from our own experience and that of friends.

Table 7.1. Months needed to develop green pod and ripe pod orchid capsules. Data from author and friends.

Species	Months to develop green pod	Months to develop ripe pod
Aerangis appendiculata	–	7
A. biloba	6–9	–
A. confusa	5.5	–
A. distincta	–	9–10
A. kirkii	6–9	–
A. montana	–	6
A. mystacidii	–	4
A. oligantha	6	–
A. verdickii	11	8
Graphorkis lurida	–	3
Habenaria procera var. *gabonensis*	–	2
Jumellea filicornoides	–	8
Microcoelia corallina	–	2.5
M. globulosa	–	2–2.5
Mystacidium brayboniae	6	2.5
M. venosum	–	5.5
Polystachya affinis	–	3
P. bella	5.5	–
P. heckmanniana	–	5
P. valentina	–	5

Sowing Seed

Orchid seed is so small as to consist of just an embryo of 100–200 cells within the seed coat. These dustlike seeds are wind-dispersed; they are so light that it is believed they can be carried in air currents for hundreds of miles. Plenty of other plants have wind-dispersed seed, but there the fruit has some adaptation, such as wings or plumes of hair, to enable it to be carried for some distance from the parent plant. The tiny seeds of orchids do not have the food reserves that other seeds have to enable them to grow until there are sufficient leaves to photosynthesize and enough root to absorb nutrients.

As already mentioned in Chapter 5, in the wild, orchids grow with an associated fungus, known as mycorrhiza. This association of orchid with fungus was first noticed and described in 1837, but the full significance was not realized until 1899, by the French botanist Noel Barnard (1874–1911). There is still much to be learned about the identity of the various fungi involved. In a few cases it seems that a particular orchid is associated with a particular fungus, but more often a fungus will associate with a group of related orchids, and sometimes one orchid, or group of orchids, are able to associate with a variety of fungi.

Orchids produce a very large number of seeds, which is obviously necessary as wind-borne seed can land anywhere, and the chances of any one seed alighting where there is already a suitable fungus, must be small. This is presumably why in the wild one often sees one tree covered in orchids, while other similar trees close by have none. In spite of the dispersal mechanism, seeds are still most likely to develop close to the parent plant, where all the right conditions exist.

The developing seed depends on food materials broken down by the fungus and available to the growing embryo. For in vitro (asymbiotic) propagation, which is by far the most widely used method, these nutrients must be supplied artificially. It was the American botanist Lewis Knudson (1884–1958) who discovered that orchids could be grown asymbiotically (that is, without the presence of fungus) on a culture medium supplying all the necessary nutrients. He published the details of Knudson Solution C in 1946, and this is still in use today, although there are many other formulas available. Fay (1994) gave an account of the classes of compound that are used under the following headings: major minerals; minor minerals; energy source; other defined organic additives (such as vitamins, amino acids); non-defined organic additives (such as yeast extract, banana pulp); support systems (including jelling agents such as agar); activated charcoal; and growth regulators (such as cytokinins, auxins, gibberellins).

While a few growers mix their own formulas from scratch, most people use ready-made preparations. Anyone who sows seed on a large scale usually finds it necessary to use more than one medium, as certain species seem to show a preference for a particular formulation. Ideally, seed being sown for the first time should be tried on three or four different media to see which suits it best, but this is a counsel of perfection. Some genera seem to be more fussy than others; there is rarely a problem with *Angraecum* species, but species of *Microcoelia* and *Aerangis* are more tricky.

In practical terms, the greatest difficulty lies in the nutrient jelly. If it is suitable for the germination of orchid seed, it is also an excellent medium for the culture of undesirable fungi and bacteria, the spores of which are everywhere in the air. If these are present, the orchid seed is soon smothered. Absolute sterility of the nutrient jelly is essential, and the seed must also be sterilized.

We are very inexpert seed sowers, but have been taught an idiot-proof method which (usually) works by a friend who is an expert. There are several other methods to choose from (see, for example, Northen 1990 or Thompson 1977), but this is the method we have used. The term *flask* is always used to describe a sealed container of orchid seedlings, but any sterilizable container with a tight fitting lid can be used—honey jars are ideal. A sterile area for sowing the seed is necessary; the ideal is a laminar flow cabinet, where a current of air blows from inside the cabinet to the outside, but many people operate successfully with glove boxes or even a glass or clear plastic tank lying on its side. Roberts (1986a, 1986b) described making a glove box and a clean air station, respectively. Whatever is used, the inside should be wiped out with household bleach to sterilize the container.

The previous day, or early on the day of sowing, add one drop of liquid detergent to 300 ml of tap water in a jug. Put seed to be sown into a very small glass bottle or specimen tube. If more than one kind of seed is being sown, make sure that bottles are labeled or color-coded. Add water plus detergent, shake and leave overnight or until the seed has settled on the bottom; this usually takes several hours.

Put 250 ml deionized water, 2 g of agar, and 4 g of Sigma phytomax medium in a *large* jam jar, leaving room for the liquid to rise. (If another type of medium is used, quantities may vary, but it should be used at half the recommended strength for the initial sowing.) Heat the jar in a 650-watt microwave on high for two minutes to simmering point, stir well to make sure the agar is properly dissolved, and simmer again. This yields enough half-strength medium to put ca. 3 cm (1 in.) of medium in the bottom of five honey jars. Screw the lids on the jars, then release by half a turn. Bayonet lids, which are used on most marmalade and pickle jars should be avoided, as even when put on loosely, they tend to pull down and become vacuum-sealed during sterilization and are then very difficult to open. Check also that any lid used has not been distorted, for example, by using an implement to open the original jar. It is possible to get polypropylene lids to fit honey jars; these are particularly suitable as they can be sterilized and reused many times.

Place the jars in a pressure cooker, along with three containers of deionized water, one with just under 50 ml of water, the others about half full, with lids on or covered with kitchen foil. For replating or green podding, two petri dishes and any instruments likely to be needed, such as forceps, scalpel, and needles, should be added as well; the instruments wrapped in kitchen foil. An empty container, such as a beaker, is useful too to receive discarded liquids, but this could be rinsed in bleach if space in the pressure cooker is short. Pressure cook for 15 to 20 minutes at full pressure (15 lbs.) and leave the pot and contents to cool naturally.

The next day, or later the same day, make up a fairly strong (about 30 percent) bleach solution in a bowl for sterilizing things outside the clean area. Put 2.5 ml of bleach in a syringe, the outside of which has been dipped in, or wiped with, bleach. Move the pressure cooker as near as possible to the clean air station. Wearing a pair of fine plastic or rubber gloves that have been wiped with bleach, open the pressure cooker and transfer the contents to the cabinet, holding the sterile jars by the edge of the lids.

Using a plastic dropper, extract most of the water from the little bottles containing the seed, carefully leaving the seed on the bottom. Any seed that is floating is likely to be non-viable and should be removed with the water. Wipe the outside of the little bottles containing seed with the strong bleach solution and transfer them to the cabinet. Wipe the rims with a gloved finger dipped in bleach.

Inside the clean work area there should be a container filled with a strong bleach solution and deep enough to hold the plastic droppers almost up to the bulb. The droppers should be kept in this container when not in use. The 2.5 ml of bleach in the syringe is added to the flask containing just under 50 ml of sterile water. Then pour the mixture into the bottles of seed, filling them completely to the brim. Allow the seed bottles to sit for 15 minutes before drawing off the bleach by the plastic droppers and refilling the bottles with sterile water. (After a dropper is used in a seed bottle, a quick fill and squeeze in the bleach will rinse out any remaining seed and kill it, thus preventing seed from being transferred from one bottle to another.) Most of the sterile water now in the seed bottles is again drawn off, and the seed, in a little water, is dropped on the agar in the jars, which are sealed immediately. When all the jars are sealed, they can be removed from the sterile cabinet and labelled with name of seed and date (and type of medium if more than one is likely to be used).

The part of the procedure that involves sterilizing the seed can be omitted if green pods are used. Orchid seed seems to be able to germinate when a capsule is about half way to being mature. The complete capsule is immersed in a strong (about 30 percent) bleach solution in a jar, the outside of which has been dipped in or wiped with bleach, and then left for half an hour. In the cabinet, rinse the capsule in sterile water and put it in a sterile petri dish. Using forceps and a scalpel, cut off the column end of the capsule, then make two longitudinal cuts so that the capsule falls into two pieces lengthwise (rather like cutting a slice of watermelon). Scrape the seed-bearing surface directly on to a jar of sowing medium; a few drops of sterile water should be added to spread the seed over the surface of the agar. Seal and label. The advantage of green podding is that there should be less risk of contamination and less risk of the seeds themselves being damaged by the bleach solution. The drawback is that seed cannot be saved, it must all be sown at once, unless the capsule contains loose seed with a developed testa, which can then be stored normally. Also, very small capsules are not easy to handle.

Whichever method is used, the sealed and labelled jars are put in a warm, dry place where the temperature does not fluctuate much, with good, diffused or artificial light. They should not be placed in direct sunlight; thus a greenhouse is not suitable. After some weeks or even months (the time seems to be very variable), a green haze should appear on the surface of the agar as protocorms start to develop. Some jars are almost bound to develop contamination; throw them away. If only one small patch of contamination appears it might be worth trying a rescue operation. It is necessary to take away a generous patch of agar around the visible patch, as fungal hyphae extend much farther out, and it must be done before any spores are produced, which can happen very quickly. Penicillins are frequent contaminants. While the patches are white they are removable; once they turn blue, it is too late. Contaminants that have reached the glass are usually intractable.

Once the seedlings seem to have stopped growing, or if they are too crowded, or if the agar is drying up, they should be replated. This involves preparing jars with sowing medium as before, but at full strength (not half strength), and with 100 g per liter of mashed, ripe banana added to the solution before the jars are pressure cooked. The pH will need to be adjusted to 5.7. This is done by adding 5-percent weight per volume potassium hydroxide solution. If pH strips are not available, 2–3 ml of 5-percent potassium hydroxide will compensate for 100 g of banana.

The original jars of seedlings are wiped with bleach on the outside and taken into the sterile sowing area, where clumps of seedlings are transferred to the new medium, using a laboratory spatula or a stainless steel dinner fork or teaspoon (sterile, of course). Seedlings are easily crushed, and any damaged tissue in the bottle will release volatile organics such as ethylene that can cause complete collapse of the rest of the seedlings. If the protocorms have proliferated and form a dense mass of tiny plants, these should be carefully teased out with sterile needles, in a petri dish. Replating may be necessary more than once; seedlings grow faster in a flask than out of it, and it is worth keeping them in flask for as long as possible. We prefer to deflask in spring or early summer, but this is not always possible.

Deflasking

When seedlings are deflasked, they are put into a bowl of warm water and any agar jelly sticking to the roots should be washed off, as it is likely to become a focus of infection. Any long roots should be trimmed off, as roots that have developed in agar will not function once the seedling has left the flask; new roots will grow. Leave enough old root to anchor the seedling in the new compost. At this stage, seedlings are often dipped in a weak solution of fungicide.

We pot newly deflasked seedlings into a mix of fine bark and perlite, sometimes with finely chopped, dried sphagnum mixed in, with polystyrene chips at the bottom of the pot. We stand the pots with the mix (but not the seedlings) in the sink and pour boiling water over them to sterilize them (to some extent), to wet the mix, and to wash through any fine dust. Fit as many seedlings into a pot as possible; at this stage they seem to do better if crowded into what is known as a community pot. The seedlings must now be enclosed in some way. We put all our newly deflasked seedlings into a Dewpoint cabinet, where they stay for at least three weeks or until space is needed for another batch of seedlings. For a few pots, it is almost as effective to put them in a large polyethylene bag with plenty of air enclosed, or under half a clear plastic lemonade bottle, with a few small holes cut in it for ventilation. When these are removed, or the seedlings transferred from Dewpoint to greenhouse, it is necessary to see that the humidity is kept high until the little plants are well established.

Terrestrial orchids tend to be more difficult to grow from seed than do epiphytic. It may be necessary to use a different medium. Much work has been done in recent years, particularly by the Sainsbury Orchid Conservation Project at the Royal Botanic

Gardens, Kew, on symbiotic germination of European terrestrial orchids. This complex procedure can be briefly summed up thus: orchid roots are examined under a microscope for pelotons of fungus (coils of fungus that look like nodules), which are dissected out and cultured on agar. Part of the culture is added to agar mix containing powdered oats along with sterile seed. Seedlings raised in this way are much more vigorous and faster growing than those of the same species grown by asymbiotic methods. Much less work has been done on the germination of African terrestrial orchids, but it seems possible that at least some species would benefit from symbiotic germination.

Seeds of *Disa uniflora* and the related species *D. cardinalis, D. caulescens* and *D. tripetaloides* are in a category of their own. As orchid seeds go, they are large (to 1.5 mm long), although still without endosperm; the embryo is large. It is thought that the seed of these species might be dispersed by water rather than wind (Kurzweil 1994). Seed of these species can be grown without recourse to nutrient mixtures (although it can be grown under sterile conditions like other orchids). It germinates well in sphagnum moss; this must be dead, for if it is living, the seed will be smothered. The sphagnum can be boiled, but this tends to turn it slimy, not that that seems to matter. We generally use sphagnum that has been dried for some months and chop it into short lengths, which are packed into a pot on top of polystyrene chips, leaving 2–3 cm (ca. 1 in.) of space at the top. Water the mixture well, then scatter the seed on the compost, cover with plastic film, and keep the seed at a temperature of 16°C (60°F) in not very bright light. After about six weeks, there should be a dense growth of grasslike seedlings that can, in due course, be potted into whatever medium is used for growing *Disa* species (see section on *Disa*).

Chapter 8

Conservation

Orchids are at risk worldwide, and the two main reasons are habitat destruction and over-collection. The Convention on International Trade in Endangered Species (CITES) was formulated to prevent over-exploitation of rare plants and animals. (In this context, trade means international movement.) Orchids constitute more than half the species covered by CITES, and they are listed in two appendices. The whole family Orchidaceae is listed in Appendix 2 of CITES where, contrary to what many people seem to believe, trade in wild and artificially propagated specimens is allowed, subject to license. This appendix controls all readily recognizable parts, except for orchid seed and pollen, tissue culture and seedlings in flask, as well as cut flowers of artificially propagated plants. Appendix 1 of CITES, which covers all *Paphiopedilum, Cypripedium,* and *Phragmipedium* species and about seven other individual species of orchid, is much more restrictive but does not concern us here as no African orchids are listed on it.

If one wants to import plants covered by Appendix 2 of CITES, it is necessary to obtain a CITES import permit and to have a CITES export permit issued by the country of origin. This is where the system can break down, as many countries, certainly in Africa, do not have any clear idea of what should be done and, if in doubt, it is easier to do nothing and refuse to give a certificate. All too often, only one person in a country is apparently able to issue the export permits; he keeps them in his locked desk, and when a permit is required, he is in a conference in some other part of the world and not due to return until too late. It is not the system that is at fault, but rather it is the way people operate it. Some addresses from which permits can be obtained are given in Appendix 1 of this volume. If an import permit is obtained, it will give the address in the exporting country from which export permits should be obtainable.

Another problem is that not all countries are signatories to CITES. In 1992, four African countries were not signatories—Angola, Lesotho, São Tomé, and Swaziland. Article X of CITES does, however, permit acceptance of comparable documents issued by states not party to the Convention, subject to certain conditions. Basically, these are that the documents should contain the name, stamp, and signature of a competent issuing authority (nature conservation authorities are considered competent unless the State concerned has designated another authority for the purpose); that there is sufficient identification of the species concerned; and, that in the case of export, certification to the effect that export will not be detrimental to the survival of the species and that the specimen was not obtained in contravention of the laws of the State of export. In these circumstances, anyone wishing to import from one of the countries mentioned above, should consult the authority who issues import permits.

It should also be mentioned here that most countries have their own regulations in addition to CITES. It is always necessary to have permits to collect in national parks and forest reserves. These are usually obtainable by residents but are difficult for visitors to obtain. Moreover, when importing plants of any kind (except for seed and seedlings in flask), a phytosanitary certificate is always required by the importing country. This is usually obtainable from the department of agriculture of the country of export (at least that is where inquiries should initially be made); this is usually more straightforward than CITES documentation.

Some species of orchid, such as *Paphiopedilum druryi* in India and *P. delenatii* in Vietnam, are believed to have become extinct in the wild through over-collection, but this is not the primary problem in Africa, where by far the biggest threat is destruction of habitat. The felling of rainforest is a worldwide problem; in Brazil, cattle ranchers take most of the blame and in the Asia, Japanese timber companies. In Africa, it is pressure of population that is responsible. The number of people in Africa is increasing at a frightening rate, and they need fuel to burn and land to cultivate. Ways of life that were valid when a small number of people occupied a large tract of land are no longer so in an overcrowded country.

Tree-felling, of course, has effects that are much more far reaching than loss of habitat for epiphytic orchids. When a hillside is covered in forest or woodland, the force of rain is absorbed largely before the rain reaches the ground, and the soil is held together by the tree roots. In temperate climates, more than 2.5 cm (1 in.) of rain per hour is considered heavy rain. In Africa, however, this rate is common in the rainy season and often the rate is 10–15 cm (4–6 in.) per hour. On a bare slope, rain falling at a rate of more than 25 mm (1 in.) per hour can cause erosion. It has been estimated that a hillside under crops, if not properly terraced, can lose 200–400 tons of soil per hectare (90–170 tons per acre) a year. In other words, in one year, 100 years' accumulation of soil can be washed away. Terracing is rarely carried out in Africa, as in most parts people have in the past not needed to cultivate hillsides and so do not have knowledge or tradition of terracing.

Another result of tree-felling that bares hillsides is the development of flash floods that can cause considerable destruction and loss of life. Without trees, the rainfall itself becomes more unreliable. The city of Blantyre, in southern Malawi, is surrounded by hills that, until quite recently, were well forested. When we lived near there, it was very noticeable how the wooded hills would often have a cap of cloud by evening, while the bare hills did not.

Anyone who is collecting plants in the wild, either to grow in their country of origin, or to take out under permit, should not take plants from living wood unless, of course, the trees are about to be felled. With a bit of hunting around, it is usually possible to pick up plants on fallen branches or on dead branches still on the tree, which will soon be shed.

Most African countries have set aside commendably large areas as national parks and game reserves. Unfortunately, land that is well suited to game is rarely suitable for orchids. Most countries also have forest reserves, but these frequently seem to be taken less seriously, or at least they come well down the list when scarce resources are allocated. Furthermore, there has to be some incentive for the local people if protection of any kind is to be successful. This is now being recognized for game. Zimbabwe is one of the pioneers.

In Malawi, and presumably in other countries, fuel-wood plantations have been set out, using fast-growing trees such as *Eucalyptus* and *Gmelina* species, but even if wood is sold cheaply, nobody in any country wants to pay for something that they can get for themselves, free. Certainly, greater prosperity would help. In Congo, which has (or had) the highest per capita annual income of any black African country, thanks to its off-shore oil, we found that people even in remote villages tended to use bottled gas for cooking and so far fewer trees were being felled for fuel than is the case in other African countries. Ideally, orchids should be thought of as a resource and grown from seed in their native countries, as happens in some Central American countries and possibly in Madagascar. However, this situation is a long way off in Africa.

Orchids raised from seed are always to be preferred to wild-collected plants; they become established much more easily in cultivation, especially when, as is usually the case, a change of hemisphere is involved. Anyone who grows orchid species should consider it almost a duty to propagate them. Many people dislike pollinating their orchids as it shortens the period the plant is in flower, and on rare occasions, the pollinated plant dies. This, however, should not happen if only vigorous plants are pollinated. As to the loss of the flower, it should seldom be necessary to pollinate a plant more than once. An orchid capsule produces thousands of seeds, and if these can be successfully raised and well distributed, that species should be safe for some time.

In Chapter 7, we give some information on propagating orchids, but many people will not have the time, or not want to take the trouble, to do this themselves. In most countries, there are nurseries that will sow seed for people, either making a charge or, in some cases doing it free if they are allowed to keep, and subsequently sell, most of the plants raised. Places that do this can be found in the advertisement pages of journals such as *The Orchid Review* and *Orchids*. Information on deflasking orchids and on how to look after newly deflasked seedlings is given in Chapter 7.

Chapter 9

Hybridization

Why hybridize? This is a question we sometimes find difficult to answer, as our preference is for species; all too often the grace and elegance of a species are lost to the size, shape, and perhaps garish colors of a hybrid. There are, however, some valid reasons for hybridizing, beyond the fact that two species just happened to flower at the same time. One is vigor. In all groups of plants, hybrids are often more vigorous, free-flowering, and easily grown than either parent, and in the case of a temperamental or short-lived species, a hybrid of similar appearance might well be a better bet. Who would not welcome a hybrid that combined the intense violet-blue color of *Herschelianthe baurii* with ease of growth?

Another reason for hybridizing is size. This is particularly relevant with several Madagascan species, where some of the most beautiful orchids, such as *Angraecum sesquipedale* and *A. eburneum*, eventually become very large plants suitable only for a very large greenhouse. By judicious hybridization, large flowers can be grown on a smaller plant. Hillerman (1994) gave two examples of this. *Angraecum* Lemforde White Beauty, a cross of *A. magdalenae* × *A. sesquipedale*, retains the large flower size of the latter species, but with wider segments, and on a smaller plant. Hillerman's second example was *Eurygraecum* Lydia (*Angraecum sesquipedale* × *Eurychone rothschildiana*), which produces flowers 10 cm (4 in.) in diameter on a plant less than 25 cm (10 in.) tall.

A third reason for hybridizing is color. Almost all African angraecoid orchids are white, if not green or yellow-green, and while white flowers have a beauty and purity of their own, variety is always welcome. It would seem that there is considerable scope for using the few angraecoid species that are colored, such as the beautiful salmon-pink

78

Eurychone galeandrae and the bright orange *Ossiculum aurantiacum.* The latter may not be in cultivation, but we have included it in the species descriptions in the hope that if it is not being grown, it might eventually become available. Incidentally, it is not the only angraecoid orchid with bright orange flowers; the Madagascan *Microcoelia gilpinae* also has these. Dull, straw-orange flowers are quite common. Two angraecoid species have white flowers and red columns: *Aerangis luteoalba* var. *rhodosticta* and *Microcoelia corallina.* The former has been used in many crosses, where the red color is often passed on, but the latter has not, as far as we know.

Of course, a hybrid could just as easily combine the least desirable features of each parent as well as the best! Intergeneric hybridization is still rather hit and miss. The chromosomes in angraecoid orchids are usually small and not too easy to differentiate; much work remains to be done in this field. For more detail on chromosome counts, see Withner (1974) and van der Laan and Cribb (1986), among others. It has been pointed out that, provided the differences are not too great, chromosome counts are of less importance in the making of primary hybrids than in secondary hybrids.

Some natural hybrids do occur, and it is probably because of the very specific pollination syndromes of most orchid species that these are not more frequent. Several natural hybrids in *Disa* have been recorded in South Africa, and one intergeneric hybrid between *D. ferruginea* and *Herschelianthe lugens,* × *Herscheliodisa vogelpoelii,* has been discovered on Table Mountain. We found one intergeneric hybrid in Malawi, between *Tridactyle tricuspis* and *Ypsilopus erectus;* the plant and its parents all grew on the same branch, and what we presumed to be a hybrid was almost exactly intermediate in appearance. We also found what seemed to be a hybrid swarm of a cross between *Aerangis kotschyana* and *A. verdickii;* again, the putative hybrids were intermediate in appearance, and different plants differed slightly in lip shape.

The greatest scope for hybridization lies in some of the terrestrial orchids, in particular with species of *Eulophia.* Many attractive species, such as the bright yellow *E. speciosa* and the pink *E. cucullata,* have very tall flower stalks. Other beautiful species of *Eulophia* have short, inflorescences with dense heads, such as *E. euantha, E. thomsonii,* and *E. zeyheri,* with pale pink, white, and lemon-yellow flowers respectively, all with a large, dark blotch on the lip. *Eulophia zeyheri* may be grown to some extent in South Africa, but the other two species are not in cultivation, and would probably be difficult to grow even if they could be obtained. If it were possible, a hybrid involving these might well be easier to grow and could impart the desirable short, dense inflorescence to other species. Some hybridization of *Eulophia* is starting to be done in America and South Africa, but few hybrids have been registered.

Likewise, the genus *Polystachya* has much potential for hybridization, but little seems to be have done. Townsend (1995) listed only three registered hybrids.

Of the species of *Aerangis,* the one used most often for hybridization seems to be *A. luteoalba* var. *rhodosticta,* which usually transmits its red column to its offspring, although the color often seems to be not quite so intense. The only *Aerangis* hybrid with which we have any experience is 'Spicusticta'; our plants have been very slow, but photographs of a plant in flower indicate this hybrid resembles more the *A. spiculata* (a Madagascan species) parent, but with an orange-red column. *Aerangis kotschyana* has also been used frequently; this could be either to transmit the broader lip, or because it is one of the more common species in cultivation.

There are many *Angraecum* hybrids, but relatively few involve African species. Among African orchids, most hybridization has been done with *Disa,* particularly in South Africa, but there are still relatively few species involved and the numbers used will undoubtedly increase in the future. The first *Disa* hybrid, *D.* Veitchii (*D. uniflora* × *D. racemosa*), was registered as long ago as 1891. It was followed by *D.* Kewensis (*D. uniflora* × *D. tripetaloides*), which flowered in May 1893 from seed sown at Kew in November 1891. Seed of two other hybrids was sown at the same time: *D.* Premier (*D. tripetaloides* × *D.* Veitchii) flowered in October 1893 and *D.* Langleyensis (*D. racemosa* × *D. tripetaloides*) flowered in 1894. Other early hybrids included *D.* Diores (*D. uniflora* × *D.* Veitchii), registered in 1898, and *D.* Watsoni (*D.* Kewensis × *D. uniflora*), registered in 1900. By 1922, only 11 *Disa* hybrids were registered, and then there were no more until 1981, when *D.* Kirstenbosch Pride (*D. uniflora* × *D. cardinalis*) appeared. This beautiful plant seemed to give hybridization a boost. Cywes and Cywes (1992) listed 75 new hybrids registered between 1981 and 1991 and pointed out that of the 86 known *Disa* hybrids (75 new and 11 older), 92 percent had *D. uniflora* in their lineage and 80 percent had *D. racemosa.* By the end of 1995, the number of registered hybrids reached 135 and was steadily increasing. Because of this, there is no point in attempting to list them in the table below. By far the majority of hybrids are registered by growers in the Cape Region of South Africa (67 of the 75 new hybrids listed by Cywes and Cywes in 1992 were created in the western Cape), where there is a thriving society, the Disa Orchid Society (see Appendix 1 for the address of this society).

The first 11 *Disa* hybrids involved only three species: *D. racemosa, D. tripetaloides,* and *D. uniflora.* Now *D. aurata* (initially a variety and then a subspecies of *D. tripetaloides*), *D. cardinalis, D. caulescens,* and *D. venosa* are also used, but almost all the hundred plus *Disa* hybrids registered are derived from these seven species. The smaller-flowered species decrease the size of flower when crossed with *D. uniflora,* but increase the number of flowers. All are beautiful but there is no space to describe them here, especially as there are numerous cultivars of the various crosses, usually involving different color forms of the species. All are cultivated in the same way as *D. uniflora.* In 1988, a cross between *D. uniflora* and *D. bivalvata* was shown at the 1st *Disa* Symposium in Cape Town, and was described and illustrated by Vogelpoel (1989). Like the other seven species already used in crossing, *D. bivalvata* belongs to section *Disa,* but it is in the series *Complanae,* which has a corymbose inflorescence, with the flowers forming an almost flat head. This character is retained in the hybrid, which has been called Warren Stoutamire in honor of its originator. It has a very different appearance from all the other hybrids.

Much is known today about the inheritance of color in *Disa* hybrids. The pigments involved, anthocyanins, which give magenta-red and purple, and carotenoids, which give orange and yellow, appear to be inherited in different ways. The genes controlling the anthocyanin pigments are located in the DNA of nuclear chromosomes and so are transmitted both in the pollen and the egg cells. Genes for carotenoids are located in primitive DNA strands in chromoplasts, which are yellow plastids in the cells. Nuclear DNA is distributed equally in pollen and egg cells, but there are very few plastids in pollen cells and many in the egg cells. When fertilization takes place, only the cell nucleus and some mitochondria (responsible for cell respiration), but no plastids, pass from the pollen into the egg. Plastid DNA, which contains the genes for carotenoids, is only inherited through the pod parent and not through the pollen parent. This has obvious relevance regarding breeding for particular colors. *Disa uniflora* can be found in several color forms, some of which contain carotenoids and some of which do not. Louis Vogelpoel has written extensively about *Disa* breeding; references are given in the Bibliography.

Considering that there are about 130 species of *Disa,* there would seem to be considerable scope for extending the range of those used for hybridization. Besides the species mentioned above, other species that are starting to be used in hybridization programs include *D. atricapilla, D. elegans, D. longicornu, D. maculata, D. marlothii, D. tenuifolia* (synonym *D. patens*). Undoubtedly, more species will become involved in *Disa* hybridization, but it is likely to be some time before they are widely available.

Intrageneric hybrids are being made with species of *Herschelianthe* and *Disa* in an attempt to develop blue flowers. These two genera are closely related; in fact, *Herschelia* was at one time considered to be a section of *Disa* rather than a genus in its own right, and these plants may well end up there again. *Herscheliodisa* Darling Blue, a cross between *Herschelianthe lugens* (blue form) and *D. longicornu,* has recently been registered by Nicolas and Wilfred Duckitt. A natural intrageneric hybrid between these two genera, × *Herscheliodisa vogelpoelii* (*Herschelianthe graminifolia* × *Disa ferruginea*), was found by Louis Vogelpoel on Table Mountain in 1985.

Hybridizing in *Disa* is less demanding of patience than in most genera, as seeds mature in four to eight weeks from pollination, and seedlings can flower 18 to 30 months after sowing. The Disa Orchid Society of South Africa has published a book with color photographs and descriptions of all 187 disas that were awarded from 1983 to 1992 (Vogelpoel 1995). A second volume, with at least 140 more awarded plants, is in preparation.

Table 9.1 lists selected hybrids whose parentage we were able to trace (although we are sure there must be more). Many of these hybrids, although they were registered, are not generally available, and there is no, or little, information on most. If any are obtained, they should be given growing conditions similar to those required by their parents. Mr. Hillerman, of Angraecum House, California, has been in the forefront of hybridizing angraecoid orchids, and there are usually some hybrids on the Angraecum House nursery list.

Table 9.1. Selected African orchid hybrids.

Hybrid
    Parentage; Year; Hybridizer
        Comment

Aerangis Brian Perkins
    A. kotschyana × *A. coriacea*; 1967; Moir

Aerangis Callikot
    A. calligera × *A. kotschyana*; 1981; F. Hillerman

Aerangis Fastyana
    A. fastuosa × *A. kotschyana*; 1985; F. Hillerman
        Flowers 5 cm (2 in.) diameter, in autumn

Aerangis Fastusticta
    A. fastuosa × *A. luteoalba* var. *rhodosticta*; 1985; F. Hillerman

Aerangis Gini
    A. luteoalba var. *rhodosticta* × *A. modesta*; 1982; Lauralin Orchids

Aerangis Hawaiian Star
    A. articulata × *A.* Brian Perkins; 1976; Moir

Aerangis Memoria Rocky Clough
    A. collum-cygni × *A. biloba*; 1995; G. Carr

Aerangis Platysticta
    A. platyphylla × *A. luteoalba* var. *rhodosticta*; F. Hillerman

Aerangis Prediction
    A. ugandensis × *A. collum-cygni*; 1992; H. Pfennig

Aerangis Quanah
    A. luteoalba var. *rhodosticta* × *A. fuscata*

Aerangis Red Necked Swan
    A. luteoalba var. *rhodosticta* × *A. collum-cygni*; 1992; H. Pfennig

Aerangis Somacalli
    A. somalensis × *A. calligera*; 1983; F. Hillerman

Aerangis Somasticta
    A. somalensis × *A. luteoalba* var. *rhodosticta*

Aerangis Spiculakot
    A. spiculata × *A. kotschyana*; 1995; (W. Neptune) F. Hillerman

Aerangis Spicusticta
    A. spiculata × *A. luteoalba* var. *rhodosticta*; 1992; F. Hillerman

Hybrid
    Parentage; Year; Hybridizer
        Comment

Aerangis Thomasticta
    A. luteoalba var. *rhodosticta* × *A. thomsonii*; 1992; F. Hillerman

Aerangis Verticosa
    A. somalensis × *A. fastuosa*; 1978; F. Hillerman

Aerangis Winter Dove
    A. kotschyana × *A.* Amado Vasquez (*A. cryptodon* × *A. articulata*); 1993; R. Ciesinski

Aerangis hybrid
    A. luteoalba var. *rhodosticta* × *A. punctata*

Angraecentrum Rumrill Prodigy
    Angraecum eichlerianum × *Ascocentrum pumilum*; 1978; J. E. Rumrill
        A dwarf plant with small pale pink flowers (Hillerman 1986).

Angraecorchis Mad
    Cyrtorchis arcuata × *A. eichlerianum*; 1974; J. E. Rumrill

Angraecostylis Blush
    Angraecum eichlerianum × *Rhynchostylis coelestis*; 1982; H. M. Wallbrunn
        See photo in *American Orchid Society Bulletin,* November 1984, p. 1172.

Angraecum Memoria George Kennedy
    A. giryamae × *A. comorense*

Angraecum Orchidglade
    A. giryamae × *A. sesquipedale*; 1964; Jones & Scully
        Plants to 1.5 m (ca. 5 ft.) tall, with flowers 6–8 cm (2–3 in.) wide in winter.

Angraecum Rose Ann Carroll
    A. eichlerianum × *A. sesquipedale*; 1995; (G. Johnson) R. Ciesinski

Angranthes Cornucopia
    Aeranthes arachnites × *Angraecum eichlerianum*; 1982; J. E. Rumrill

Angranthes Luma
    Angraecum infundibulare × *Aeranthes ramosa*; 1985; Levy

Angranthes Primera
    Angraecum giryamae × *Aeranthes ramosa*; 1982; F. Hillerman

Ansidium Tessa Hedge
    Cymbidium pumilum × *A. gigantea*; 1993; G. Russell

(continued)

Table 9.1 continued.

Hybrid
    Parentage; Year; Hybridizer
        Comment

Diaphangis Kotschycida
    Diaphananthe pellucida × *Aerangis kotschyana*
        The photo in Hillerman (1992) shows an attractive plant very much intermediate
        between the parents.

Euclades Saint Leger
    Oeceoclades cordylinophylla × *Eulophia guineensis*; 1995; M. Lecoufle

Eulophia Jeannie Wolff
    E. streptopetala × *E. speciosa*; 1992; (J. Agnew) N. Wolff

Eulophia Michael Tibbs
    E. guineensis × *E. speciosa*; 1992; Paphanatics

Euryangis Grass Valley
    Aerangis coriaceae × *Eurychone rothschildiana*; 1992; R. Robinson (F. Hillerman)
        Euryangis is the genus name given to crosses between *Eurychone* and *Aerangis.*

Euryangis Spicychild
    Aerangis spiculata × *Eurychone rothschildiana*; 1988; F. Hillerman

Euryangis Victoria Nile
    Aerangis kotschyana × *Eurychone rothschildiana*; 1980; H. Pfennig
        This hybrid looks rather like *Aerangis kotschyana*, but has a much shorter spur and a
        broader lip, with no trace of the dark blotch of *Eurychone rothschildiana*. The plant was
        raised in Germany by Dr. Pfennig and exhibited as Victoria Nile 'Lisa' by Joyce Stewart
        at the Royal Horticulture Society in London, where it won an Award of Merit. It is
        illustrated in *Orchid Review,* February 1992, p. 71.

Euryangis hybrid
    Eurychone galeandrae × *Aerangis somalensis*
        Not yet registered, but offered in Angraecum House list.

Eurychone Virginie Moulin
    E. galeandrae × *E. rothschildiana*
        The photo in *American Orchid Society Bulletin,* August 1994, p. 894, shows a plant very
        much intermediate between the parents, with pink-tinged flowers paler than those of
        E. galeandrae and a dark-blotched lip like that of *E. rothschildiana*.

Eurygraecum Lydia
    Angraecum sesquipedale × *Eurychone rothschildiana*; 1986; F. Hillerman
        Eurygraecum is the genus name given to crosses between *Eurychone* and *Angraecum.*

Hybrid
    Parentage; Year; Hybridizer
        Comment

Eurygraecum hybrid
    E. Lydia × *Angraecum magdalenae*

Eurynopsis Fort Caroline
    Eurychone rothschildiana × *Phalaenopsis* Terri Cook; 1979; Fort Caroline Orchids

Herscheliodisa Darling Blue
    Herschelianthe lugens (blue form) × *Disa longicornu*; Nicolas and Wilfred Duckitt

× *Herscheliodisa vogelpoelii*
    Herschelianthe graminifolia × *Disa ferruginea*; Found on Table Mountain 1995; Louis Vogelpoel

Jumellea Filicomo
    J. comorensis × *J. filicornoides*; 1981; F. Hillerman

Plectrelgraecum Manerhill
    Plectrelminthus caudatus × *Angraecum scottianum*; 1984; F. Hillerman

Polystachya Alpha
    P. pubescens × *P. ottoniana*; 1995
        Said to be disappointing with a habit of self-pollinating.

Polystachya Estelle Truter
    P. vulcanica var. *aconitiflora* × *P. pubescens*; 1995; J. Truter
        Resembles a white form of *Polystachya pubescens* but with larger, more open flowers.

Polystachya Jesse Truter
    P. vulcanica var. *aconitiflora* × *P. transvaalensis*; 1995; J. Truter
        A green form of *Polystachya transvaalensis* was used. The flowers of the hybrid are white with a light purple anther cap.

Stenoglottis Bill Fogarty
    S. woodii × *S. fimbriata*; 1993; H. Koopowitz

Thesaera Rex Van Delden
    Aeranthes arachnites × *Aerangis kotschyana*; 1967; Rex Van Delden
        Said to be 20–30 cm (8–12 in.) tall, with greenish-white flowers, more or less intermediate between the parents. *Thesaera* is the genus name given to crosses between *Aeranthes* and *Aerangis*

Thesaera Enny
    Aerangis articulata × *Thesaera* Rex Van Delden; 1976; Rex Van Delden

Part 2

Chapter 10

Plant Descriptions
A to Z

Acampe Lindley

The genus *Acampe* was established by John Lindley in 1853. The name is derived from the Greek word *akampes* (rigid), referring to the brittle, fleshy flowers. There are about 10 species in India, China, Southeast Asia, and the Indian Ocean Islands; only one occurs in Africa. The African species is close to the Indian species *A. praemorsa* (Roxburgh) Blatter & McCann and may even be conspecific with it, but here we are following Cribb (1989) and keeping it as a separate species.

DESCRIPTION: Robust, monopodial epiphytes with small to medium-sized flowers. Sepals and petals similar. Lip saccate or spurred. Pollinia four, in two unequal pairs, with one long stipes and one very small viscidium.

Acampe pachyglossa Reichenbach f. PLATE 7
SYNONYMS: *Acampe mombasensis* Rendle, *Acampe nyassana* Schlechter

DESCRIPTION: A robust species, sometimes forming large, tangled colonies; stems woody, to 40 cm (18 in.) long; roots thick, 5–9 mm in diameter. Leaves distichous, in four to eight pairs, 15–25 × 1.5–3.5 cm (6–10 × 1 in.), strap-shaped, unequally and obtusely bilobed at the apex, folded, stiff, rather fleshy, dark green. Inflorescences axillary, erect, to 20 cm (8 in.) long but usually shorter, sometimes branched, densely several-flowered. Flowers fleshy, 2 cm (1 in.) in diameter, creamy-yellow blotched with red-brown, the lip white with red-brown spots, with a strong, sweet, diurnal scent. Pedicel and ovary 10 mm long; bracts 2–4 mm long. Sepals 9–14 × 5–7 mm, ovate or obovate, obtuse. Petals 8–12 × 3–4 mm, spathulate. Lip very fleshy, saccate at the base, 7–12 × 3–4 mm, rather obscurely trilobed; side lobes erect, midlobe ovate, papillose, the edge undulate. Column stout, 2–3 mm long.

HABITAT: Epiphytic on the trunks and main branches of trees in deciduous woodland, usually in hot, rather dry, low-lying areas; sometimes lithophytic; occasionally found in riverine forest, to 800 m (2600 ft.).

CULTIVATION: Seems to be most suited to culture in a basket, in a mix of very coarse bark and charcoal. It might also do well in a clay pot; if mounted, it would require a large mount. It needs bright light and intermediate to warm temperatures.

DISTRIBUTION: Angola, Kenya, Malawi, Mozambique, South Africa (KwaZulu-Natal, Mpumalanga), Swaziland, Tanzania, Zaire, Zambia, Zimbabwe. Also in Comoro Islands, Madagascar, Seychelles.

Aerangis Reichenbach f.

The genus *Aerangis* was established by H. G. Reichenbach in 1865 for species that had a long, slender rostellum and a lip that did not envelop the column at the base, but otherwise resembled *Angraecum*. The name is derived from the Greek words *aer* (air) and *angis* (vessel), presumably in reference to the long, hollow spurs. The type species was *Aerangis flabellifolia* from Angola, a name that is now considered a synonym of *A. brachycarpa*. Several species now placed in *Aerangis* were known before 1865, but had been put in other genera, usually *Angraecum*. The first species known, the West African *Aerangis biloba,* was described as *Angraecum bilobum.*

There are 29, possibly 30, species of *Aerangis* known from mainland Africa, with an additional 19 in Madagascar and the Comoro Islands. As far as is known, no species occurs both on the mainland and in Madagascar and the islands, but *A. hologlottis* is found in East Africa and in a few localities in Sri Lanka. Some of the African species have a restricted distribution, while others are widespread on the continent. Many have been described several times under different names; Joyce Stewart's (1979) revision of the genus has been invaluable. Since that time, 3 new species have been added to the 26 species Stewart discussed: *Aerangis distincta* and *A. splendida,* both new species described from Malawi (Stewart and la Croix 1987), and *A. gracillima,* which was transferred from the genus *Barombia* in 1989 (Arends and Stewart 1989).

Aerangis seems to be a natural grouping of species; even sterile plants are usually easily recognizable as belonging to the genus. Although *Aerangis* has not been formally subdivided, species seem to fall into two groups, most easily recognized by capsule shape. In one group, the capsule is ellipsoid and relatively short, perhaps three to four times as long as broad: *A. appendiculata, A. kotschyana, A. luteoalba, A. montana, A. mystacidii, A. oligantha, A. somalensis, A. thomsonii, A. ugandensis,* and *A. verdickii.* In the other group. the capsule is cylindrical and elongated, perhaps 10 to 30 times as long as broad: *A. arachnopus, A. biloba, A. brachycarpa, A. carnea, A. collum-cygni, A. confusa, A. distincta, A. gravenreuthii, A. kirkii,* and *A. splendida.*

Aerangis is probably the most popular and desirable of all African genera. The plants are rarely too large, most species flower freely, and the flowers of all of them have a grace and elegance rivalled by few other orchids. Unlike in *Angraecum,* the largest flowers in the genus occur in African species: *Aerangis distincta, A. splendida,* and *A. stelligera* all have flowers in which the lateral sepals may be more than 5 cm (2 in.) long and the spur to 25 cm (10 in.) long. All species seem to be strongly night-scented and are almost certainly pollinated by night-flying moths such as sphingids (hawk moths). All but four species are or have been in cultivation, and it would not surprise us if someone, somewhere, grew these. Thus all the African species are described here in the hope that at some time all will be available.

DESCRIPTION: Epiphytic plants, with a few lithophytic on occasion (*A. appendiculata, A. verdickii*). Roots of woodland species, where there is a pronounced dry season, thick (*A. kotschyana, A. verdickii*); roots of forest species, where humidity tends to be high even in the dry season, more slender. Stems usually short, sometimes elongating with age, only a few consistently long (*A. thomsonii*). Leaves fleshy or leathery, usually oblanceolate or obovate, sometimes strap-shaped (*A. thomsonii*); apex usually markedly bilobed. Flowers predominantly white, sometimes very strongly tinged with salmon-pink towards the tips of the floral parts and on the spur (*A. arachnopus, A. carnea, A. distincta, A. kirkii*), the pink coloring more intense when plants are grown in a greenhouse than in the wild; only *A. luteoalba* var. *rhodosticta* has a bright red column. Sepals and petals similar in shape, often reflexed depending on age of flower; the sepals, particularly the lateral sepals, often slightly longer. Lip similar to sepals and petals or wider and differently shaped (*A. kotschyana, A. luteoalba*). Spur relatively long, arising at the base of the lip, sometimes straight, sometimes flexuous, usually slender throughout, occasionally slightly swollen towards the apex; only *A. flexuosa* has a wide-mouthed spur, quickly tapering.

CULTIVATION: In general, species of *Aerangis* are easily grown, either mounted on a vertical piece of bark or in a pot. Most are better mounted, as this allows the long spurs to hang freely and most species have long roots that dislike being confined to a pot. If they are grown in pots, it is important that the mixture should be coarse and free-draining. The finer rooted species, such as *A. biloba,* are more likely to do well in a pot. We grow all our species in intermediate conditions, but some might be happier on the warm or the cool side of that and this will be mentioned when individual species are described. All species, even the forest ones, benefit from being kept cooler and drier in winter.

Key to *Aerangis* Species

Because the genus is complete, a key is included to help identify plants (which are often wrongly named in commerce). The key is based on keys in Stewart (1979) and Stewart and la Croix (1987).

1 Flowers with spur more than 10 cm (4 in.) long 2
   Flowers with spur up to 9 cm (4 in.) long 12

2 Column more than 25 mm long .... *A. gracillima*
   Column less than 15 mm long 3

3   Sepals narrowly lanceolate, long acuminate 4
     Sepals acute or apiculate but not long acuminate 8

4   Column 10–12.5 mm long; spur 20–24 cm (8–9 in.) long .... *A. stelligera*
     Column up to 9 mm long 5

5   Sepals less than 4 mm wide; spur not more than 10 cm (4 in.) long ....
     .... *A. megaphylla*
     Sepals 4 mm wide or more; spur more than 12 cm (5 in.) long 6

6   Sepals 8–12 mm wide, spur twisted, 20–25 cm (8–10 in.) long ..... *A. splendida*
     Sepals 4–9 mm wide; spur straight 7

7   Leaves obovate, but narrowing towards the tip; lip tapering gradually from the
       middle to a long acuminate tip; column 6–8 mm long .... *A. brachycarpa*
     Leaves narrowly triangular, widest at the apex and deeply bilobed like a fish-tail;
       lip becoming abruptly acuminate at about halfway; column 5 mm long ....
       .... *A. distincta*

8   Lip with 2 or more ridges at the base, in the mouth of the spur 9
     Lip smooth at the base 10

9   Lip oblong or obovate; spur 11.5–16 cm (4–6 in.) long .... *A. verdickii*
     Lip fiddle-shaped; spur 20–24 cm (8–9 in.) long .... *A. kotschyana*

10   Leaf venation not conspicuous; column 6–8 mm long; stems usually more than 15
       cm (6 in.) long; leaves parallel-sided .... *A. thomsonii*
     Leaf venation markedly reticulate, raised above the leaf surface; stems long or
       short; column short and thick, 5 mm long 11

11   Leaves dark green; dorsal sepal at least 13 mm long, usually 15–20 mm long ....
       .... *A. coriacea*
     Leaves gray-green; dorsal sepal not more than 10 mm long .... *A. somalensis*

12   Lip narrow and elongated, at least 3 times as long as wide, or nearly so 13
     Lip short, not more than twice as long as wide 26

13   Spur more than 4 cm (2 in.) long, straight or only slightly curved 14
     Spur less than 4 cm (2 in.) long, or if 4 cm long, then the tip curved in a distinct
       hook 25

14   Lip lanceolate, ovate, obovate or elliptic, with a long acuminate tip 15
     Lip of various shapes, but acute, cuspidate or apiculate, not acuminate 19

15 Inflorescences 30–60 cm (12–24 in.) long; flowers set 3–5 cm (1–2 in.) apart ....
.... *A. arachnopus*
Inflorescences to 20 cm (8 in.) long; flowers set 1–3 cm (0.5–1 in.) apart 16

16 Petals usually narrower than sepals; column 4 mm long .... *A. kirkii*
Petals and sepals of similar width; column 5–6 mm long 17

17 Sepals and petals more than 33 mm long .... *A. carnea*
Sepals and petals less than 33 mm long 18

18 Inflorescences 4- to 10-flowered; column 6-8 mm long .... *A. confusa*
Inflorescences 2- to 5-flowered; column 5 mm long .... *A. gravenreuthii*

19 Column more than 3 mm long, measured along the upper surface 20
Column 3 mm long or less, measured along the upper surface 23

20 Plants with very short stems; column 2–4 mm long .... *A. mystacidii*
Plants usually with conspicuous stems; column at least 4 mm long 21

21 Apical flowers of inflorescence opening first; anther cap with crested beak ....
.... *A. biloba*
Flowers at base of inflorescence opening first; anther cap with short, smooth beak
.... 22

22 Leaves 1.5–5.5 cm (1–2 in.) wide; spur usually 6–7.5 cm (2–3 in.) long; column
5–8 mm long .... *A. collum-cygni*
Leaves 1–2.3 cm (1 in.) wide; spur usually 4–5.5 cm (2 in.) long; column 4 mm
long .... *A. jacksonii*

23 Pedicels of flowers attached to short projections of rachis a few mm above each
bract; flowers saucer-shaped, the sepals and / or petals not reflexed ....
.... *A. montana*
Pedicels of flowers attached to rachis at the base of each bract; sepals and / or petals
reflexed 24

24 Inflorescences 4- to 15-flowered; dorsal sepal 7–13 mm long; spur usually 6–8 mm
long; column 2–4 mm long .... *A. mystacidii*
Inflorescences 1- to 7-flowered; dorsal sepal 5–8 mm long; spur usually 4–6 cm
(2 in.) long; column 1.5–2 mm long .... *A. appendiculata*

25 Column less than 3 mm long; spur slender throughout, often hooked at the tip
.... *A. calantha*
Column 5–8 mm long; spur tapering from a wide mouth ....
.... *A. flexuosa*

26 Lip less than 6 mm wide 27
    Lip more than 7 mm wide 31

27 Flowers crowded on rachis, less than 3 mm apart .... *A. oligantha*
    Flowers more than 5 mm apart (rarely solitary) 28

28 Spur more than 4 cm (2 in.) long 29
    Spur less than 4 cm (2 in.) long 30

29 Inflorescences 4- to 15-flowered; dorsal sepal 7–13 mm long; spur usually 6–8 mm
    long; column 2–4 mm long .... *A. mystacidii*
    Inflorescences 1- to 7-flowered; dorsal sepal 5–8 mm long; spur usually 4–6 cm
    (2 in.) long; column 1.5–2 mm long .... *A. appendiculata*

30 Spur 10–25 mm long; column 2 mm long .... *A. ugandensis*
    Spur 3–7 mm long; column 1 mm long .... *A. hologlottis*

31 Leaves linear-oblanceolate, widest near the apex ; lip suborbicular or fan-shaped ...
    .... *A. alcicornis*
    Leaves linear or strap-shaped, narrowing at the apex; lip obovate; column usually
    red .... *A. luteoalba*

Aerangis alcicornis (Reichenbach f.) Garay

DESCRIPTION: Stems short, to 3 cm (1 in.) long; roots 2–3 mm in diameter. Leaves narrowly oblanceolate. Inflorescences to 30 cm (12 in.) long, 3- to 15-flowered. Pedicel and ovary 13–15 mm long. Sepals 10–18 × 4–7 mm, oblong-elliptical, apiculate. Petals 9–15 × 5–8 mm, elliptical from a narrow base. Lip 10–20 × 10–15 mm, suborbicular or fan-shaped; spur 2.5–4 cm (1–2 in.) long, slender but slightly swollen near apex, gently incurved. Column 2–4 mm long.

HABITAT: Epiphytic on trees, shrubs, and climbers in thicket, 200–1000 m (660–3300 ft.).

CULTIVATION: This is one of the species not in cultivation, although it must be an attractive one, with a broad lip not unlike the Madagascan *Aerangis citrata*. It seems likely *A. alcicornis* would like fairly heavy shade and temperatures on the warm side of intermediate.

DISTRIBUTION: Mozambique, Tanzania.

NOTE: The type specimen was collected by John Kirk in 1859 while on David Livingstone's Zambezi expedition. La Croix and la Croix (1991) described how confusion arose over the collection locality. We do not propose to repeat that discussion here, except to say that some of the leaves on the type sheet, which must have given rise to the specific epithet *alcicornis* (like an elk's antlers), do not belong to that species but to *Aerangis distincta,* a species not described until 1987.

Aerangis appendiculata (De Wildeman) Schlechter

DESCRIPTION: Stems short; roots relatively stout, 3–5 mm in diameter. Leaves three to four, to 8 × 3 cm (3 × 1 in.), oblanceolate, dark green, either fleshy or leathery, often with noticeable reticulate venation. Inflorescences pendent, 8–14 cm (3–6 in.), to 10-flowered. Pedicel and ovary 11–14 mm long. Flowers white. Sepals and petals 5–8 × 2–4 mm, elliptic to obovate, the lateral sepals strongly reflexed. Lip 7–8 × 3–4 mm, elliptic or oblong, slightly apiculate; spur 4–6 cm (2 in.) long, slightly incurved. Column 1.5–2 mm long, with a long rostellum. Capsules ovoid, 15 × 6 mm.

HABITAT: Occurs in a variety of habitats, such as evergreen forest, high rainfall woodland, and in patches of thicket, 1150–1850 m (3800–6100 ft.). Usually epiphytic at a low level on tree trunks in heavy shade, but occasionally lithophytic (usually at higher altitudes) in bright light.

CULTIVATION: *Aerangis appendiculata* seems to be more successful when mounted on bark than when grown in a pot. It is not too demanding, but moderate shade is probably best and it needs to be kept drier in winter, as there is a risk of the crown rotting if it is too wet when the temperatures are relatively low. In our greenhouse, it usually flowers in spring (June).

DISTRIBUTION: Malawi, Mozambique, Zambia, Zimbabwe.

NOTE: This species closely resembles *Aerangis mystacidii,* differing in the slightly smaller flowers with a longer rostellum, and shorter spur. Some specimens seem to be on the borderline between the two species.

Aerangis arachnopus (Reichenbach f.) Schlechter   PLATE 8, FIGURE 10-1

DESCRIPTION: Stems short; roots fine, 2–3 mm in diameter, long, gray. Leaves four to six, borne in a fan, to 14 × 4.5 cm (6 × 2 in.), oblanceolate or obovate, unequally and obtusely bilobed at the apex, rather light green, sometimes dotted with black. Inflorescences pendent, very slender, to 60 cm (24 in.) long, with three to eight flowers set 3–5 cm (1–2 in.) apart on a rather zigzag rachis. Pedicel and ovary 4 cm (2 in.) long, salmon-pink, slender; bracts black, 3 mm long. Flowers white, strongly tinged with pink towards the tips of the floral parts, or pale pink. Sepals, petals, and lip all narrowly lanceolate, acuminate. Dorsal sepal 22 × 4 mm, curving forwards, the edges slightly recurved; lateral sepals similar, but slightly curved and deflexed. Petals 22 × 3 mm, reflexed. Lip 25 × 4 mm, deflexed, the edges curved back; spur 6–7 cm (2–3 in.) long, at first parallel to the ovary, then forming almost a right angle bend and narrowing in diameter from 2 mm to 1 mm at the bend. Column 7 mm long, slender, pink at base.

HABITAT: Evergreen forest, below 1000 m (3300 ft.). We found this species in Congo, growing profusely on old citrus trees in an abandoned garden, at 400 m (1300 ft.).

CULTIVATION: Although first described as *Angraecum arachnopus* as long ago as 1854, this species is not common in cultivation. We find it an obliging plant and grow it in moderate shade in intermediate conditions, but it might do even better slightly warmer. In our greenhouse, it usually flowers in summer (late July).

Figure 10-1. *Aerangis arachnopus.* Plant, ×0.75.

DISTRIBUTION: Cameroon, Congo, Gabon, Zaire. Possibly Ghana: the type specimen was said to come from there, but the species has never been found there since.

Aerangis biloba (Lindley) Schlechter

DESCRIPTION: First described in 1840 by John Lindley as *Angraecum bilobum*, from a specimen originating in Ghana. Stems usually short, but can be to 20 cm (8 in.) long; roots 2–3 mm in diameter. Leaves 4 to 10, to 18 × 3–6 cm (7 × 1–2 in.) long, distichous, obovate, obtusely bilobed at apex, dark green with black dots. Inflorescences pendent, 10–40 cm (4–16 in.) long, 8- to 10-flowered. Pedicel and ovary 2–3 cm (1 in.) long; bracts 3–4 mm long. Flowers white, the spur pinkish. Sepals and petals spreading, all narrowly lanceolate, acute, 12–25 × 5–6 mm. Lip 15–25 × 6–8 mm, deflexed, oblanceolate, cuspidate; spur 5–6 cm (2 in.) long, straight or slightly curved. Column 3–6 mm long, the anther cap with a median crest. Capsules elongated, cylindrical.

HABITAT: Forest, woodland and thicket, often found on plantation crops such as cocoa, to 700 m (2300 ft.).

CULTIVATION: An easy species that flowers regularly. Does well in a pot with bark mix, but can also be mounted. Needs intermediate to warm temperatures and high humidity. We are told that this species does particularly well in a case. In our greenhouse, it flowers in winter (November and December).

DISTRIBUTION: Cameroon, Ghana, Guinea, Ivory Coast, Liberia, Nigeria, Senegal, Sierra Leone, Togo.

Aerangis brachycarpa (A. Richard) Dur. & Schinz   FIGURE 10-2
SYNONYM: *Aerangis flabellifolia* Reichenbach f.

DESCRIPTION: Stems woody, to 20 cm (8 in.) long but usually shorter; roots 4–5 mm in diameter. Leaves 4 to 12, to 25 (10 in.) long, 2–6 cm (1–2 in.) wide near the apex, obovate, unequally bilobed at the apex, the lobes rounded, fleshy or leathery, dull green with black dots. Inflorescences to 25 cm (10 in.) long, arching or pendent, 2- to 12-flowered. Flowers white, sometimes tinged with pink. Pedicel and ovary 3.5–7 cm (2–3 in.) long; bracts to 9 mm long. Sepals and petals narrowly lanceolate, acuminate, often with the margins recurved so that they look even narrower, 20–45 × 4–8 mm, the dorsal sepal erect and the lateral sepals and petals reflexed. Lip deflexed, 20–45 × 5–10 mm, lanceolate, acuminate; spur 12–24 cm (5–9 in.) long, straight or slightly curved. Column 6–8 mm long. Capsule narrowly cylindrical, to 20 cm (8 in.) long.

HABITAT: In dense shade, usually epiphytic at a low level on tree trunks, branches, and large shrubs, 1500–2300 m (5000–7600 ft.).

CULTIVATION: Given shade, high humidity and intermediate temperatures, generally does well mounted. In our greenhouse, it flowers in fall (September and October).

DISTRIBUTION: Angola, Ethiopia, Kenya, Tanzania, Uganda, Zambia.

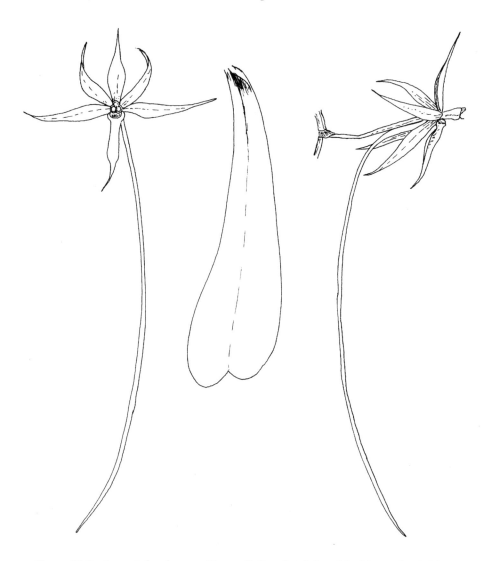

Figure 10-2. *Aerangis brachycarpa.* Flower (left and right) and leaf (center), ×0.75.

Aerangis calantha (Schlechter) Schlechter

DESCRIPTION: A small species; stems short, woody; roots slender, 1–1.5 mm in diameter. Leaves two to six, 3–8 cm (1–3 in.) × 4–8 mm, linear, often curved, unequally bilobed at apex, the lobes acute, the shorter lobe sometimes absent, dark green. Inflorescences to 11 cm (4 in.) long, 2- to 8-flowered. Flowers white, the spur and ovary often pink-tinged. Pedicel and ovary 12–17 mm long; bracts 1–3 mm long. Sepals 7–12 × 2–3.5 mm, oblong-lanceolate, subacute, the lateral sepals slightly longer and narrower than the dorsal. Petals 7–10 × 2–2.5 mm, narrowly oblong, spreading or somewhat reflexed. Lip 7–10 × 2–3.5 mm, oblong-lanceolate, apiculate; spur 2.5–4 cm (1–2 in.) long, slender, often curved forward like a hook in the apical 5–10 mm. Column short and stout, 1.5–2 mm long. Capsule cylindrical, to 5 × 0.5 cm (2 × 0.25 in).

HABITAT: Usually epiphytic on small branches and twigs in deep shade, often found on plantation trees such as cocoa, coffee, and citrus, 1000–1650 m (3300–5500 ft.).

CULTIVATION: Probably requires intermediate temperatures, with shade and high humidity. With its fine roots, it should be one of those species that will do well in a pot.

DISTRIBUTION: Angola, Cameroon, Central African Republic, Equatorial Guinea, Ghana, Tanzania, Uganda, Zaire.

Aerangis carnea J. Stewart PLATE 9

DESCRIPTION: Stems short, occasionally to 8 cm (3 in.) long; roots numerous, 2–3 mm in diameter. Leaves several, to 15 × 3 cm (6 × 1 in.), dark green, oblanceolate with a sheathing base, unequally bilobed at the apex, the lobes 3–20 mm long, triangular acute. Inflorescences 2- to 7-flowered. Flowers pinkish, or white very strongly tinged with salmon-pink. Pedicel and ovary 25–35 mm long; bracts 5–7 mm long. Sepals lanceolate or narrowly ovate, long acuminate; dorsal sepal erect or arching over column, 33–35 × 3–6 mm; lateral sepals 35–42 × 3–5 mm, reflexed or spreading. Petals 23–28 × 3.5–4 mm, oblanceolate, acuminate. Lip 26–30 × 5–7 mm, obovate, long acuminate; spur 5–6.5 cm (2 in.) long, somewhat incurved, slender but slightly swollen in the apical half and narrowing again towards the tip. Column 5–6 mm long. Capsule cylindrical, 7 cm long (3 in.), 3 mm in diameter.

HABITAT: In deep shade at high and low levels in submontane and riverine forest, growing on trunks, branches and small twigs, 1600–1900 m (5300–6300 ft.), occasionally as low as 1300 m (4300 ft.).

CULTIVATION: Intermediate to cool conditions, in heavy shade and with high humidity. Plants seem to do better mounted. The species is not common in cultivation; some plants that have been offered for sale under the name *Aerangis carnea* turned out to be *A. distincta*. The latter has leaves that are widest at the apex, while leaves of *A. carnea* are widest below the apex, and narrow again slightly towards the tip. In flower, *A. distincta* can be recognized easily by the larger flowers with a much longer spur.

DISTRIBUTION: Northern Malawi, southern Tanzania.

Aerangis collum-cygni Summerhayes FIGURE 10-3
SYNONYM: *Aerangis compta* Summerhayes

DESCRIPTION: Stems short, occasionally to 10 cm (4 in.) long; roots 2–4 mm in diameter. Leaves three to seven, 6–17 × 1.5–5.5 cm (2–7 × 1–2 in.), broadly oblanceolate, unequally bilobed at the apex, the lobes rounded or subacute. Inflorescences arching or pendent, 4- to 16-flowered. Flowers white, the sepals and petals tipped with

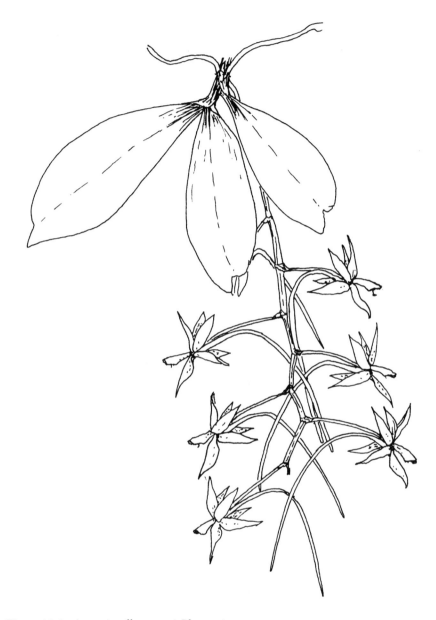

Figure 10-3. *Aerangis collum-cygni.* Plant, ×1.

brownish-pink, the lip brownish-pink in the apical half, the spur pale salmon-pink. Pedicel and ovary 20–35 mm long; bracts 3–5 mm long. Dorsal sepal erect or slightly reflexed, 12–15 × 3.5–5 mm, lanceolate or oblanceolate, acute or acuminate; lateral sepals 11–17 × 2.5–4 mm, reflexed, narrowly lanceolate, acuminate, slightly keeled on the back. Petals 9–15 × 2.5–4 mm, lanceolate, acuminate, strongly reflexed. Lip deflexed, 10–14.5 × 3.5–6 mm, lanceolate, acuminate, the lateral margins recurved. Spur 6–7.5 cm (2–3 in.) long, at first parallel to the ovary, then pendent or incurved. Column 6–8 mm long., with a short tooth on the underside pointing towards the mouth of the spur. Capsules cylindrical, 6 cm (2 in.) long, 4 mm in diameter.

HABITAT: Rainforest, high rainfall woodland and on plantation trees, 800–1200 m (2600–4000 ft.).

CULTIVATION: Mounted, in intermediate temperatures, with shade and humidity. In our greenhouse, it flowers in spring (April).

DISTRIBUTION: Cameroon, Central African Republic, Tanzania, Uganda, Zaire, Zambia.

NOTE: This species is not common in cultivation. It has a distinctive appearance, with all the floral parts except the dorsal sepal swept back. Presumably the elegant curve of the spur gave rise to the specific epithet, referring to a swan's neck.

Aerangis confusa J. Stewart   PLATE 10

DESCRIPTION: Stems short, to 10 cm (4 in.) long; roots long, numerous, 3–4 mm in diameter. Leaves several, 5–24 × 1.5–5.5 cm (2–9 × 1–2 in.), obovate or oblanceolate, leathery, dark green with numerous black dots, equally or unequally bilobed at the apex. Inflorescences spreading or pendent, 4- to 10-flowered. Flowers white, usually quite strongly pink-tinged. Pedicel and ovary 2–6 cm (1–2 in.) long; bracts black, 4–7 mm long. Sepals lanceolate, acuminate; dorsal sepal 15–25 × 4–7.5 mm, arching over column; laterals 18–26 × 2.5–5 mm, more or less spreading. Petals reflexed, 15–22 × 3–5 mm, lanceolate, acuminate. Lip 15–23 × 5–7 mm, oblong to lanceolate, acuminate or cuspidate, the margins reflexed; spur 4–6 cm (2 in.) long, almost straight. Column 6–8 mm long. Capsules cylindrical.

HABITAT: Epiphytic at low level on tree trunks and small bushes in shade, often in hilly areas, 1600–2100 m (5300–7000 ft.).

CULTIVATION: One of the best species of *Aerangis,* flowering reliably twice a year, in spring (May and June) and again in fall (October and November). We grow it mounted, in intermediate temperatures, in moderate shade and high humidity.

DISTRIBUTION: Kenya, Tanzania.

NOTE: When not in flower, this species closely resembles *Aerangis brachycarpa,* with which it was confused for many years (hence the name). In flower, the slightly smaller flowers with the spreading, not reflexed sepals and the much shorter spur, easily distinguish it.

Aerangis coriacea Summerhayes

DESCRIPTION: Stems stout, woody, to 40 cm (16 in.) long in old plants, leafy in the apical part; roots to 5 mm in diameter. Leaves several, to 22 × 2–4.5 cm (9 × 1–2 in.), ligulate or ligulate-oblanceolate, unequally bilobed at apex, dark green with noticeable reticulate veining, rather fleshy, the edges often undulate. Inflorescences arching, arising from upper leaf axils, to 40 cm (16 in.) long, 4- to 22-flowered. Flowers white, tinged with pink or greenish. Pedicel and ovary 2–3 cm (1 in.) long; bracts to 1 cm (0.5 in.) long. Dorsal sepal erect, 13–20 × 7–10 mm, lanceolate, acute, the margins recurved; lateral sepals strongly reflexed, 14–19 × 5–7 mm, oblanceolate, apiculate, the margins recurved. Petals also reflexed, similar but slightly shorter. Lip deflexed, 14–18 × 6–10 mm, lanceolate, acute, the margins recurved in the middle, the apex reflexed. Spur 11–17 cm (4–7 in.) long, flexuous, somewhat thickened in the apical half. Column stout, 4 mm long.

HABITAT: Epiphytic at low level in shade in upland forests, often near a river, 1300–2300 m (4300–7600 ft.).

CULTIVATION: Another species that is not common in cultivation. With its thick roots, it is likely to do better mounted on bark and kept drier in winter. Intermediate to cool temperatures in shade.

DISTRIBUTION: Kenya, Tanzania.

Aerangis distincta J. Stewart & I. F. la Croix   PLATE 11, FIGURE 10-4

DESCRIPTION: Stems woody, short, occasionally to 15 cm (6 in.) long; roots 3–4 mm in diameter. Leaves several, lying in one plane, borne in a fan, 4–16 cm (2–6 in.) long, 2–4.8 cm (1–2 in.) wide near the apex, triangular, the apex deeply and acutely bilobed, the lobes often diverging, the longer lobe to 3 cm (1 in.) long, dark olive green usually dotted with black, and usually with longitudinal ridging. Inflorescences spreading or pendent, to 27 cm (11 in.) long, 2- to 5-flowered, the flowers set 2–3 cm (1 in.) apart. Flowers white, the sepals, petals, and lip usually strongly pink-tinged in the apical half; spur and ovary salmon-pink. Sepals and petals narrowly lanceolate, long acuminate. Dorsal sepal 25–50 × 7–9 mm, erect or arching over the column; lateral sepals 35–65 × 5–7 mm, reflexed, rather oblique. Petals 25–45 × 4.5–6 mm, at least 10 mm shorter than the lateral sepals. Lip deflexed, 30–45 × 7–10 mm, elliptic, abruptly constricted in the apical half into a long, narrow acumen. Spur 13–23 cm (5–9 in.) long, pendent, straight. Column 5 mm long. Capsule cylindrical, 13 cm (5 in.) × 6 mm.

HABITAT: Epiphytic on tree trunks and small branches, usually at a low level, in riverine or evergreen forest, usually near a river, usually 1000–1750 m (3300–5800 ft.), but occasionally as low as 650 m (2100 ft.).

CULTIVATION: Although only described in 1987, this species has become well established in cultivation, to which it is well adapted. It is better mounted, to allow the long spurs to hang freely, and does well in intermediate temperatures. It is best in moderate shade, although in the wild we have seen it growing in forest where it was so dark that a light meter did not register at all; it will grow and flower in more light, but the leaves become rather yellow. Plants from the Northern Region of Malawi flower in the wild in March and April, while those from the Central and Southern Regions flower in November and December. In cultivation, these differences persist; in the Northern Hemisphere the northern plants still flower in winter (November and December) and the central and southern plants flower in spring and early summer (May and June).

Figure 10-4. *Aerangis distincta*. Plant, ×0.75. →

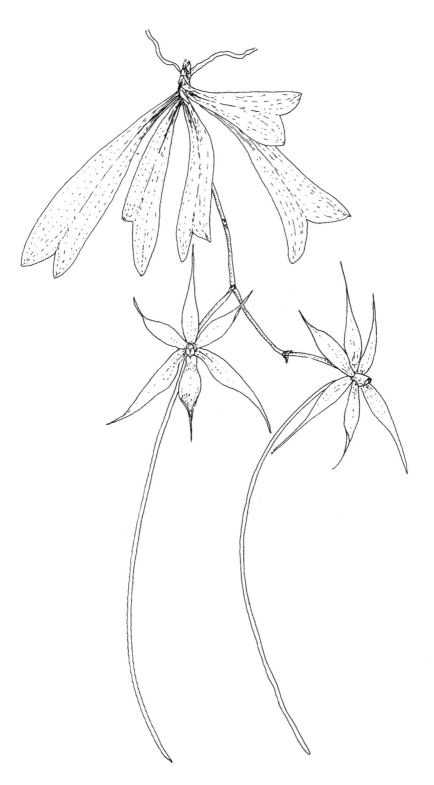

DISTRIBUTION: Malawi. Although this species is widely distributed in Malawi, occurring in all three regions, it has not yet been found elsewhere.

Aerangis flexuosa (Ridley) Schlechter

DESCRIPTION: A small species; stems short; roots numerous, long. Leaves three to five, 5–15 × 1.5–3 cm (2–6 × 1 in.), oblanceolate, unequally bilobed at the apex, with one lobe acute, the other almost absent. Inflorescences spreading or pendent, to 26 cm (10 in.) long, 10- to 18-flowered. Flowers white. Pedicel and ovary 2–2.5 cm (1 in.) long; bracts 3–6 mm long. Sepals and petals 10–13 × 2.5–3 mm long, lanceolate, acute. Lip 10–11 × 2–3 mm, lanceolate, acute or apiculate; spur 19–25 mm long, wide at the mouth but soon tapering. Column 5–8 mm long.

HABITAT: Evergreen forest, to 700 m (2300 ft.).

CULTIVATION: This little species which, with its wide-mouthed spur and relatively long column, is very distinctive, has not, as far as we know, been collected since 1894. Thus, there must be some doubt whether it still exists, especially as one of its collection sites is now covered by an airport. However, there is still much forest left on São Tomé, and it is to be hoped that the species is still growing there and might, at some time, come into cultivation. If it does, it seems probable that it would like humid shade in intermediate to warm temperatures.

DISTRIBUTION: São Tomé.

Aerangis gracillima (Kränzlin) J. C. Arends & J. Stewart

SYNONYM: *Barombia gracillima* (Kränzlin) Schlechter

DESCRIPTION: Stems short, to 8 cm (3 in.) long; roots 3 mm in diameter. Leaves several, distichous, 11–24 × 2.5–6 cm (4–9 × 1–2 in.), narrowly obovate, unequally bilobed at apex, leathery, dull green. Inflorescences pendent, to 75 cm (30 in.) long, 7- to 12-flowered; rachis zigzag. Flowers white, the lip and the tips of the sepals and petals pale pinkish-brown; spur and ovary pale brown. Pedicel and ovary S-shaped, 5–6 cm (2 in.) long. Sepals and petals spreading, or the petals slightly reflexed, narrowly elliptic-obovate, acuminate, with the margins reflexed in the basal half; dorsal sepal 35–50 × 4–6 mm; lateral sepals 40–45 × 3–5 mm. Petals 35–45 × 3–4 mm. Lip 35–45 × 4–6 mm; spur 18–25 cm (7–10 in.) long, straight or slightly incurved, slender but swollen at apex. Column 30–37 mm long. Capsule cylindrical, 10–12 cm (4–5 in.) long.

HABITAT: Shady forest in humid areas, 400–800 m (1300–2600 ft.).

CULTIVATION: This species has been cultivated in Europe, but we do not know of anyone who is currently growing it. With the long inflorescence, it is likely to be better mounted and presumably requires warm to intermediate temperatures, in a shaded position, with high humidity.

DISTRIBUTION: Cameroon, Gabon.

NOTE: This species was placed in *Aerangis* in 1989 (Arends and Stewart 1989) as it differs from other species only in the unusually long column.

Figure 10-5. *Aerangis gravenreuthii.* Plant (left) and flower (right), ×0.75.

Aerangis gravenreuthii (Kränzlin) Schlechter FIGURE 10-5

DESCRIPTION: Stems short, to 7 cm (3 in.) long; roots numerous, to 3 mm in diameter. Leaves several, to 22 × 1.5–3 cm (9 × 1 in.), narrowly oblanceolate, unequally bilobed at apex, the larger lobe acute or obtuse, the smaller sometimes almost absent, dark, glossy green with slightly raised reticulate venation. Inflorescences 10–20 cm (4–8 in.) long, 2- to 5-flowered. Flowers white, with a greenish tinge, sometimes pink-tinged; spur greenish-pink towards apex. Pedicel and ovary 3.5–4 cm (1–2 in.) long;

bracts to 5 mm long. Sepals and petals lanceolate or narrowly ovate, long acuminate. Dorsal sepal erect or arching over the column, 20–32 × 5–7 mm; lateral sepals 20–35 × 5 mm, spreading. Petals 15–25 × 4–4.5 mm, slightly reflexed. Lip 17–26 × 5 mm, oblong-ovate, long acuminate, with the margins of the apical half rolled back so that it seems to narrow abruptly. Spur 4–9 cm (2–4 in.) long, slender, curving forwards. Column 5 mm long, anther cap very slightly beaked. Capsule cylindrical, to 12 cm (5 in.) × 6 mm.

HABITAT: Evergreen forest, in deep shade, 1500–2200 m (5000–7300 ft.).

CULTIVATION: Heavy shade and high humidity; temperature intermediate. In our greenhouse, it flowers regularly in summer (July and August).

DISTRIBUTION: Cameroon, Equatorial Guinea (Bioko), Nigeria, Tanzania.

Aerangis hologlottis (Schlechter) Schlechter

DESCRIPTION: Stems short, to 3 cm (1 in.) long; roots numerous, fine, 1–2 mm in diameter. Leaves two to six, 5–9 cm (2–4 in.) × 7–18 mm, linear or strap-shaped, often curved, unequally bilobed at the apex, rather fleshy, dark green. Inflorescences erect or spreading, to 18 cm (7 in.) long, 6- to 15-flowered. Flowers white, the ovary and spur pale green. Pedicel and ovary 5–7 mm long; bracts to 2 mm long. Sepals and petals all spreading, narrowly elliptical, apiculate. Dorsal sepal 6–7 × 1.5–3 mm; laterals very slightly smaller. Petals 5–6 × 2–4 mm. Lip 5–6 × 2.5–3 mm, obovate, apiculate; spur 3.5–7 mm long, straight, slender. Column short and stout, 1 mm long.

HABITAT: Epiphytic on twigs and small branches of trees in coastal forest, to 500 m (1650 ft.).

CULTIVATION: Not known to be cultivated. Presumably it should like shade, in intermediate to warm temperatures.

DISTRIBUTION: Kenya, Mozambique, Tanzania. Also known from Sri Lanka. This is the only species of *Aerangis* found outside Africa and Madagascar and its adjacent islands. Its distribution is paralleled to some extent by *Angraecum zeylanicum*, which occurs in Sri Lanka and the Seychelles.

Aerangis jacksonii J. Stewart

DESCRIPTION: Stems woody, to 20 cm (8 in.) long, leafy; roots 3–4 mm in diameter. Leaves numerous, distichous, to 15 × 1–2.5 cm (6 × 0.5–1 in.), ligulate, linear-lanceolate, or oblanceolate, often curved, unequally bilobed at the apex, the longer lobe obtuse or subacute, the other often almost absent, dark green with numerous black dots. Inflorescences arching, to 17 cm (7 in.) long, 4- to 8-flowered, arising opposite the leaves from the same place in successive years. Flowers white, tinged with greenish or pinkish, set 1–2 cm (1 in.) apart. Pedicel and ovary 3 cm (1 in.) long; bracts 5–6 mm long, black when the flowers open. Sepals and petals all narrowly elliptical, acute; dorsal sepal erect, 10–12 × 5 mm; lateral sepals 12–15 × 4 mm, reflexed. Petals similar but slightly shorter, also reflexed. Lip 13–15 × 5 mm, narrowly obovate, apiculate, the sides reflexed; spur 4–5.5 cm (2 in.) long, pendent or slightly incurved, slightly thickened in the apical half but tapering again towards the tip. Column 4 mm long. Capsule not seen.

HABITAT: Rainforest, 1200–1600 m (4000–5300 ft.).

CULTIVATION: Not known to be cultivated, although it must be grown in East Africa. It should like shade and high humidity, and intermediate temperatures.

DISTRIBUTION: Uganda.

Figure 10-6. *Aerangis kirkii.* Plant (left) and flower (right), ×0.75.

Aerangis kirkii (Reichenbach f.) Schlechter PLATE 12, FIGURE 10-6

DESCRIPTION: Stems short, to 5 cm (2 in.) long; roots numerous, fine, 1–2 mm in diameter. Leaves two to seven, to 15 × 3 cm (6 × 1 in.), oblanceolate, unequally bilobed at the apex, the lobes rounded or acute, dark green or gray-green, sometimes with a reddish tinge, usually leathery but occasionally fleshy, often with a rather shrivelled appearance. Inflorescences to 17 cm (7 in.) long, spreading or pendent, 2- to 6-flowered, the apical flower opening first and usually larger than the rest. Flowers white, strongly tinged with salmon pink. Pedicel and ovary 18–25 mm long; bracts 4–8 mm long. Sepals lanceolate, acuminate, the dorsal sepal erect, 18–27 × 5–7 mm; the laterals spreading, 22–28 × 4–6 mm. Petals spreading or slightly reflexed, 16–22 × 5–6 mm, oblanceolate, acuminate. Lip 16–23 × 7–8 mm, oblong, abruptly acuminate, the narrow tip 10 mm long; spur 6–7.5 cm (2–3 in.) long, pendent, straight or slightly curving forwards, usually slightly swollen in the apical half but narrowing towards the tip. Column 4–5 mm long; anther cap with a short beak. Capsule elongated, cylindrical.

HABITAT: Coastal bush and riverine forest, on shrubs and small trees, usually in deep shade, to 450 m (1500 ft.).

CULTIVATION: We have always grown this mounted, but with the fine roots, it should also grow in a pot. Moderate shade, intermediate to warm temperatures.

DISTRIBUTION: Kenya, Mozambique, South Africa (Natal coast), Tanzania.

Aerangis kotschyana (Reichenbach f.) Schlechter   FIGURE 10-7

DESCRIPTION: Stems stout, woody, to 20 cm (8 in.) long in old plants. Roots numerous, 7–9 mm in diameter. Leaves 3 to 20 (usually fewer), set close together, 6–30 × 2–8 cm (2–12 × 1–3 in.), obovate, the apex unequally bilobed, the longer lobe subacute or obtuse, the other lobe usually almost absent; dark green, the edges undulate, usually leathery but sometimes rather fleshy. Inflorescences arching or pendent, 30–45 cm (12–18 in.) long, to about 20-flowered. Flowers white, in two rows, often tinged with salmon-pink. Pedicel and ovary 2–3 cm (1 in.) long; bracts to 8 mm long. Sepals lanceolate or narrowly ovate, apiculate, slightly winged on the back near the tips; dorsal sepal erect or arching over the column, 20–25 × 9–10 mm; laterals spreading, 20–28 × 7–8 mm. Petals reflexed, 10–23 × 7–8 mm, oblanceolate, apiculate. Lip deflexed, 15–20 × 8–15 mm, fiddle-shaped, apiculate, the margins recurved in the lower half, with two prominent ridges at the base at the mouth of the spur; spur 13–24 cm (5–9 in.) long, pendent, with a loose corkscrew twist about the middle, thickened in the apical third. Column stout, 3–6 mm long. Capsule ellipsoid, 3–5 × 1.5 cm (1–2 × 1 in.).

HABITAT: Epiphytic at mid and high levels, often on smooth-barked trees such as figs, in woodland in hot but high rainfall areas, or on riverine trees in hot but fairly dry areas, to 1500 m (5000 ft.), but usually below 900 m (3000 ft.).

CULTIVATION: This is one of the best-known species of *Aerangis* in cultivation. Although the flowers are not so large as those of some species, the floral parts are broader, giving them much "substance," and a well-flowered plant is a magnificent sight. It can be reluctant to flower in cultivation. It needs to be kept fairly dry in winter, as the hot, high-rainfall areas where it often grows are ones where the rainfall is very seasonal, and the dry season is long. Otherwise, it is better mounted and requires moderate shade and intermediate to warm temperatures. It can stand bright light and probably flowers more readily then, but the leaves turn very yellow and lose the luxuriant look that they should have.

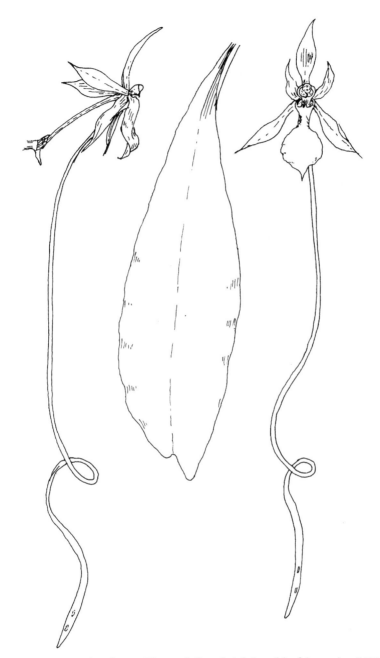

Figure 10-7. *Aerangis kotschyana.* Flower (left and right) and leaf (center), ×0.75.

DISTRIBUTION: Burundi, Central African Republic, Ethiopia, Guinea, Kenya, Malawi, Mozambique, Nigeria, Rwanda, Sudan, Tanzania, Uganda, Zaire, Zambia, Zimbabwe.

Aerangis luteoalba (Kränzlin) Schlechter   PLATE 13

DESCRIPTION: Stems short; roots numerous, long and slender. Leaves two to eight, twisted at the base to lie in one plane, to 15 × 0.6–1.5 cm (6 × 1 in.), linear-ligulate, sometimes curved, unequally bilobed at the apex, the lobes rounded, dark green. Inflorescences arching or pendent, to 35 cm (14 in.) long, with to 25 flowers borne in two rows and all facing the same way. Flowers creamy white to yellowish-white, the column white or bright red; all the floral parts spreading. Sepals 10–15 × 3–7 mm, oblanceolate, acute; petals similar but slightly wider. Lip 15–20 × 7–15 mm, obovate, acute; spur 2.5–4 cm (1–2 in.) long, incurved, slender but slightly thickened in the apical half. Column 2–3 mm long. Capsule ellipsoid, 2–2.5 cm (1 in.) long.

HABITAT: On twigs and branches of shrubs and small trees, often near a river, 800–2200 m (2600–7300 ft.).

CULTIVATION: Intermediate to cool temperatures, deep shade, and high humidity. It seems to do better mounted. It usually flowers in autumn (September).

DISTRIBUTION: Cameroon, Central African Republic, Ethiopia, Kenya, Tanzania, Uganda, Zaire.

NOTE: Two varieties have been described: var. *luteoalba,* with a white or yellowish-white column, and var. *rhodosticta* (Kränzlin) J. Stewart, synonym *Aerangis rhodosticta* (Kränzlin) Schlechter, with a vermilion-red column. Variety *rhodosticta* is the one so popular in cultivation. Its red column is unique in the genus; the only other orchid with similar coloration is *Microcoelia corallina.*

Aerangis megaphylla Summerhayes

DESCRIPTION: Stems to 10 cm (4 in.) long; roots numerous, rather slender, to 3 mm in diameter. Leaves six to seven, 15–22 × 3–6 cm (6–9 × 1–2 in.), oblanceolate, unequally bilobed at the apex, the longer lobe acute, the other rounded or almost absent. Inflorescences pendent, 15–30 cm (6–12 in.) long, 5- to 7-flowered, the flowers set well apart. Flowers greenish-white. Pedicel and ovary 3–4 cm (1–2 in.) long; bracts 3–7 mm long. Sepals and petals all narrowly lanceolate, acuminate. Dorsal sepal erect, 20–27 × 3–3.5 mm; lateral sepals deflexed, 30–35 × 3–3.5 mm. Petals reflexed, 20–22 × 3–3.5 mm. Lip 25–30 × 5 mm, lanceolate, acuminate, somewhat recurved; spur pendent, 9–10 cm (4 in.) long, slightly thickened in the apical half. Column 9 mm long.

HABITAT: Forest, 300–1000 m (1000–3300 ft.).

CULTIVATION: Not known to be in cultivation. From the habitat and distribution, it could be expected to require shade, high humidity and intermediate to warm temperatures.

DISTRIBUTION: Cameroon, Central African Republic, Equatorial Guinea (Pagalu Island).

Aerangis montana J. Stewart   PLATE 14

DESCRIPTION: Stems woody, to 10 cm (4 in.) long, occasionally longer in old plants; roots numerous, 2–3 mm in diameter. Leaves two to several, 7–19 × 2–3.8 cm

(3–8 × 1 in.), ligulate or oblanceolate, unequally bilobed at the apex, the lobes rounded, dark green with darker reticulate venation, rather fleshy. Inflorescences spreading or pendent, to 20 cm (8 in.) long, 4- to 10-flowered, the flowers borne on short projections from the rachis 3–5 mm above each bract. Flowers white, usually faintly tinged with pink, particularly on the spur. Pedicel and ovary 1.5–2 cm (1 in.) long; bracts to 4 mm long. Sepals, petals, and lip narrowly ovate or obovate, apiculate, all spreading so that the flower is saucer-shaped; dorsal sepal 13–16 × 5–7 mm; lateral sepals and petals 11–15 × 4–6 mm. Lip 11–18 × 5.5–7.5; spur 5–6 cm (2 in.) long, curving forwards, slightly thicker in the apical half. Column to 3 mm long. Capsules ellipsoid, 2 cm (1 in.) long.

HABITAT: Montane forest, often on tree trunks at low levels, where old plants sometimes stand out horizontally, or form large, tangled masses; also on lower branches or creepers, usually in very deep shade; rarely lithophytic; 1370–2400 m (4500–8000 ft.), but usually over 2200 m (7300 ft.).

CULTIVATION: This attractive species does well in cultivation. We grow it mounted, at intermediate temperatures, but it might do even better in cool temperatures, as where it grows on the Nyika plateau in Malawi, the ground is frequently white with frost in winter, although the frost never penetrates the forest. It needs deep shade and high humidity, and should be kept drier in winter. In our greenhouse, it flowers rather erratically, in May and September, in different years.

DISTRIBUTION: Malawi, southern Tanzania, Zambia.

Aerangis mystacidii (Reichenbach f.) Schlechter   PLATE 15
SYNONYM: *Aerangis pachyura* Schlechter

DESCRIPTION: Stems usually short, but occasionally to 10 cm (4 in.) long; roots numerous, 2–4 mm in diameter. Leaves two to eight, usually 4–15 × 1–3 cm (2–6 × 0.5–1 in.), but rarely as much as 25 × 5 cm (10 × 2 in.), oblanceolate to obovate, the apex unequally or subequally bilobed, leathery or slightly fleshy. Inflorescences horizontal or pendent, to 30 cm (12 in.) long, 3- to 24-flowered. Flowers white, the spur tinged with pink. Sepals and petals oblong, acute or apiculate; dorsal sepal erect or arching over column, 7–13 × 2–6 mm; laterals deflexed, 8–14 × 2.5–5 mm. Petals strongly reflexed, 6–13 × 2–4.5 mm. Lip deflexed, 7–14 × 3–5 mm (rarely to 8 mm wide), oblong or ovate-oblong, obtuse or apiculate; spur usually 6–8 cm (2–3 in.) long, rarely to 1.5 cm (1 in.) either longer or shorter. Column 2–4 mm long. Capsule ellipsoid, 3 cm (1 in.) long.

HABITAT: Most often in riverine forest, where it can occur profusely on small twigs overhanging the water, but also in evergreen forest, well away from a river, and in high-rainfall woodland, 60–1800 m (200–6000 ft.).

CULTIVATION: As might be expected from a plant occupying such a range of habitats, it grows very easily, either mounted or in a pot. It seems to like moderate shade, intermediate temperatures, and high humidity in the growing season, with a cooler and drier rest.

DISTRIBUTION: Malawi, Mozambique, South Africa (Eastern Cape, KwaZulu-Natal, Northern Province), Swaziland, Tanzania, Zambia, Zimbabwe.

NOTE: This species is very variable in size of both leaf and flower. This variation in size is not entirely related to growing conditions, although the biggest plants are found in the most favorable situations, as large and small plants tend to remain like that even when grown together in cultivation.

Aerangis oligantha Schlechter   PLATE 16

DESCRIPTION: A dwarf species; stems short; roots numerous, 2–2.5 mm in diameter. Leaves four to eight, to 8 × 2 cm (3 × 1 in.), leathery, oblanceolate, unequally or subequally bilobed at apex, the lobes acute, dark green with black dots. Inflorescences 1.5–4 cm (1–2 in.) long, densely to 12-flowered, the flowers crowded towards the end of the rachis. Flowers white, including the ovary. Pedicel and ovary 10–16 mm long, slender; bracts 2 mm long. Sepals and petals spreading; dorsal sepal 6–9 × 3–3.5 mm, ovate, apiculate; lateral sepals 6–10 × 2–3 mm, oblanceolate, slightly curved. Petals 6–9 × 3–3.5 mm, lanceolate or oblanceolate, acute. Lip 6–8.5 × 4–4.5 mm, ovate, apiculate; spur 8–13 mm long, parallel to the ovary, slender, slightly swollen in the apical half. Column 2 mm long. Capsule ellipsoidal, 1 cm (0.5 in.) long.

HABITAT: Montane or submontane forest, sunk in moss at 2–9 m (6–30 ft.) above ground level, 1800–2100 m (6000–7000 ft.).

CULTIVATION: Mounted, in deep shade and with high humidity, at intermediate to cool temperatures. In our greenhouse, it flowers in spring (April and May).

DISTRIBUTION: Northern Malawi, southern Tanzania.

Aerangis somalensis (Schlechter) Schlechter

DESCRIPTION: Stems short; roots numerous, thick, 5–7 mm in diameter. Leaves two to six, distichous, 2–11 × 1.5–3.5 cm (1–4 × 1 in.), occasionally to 15 cm (6 in.) long, oblong ligulate to suborbicular, unequally or subequally bilobed at the apex, the lobes subacute or rounded, gray-green, olive green, or purple-green with darker raised reticulate venation. Inflorescences 10–20 cm (4–8 in.) long, 2- to 17-flowered. Flowers white, sometimes pink-tinged. Pedicel and ovary 1.5–2 cm (1 in.) long; bracts to 5 mm long. Dorsal sepal arching over column, 8–12 × 4–6 mm, ovate, apiculate; lateral sepals 9–14 × 3–5 mm, somewhat reflexed, oblong or oblanceolate, apiculate. Petals spreading, 8–12 × 3–5.5 mm, oblong, apiculate. Lip 9–13 × 4-7 mm, oblong-ligulate, apiculate, the margins reflexed in the lower half; spur 10–15 cm (4–6 in.) long, straight or slightly curved, sometimes coiled in bud, slightly swollen in the apical half but narrowing towards the tip. Column stout, to 4 mm long. Capsules ellipsoid.

HABITAT: Woodland, often in rather dry areas, 1000–1800 m (3300–6000 ft.).

CULTIVATION: This species is better mounted, as the thick roots tend to rot in a pot. We find it grows well, but can be reluctant to flower; good light and a prolonged dry spell in winter are important. Intermediate to warm temperatures.

DISTRIBUTION: Ethiopia, Kenya, Malawi, South Africa (Mpumalanga), Tanzania, Zimbabwe.

Note: The foliage of this species varies considerably, but the flowers are very consistent throughout the species' range. Kenya plants have very gray leaves, while Malawi plants have purplish, almost round leaves.

Aerangis splendida J. Stewart & I. F. la Croix   plate 17, figure 10-8

Description: Stems woody, to 20 cm (8 in.) long, but usually less; roots long, 4–6 mm in diameter. Leaves three to eight, pendent, 12–30 × 5–8 cm (5–12 × 2–3 in.), oblanceolate or obovate, unequally bilobed at the apex, the lobes rounded, dark, glossy green, leathery. Inflorescences pendent, to 30 cm (12 in.) long, rather laxly 2- to 7-flowered. Flowers white, set 3–5 cm (1–2 in.) apart, in two rows. Pedicel and ovary 6–8 cm (2–3 in.) long; bracts 2–3 mm long. Sepals and petals all lanceolate, ovate, acuminate. Dorsal sepal erect, curving forward at the tip, 35–50 × 8–12 mm; lateral sepals similar but slightly narrower, spreading. Petals similar but slightly shorter, reflexed. Lip deflexed, 40–45 × 10–14 mm, the basal part obovate, then narrowing abruptly to a slender acumen 10–15 mm long. Spur 20–25 cm (8–10 in.) long, slender but sometimes slightly inflated towards the apex, with a single, loose coil about the middle. Column 6–8 mm long. Capsule cylindrical, 15 cm (6 in.) × 8 mm.

Habitat: In deep shade in evergreen forest, usually epiphytic at a fairly low level on trunks and larger branches, often near a river, 1000–1500 m (3300–5000 ft.).

Cultivation: This species, with its large flowers and gracefully coiling spur, is one of the most beautiful species of *Aerangis,* but it is much less often grown than its sister species, *A. distincta.* We grow plants both mounted and in pots, but the latter tend to root on top of and around the pot rather than in it. If grown in a pot, the pot must be hung up, as good ventilation seems to be essential to the plant, otherwise black blotches appear on the leaves. Apart from this, *A. splendida* is not difficult, requiring shade and high humidity in the growing season, at intermediate temperatures. It can be reluctant to flower unless given a cooler and dry rest in winter. In our greenhouse, it flowers in autumn (September and October).

Distribution: Malawi, Zambia. This species is under a real threat, as it is known from only three sites in southern Malawi, and is common in only one of these. We do not know its status in Zambia, but suspect that it is rare there, as it has seldom been collected.

Aerangis stelligera Summerhayes

Description: Stems short, to 5 cm (2 in.) long; roots numerous, 2–3 mm in diameter. Leaves three to five, distichous, 7–15 × 1.5–4 cm (3–6 × 1–2 in.), oblanceolate or oblong, unequally bilobed at the apex, the lobes acute. Inflorescences pendent, 10–25 cm (4–10 in.) long, 3- to 6-flowered, the flowers set 2–4 cm (1–2 in.) apart. Flowers white. Pedicel and ovary 3–6 cm (1–2 in.) long; bracts 5–10 mm long. Sepals and petals lanceolate, acuminate, all spreading, later becoming somewhat reflexed; dorsal sepal 40–50 × 7 mm; laterals slightly longer and narrower. Petals 37–40 × 4–5 mm.

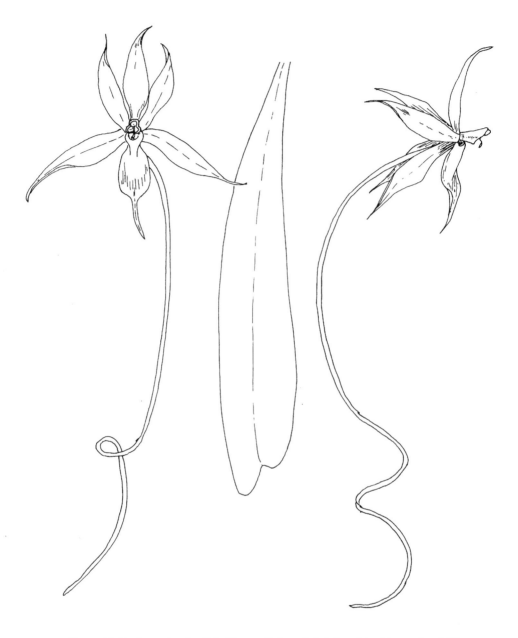

Figure 10-8. *Aerangis splendida*. Flower (left and right) and leaf (center), ×0.75.

Lip to 40 × 5 mm, lanceolate, long acuminate; spur 20–24 cm (8–9 in.) long, slightly inflated towards the apex but narrowing again to the tip. Column 10–12.5 mm long, slender but slightly enlarged at the apex.

HABITAT: Forest undergrowth, in dense shade, 400–1100 m (1300–3600 ft.).

CULTIVATION: We have not heard of anyone growing this species in Europe or America, one can only hope that it will at some time be introduced into cultivation there, as it is very beautiful. It probably requires warm to intermediate temperatures, heavy shade, and high humidity.

DISTRIBUTION: Cameroon, Central African Republic, Zaire.

Aerangis thomsonii (Rolfe) Schlechter

SYNONYM: *Aerangis friesiorum* Schlechter

DESCRIPTION: Stems woody, 10–100 cm (4–40 in.) long, the lower part covered with old leaf bases; roots numerous, 4–9 mm in diameter. Leaves 8 to 20, distichous, 8–28 × 1.5–4.5 cm (3–11 × 1–2 in.), ligulate, unequally bilobed at the apex, the lobes obtuse, dark green, fleshy or leathery. Inflorescences arching, to 30 cm (12 in.) long, 4- to 10-flowered. Flowers white. Pedicel and ovary 3–6 cm (1–2 in.) long; bracts 10–15 mm long. Sepals and petals lanceolate-elliptic, acute; dorsal sepal erect, 22–30 × 7–9 mm; lateral sepals reflexed, 25–32 × 5–6 mm, somewhat winged on the back in the apical half. Petals 20–25 × 6–8 mm, reflexed. Lip 20–25 × 7–8 mm, deflexed, elliptic-lanceolate, acuminate, the margins reflexed; spur 10–15 cm (4–6 in.) long, pendent, flexuous, thickened in the apical half. Column 6–8 mm long.

HABITAT: Epiphytic at low level on trunks and branches of upland forest, in deep shade, 1600–2600 m (5300–8600 ft.).

CULTIVATION: This is the coolest growing of the *Aerangis* species; it will grow in intermediate conditions, if given a shaded but airy place, but cool temperatures would be better.

DISTRIBUTION: Ethiopia, Kenya, Tanzania, Uganda.

Aerangis ugandensis Summerhayes   PLATE 18, FIGURE 10-9

DESCRIPTION: Stems woody, to 20 cm (8 in.) long, but usually shorter; roots numerous, long, 3–4 mm in diameter. Leaves 4 to 12, distichous, 5–15 × 1–2 cm (2–6 × 1 in.), narrowly oblanceolate, often curved, unequally bilobed at the apex, the lobes rounded, the shorter one sometimes absent, leathery, dark green dotted with black. Inflorescences pendent, to 15 cm (6 in.) long, 7- to 10-flowered. Flowers white, sometimes tinged with green, set 5–12 mm apart, the apical flowers usually opening first, with those in the middle of the inflorescence the largest. Pedicel and ovary 1–2.5 cm (1 in.) long, green; bracts 2–3 mm long. Sepals and petals oblong-lanceolate, acute; sepals 6–12 × 3–4 mm, the dorsal sepal erect, the laterals slightly reflexed. Petals reflexed, 6–10 × 3 mm. Lip 6–10 × 3–5 mm, oblong, suddenly acute; spur 10–25 mm long, straight, pendent. Column 2 mm long. Capsule narrowly ellipsoid, 2 cm (1 in.) long.

Plants of this species have been sold under the name of *Aerangis laurentii*. It is difficult to see how this arose, as the plant that was originally called *Angraecum laurentii* De Wildeman and was placed in *Aerangis* by Schlechter in 1918, becoming *Aerangis laurentii* (De Wildeman) Schlechter, is now placed in the genus *Summerhayesia*, and is correctly *Summerhayesia laurentii* (De Wildeman) Cribb. This species, with narrow, folded leaves, is described later; it does not resemble *Aerangis ugandensis* in any way.

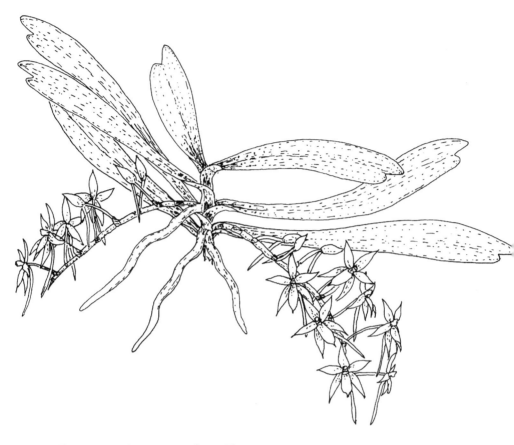

Figure 10-9. *Aerangis ugandensis.* Plant, ×0.75.

HABITAT: Epiphytic at low level in evergreen forest, often near a river, usually growing on tree trunks among moss, 1500–2000 m (5000–6600 ft.).

CULTIVATION: It grows well at intermediate temperatures, in deep shade, with high humidity. It flowers regularly, usually in autumn (September and October).

DISTRIBUTION: Burundi, Kenya, Uganda, Zaire.

Aerangis verdickii (De Wildeman) Schlechter   PLATE 19, FIGURE 10-10

DESCRIPTION: Stems short; roots numerous, stout, 8–9 mm in diameter. Leaves two to six, 5–20 × 2–5 cm (2–8 × 1–2 in.), oblong-ligulate, the edges undulate, subequally bilobed at the apex, the lobes acute or obtuse, thick and fleshy, gray-green, sometimes with a reddish margin, in the wild sometimes deciduous in the dry season. Inflorescences to 40 cm (16 in.) long, 4- to 16-flowered. Flowers white, the spur tinged with green or pink. Pedicel and ovary 2–4 cm (1–2 in.) long; bracts 10 mm long. Dorsal sepal 10–20 × 4–8 mm, arching over column, ovate, apiculate; lateral sepals

Figure 10-10. *Aerangis verdickii.* Plant, ×0.75. →

spreading or deflexed, 14–22 × 3–8 mm, oblong, apiculate. Petals reflexed, 12–20 × 3–8 mm, obovate or oblong, apiculate. Lip 11–20 × 5–9 mm, oblong-obovate, somewhat constricted towards the base, with two ridges at the base at the mouth of the spur. Spur 12–20 cm (5–8 in.) long, pendent, flexuous, thickened in the apical half. Column 3–5 mm long. Capsule ellipsoid, 3 × 1 cm (1 × 0.5 in.).

HABITAT: Open woodland, often, but not always, in hot, dry areas, usually on high branches, occasionally on rocks, 100–1800 m (330–6000 ft.).

CULTIVATION: This is a species we would not be without. It grows easily (as perhaps might be expected from its wide altitudinal range) and flowers regularly. Intermediate temperatures seem to suit it, but it needs fairly good light and must be kept dry in winter to avoid stem rot, the greatest risk. Our plants are all mounted, but the species can be grown in a pot if the mix is sufficiently coarse. As with *Aerangis distincta,* plants in the wild have two flowering times depending on their geographic location. In Malawi, plants from the northern and central regions flower in summer, and those originating in the southern region, in spring; this pattern seems to persist in cultivation.

DISTRIBUTION: Angola, Malawi, Mozambique, Rwanda, South Africa (Mpumalanga), Tanzania, Zaire, Zambia, Zimbabwe.

Aeranthes Lindley

The genus *Aeranthes* was created by John Lindley in 1824. The name is derived from the Greek words *aer* (air, mist) and *anthos* (flower); it has been suggested that the name means "mist flower," referring to the humid places where these species grow, or to the epiphytic habit. We think the name was suggested by the way the translucent flowers seem poised in the air, moving in every breeze, on their very slender, almost wiry peduncles.

Aeranthes is a large genus, with more than 30 species once thought to be confined to Madagascar, the Comoro Islands, and the Mascarene Islands. In 1978, however, one species was described from mainland Africa, followed by a second in 1990, both from Zimbabwe. Neither is known to be in general cultivation, but as *Aeranthes* is a popular genus, the two are likely to become available.

DESCRIPTION: Monopodial epiphytes with short stems. Roots usually fine. Inflorescences axillary, one- to several-flowered, usually unbranched, often pendent, with very slender stalks. Flowers translucent, green or yellowish, rarely white, with the lateral sepals joined to the column foot. Sepals and petals similar, usually acuminate. Lip unlobed, the spur arising from the column foot. Column long or short; pollinia two, stipites two, viscidia two; rostellum side lobes longer than the midlobe.

CULTIVATION: Species of *Aeranthes* like high humidity and should never be allowed to dry out completely. All, however, seem very prone to developing fungal spots on the leaves in stagnant air, which can eventually lead to defoliation and death, so good ventilation is important. This would seem to suggest that they would do well mounted, especially with their pendent inflorescences, but the fine roots dry out very easily and we have had most success in growing them in a standard bark mix in pots, which are then suspended. Intermediate temperatures and fairly heavy shade are suitable.

Aeranthes africana J. Stewart

DESCRIPTION: A dwarf species; stems woody, 2–4 cm (1–2 in.) long. Leaves several, 4–7 cm (2–3 in.) × 4–8 mm, gray-green, distichous, linear to ligulate, leathery, unequally and obtusely bilobed at the tip. Inflorescences about the same length as the leaves, erect or spreading, one-flowered. Peduncle very slender with several brownish sheaths. Flowers whitish. Sepals 7–8 × 3–4 mm, ovate, acuminate, the laterals slightly longer than the dorsal. Petals 4–5 × 2 mm, ovate, acuminate. Lip 4 × 3 mm, more or less diamond-shaped, with a small apicule; spur 3 mm long, straight, tapering. Column 1 mm long; column foot 2 mm long.

HABITAT: Montane forest, often on species of *Podocarpus*. Altitude not recorded.

DISTRIBUTION: Zimbabwe.

Aeranthes parkesii G. Williamson

DESCRIPTION: Stems woody, to 12 cm (5 in.) long, covered with old leaf bases and the remains of old inflorescences. Leaves several, to 17 × 1.5 cm (7 × 1 in.), linear, the base folded, leathery, rather gray-green. Inflorescences arising from base of stem, to 20 cm (8 in.) long, erect or pendent, sometimes branched, each branch one-flowered. Flowers greenish-cream, the tips of the sepals, petals, and spur darker. Sepals to 20 × 7 mm, ovate, acuminate, curving forwards. Petals to 12 × 7 mm, ovate or acuminate, sometimes recurved. Lip 10 × 10 mm, quadrate, with an acumen 2 mm long at the tip; spur conical, to 10 mm long. Column 3 mm long. Capsule to 3 cm (1 in.) long, persisting for more than a year.

HABITAT: Low-altitude riverine forest, in deep shade, usually in mid-canopy.

DISTRIBUTION: Zimbabwe.

Ancistrochilus Rolfe

The genus *Ancistrochilus* was established by Robert Rolfe in 1897. The name is derived from the Greek words *ankistron* (hook) and *cheilos* (lip), referring to the hooklike mid-lobe of the lip. Some botanists (Geerinck 1984) consider that there is only one species in this genus, but two are generally accepted.

DESCRIPTION: Sympodial, epiphytic, with round or pear-shaped pseudobulbs, 1- to 2-leaved at the apex. Leaves deciduous, thin-textured, pleated. Inflorescences arising from the base of the pseudobulb, 1- to few-flowered. Flowers showy; sepals and petals spreading; lip trilobed. Pollinia eight, of two sizes.

Ancistrochilus rothschildianus O'Brien PLATE 20

SYNONYM: *Ancistrochilus thomsonianus* var. *gentilii* De Wildeman

DESCRIPTION: Pseudobulbs clustered, round to pear-shaped, rather squat, to 5 cm (2 in.) in diameter. Leaves one to (usually) two, 10–30 × 3–7 cm (4–12 × 1–3 in.), lanceolate or oblanceolate, acuminate, ribbed, deciduous. Inflorescences pubescent, to

20 cm (8 in.) long, 1- to 5-flowered. Flowers 5–8 cm (2–3 in.) in diameter, pale to deep pink, the lip pink or purple. Sepals pubescent on the outside, 25–30 × 10 mm, elliptic, acute. Petals 28 × 6 mm, oblanceolate, acute. Lip 17 × 14 mm, trilobed, with three to five ridges in the center, recurved in the apical half; side lobes oblong, erect; midlobe 10 mm long, narrowly triangular, acute. Column 17 mm long, curved, pubescent.

HABITAT: Evergreen forest, usually epiphytic on big, horizontal branches of large, old trees, at 500–1100 m (1650–3600 ft.). We saw big colonies of this species in Congo, where it was in flower and the pink sprays were very obvious, but, alas, always 25 m (80 ft.) above our heads. Whenever possible, we hunted below the tree in case a branch had come down or a piece of orchid had become detached, but that never happened. The species occasionally grows on mossy rocks.

CULTIVATION: Intermediate or intermediate to warm temperatures, in a pan in a standard bark mix, or a standard mix with extra leaf mold, in moderate shade. This species needs plenty of water while the new pseudobulbs are developing, but once these are mature and the leaves fall, plants should only receive occasional water, enough to stop the pseudobulbs from shrivelling. The inflorescences start to develop just before the leaves fall. As with so many species, especially those with rather thin leaves, this species is prone to rot if water lodges on the newly developing leaves. In cultivation this species flowers in autumn and winter (October to December), which seems to be the same time it flowers in the wild, as it was in late November that we saw it in flower in Congo.

DISTRIBUTION: Cameroon, Congo, Gabon, Guinea, Ivory Coast, Liberia, Nigeria, Sierra Leone, Uganda, Zaire.

Ancistrochilus thomsonianus (Reichenbach f.) Rolfe

DESCRIPTION: Pseudobulbs to 2.5 cm (1 in.) in diameter, orbicular, flattened. Leaves to 20 × 3 cm (8 × 1 in.), narrowly lanceolate, ribbed. Inflorescences erect or arching, 2- to 3-flowered. Flowers white, the midlobe of the lip bright purple, the side lobes green. Sepals and petals 35–45 mm long, lanceolate, acuminate. Lip side lobes erect, oblong, obtuse; midlobe 16–25 mm long, very slender, often recurved. Column slender, 15 mm long.

HABITAT: In forest.

CULTIVATION: May not be in cultivation, but if it is, it is certainly less common than *Ancistrochilus rothschildianus*. It grows in a similar habitat, so should thrive in the same conditions.

DISTRIBUTION: Cameroon, Nigeria.

Ancistrorhynchus Finet
SYNONYM: *Cephalangraecum* Schlechter

The genus *Ancistrorhynchus* was established by the French botanist Achille Finet in 1907; many of the species were already known but had been described in other genera, such as *Angraecum*. The name derives from the Greek words *ankistron* (hook) and *rhynchos* (beak, snout), referring to the distinctively shaped rostellum, which curves back on itself forming a hook. Species of *Ancistrorhynchus* are not showy plants; one would not want to grow too many of them, but there should be at least one species in any representative collection of African orchids as they are an important part of the orchid flora, particularly in West Africa. The dense heads of green and white flowers can be rather attractive. There are about 16 species in tropical Africa, reaching their most southerly point in northern Malawi. A surprising number of species is sometimes available in cultivation.

DESCRIPTION: Large or small, epiphytic, with long or, more often, short stems. Leaves usually linear, bilobed at the apex, with the lobes and sometimes the sides of the leaves just below the apex usually toothed, making the genus easy to identify even when plants are not in flower. Inflorescences arising at the base of the plant among old leaf sheaths, very dense, almost round, surrounded by large, papery bracts. Flowers white, often with a green mark on the lip. Sepals and petals fairly similar. Lip larger, entire or rather obscurely trilobed, with a wide-mouthed spur at the base. Spur often swollen at the apex, sometimes with a sharp bend in the middle. Column very short; rostellum pointed downwards, then sharply bent up so that the tip is pointing upwards—this is quite easily seen with a hand lens. Pollinia two, stipites two or one stipes that divides into two, viscidium one.

CULTIVATION: Almost all species of *Ancistrorhynchus* are forest plants, growing in deep shade, where the humidity is high for most of the year. They grow well in pots with a standard bark mix, but we also have a few plants mounted on bark, and that is satisfactory as well. They grow well at intermediate temperatures, although they probably prefer the warm side of intermediate. Generally, they are not too fussy and most species flower regularly, sometimes more than once a year.

Figure 10-11. *Ancistrorhynchus capitatus.* Flower, ×3.5.

Ancistrorhynchus capitatus (Lindley) Summerhayes

PLATE 21, FIGURE 10-11

DESCRIPTION: One of the more attractive species. Stems short, to 10 cm (4 in.) long. Leaves several, 15–30 × 1.5–2 cm (6–12 × 1 in.), linear, stiff and leathery, unequally bilobed at the apex, each lobe with two to three sharp teeth. Inflorescences 1.5 × 2.5 cm (1 × 1 in.), densely many-flowered; bracts brown and papery, to 1 cm (0.5 in.) long. Flowers white, the lip with a green blotch. Sepals 5–6 × 2–3 mm, oblong, obtuse; petals slightly smaller. Lip 4.5–6 × 4–5 mm, ovate, concave; spur 7–8.5 mm long, straight or slightly incurved, swollen at the tip. Column 2–3 mm long.

HABITAT: Evergreen forest, in heavy shade, 500–1300 m (1650–4300 ft.).

CULTIVATION: It usually flowers in early spring (March and April).

DISTRIBUTION: Cameroon, Central African Republic, Congo, Equatorial Guinea (Bioko), Gabon, Liberia, Nigeria, Sierra Leone, Togo, Uganda, Zaire.

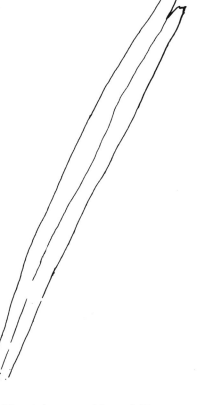

Figure 10-12. *Ancistrorhynchus cephalotes.* Flower (upper and lower left), ×3; leaf (right), ×1.

Ancistrorhynchus cephalotes (Reichenbach f.) Summerhayes

FIGURE 10-12

DESCRIPTION: Stems 5–20 cm (2–8 in.) long, erect. Leaves several, 7–40 × 1–2 cm (3–16 × 1 in.), linear, slightly folded at the base, bilobed at the apex, the lobes almost entire. Inflorescences densely many-flowered, surrounded by large, chaffy bracts. Flowers scented, white, the lip with a green or yellow blotch. Sepals and petals 4–7 ×

2–3 mm, oblong or elliptic, obtuse. Lip 4–7 × 4–9 mm, obscurely trilobed, side lobes rounded, midlobe suborbicular; spur 6–10 mm long, almost straight, slightly swollen at the apex. Column 1 mm long.

Habitat: Epiphytic in evergreen forest.

Distribution: Ghana, Guinea, Ivory Coast, Liberia, Nigeria, Sierra Leone.

Ancistrorhynchus clandestinus (Lindley) Schlechter

Description: Stems to 7 cm (3 in.) long, erect or pendent. Leaves 5 to 10, borne in a fan, 15–100 × 1–2 cm (6–40 × 1 in.), linear, acuminate, the apex very unequally bilobed, with one lobe often almost absent. Inflorescences 2 cm (1 in.) long, densely many-flowered. Pedicel and ovary 7–9 mm long; bracts 2–3 mm long. Flowers white, the lip with green marks in the throat. Sepals and petals 2–5 × 1–2.5 mm, elliptic, obtuse. Lip 4– 9 × 2–4 mm, obscurely trilobed; side lobes rounded, midlobe ovate, obtuse, the edges wavy; spur 3–7 mm long, S-shaped, wide-mouthed and swollen again at the apex. Column 2 mm long.

Habitat: Epiphytic in evergreen forest, 900–1100 m (3000–3600 ft.).

Distribution: Cameroon, Gabon, Ghana, Ivory Coast, Liberia, Nigeria, Sierra Leone, Togo, Uganda, Zaire.

Ancistrorhynchus ovatus Summerhayes

Description: Stems to 20 cm (8 in.) long, erect or pendent. Leaves to twelve, 7–20 × 0.5–1.5 cm (3–8 × 0.25–1 in.), linear, unequally bilobed at the apex, each lobe with two teeth. Inflorescences forming a dense head, 1–2 cm (1 in.) long and wide; pedicel and ovary 6–8 mm long; bracts 6–12 mm long. Flowers white. Sepals 3–5 × 1–2 mm, oblong to elliptic, rounded. Petals 3–4.5 × 2.5–4.5 mm, broadly oblanceolate, rounded. Lip 3–5 × 2.5–4.5 mm, concave, broadly ovate to orbicular, with wavy margins; spur 4.5–6 mm long, almost straight, swollen at the apex. Column 1 mm long.

Habitat: Epiphytic in evergreen forest, 1200–1600 m (4000–5300 ft.).

Distribution: Congo, Gabon, Uganda, Zaire.

Ancistrorhynchus recurvus Finet   FIGURE 10-13

Description: Stems short, 1–6 cm (0.5–2 in.) long. Leaves several, 12–40 × 1–2 cm (5–16 × 1 in.), unequally bilobed at the apex, each lobe with two teeth. Inflorescence a dense head to 3 cm (1 in.) long; pedicel and ovary 5 mm long; bracts 2–3 mm long. Flowers white, with scurfy hairs on the outside. Sepals 3.5–4.5 × 2 mm, elliptic, obtuse. Petals 4 × 1 mm, oblong. Lip 4.5–7.5 × 3–4.5 mm, obscurely trilobed; side lobes rounded, midlobe ovate, acute, recurved; spur wide-mouthed, 5–6 mm long, sharply bent in the basal half and recurved towards the swollen apex. Column 2 mm long.

Habitat: Epiphytic in evergreen forest, 1100–1300 m (3600–4300 ft.).

Distribution: Cameroon, Gabon, Ghana, Guinea, Liberia, Nigeria, Sierra Leone, Uganda, Zaire.

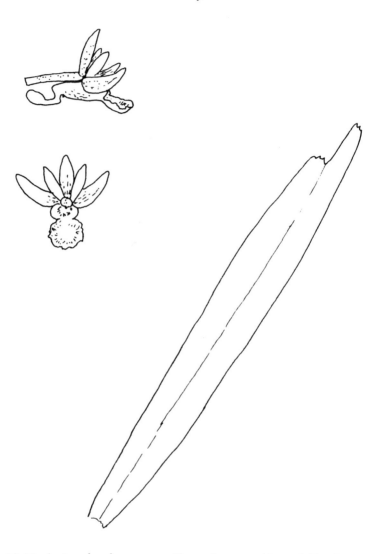

Figure 10-13. *Ancistrorhynchus recurvus.* Flower (upper and lower left), ×3; leaf (right), ×1.

Ancistrorhynchus refractus (Kränzlin) Summerhayes

DESCRIPTION: Stems short, erect when young but sometimes pendent when older, to 4 cm (2 in.) long. Leaves six to eight, 6–40 × 1 cm (2–16 × 0.5 in.), linear, fleshy or leathery, folded, linear, unequally bilobed at the apex. Inflorescences dense, 3–3.5 cm (1 in.) long; pedicel and ovary 12–14 mm long; bracts 7–8 mm long. Flowers shining white. Dorsal sepal 10–12 × 4 mm, narrowly oblong, obtuse; lateral sepals slightly longer. Petals 12–13 × 3–4 mm, oblong, obtuse. Lip 15–17 × 7 mm, obscurely trilobed, concave, ovate, obtuse; spur 13–17 mm long, S-shaped, tapering from a wide mouth, then swollen at the apex. Column 7–8 mm long.

HABITAT: Epiphytic in submontane to montane evergreen forest, 900–2100 m (3000–7000 ft.).

DISTRIBUTION: Tanzania.

Ancistrorhynchus serratus Summerhayes

DESCRIPTION: Stems fairly elongated, occasionally branched, leafy in the apical half. Leaves 7–11 × 1 cm (3–4 × 0.5 in.), linear, V-shaped in cross-section, unequally bilobed at the apex, the lobes irregularly toothed. Inflorescences short, dense, several to many-flowered. Flowers white. Sepals 3–3.5 × 1–1.5 mm, oblong-elliptic, obtuse. Petals 3 × 1 mm, oblanceolate. Lip 2.5 × 4–4.5 mm, obscurely trilobed, concave, transversely elliptic, apiculate; spur 4–4.5 mm long, almost straight, tapering from a wide mouth, then swollen at the apex.

HABITAT: Epiphytic in evergreen forest, 1200–1500 m (4000–5000 ft.).

DISTRIBUTION: Cameroon, Equatorial Guinea (Bioko), Nigeria.

Angraecopsis Kränzlin

The genus *Angraecopsis* was established by the German botanist Fritz Kränzlin in 1900. The name comes from *Angraecum* and the Greek word *opsis* (looking like), referring to the resemblance of the plants to some *Angraecum* species. There are about 15 species in tropical Africa, Madagascar, and the Mascarene Islands. They are not showy, but some are attractive.

DESCRIPTION: Monopodial epiphytes with short stems. Leaves distichous, linear, oblanceolate or strap-shaped, often twisted at the base to face the same way. Inflorescences axillary, unbranched, one- to several-flowered, with a wiry peduncle, often long in relation to the rachis. Flowers small, white, green, or yellow-green. Lateral sepals often longer than dorsal sepal and often joined at the base to the petals; petals usually triangular. Lip usually trilobed but sometimes entire, spurred at the base. Column short and fleshy; rostellum trilobed; pollinia two, stipites two, viscidium usually two.

Angraecopsis amaniensis Summerhayes   PLATE 22

DESCRIPTION: A small, virtually stemless species, with many long roots radiating from the base and clinging to the bark, 2–3 mm in diameter, gray-green. Leaves two to four, to 4 × 0.7 cm (2 × 0.25 in.), narrowly elliptic, blue-green, almost fleshy, sometimes deciduous in the dry season. Inflorescences several, pendent, 4–10 cm (2–4 in.) long, densely to 20-flowered. Flowers in two ranks, green or yellow-green, scented like lily-of-the-valley. Pedicel and ovary arched, 5 mm long; bracts 2 mm long, sheathing, dark brown. Dorsal sepal erect, 4–5 × 1.5 mm, lanceolate, acute; laterals deflexed, 7 × 1.5 mm, obliquely lanceolate, rather curved. Petals 4 × 1.5 mm, triangular. Lip 4–7 × 2 mm, rather obscurely trilobed at the base, triangular, acute, channelled. Spur 7–13 mm long, slender, pendent. Column less than 1 mm long.

HABITAT: Epiphytic in woodland in high rainfall areas, sometimes in evergreen forest, occasionally on rocks, often forming large colonies where it occurs, 750–2100 m (2500–7000 ft.), but usually 1000–1500 m (3300–5000 ft.).

CULTIVATION: Mounted, in intermediate conditions, in moderate shade. It likes high humidity while growing, but is better with a cooler and drier rest. This little species is a great favorite of ours, as when it is in flower, it is smothered in a mass of scented, yellow-green flowers.

DISTRIBUTION: Kenya, Malawi, Mozambique, Tanzania, Zambia, Zimbabwe.

Angraecopsis breviloba Summerhayes

DESCRIPTION: This species is very similar to *Angraecopsis amaniensis*, except that the spur is only 4–5 mm long, and swollen at the tip.

HABITAT: Montane forest, often near a stream; also in citrus plantations, 1300–2400 m (4300–8000 ft.).

CULTIVATION: Mounted, in intermediate conditions, in moderate shade. It likes high humidity while growing, but is better with a cooler and drier rest.

DISTRIBUTION: Kenya, Tanzania.

Angraecopsis gracillima (Rolfe) Summerhayes   FIGURE 10-14

DESCRIPTION: Stems to 7 cm (3 in.) long, usually pendent. Leaves several, 6–15 × 1–2 cm (2–6 × 1 in.), linear, curved, unequally and obtusely bilobed at the apex, twisted at the base to lie in one plane. Inflorescences 4–16 cm (2–6 in.) long, 4- to 15-flowered. Flowers white, the sepals and petals orange right at the base. Pedicel and ovary 17–27 mm long; bracts 2–3 mm long. Dorsal sepal 2–3 × 1.5 mm, ovate, obtuse; lateral sepals 7–9 × 1.5–2 mm, reflexed and deflexed, spathulate. Petals 2–5 × 3–5 mm, obliquely triangular. Lip 5–6 mm long, trilobed in the basal half; side lobes reflexed, 1.5 mm long, linear, midlobe 4.5–5 × 1–1.5 mm, oblanceolate, rounded. Spur 4 cm (2 in.) long, pendent, very slender. Column 1 mm long.

HABITAT: Epiphytic in deep shade in forest, often near a stream, 1500–1850 m (5000–6100 ft.).

CULTIVATION: Intermediate temperatures, either mounted or in a pot, in deep shade. It should not be allowed to dry out too much, even in the resting season.

DISTRIBUTION: Kenya, Uganda, Zaire, Zambia.

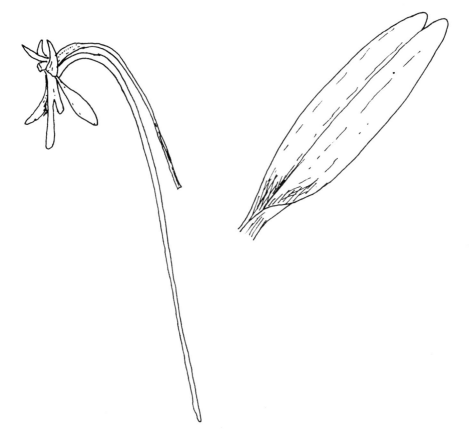

Figure 10-14. *Angraecopsis gracillima.* Flower (left), ×2.5; leaf (right), ×1.

Angraecopsis ischnopus (Schlechter) Schlechter FIGURE 10-15

DESCRIPTION: Stems short. Leaves 2–11 × 0.5–1.5 cm (1–4 × 0.25–1 in.), strap-shaped or oblong-elliptical, unequally bilobed at the apex, the lobes rounded. Inflorescences arising at base of plant, 3–9 cm (1–4 in.) long, 5-flowered. Flowers white; pedicel and ovary salmon pink, 15–16 mm long, arched or almost straight. Dorsal sepal erect, 2–3 × 2 mm, broadly ovate; lateral sepals 7 × 2 mm, spathulate, spreading and deflexed. Petals 2 × 3 mm, triangular, broader than long. Lip 7 mm long, trilobed at about halfway; midlobe 4 × 1.5 mm, lanceolate, obtuse; side lobes similar but slightly narrower, not reflexed. Spur 12–38 mm long, slender, parallel to the ovary and pedicel at first, then pendent.

HABITAT: Evergreen forest, often near a river, 1650 m (5500 ft.).

CULTIVATION: Intermediate temperatures, either mounted or in a pot, in deep shade. It should not be allowed to dry out too much, even in the resting season.

DISTRIBUTION: Cameroon, Guinea, Nigeria, Sierra Leone.

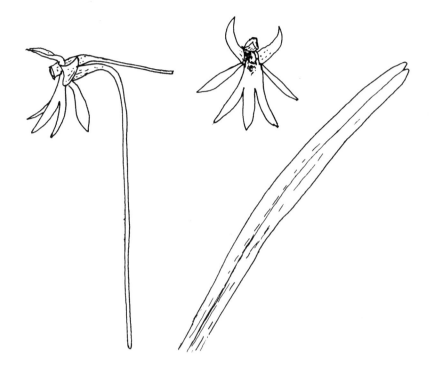

Figure 10-15. *Angraecopsis ischnopus.* Flower (left and center), ×2.5; leaf (right), ×1.

Angraecopsis parviflora (Thouars) Schlechter

DESCRIPTION: Stems short, pendent; roots slender. Leaves several, 6–25 × 0.5–1.5 cm (2–10 × 0.25–1 in.), linear or narrowly oblanceolate, curved, slightly fleshy, unequally and acutely bilobed at the apex. Inflorescences 5–10 cm (2–4 in.) long, densely 5- to 10-flowered, the peduncle to 9 cm (4 in.) long, very slender and wiry. Flowers greenish-white, turning yellowish as they age. Pedicel 5 mm long, ovary 3 mm long; bracts 1 mm long. Dorsal sepal erect, 2 × 1 mm, ovate; laterals deflexed, 4 × 1 mm, obliquely oblanceolate. Petals 1.5–2 × 1–1.5 mm, obliquely triangular, acute. Lip 4 mm long, trilobed near the base; midlobe 3 × 1, linear, acute; side lobes similar but slightly shorter, spreading, slightly upcurved. Spur 5–10 mm long, occasionally longer, incurved, slender but swollen at the apex. Column 1 mm long.

HABITAT: Epiphytic in deep shade on trunks and lower large branches of trees in evergreen forest, usually near a river; occasionally on rocks, 600–1800 m (2000–6000 ft.). Where it occurs, it is usually plentiful.

CULTIVATION: With its pendent habit, this species needs to be mounted—in the wild, the leaves are usually hanging down and pressed against the tree trunk. Otherwise, intermediate temperatures, heavy shade, and high humidity suit it. It should not be allowed to dry out too much. In our greenhouse, it flowers in early winter (November).

DISTRIBUTION: Cameroon, Malawi, Mozambique, Tanzania, Zimbabwe. Also in Madagascar, Mascarene Islands.

Angraecopsis tenerrima Kränzlin

DESCRIPTION: Stems pendent, short, occasionally to 7 cm (3 in.) long. Leaves several, 6–20 × 1.5–2 cm (2–8 × 1 in.), linear to oblanceolate, curved, unequally and roundly bilobed at the apex, twisted at the base to lie in one plane, very dark green. Inflorescences 8–20 cm (3–8 in.) long, rather laxly 3- to 7-flowered, with a slender peduncle 6–13 cm (2–5 in.) long. Flowers white, the spur green-tipped. Pedicel and ovary 2–3 cm (1 in.) long; bracts sheathing, 2–4 mm long. Dorsal sepal 3 × 2 mm, elliptic, obtuse; lateral sepals 8–12 × 2–2.5 mm, spathulate. Petals 3 × 4 mm, obliquely triangular, joined at the base to the lateral sepals. Lip 9–10 mm long, trilobed about halfway along, all lobes 4–5 mm long. Spur pendent, 5–6 cm (2 in.) long, fairly wide-mouthed but becoming slender. Column 1 mm long.

HABITAT: Epiphytic in submontane forest, 400–1600 m (1300–5300 ft.).

CULTIVATION: With its pendent habit, this species needs to be mounted. Otherwise, intermediate temperatures, heavy shade, and high humidity suit it. It should not be allowed to dry out too much.

DISTRIBUTION: Tanzania.

Angraecum Bory

The genus *Angraecum* was established in 1804 by Colonel Bory de St. Vincent. The name derives from a Malayan word, *angurek,* used for epiphytic orchids with growth similar to that of *Vanda. Angraecum* is a large genus of about 200 species, about a quarter of which occur on mainland Africa, with the rest growing in Madagascar and other Indian Ocean islands, except for *A. zeylanicum,* which is found in Sri Lanka as well as the Seychelles. As *Angraecum* was one of the first genera of African orchids to be described, many species that are now placed in other genera such as *Aerangis, Jumellea,* and *Rangaeris* were originally described as *Angraecum.*

Several botanists have at various times revised *Angraecum* and endeavored to divide it into sections, the most recent being the American botanist Leslie Garay, who in 1973 proposed 19 sections. Garay's arrangement is still generally followed. Of his 19 sections, 7 occur only in Madagascar and the other islands, 10 are found both there and in Africa, and only 2 sections, *Afrangraecum* and *Dolabrifolia,* are confined to mainland Africa. Of the 10 sections occurring on the mainland and on the Indian Ocean islands, only two species are common to both areas, *A. calceolus* in Mozambique and Madagascar, and *A. eburneum* in East Africa, Madagascar, the Mascarene Islands, and the Comoro Islands. *Angraecum eburneum,* however, is represented by a different subspecies in each of these areas, and some people consider each of these to be a species in its own right.

Angraecum is a genus showing great diversity in size and in foliage, including probably the largest, and some of the smallest, of all African orchids. In spite of this, it is usually easy to recognize a plant as belonging to this genus when it is in flower. While many African species have small flowers, there are some, particularly in section *Arachnangraecum,* that rival the well-known Madagascan species for size and beauty of flower, yet are seldom grown. Only half the African species of *Angraecum* are in cultivation—and many of these to only a limited extent—and so it seems worth giving a complete list of species, in their sections, so that if anyone manages to obtain a species not described here, at least it will be possible to find out which other species are similar.

DESCRIPTION: Tiny or very large, almost stemless or with a long, sometimes climbing, stem; leaves thin-textured or fleshy, flattened in the usual way, bilaterally flattened, or needle-shaped—almost every variation is represented. Flowers green, white, yellowish, or dull orange-salmon, scented in the evening and at night. Lip unlobed, deeply concave, spurred at the base, although the spur may be slender or saclike. Sepals and petals similar in size and shape; column deeply divided in front.

CULTIVATION: Because there is such diversity in the genus, it is difficult to give any general advice on cultivation, except to say that most are forest species and appreciate fairly dense shade and high humidity. All are epiphytic, or rarely, lithophytic. We grow most species in pots, in a standard bark mix, but some of the species with trailing stems, such as *Angraecum doratophyllum,* have to be mounted. It is even more important, in that case, to maintain the humidity. Species with climbing stems, such as *A. infundibulare,* need something like a stick or a moss pole in their pot so that they can scramble up it. Other details of habitat are given in the descriptions that follow.

African Species of *Angraecum*

***Angraecum* Section *Afrangraecum* Summerhayes.** Stems long, leafy. Inflorescences fairly long, but usually shorter than the leaves, several-flowered. Flowers rather fleshy, usually medium-sized. Confined to mainland Africa. Of the 10 known species, several sound attractive, but only one is known to be in cultivation.

    A. angustum (Rolfe) Summerhayes (Nigeria)
    A. affine Schlechter (West Africa)
    A. astroarche Ridley (São Tomé)
    A. claessensii De Wildeman (Liberia, Nigeria, Zaire)
    A. firthii Summerhayes (Cameroon, Uganda, Kenya)
    A. mofakoko De Wildeman (Zaire)
    A. multinominatum Rendle (West Africa)
    A. pyriforme Summerhayes (Ivory Coast, Nigeria)
    A. reygaertii De Wildeman

***Angraecum* Section *Angraecoides* (Cordemoy) Garay.** Stems usually somewhat elongated. Inflorescences 1- to 2-flowered. Peduncle slender, usually much longer than the spaces between the leaves, with one to two appressed sheaths covering the base. Flowers small, green, greenish-yellow, or dull orange, rarely white. Spur cylindrical or club-shaped. In his description of the section, Garay (1973) said that the inflorescence is one-flowered, but several species, for example, *Angraecum cultriforme,* have inflorescences with two buds, of which one usually, but not always, aborts.

A. *chevalieri* Summerhayes (?= A. *moandense* De Wildeman)
A. *cultriforme* Summerhayes
A. *curvipes* Schlechter (Cameroon)
A. *egertonii* Rendle (Nigeria, Gabon)
A. *modicum* Summerhayes (Liberia)
?A. *petterssonianum* Geerinck (Zaire)
A. *stolzii* Schlechter
A. *umbrosum* Cribb (Malawi)

Angraecum* Section *Angraecum. Plants usually large; stems well developed, leafy. Inflorescences long, occasionally branched, several to many-flowered. Flowers large, fleshy, white or greenish-white. About a dozen species, with one found in Africa.

A. *eburneum* subsp. *giryamae* (Rendle) Senghas & Cribb

***Angraecum* Section *Arachnangraecum* Schlechter.** Stems usually very long. Inflorescences 1- to 2-flowered; peduncle long, covered with one to two sheaths at the base. Flowers usually large and white; lip suborbicular, acuminate; spur long and slender. This section has about 17 species, 5 of which are from Africa. It is one of the most attractive sections, and any species that can be obtained, is worth growing. Except for *Angraecum conchiferum,* they are large plants with a climbing habit, almost like *Vanilla* species. A good way to grow them (except for A. *conchiferum*) is in a bark mix in a fairly large pot that contains a moss pole (of the type used for climbing indoor plants) to which the stem can be tied until it attaches itself by its roots.

A. *birrimense* Rolfe
A. *conchiferum* Lindley
A. *eichlerianum* Kränzlin
A. *infundibulare* Lindley
A. *spectabile* Summerhayes (Tanzania)

***Angraecum* Section *Boryangraecum* Schlechter.** Stems very short. Inflorescences several-flowered, not usually secund. Flowers usually thin-textured, small, or rarely medium-sized. Members of this section are similar to members of section *Nana,* and indeed Garay (1973) predicted that in the future the two sections would be merged. About a dozen species are included in this section, with three occurring in Africa.

A. *dives* Rolfe
?A. *geniculatum* Williamson
A. *sacciferum* Lindley
A. *teres* Summerhayes (Tanzania)

Angraecum Section *Conchoglossum* **Schlechter.** Stems long. Inflorescences 1- to 2-flow-ered, the peduncle short and covered at the base with one or two sheaths. Flowers small or more rarely, medium-sized. Spur usually shorter than, or as long as, the ovary.

A. *angustipetalum* Rendle
A. *brevicornu* Summerhayes (Tanzania)
A. *erectum* Summerhayes
A. *keniae* Kränzlin (Kenya)
A. *viride* Kränzlin (Tanzania)

Angraecum Section *Dolabrifolia* **(Pfitzer) Garay.** Stems elongated, leafy. Leaves dis-tichous, short, fleshy, bilaterally compressed with a groove on the upper surface, over-lapping. Inflorescences one-flowered, with a very short peduncle. Flowers small, white. This small section is one of those confined to mainland Africa. The plants are not showy, but have interesting and unusual foliage and usually attract attention.

A. *aporoides* Summerhayes
A. *bancoense* Van der Burg
A. *distichum* Lindley
A. *podochiloides* Schlechter (Nigeria, Cameroon, Zaire)

Angraecum Section *Gomphocentrum* **(Bentham) Garay.** Stems short but distinct. Inflorescences several to many-flowered, simple or branched. Flowers small or medium-sized, thin-textured, usually greenish-yellow.

A. *calceolus* Thouars
A. *tenuipes* Summerhayes

Angraecum Section *Lemurangis* **Garay.** Plants small; stems usually elongated. Leaves distichous. Inflorescences few-flowered, arising from axils of upper leaves, and shorter than leaves. Flowers small, thin-textured. Only one African species falls into this section.

A. *humile* Summerhayes

Angraecum Section *Nana* **(Cordemoy) Garay.** Stems very short. Inflorescences arising from lower leaf axils, few- to many-flowered, often secund. Flowers very small, thin-textured.

A. *chamaeanthus* Schlechter
A. *decipiens* Summerhayes (Kenya, Tanzania)
A. *minus* Summerhayes (Tanzania, Zambia, Zimbabwe)
A. *pusillum* Lindley

Angraecum Section *Pectinaria* **(Bentham) Schlechter.** Stems long, leafy. Leaves not overlapping or bilaterally flattened. Inflorescences one-flowered; peduncle very short. Flowers small or smallish with a sessile ovary.

A. *doratophyllum* Summerhayes
A. *gabonense* Summerhayes
A. *pungens* Schlechter
A. *subulatum* Lindley

Angraecum Section *Perrierangraecum* Schlechter. Stems short or of medium length. Inflorescences one-flowered; peduncle covered completely with three to four compressed sheaths. Flowers large for size of plant, long-spurred; lip ovate, prominent; ovary and capsule usually triangular in cross-section. This is one of the most attractive sections, with showy but compact plants; it includes such favorite Madagascan species as *Angraecum compactum, A. didieri,* and *A. rutenbergianum.* Although it is a large section with almost 30 members, only two species, both of limited distribution, are known from mainland Africa and probably neither is in cultivation. Because of their beauty, it is hoped that they might become generally available in the future.

A. chimanimaniense Williamson

A. stella-africae Cribb

Angraecum angustipetalum Rendle

DESCRIPTION: Stems leafy, to 60 cm (24 in.) long. Leaves distichous, 3–10 × 1–2 cm (1–4 × 0.5–1 in.), elliptic, deeply, unequally and acutely bilobed at the apex. Inflorescences arising along the stem, one-flowered, 1–2 cm (1 in.) long, shorter than leaves. Flowers white or pale buff. Sepals 12–15 × 1–1.5 mm, linear, acuminate; petals 10 mm long, almost threadlike from a broader base. Lip 12–20 × 4–5 mm, triangular-ovate, acute; spur 12–20 mm long, slender from a wide mouth, but inflated again at apex, somewhat recurved.

HABITAT: Dense forest. Altitude not known.

CULTIVATION: We have not grown this species, but it would seem that it should be mounted on bark, in a shaded and humid situation, at intermediate to warm temperatures.

DISTRIBUTION: Cameroon, Gabon, Ghana, Nigeria, Zaire. Two collections of what appears to be this species were made in Malawi around Mount Mulanje in 1914, but the species has not been found there since.

Angraecum aporoides Summerhayes   FIGURE 10-16

SYNONYM: *Angraecum distichum* var. *grandifolium* (De Wildeman) Summerhayes

DESCRIPTION: A splendid plant, like an oversized plant of *Angraecum distichum;* stems branched, 20–30 cm (8–12 in.) long, becoming pendent, covered with leaves; roots very slender. Leaves fleshy, bright green, distichous, 1–2.5 cm (0.5–1 in.) × 6–10 mm, with a groove running most of the way along the upper surface. Flowers white, scented, arising along the stem, mostly towards the apex. Pedicel and ovary 8 mm long, greenish-white. Sepals and petals spreading. Sepals 4–9 × 2–3 mm, elliptic, obtuse; petals similar but slightly smaller. Lip rather obscurely trilobed, concave, acute, the apex curved back, 4 mm × 5 mm if flattened; spur 6–7 mm long, more or less straight, very slender, acute.

HABITAT: Rainforest, in deep shade, at low altitudes.

CULTIVATION: Although much less widespread than *Angraecum distichum* and apparently growing at lower altitudes, this species seems to like similar conditions in cultivation. It does well in a pot in a bark mix, but because of its rather floppy habit, larger plants need to be hung in a shady place.

DISTRIBUTION: Cameroon, Equatorial Guinea (Bioko), Nigeria, Príncipe, Zaire.

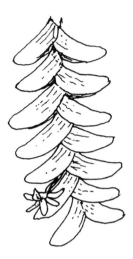

Figure 10-16. *Angraecum aporoides.* Branch (left), ×1; flower (right), ×3.

Angraecum bancoense Van der Burg

DESCRIPTION: This species was described in 1980; it has been, and still is, confused with *Angraecum distichum.* Vegetatively, the two species are indistinguishable, so no further description of the foliage and plant habit is needed here. The flowers, however, are smaller and the spur is of a different shape. The flowers are white, 3.7–6 mm from tip of spur to the apex of the lip, about the same length as the leaves. Sepals 1.5–2 × 1 mm, elliptic or obovate. Petals 1.5 × 0.5 mm, narrowly elliptical. Lip 1 mm long, obscurely trilobed; spur 2.5–5 mm long, straight, tapering gradually to a blunt apex.

HABITAT: Forms dense mats on the branches of trees in rainforest, in deep shade, 200–1600 m (660–5300 ft.).

CULTIVATION: Grows well for us in a pot with a standard bark mix, in intermediate conditions, in fairly heavy shade. It would do as well, perhaps better, in warm temperatures. If the humidity is not sufficiently high, the leaves start to look shrivelled.

DISTRIBUTION: Cameroon, Congo, Ivory Coast.

Angraecum birrimense Rolfe

DESCRIPTION: Stems elongated, sometimes as much as 2 m (6 ft.) long, somewhat flattened. Leaves distichous, 7–15 × 1.5–4.5 cm (3–6 × 1–2 in.), oblong-lanceolate, unequally and obtusely bilobed at the apex. Inflorescences usually 2-flowered. Flowers to 12 cm (5 in.) in diameter, scented, pale green, the lip white with a green central mark. Sepals and petals 3–6 cm (1–2 in.) × 3–9 mm, narrowly lanceolate. Lip 3–4 cm (1–2 in.) long and wide, suborbicular to squarish, not including an apicule 1–1.5 cm (0.5–1 in.) long. Spur 3.5–5 cm (1–2 in.) long, tapering from a wide mouth.

HABITAT: Evergreen forest. Altitude not known.

CULTIVATION: In shaded, humid, and warm to intermediate conditions. Grows well in a bark mix in a fairly large pot that contains a moss pole (of the type used for climbing indoor plants) to which the stem can be tied until it attaches itself by its roots.

DISTRIBUTION: Cameroon, Ghana, Ivory Coast, Liberia, Nigeria, Sierra Leone.

Angraecum calceolus Thouars   FIGURE 10-17
SYNONYM: *Angraecum anocentrum* Schlechter

DESCRIPTION: Stems woody, erect, to 9 cm (4 in.) long, sometimes forming clumps; roots numerous, 1.5–2 mm in diameter. Leaves numerous, 17–22 × 1.5–2.5 cm (7–9 × 1 in.), strap-shaped, very unequally lobed at apex, with one lobe almost absent. Inflorescences 15–25 cm (6–10 in.) long, with up to five branches, each several-flowered. Flowers pale yellow-green. Sepals 7–8 × 2–4 mm, lanceolate, acute; petals similar but slightly smaller. Lip 7 × 3 mm, including an acumen 2 mm long, very concave, ovate, acuminate; spur 12 mm long, slender, slightly swollen at apex, often pointing upwards.

HABITAT: Coastal forest, 30–60 m (100–200 ft.).

CULTIVATION: Although growing at such a low altitude it might be expected to like much heat, this is one of the most amenable species in cultivation. It does well in a pot at intermediate temperatures and seems to like fairly bright light.

DISTRIBUTION: Mozambique. Also in Comoro Islands, Madagascar, Mascarene Islands, Seychelles.

NOTE: One of two species common to both the Indian Ocean islands and mainland Africa, this is not one of the showier species, but the branched inflorescence, seen only in older plants, is unusual. Young plants have a simple raceme. The species flowers over a long period from summer through autumn and even into winter.

Angraecum chamaeanthus Schlechter

DESCRIPTION: Probably the smallest of all the species of *Angraecum* and an interesting species for anyone who likes very miniature orchids. Stems only 1–4 mm long. Leaves two to four, 10–18 × 1.5–3 mm, linear-ligulate to elliptic. Inflorescences 1–3 cm (0.5–1 in.) long, more or less secund, 4- to 10-flowered. Flowers white. Sepals and petals 1.5–2 × 1 mm, ovate, rounded, the lateral sepals slightly longer than the other parts. Lip 1.5 × 1–1.3 mm, broadly ovate, rounded; spur 1–1.5 mm long, conical, rounded at apex.

HABITAT: Montane and submontane forest, 1400–2300 m (4600–7600 ft.), where it grows on the smallest twigs.

CULTIVATION: Not easy because of its small size. Shade and high humidity are essential, and it is probably better mounted. Intermediate to cool temperatures.

DISTRIBUTION: Kenya, Malawi, South Africa (Mpumalanga, Northern Province), Tanzania, Zimbabwe.

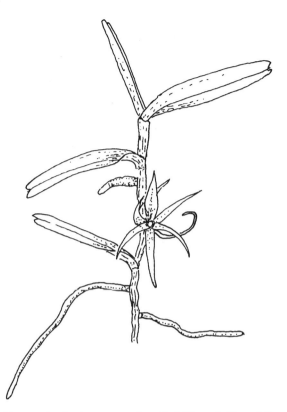

Figure 10-18. *Angraecum chevalieri*. Plant (left) and flower right), ×1.

Angraecum chevalieri Summerhayes   FIGURE 10-18

DESCRIPTION: Stems to 15 cm (6 in.) long, sometimes branched; roots 2 mm in diameter, arising along the stem. Leaves several, distichous, on the upper half of the stem, 3–5 × 0.5–0.7 cm (1–2 × 0.25 in.), slightly fleshy, narrowly strap-shaped, twisted at the base to face the same way. Inflorescences arising along the stem opposite the leaves, to 2.5 cm (1 in.) long, 1- to 2-flowered. Flowers nonresupinate, greenish-straw. Sepals and petals 8–16 × 1–2 mm, all lanceolate, acuminate, the petals slightly shorter and narrower than the sepals. Lip 7–11 × 2–3 mm, very concave, ovate, acuminate, the tip recurved. Spur 15–20 mm long, slender, slightly S-shaped.

HABITAT: Rainforest, 1100–1200 m (3600–4000 ft.).

CULTIVATION: Mounted on bark, in a shady, humid situation; intermediate temperatures. This rather unshowy species seems to be well established in cultivation. In our experience, plants do not appreciate being divided.

DISTRIBUTION: Cameroon, Gabon, Guinea, Equatorial Guinea (Bioko), Ivory Coast, Liberia, Nigeria, Tanzania, Uganda, Zaire.

NOTE: This species may be the same as *A. moandense* De Wildeman. If that is so, *A. moandense* would be the correct name.

← Figure 10-17. *Angraecum calceolus*. Plant, ×0.75.

Angraecum chimanimaniense G. Williamson

DESCRIPTION: Stems to 15 cm (6 in.) long, sometimes branched; roots verrucose, 2 mm in diameter. Leaves several, 7–10 cm (3–4 in.) × 4–8 mm, distichous, linear, glossy green, almost triangular in cross-section. Pedicel and ovary 5 cm (2 in.) long, S-shaped. Flowers 7 cm (3 in.) diameter, fleshy, white, slightly tinged with green and straw-color. Sepals and petals narrowly lanceolate, acute; sepals 35–40 × 5–6 mm; petals similar but slightly narrower and somewhat reflexed. Lip 40 × 15 mm, concave, narrowly ovate, long acute; spur 10–14 cm long (4–6 in.) long, pendent, very slender.

HABITAT: Epiphytic or lithophytic in riverine forest, 1800 m (6000 ft.).

CULTIVATION: Not known to be in cultivation, but so attractive we hope it might at some time become available. From its habitat, it should like a shady, humid situation, and intermediate temperatures.

DISTRIBUTION: Zimbabwe (Chimanimani Mountains in the eastern highlands).

NOTE: This attractive species will be familiar to anyone who has seen Ball (1978), where it is illustrated as *Angraecum* sp. no. 2.

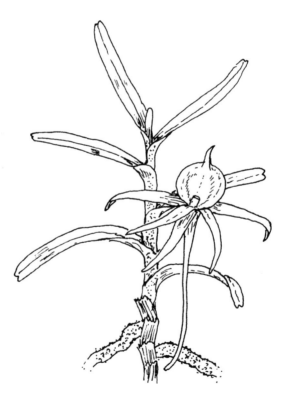

Figure 10-19. *Angraecum conchiferum*. Plant, ×1.

Angraecum conchiferum Lindley

PLATE 23, FIGURE 10-19

DESCRIPTION: Stems branching, to 60 cm (24 in.) long, often shorter; roots many, pale gray, warty, 2 mm in diameter. Leaves distichous, to 6 cm (2 in.) × 7 mm, linear, dark green, rather stiff. Inflorescences arising along the stem, usually one-flowered but sometimes 2-flowered; peduncle 2.5 cm (1 in.) long; pedicel and ovary 2 cm (1 in.) long. Flowers nonresupinate, white, the spur greenish towards the apex. Sepals and petals spreading, linear, long acuminate; sepals 20–30 × 2–3 mm; petals slightly narrower. Lip 10 mm long and wide, not including an acumen 3–9 mm long, the basal part concave, orbicular (*conchiferum* means "shell-like"); spur 3.5–5 cm (1–2 in.) long, slender and tapering, straight or slightly S-shaped.

HABITAT: Montane forest, sometimes on isolated trees and rocks, 1250–2400 m (4100–8000 ft.).

CULTIVATION: This beautiful species must have high humidity to grow well. Although in the wild it can grow in exposed positions, at these altitudes, there will be frequent mist and drizzle, even in the dry season. It can be grown either mounted on bark or in a pot, but good ventilation is essential. It is not easy to get the conditions just right, but it is well worth persevering with it, as it is a lovely species, not so big as the others in its section. Intermediate to cool temperatures seem to be best.

DISTRIBUTION: Kenya, Malawi, Mozambique, South Africa (Eastern Cape, KwaZulu-Natal, Mpumalanga, Northern Province, Western Cape), Tanzania, Zimbabwe.

Angraecum cultriforme Summerhayes

FIGURE 10-20

DESCRIPTION: A species very variable in flower size; plants with smaller flowers similar to *Angraecum stolzii* (which see). Stems elongated, to 20 cm (8 in.) long; roots many, wiry, 1.5–2 mm in diameter. Leaves to 6 cm (2 in.) × 8 mm, curved, strap-shaped, acutely and unequally bilobed at the apex, twisted at the base to lie in one plane, dull olive green, sometimes tinged with reddish or orange. Flowers often non-resupinate, light orange to greenish-yellow, arising along the stem opposite leaves. Inflorescences to 3.5 cm (1 in.) long, 1- to 2-flowered but usually one flower aborts. Ovary 5 mm long, forming a right angle with the 7-mm-long pedicel. Sepals and petals all linear-lanceolate, acuminate; sepals 10–19 × 2–4 mm; petals 8–14 × 2 mm. Lip 8–12.5 × 4.5–6 mm, boat-shaped, acuminate, somewhat recurved; spur 1–2.7 cm (1 in.) long, straight or slightly S-shaped, slender but slightly inflated towards the apex.

HABITAT: Thicket or riverine forest, often growing low down in rather dry, low-lying areas (although it has been collected at 1800 m, 6000 ft.), usually near a river. Plants form dense tangles, often dangling from small branches, usually 350–650 m (1150–2100 ft.).

CULTIVATION: This species does better when mounted, particularly on smooth pieces of wood, such as bogwood or freshwater driftwood. It likes intermediate to warm temperatures and flowers off and on throughout the year.

DISTRIBUTION: Kenya, Malawi, Mozambique, South Africa (KwaZulu-Natal), Tanzania, Zambia, Zimbabwe.

Figure 10-20. *Angraecum cultriforme*. Plant (upper center), ×1;
flower (lower left and right), ×3.

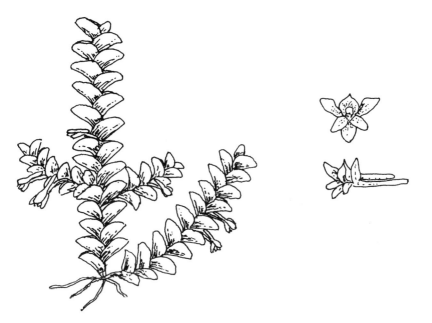

Figure 10-21. *Angraecum distichum.* Plant (left), ×1; flower (upper right), ×6; flower (lower right), ×5.

Angraecum distichum Lindley

FIGURE 10-21

DESCRIPTION: A dwarf species, often forming large clumps, with an unusual and attractive appearance; it flowers several times a year. Stems sometimes branched, usually 10 cm (4 in.) long but sometimes longer. Leaves many, fleshy, bilaterally flattened, dark green, 5–10 × 3–5 mm, with a groove along the basal half of the upper surface. Flowers borne singly along the stem opposite leaves, white, nonresupinate, 7.5–10.5 mm long from the tip of the spur to the apex of the lip, longer than the leaves. Pedicel and ovary 5–6 mm long. Sepals and petals 3–5 × 1–2 mm, ovate or elliptic, rounded; lip 3–4 × 3–4 mm, obovate, concave; spur 5–6 mm long, slender, suddenly narrowing to the apex, more or less straight.

HABITAT: Forms dense mats on the branches of trees in rainforest, in deep shade, 200–1600 m (660–5300 ft.).

CULTIVATION: Grows well for us in a pot with a standard bark mix, in intermediate conditions, in fairly heavy shade. It would do as well, perhaps better, in warm temperatures. If the humidity is not sufficiently high, the leaves start to look shrivelled. Side branches can be used as cuttings, as they strike readily in perlite.

DISTRIBUTION: Angola, Cameroon, Congo, Gabon, Ghana, Guinea, Ivory Coast, Liberia, Nigeria, Sierra Leone, Uganda, Zaire.

Angraecum dives Rolfe

DESCRIPTION: Stems to 4 cm (2 in.) long. Leaves two to six, 5–25 × 0.5–1.5 cm (2–10 × 0.25–1 in.), linear, leathery. Inflorescences many, 3–25 cm (1–10 in.) long, 8- to 25-flowered. Flowers pale greenish-yellow, fleshy. Sepals and petals 5 × 1.2–1.5 mm, lanceolate, acuminate, recurved, the petals slightly narrower than the sepals. Lip 4 × 2.5 mm, ovate, acuminate, very concave, slightly recurved; spur 2.5–3 mm long, slightly swollen at the apex, curving up.

HABITAT: Coastal forest and woodland, and on coral rocks in the open, to 50 m (165 ft.).

CULTIVATION: We have not grown this species, but from its habitat, it should like fairly good light and warm to intermediate temperatures.

DISTRIBUTION: Kenya, Tanzania. Also in Socotra Island (South Yemen).

Angraecum doratophyllum Summerhayes

DESCRIPTION: Vegetatively, very similar to the more widespread *Angraecum pungens,* but with very different flowers. An epiphyte; stems pendent, branched, leafy, to 35 cm (14 in.) long, rooting at intervals along their length; roots very slender, scarcely 1 mm in diameter. Leaves 2–3 cm (1 in.) × 3–5 mm, linear-lanceolate, sharply pointed, fleshy, if dry seeming almost terete. Flowers white, arising along the stem. Ovary 10 mm long. Sepals 8–11 × 1.5 mm, linear; petals slightly shorter and narrower. Lip 6.5 × 7.5 mm, very concave, broadly ovate, the apex acuminate and recurved, gradually tapering into the spur. Spur 10–14 mm long, narrowing suddenly after the wide mouth, abruptly recurved in the middle and somewhat inflated at apex.

HABITAT: Rainforest, 1000–1250 m (3300–4100 ft.).

CULTIVATION: Heavy shade and high humidity are essential; if the atmosphere is too dry, the leaves soon start to look shrivelled. Because of the pendent habit, this species looks better if mounted on bark, but the fine roots quickly dry out. If it is not possible to keep the humidity high, plants can be grown in a pot and allowed to fall over the edge.

DISTRIBUTION: São Tomé.

Angraecum eburneum subsp. *giryamae* (Rendle) Senghas & Cribb
SYNONYM: *Angraecum giryamae* Rendle

DESCRIPTION: A robust species; stems to 1 m (3 ft.) long; roots thick, fleshy, 5 mm in diameter, eventually forming large clumps. Leaves numerous, to 50 × 7 cm (20 × 3 in.), distichous, strap-shaped, unequally and roundly bilobed at the apex. Inflorescences erect, 30–75 (12–30 in.) long, 8- to 20-flowered. Flowers nonresupinate, night-scented; sepals and petals greenish-white; lip white. Pedicel and ovary 1.5–2 cm (1 in.) long. Sepals and petals 32–45 × 5–7 mm, linear-lanceolate, acuminate. Lip 20–30 × 30–40 mm, transversely oblong, with an apicule 5 mm long; spur 4–6 cm (2 in.) long.

HABITAT: Near the sea it often grows on coral rocks, but inland tends to be epiphytic; usually below 350 m (1150 ft.) but it has been recorded to 1700 m (5600 ft.).

CULTIVATION: Warm or intermediate conditions, in fairly good light. It needs a pot or a basket with a coarse mix.

DISTRIBUTION: Kenya, Tanzania.

NOTE: Some authorities still recognize this as a species in its own right, *Angraecum giryamae,* but it differs from the other three subspecies that occur in various Indian Ocean islands in relatively minor details, such as the proportions of the lip and the length of the spur.

Angraecum eichlerianum Kränzlin

DESCRIPTION: Stems elongated, sometimes reaching as much as 5 m (16 ft.) in the wild. Leaves distichous, arising along the stem, 6–15 × 1.5-4.5 cm (2–6 × 1–2 in.), oblong or elliptical, unequally and obtusely bilobed at apex, rather pale green. Inflorescences 1- to 4-flowered, 10–20 cm (4–8 in.) long. Flowers pale greenish, the lip white, green in the center. Sepals and petals 3.5–6 × 4–12 mm, narrowly oblong or elliptical. Lip 3–5 × 4–5 cm (1–2 × 2 in.), obovate with a central apicule, the edges of the lip projecting beyond the apicule. Spur 3.5–4 cm (1–2 in.) long, slender from a narrowly conical mouth, sometimes slightly inflated at the apex.

HABITAT: Thick forest, sometimes forming a dense mass. Altitude not known.

CULTIVATION: Grows well in a bark mix in a fairly large pot that contains a moss pole (of the type used for climbing indoor plants) to which the stem can be tied until it attaches itself by its roots. Intermediate to warm temperatures.

DISTRIBUTION: Angola, Cameroon, Gabon, Nigeria, Zaire.

Angraecum erectum Summerhayes

DESCRIPTION: Stems scandent, leafy, to 40 cm (16 in.) long; roots slender, arising along the stem. Leaves distichous, 3–6 × 0.5–1.5 cm (1–2 × 0.25–1 in.), linear-lanceolate, unequally and acutely bilobed at the tips. Inflorescences arising at nodes, 1- to 2-flowered, to 4–5 (2 in.) long. Flowers yellow-green, greenish-white or dull salmon. Sepals 11–14 × 2.5–4 mm, lanceolate, acuminate; petals similar but slightly smaller. Lip 8.5–11.5 × 3.3–4.5 mm, lanceolate, acuminate, very convex, with a longitudinal ridge towards the base; spur 1.5–3 cm (1 in.) long, very slender, slightly S-shaped.

HABITAT: Forest, particularly riverine forest, where it grows on vertical tree trunks in shade, 1300–2100 m (4300–7000 ft.).

CULTIVATION: We have not grown this species, but it would seem that it should be mounted on bark, in a shaded and humid situation, at intermediate to cool temperatures.

DISTRIBUTION: Kenya, Tanzania, Uganda, Zambia.

Angraecum gabonense Summerhayes

DESCRIPTION: Stems leafy, to 35 cm (14 in.) long. Leaves 1–2 cm (0.5–1 in.) × 2–4 mm, fleshy, linear-lanceolate. Flowers white. Sepals 6 × 1.5 mm, oblong, obtuse; petals slightly shorter and wider. Lip 3.5 × 5 mm, transversely oval; spur 2.5–3.5 mm long, slender, but thicker in the apical half.

HABITAT: Rainforest, to 1350 m (4450 ft.).

CULTIVATION: Intermediate to warm conditions, in fairly heavy shade, with high humidity.

DISTRIBUTION: Gabon, Zaire.

Angraecum humile Summerhayes

DESCRIPTION: A dwarf species; stems leafy, 1–4 cm (1–2 in.) long, sometimes branched, rooting at base and where branches arise. Leaves 6–7 × 2–3 mm, fleshy, bilaterally flattened, with a groove along the upper surface, distichous, almost overlapping. Inflorescences 2- to 4-flowered, 2–3 mm long. Flowers white or greenish-white, very small, not opening wide. Sepals and petals 1.5 mm long, less than 1 mm wide, ovate. Lip 1.5 mm long and wide, broadly ovate, acute; spur 1.5–2 mm long, somewhat inflated at apex, parallel to the ovary.

HABITAT: Riverine and montane forest, growing high in the canopy, 1650–2500 m (5500–8250 ft.).

CULTIVATION: Shade and high humidity are important. We grow it in a pot, but it would probably grow mounted provided the humidity could be kept high enough. Intermediate temperatures.

DISTRIBUTION: Kenya, northern Tanzania, Zimbabwe.

NOTE: This little species, almost the ultimate in miniatures, has only recently been found in Zimbabwe, apparently skipping over southern Tanzania and Malawi; it would, however, be very easy to overlook. It is a charming little species and certainly does not occupy much space.

Angraecum infundibulare Lindley

DESCRIPTION: Stems long, to 2 m (6 ft.) or more; Stewart and Campbell (1970) said that stems can scramble through trees to 10 m (33 ft.) in the wild. Leaves distichous, 10–22 × 1.5–4 cm (4–9 × 1–2 in.), elliptic or oblanceolate, unequally and obtusely bilobed at apex. Inflorescences 1-flowered, 15–20 cm (6–8 in.) long. Flowers pale green with a white lip, strongly scented, 15 cm (6 in.) long from apex of dorsal sepal to tip of lip, which makes them the largest of any orchid of mainland Africa. Sepals and petals linear-lanceolate, acuminate, all spreading; sepals 6–8.5 cm (2–3 in.) × 3–10 mm; petals 5.5–6 × 4–5 mm. Lip 6.5–8.5 × 5–5.5 cm (2–3 × 2 in.), concave, oblong-ovate, with an apicule 1 cm (0.5 in.) long. Spur 10–20 cm (4–8 in.) long, slender from a funnel-shaped mouth.

HABITAT: Forest, usually in hot and humid areas, 1150–1300 m (3800–4300 ft.).

CULTIVATION: Grows well in a bark mix in a fairly large pot that contains a moss pole (of the type used for climbing indoor plants) to which the stem can be tied until it attaches itself by its roots.

DISTRIBUTION: Cameroon, Ethiopia, Kenya, Nigeria, Príncipe, Uganda.

Angraecum pungens Schlechter

DESCRIPTION: Stems pendent, leafy, to 50 cm (20 in.) long. Leaves 2–4 cm (1–2 in.) × 3–6 mm, oblong-lanceolate, fleshy, with sharp points. Inflorescences shorter than the leaves. Flowers white. Sepals and petals 6–7 × 2 mm, the sepals elliptic, the petals obovate. Lip 4 × 5 mm, concave, almost orbicular or transversely oval, apiculate; spur slender, 4–5 mm long.

HABITAT: Dense forest, to 1250 m (4100 ft.).

CULTIVATION: Heavy shade and high humidity. Because of the pendent habit, this species looks better if mounted on bark, but the fine roots quickly dry out. If it is not possible to keep the humidity high, plants can be grown in a pot and allowed to fall over the edge.

DISTRIBUTION: Cameroon, Equatorial Guinea (Bioko), Nigeria, Zaire.

Angraecum pusillum Lindley   PLATE 24, FIGURE 10-22

SYNONYM: *Angraecum burchellii* Reichenbach f.

DESCRIPTION: A dwarf species; stems to 10 mm long. Leaves four to six, 6–12 cm (2–5 in.) × 2–5 mm, distichous, linear, borne in a fan. Inflorescences several, arising from base of plant, 5–10 cm (2–4 in.) long, several- to many-flowered. Flowers very small, yellow-green or white, secund. Sepals and petals ovate, obtuse; sepals 1.5 × 0.8 mm; petals slightly smaller. Lip 1–1.5 mm long and wide, very concave; spur 1 mm long, saccate.

HABITAT: Forest and scrub, usually in deep shade, to 1200 m (4000 ft.).

CULTIVATION: Seems fairly undemanding. We grow it potted in bark at intermediate temperatures, in moderate shade. In our greenhouse, it flowers in autumn (October).

DISTRIBUTION: South Africa (Eastern Cape, KwaZulu-Natal, Northern Province, Western Cape), Swaziland, Zimbabwe.

Angraecum reygaertii De Wildeman

DESCRIPTION: Stems to 20 cm (8 in.) long, usually pendent. Leaves distichous, 10–16 × 2–3 cm (4–6 × 1 in.), strap-shaped to oblanceolate, unequally and obtusely bilobed at apex. Inflorescences to 18 cm (7 in.) long, 3- to 6-flowered. Flowers white. Pedicel and ovary 12–14 mm long. Sepals 26–28 × 3–6 mm, linear-lanceolate, acuminate; petals similar but slightly smaller. Lip 15–17 × 6 mm, concave, elliptic-lanceolate, acute, with a central, longitudinal ridge in the basal half; spur 6.5–8 cm (2–3 in.) long, slender, S-shaped.

HABITAT: Riverine forest, 1200–1250 m (4000–4100 ft.).

CULTIVATION: Intermediate conditions, with shade and high humidity.

DISTRIBUTION: Cameroon, Uganda, Zaire.

Figure 10-22. *Angraecum pusillum*. Plant (center), ×1; flower (upper right), ×3; lip and spur (lower right), ×4.

Angraecum sacciferum Lindley

DESCRIPTION: A dwarf species; stems to 2 cm (1 in.) long. Leaves four to six, 1–6 cm (0.5–2 in.) × 3–7 mm, distichous, linear, dark green. Inflorescences arising below leaves, 2–8 cm (1–3 in.) long, one- to several-flowered, with a wiry peduncle. Flowers green, yellow-green or yellow. Sepals 2–4 × 1–2 mm, ovate, obtuse; petals slightly smaller, and lanceolate. Lip 2–4 mm long and broad, broadly ovate, acute, very concave; spur 1.5–2 mm long, saccate, curved round the ovary.

HABITAT: Montane and submontane forest, occasionally in riverine forest and high-rainfall woodland, 1100–2300 m (3600–7600 ft.), always in deep shade.

CULTIVATION: Potted, in a shaded and humid location, at intermediate temperatures.

DISTRIBUTION: Cameroon, Kenya, Malawi, South Africa (Eastern Cape, KwaZulu-Natal, Mpumalanga, Northern Province, Western Cape), Swaziland, Tanzania, Uganda, Zaire, Zambia, Zimbabwe.

Angraecum spectabile Summerhayes

DESCRIPTION: A little-known species with a habit similar to that of *Angraecum infundibulare* and with flowers resembling *A. eichlerianum* but larger (Piers 1968). Stems to 30 cm (12 in.) long, rather flattened; roots 2.5 mm in diameter. Leaves distichous, 5–10 × 1.5–3 cm (2–4 × 1 in.), elliptic, unequally and obtusely bilobed at apex, twisted at the base to lie in one plane. Inflorescences one-flowered; peduncle 3 cm (1 in.) long; pedicel and ovary 3.5 cm (1 in.) long. Flowers greenish-white with a white lip. Sepals 4–5 × 1 cm (2 × 0.5 in.), narrowly lanceolate, acuminate; petals slightly shorter and narrower. Lip 3–3.5 × 4–5 cm (1 × 2 in.), funnel-shaped, obscurely trilobed at the apex with an apicule 2–3 cm (1 in.) long. Spur 6–6.5 cm (2 in.) long, funnel-shaped at base, becoming slender.

HABITAT: Known only from the western shores of Lake Victoria, where it is said to scramble over rocks, 1150–1200 m (3800–4000 ft.).

CULTIVATION: May be grown by orchid enthusiasts in East Africa, but not known to be grown in Europe or America. Obviously it would be well worth growing if it could be introduced to cultivation. Should grow well in a bark mix in a fairly large pot that contains a moss pole (of the type used for climbing indoor plants) to which the stem can be tied until it attaches itself by its roots.

DISTRIBUTION: Tanzania.

Angraecum stella-africae Cribb   PLATE 25, FIGURE 10-23

DESCRIPTION: A small species; stems very short; roots 2–3 mm in diameter. Leaves usually three to four, 3–5 cm (1–2 in.) × 6–8 mm, dark green, linear, thick-textured. Inflorescences one to two per plant. Flowers glistening white, large for such a tiny plant. Sepals 25 × 5 mm, lanceolate, acute; petals similar but slightly smaller. Lip 25 × 15 mm, ovate, concave; spur 12–15 cm (5–6 in.), coiled while developing but finally almost straight. Capsule 2.5 cm (1 in.) long, bright green, winged, remaining on the plant for more than a year before ripening.

HABITAT: Woodland, in fairly high rainfall areas, with a single record from riverine forest, 1250–1500 m (4100–5000 ft.).

CULTIVATION: Does better mounted on bark, where the spur can hang freely. It likes moderate shade, and a drier period in winter.

DISTRIBUTION: Malawi, South Africa (Northern Province), Zimbabwe. Although this may seem a relatively wide geographical distribution, *Angraecum stella-africae* is very local in its occurrence, being known from only one or two places in each country.

NOTE: Beautiful though it is, this species has its drawbacks. Sometimes the flowers do not open, but just seem to collapse when they are apparently on the point of opening; apparently they self-pollinate, as capsules generally still develop. Poor ventilation may contribute to this problem. Even when the flowers do open, they are short-lived, lasting only one to two days, which is strange as it is not the case with *Angraecum rutenbergianum* and related species.

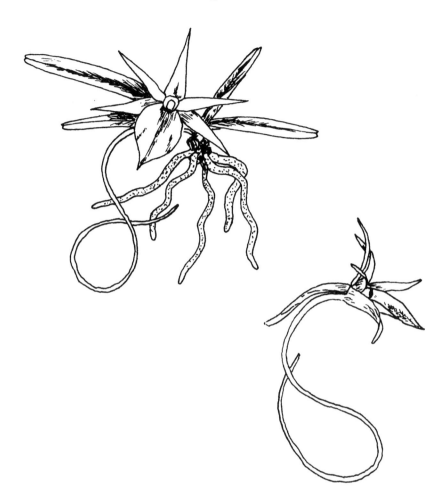

Figure 10-23. *Angraecum stella-africae.* Plant (upper) and flower (lower), ×1.

Angraecum stolzii Schlechter

DESCRIPTION: Stems to 40 cm (16 in.) long, usually pendent; roots 0.5–2 mm in diameter, arising along the stem. Leaves numerous, distichous, 4.5–7.5 cm (2–3 in.) × 4–9 mm, linear, curved, acutely and unequally bilobed at the apex, dark green. Inflorescences one-flowered, arising opposite the leaves from the same place in successive years, so that the bases often form a woody spur. Flowers cream, greenish, or straw-colored, 17–20 mm in diameter. Peduncle to 17 mm long; pedicel and ovary 6 mm. Sepals 7–9 × 1.5–3 mm, lanceolate, acuminate; petals similar but slightly narrower. Lip boat-shaped, 5–8 × 3–5 mm, including an acumen 2 mm long. Spur 5.5–9 mm long, slender, usually slightly swollen at apex.

HABITAT: Epiphytic at high and low levels in submontane, evergreen forest, 1600–2500 m (5300–8250 ft.).

CULTIVATION: Mounted on smooth pieces of wood in a shaded, humid situation, at intermediate temperatures.

DISTRIBUTION: Malawi, Tanzania, Zaire.

NOTE: May be confused with *Angraecum cultriforme,* which has larger flowers, a longer spur, and shorter and broader leaves. In *A. cultriforme,* woody spurs are rarely, if ever, formed where the inflorescences arise. Furthermore, in the wild, *A. cultriforme* tends to grow at lower altitudes, in areas of lower rainfall, in riverine trees and thicket rather than in submontane forest where *A. stolzii* grows. There are specimens, however, that are intermediate and difficult to assign to one species or the other. In Malawi, a third species, *A. umbrosum* Cribb, also occurs at higher altitudes and has longer and narrower, almost grasslike, leaves. Again, specimens can grade into *A. stolzii.* It is not impossible that detailed work would show all three species to be conspecific, in which case, *A. stolzii,* as the oldest name, would be correct.

Angraecum subulatum Lindley

DESCRIPTION: Stems leafy, usually pendent, to 50 cm (20 in.) long. Leaves 3–13 cm (1–5 in.) × 1–3 mm, needle-shaped but grooved on the upper surface, curved, with a sharp point. Inflorescences shorter than leaves. Flowers white. Sepals 4–6 × 2–2.5 mm, oblong or elliptic; petals 4–5 × 1–1.5 mm, linear. Lip 2–3 mm long and wide, boat-shaped, apiculate; spur 5 mm long, slightly inflated in the middle.

HABITAT: Dense forest.

CULTIVATION: Heavy shade and high humidity. Because of the pendent habit, this species looks better if mounted on bark, but the fine roots quickly dry out. If it is not possible to keep the humidity high, plants can be grown in a pot and allowed to fall over the edge.

DISTRIBUTION: Cameroon, Equatorial Guinea (Bioko), Ghana, Nigeria, Sierra Leone, Zaire.

Ansellia Lindley

The genus *Ansellia* was established in 1844 by John Lindley and named in honor of John Ansell, who collected the type species on the island then called Fernando Po, now Bioko and part of Equatorial Guinea. There has long been argument as to how many species belong in this genus, but today the consensus is that there is only one variable species. Although it would be easy to select two specimens that could be described as different species and keyed out without difficulty, the variation is continuous and different characters are not consistently linked, so that there is a complete range of intermediates. Perhaps, someone will yet find some characters that can be used consistently.

Ansellia africana Lindley   PLATE 26

COMMON NAME: Leopard Orchid
SYNONYMS: *Ansellia africana* var. *nilotica* Baker, *Ansellia gigantea* Reichenbach f., *Ansellia gigantea* var. *nilotica* (Baker) Summerhayes, *Ansellia nilotica* Baker

DESCRIPTION: A large epiphyte, forming big clumps. Pseudobulbs erect, 10–50 cm (4–20 in.) tall, spindle-shaped or cylindrical, yellowish, ribbed, with several nodes, leafy towards the apex. Roots of two kinds: "normal" roots that cling to the substrate or wander through compost, and slender, stiff erect roots that surround the base of the plant, trapping fallen leaves and presumably having a function in the plant's nutrition. Leaves several, distichous, 15–50 × 1.5–5 cm (6–20 × 1–2 in.), dark green, ribbed, linear or narrowly lanceolate, acute. Inflorescences branched, apparently terminal, but arising from nodes near the apex of the pseudobulb, to 80 cm (32 in.) long, rather laxly many-flowered. Flowers with a strong, rather strange, musky scent; yellow, variably blotched with maroon-brown so that in some forms the whole flower is almost dark brown while on others it is very lightly marked, to plain yellow or greenish-yellow. Pedicel and ovary slender, 4 cm (2 in.) long. Sepals and petals spreading, elliptic, obtuse; dorsal sepal 16–35 × 5–10 mm; lateral sepals slightly longer; petals slightly shorter and broader, 16–30 × 12–14 mm. Lip 14–22 × 12–19 mm, trilobed, with two to three longitudinal keels in the center; side lobes erect, midlobe almost orbicular, 11 × 10 mm, the margins undulate. Column to 12 mm long.

HABITAT: Most often open woodland in hot, dry areas, frequently growing wedged into the fork of a tree, but also sometimes occurring in forest and wetter woodland, to 2200 m (7300 ft.) but usually below 700 m (2300 ft.).

CULTIVATION: Does best in a basket in intermediate to warm temperatures, probably better in warm. It needs good light to flower and plenty of water while growing, but should be kept almost dry in the resting season. In our greenhouse, it flowers in spring (March and April). The flowers are long lasting.

DISTRIBUTION: Widespread throughout tropical Africa, and in South Africa (KwaZulu-Natal, Mpumalanga, Northern Province).

NOTE: The various species have been differentiated in the past by the proportions of the petals to the sepals, the shape of the midlobe, and the degree of blotching of the flowers, but as noted previously, these characters all show continuous variation and intermediates always occur.

Bolusiella Schlechter

The genus *Bolusiella* was established by Rudolf Schlechter in 1918 and named in honor of the South African botanist Harry Bolus (1834–1911). It comprises four species in tropical Africa, with one extending into South Africa. These species are not showy, but they are unusual in appearance.

DESCRIPTION: Monopodial, epiphytic herbs with short stems, sometimes branched at the base to form clumps. Roots very fine. Leaves bilaterally flattened, fleshy, *Iris*-like, arranged in a fan. Inflorescences many-flowered, arising from the base of the plant. Flowers small, white. Sepals and petals free, similar. Lip entire or very obscurely trilobed, with a short spur at the base. Pollinia two, stipites two, viscidium one.

CULTIVATION: Like many orchids with fleshy leaves, species of *Bolusiella* are not easy to get established, although once they are, they do quite well. The problem is maintaining high humidity without letting the plant rot. If plants are mounted, it is difficult to give them high enough humidity, but if they are potted, they are prone to rot, at least until the roots have become well established. Intermediate temperatures and moderate shade are appropriate.

Bolusiella batesii (Rolfe) Schlechter

DESCRIPTION: Differs from *Bolusiella talbotii* in having parallel-sided leaves to 6 cm (2 in.) long, with obtuse apices and inflorescences to 20 cm (8 in.) long, densely many-flowered, with the peduncle longer than the rachis. Sepals, petals, lip, and spur are all 3 mm long.

HABITAT: Epiphytic in forest.

DISTRIBUTION: Cameroon, Ghana, Ivory Coast.

Bolusiella iridifolia (Rolfe) Schlechter

DESCRIPTION: A small epiphyte; stems short. Leaves several, borne in a fan, 1–4.5 cm (0.5–2 in.) × 2–5 mm, fleshy, bilaterally flattened, with a groove along the upper surface. Inflorescences 2–6 cm (1–2 in.) long, densely several- to many-flowered. Pedicel and ovary 2 mm long, bracts brown or black, shorter or longer than the flowers, 1–4 mm long. Flowers very small, white. Sepals and petals 1–3 × 0.5–1.5 mm, oblong, obtuse. Lip 1–5 × 1–2 mm, oblong, with a spur to 2 mm long. Column less than 1 mm long.

Subsp. *iridifolia*

DESCRIPTION: Bracts brown, shorter than the flowers; spur cylindrical, more than 1 mm long, at right angles to the lip.

HABITAT: Epiphytic in forest and woodland, to 2300 m (7600 ft.).

DISTRIBUTION: Angola, Cameroon, Ghana, Equatorial Guinea, Ivory Coast, Kenya, Tanzania, Uganda, Zaire. Also in Comoro Islands.

Subsp. *picea* Cribb

DESCRIPTION: Bracts black, longer than the flowers; spur straight, conical or saccate, less than 1 mm long.

HABITAT: Usually epiphytic in montane and submontane forest, occasionally in high rainfall woodland, on small branches, embedded in lichen, rarely on rocks, 1350–2400 m (4450–8000 ft.).

DISTRIBUTION: Kenya, Tanzania, Malawi, Zambia, Zimbabwe.

Figure 10-24. *Bolusiella maudiae.* Plant, ×1.

Bolusiella maudiae (Bolus) Schlechter PLATE 27, FIGURE 10-24
SYNONYM: *Bolusiella imbricata* (Rolfe) Schlechter

DESCRIPTION: A small species. Leaves to eight, borne in a fan, 1–5 × 1 cm (0.5–2 × 0.5 in.), sword-shaped, obtuse, very fleshy, dark green, the sides convex, with no groove along the upper surface. Inflorescences to 6 cm (2 in.) long, densely many-flowered. Flowers white. Pedicel and ovary 1–2 mm long; bracts 3–4 mm long, overlapping, greenish-brown. Sepals and petals 3–4 × 1–1.5 mm, oblong, obtuse. Lip 2–3 × 1 mm, very obscurely trilobed, ovate, acute. Spur 1–2 mm long, conical to cylindrical, obtuse, pointing forwards. Column less than 1 mm long.

HABITAT: Riverine forest and high rainfall woodland, usually on large branches, 550–1900 m (1800–6300 ft.).

DISTRIBUTION: Ghana, Ivory Coast, Kenya, Malawi, South Africa (KwaZulu-Natal), Tanzania, Uganda, Zaire, Zambia, Zimbabwe.

Bolusiella talbotii (Rendle) Summerhayes FIGURE 10-25

DESCRIPTION: Stems short. Leaves to 12, although usually fewer, borne in a fan, 2–8 × 0.5–1 cm (1–3 × 0.25–0.5 in.), fleshy, but not so thick as in *Bolusiella iridifolia* or *B. maudiae,* without groove along the upper surface, sword-shaped, acute, the sides not convex. Inflorescences to 10 cm (4 in.) long, rather laxly several-flowered, the peduncle shorter than the rachis or of equal length. Flowers white, sometimes pinkish

Figure 10-25. *Bolusiella talbotii.* Plant (left), ×1; flower (right), ×6.

in the center, with a green spur. Pedicel and ovary 1 mm long. Bracts 1–3 mm long, shorter than the flowers and not overlapping. Sepals and petals 2–4 × 0.5–1 mm, oblong, obtuse. Lip 1.5–2.5 × 1 mm, very obscurely trilobed, triangular; spur conical, obtuse, of similar length to the lip, or slightly longer. Column less than 1 mm long.

HABITAT: Epiphytic in forest and in coffee plantations, 900–1350 m (3000–4450 ft.).

DISTRIBUTION: Congo, Equatorial Guinea (Bioko and Pagalu Islands), Ghana, Ivory Coast, Liberia, Nigeria, Sierra Leone, Tanzania, Togo.

Bonatea Willdenow

The genus *Bonatea* was created by C. L. Willdenow in 1805 and named in honor of Guiseppe Antonio Bonato (1753–1836), professor of botany at the University of Padua in Italy. It is closely related to *Habenaria*, differing mainly in having the basal parts of the lower petal lobes, the lip and the stigmatic arms joined, and in having a tooth in the mouth of the spur. The genus contains about 20 species in tropical and South Africa, with one species extending into Yemen. They do not have brightly colored flowers, but they are striking plants nonetheless. Several species are grown in South Africa, not so many elsewhere, but they deserve to be better known.

DESCRIPTION: Terrestrial, with fleshy, tuberous roots and leafy stems. Leaves sometimes more or less withered by the time the flowers open. Flowers large, green and white. Dorsal sepal very convex, forming a hood; lateral sepals deflexed, sometimes rolled up lengthwise. Petals bilobed, the lobes most often linear; the upper lobe is joined to the edge of the dorsal sepal. Lip with a basal claw, then trilobed, usually with a tooth in the mouth of the spur. Spur cylindrical, sometimes swollen near the apex.

CULTIVATION: Most species of *Bonatea* tend to grow in rather hot, dry areas, and it is vitally important to avoid over-watering. They can be grown in a free-draining mix of equal parts of fibrous peat, loam, coarse sand, and fine bark, with plenty of drainage material at the bottom of the pot. The stem and leaves are prone to rot, especially when the year's growth is just developing, when the leaves are funnel-shaped and water can easily lodge there. If possible, try to avoid getting water on the leaves at all. Plants die back after flowering and then should be kept almost dry with only an occasional watering; they should not be kept too dry, as then the tubers shrivel. If plants are grown in clay pots, the pots can be plunged in sand, like alpines, and the sand can be watered from time to time. Even when the plant is in full growth, the pot should be allowed to dry out between watering. Unlike most orchids, species of *Bonatea* do not appreciate too humid an atmosphere—keep them well away from a humidifier or nebulizer. Most will grow in intermediate temperatures, with light shade.

Bonatea antennifera Rolfe

SYNONYM: *Bonatea speciosa* var. *antennifera* (Rolfe) Sommerville

DESCRIPTION: A robust species, to 1 m (3 ft.) high; stems leafy. Leaves several, to 10 × 3 cm (4 × 1 in.), ovate, acute, decreasing in size up the stem, usually partly withered by flowering time. Inflorescences many-flowered; flowers green and white, 5 cm (2 in.) in diameter. Dorsal sepal 16–18 × 12 mm, ovate, acute, very convex; lateral sepals to 25 mm long, rolled up lengthwise when the flowers open. Petal lobes both narrowly linear; upper lobe 16–18 mm long, joined to dorsal sepal; lower lobe 20–25 mm long. Lip 40–45 mm long, joined to the stigmatic arms for 8 mm at the base; midlobe 25–35 mm long, side lobes 18–30 mm long, all lobes very slender and almost threadlike. Spur 3–5 cm (1–2 in.) long, slender, swollen at the apex. Stigmatic arms 15–20 mm long.

HABITAT: Woodland, usually in drier areas, but with summer rainfall, 1300 m (4300 ft.).

DISTRIBUTION: Botswana, Mozambique, South Africa (Transvaal, Northern Cape), Zimbabwe.

NOTE: This species is sometimes treated as a variety of *Bonatea speciosa,* to which it is certainly closely related. It differs, however, in having more numerous flowers with narrower petal lobes and longer lip lobes, and in the leaves being more or less withered by flowering time. It usually, although not always, grows in drier areas and at higher altitudes than *B. speciosa.*

Bonatea bracteata McDonald & McMurtry   PLATE 28

SYNONYM: *Bonatea liparophylla* Schelpe, *nomen nudum*

DESCRIPTION: A slender species, to 40 cm (16 in.) tall; tubers ovoid, 6 × 4 cm (2 in.); stems producing stolons at the base; these stolons first arch above ground, then go below ground and develop tubers at the end. Leaves several, to 9 × 3 cm (4 × 1 in.), elliptic, acuminate. Inflorescences laxly 10- to 15-flowered; sepals green, petals and lip white. Pedicel and ovary 25–30 mm long; bracts leafy, 10–40 mm long. Dorsal sepal

11 × 8 mm, erect, ovate, acute, convex, with three keels on the outside; lateral sepals 10–12 × 5 mm, obliquely ovate, with a prominent median keel, the lower edge rolled in. Petal lobes linear; upper lobe 10 × 1 mm, joined to the dorsal sepal; lower lobe 10–12 × 1 mm, joined to the base of the lip for 2–4 mm, then curving out and up. Lip 17–18 mm long with a claw 5 mm long; midlobe 10–12 × 1.5 mm; side lobes spreading, slightly longer and narrower. Spur 2–2.5 cm (1 in.) long, slender, bent in the middle. Stigmatic arms 6 mm long.

HABITAT: Grassland and thicket, 1800 m (6000 ft.).

CULTIVATION: This species is apparently unique in the genus in its stoloniferous habit. When the plants are dormant and we have turned out a pot, we have found a cluster of tubers right at the bottom of the pot. When repotting, it is advisable to put the tubers just about an inch below the soil surface, otherwise the shoots may not make it to the surface at all, unless the pot is very shallow.

DISTRIBUTION: South Africa (KwaZulu-Natal, Mpumalanga).

NOTE: This is the species described as *Bonatea liparophylla* in *Wild Orchids of Southern Africa* (Stewart et al. 1982), but that name was never validly published.

Bonatea cassidea Sonder

DESCRIPTION: A slender species, 25–50 cm (10–20 in.) tall; stems leafy. Leaves ten to twelve, 10–40 × 1–3 cm (4–16 × 0.5–1 in.), linear to lanceolate, acute, sometimes starting to wither by flowering time. Inflorescences 5–20 cm (2–8 in.) long, several to many-flowered. Flowers green, the lower petal lobes and side lobes of the lip white. Pedicel and ovary 2–3 cm (1 in.) long; bracts 2–3 cm (1 in.) long. Sepals 8–11 × 3–8 mm, ovate, acute, the dorsal very convex, the laterals rolled up lengthwise. Upper petal lobe 10–20 mm long, linear, joined to the dorsal sepal; lower lobe 10–15 × 4–6 mm, obovate from a narrow base, spreading. Lip 16–20 mm long, with a claw 8 mm long; midlobe 7–10 mm long, less than 1 mm wide; side lobes like lower petal lobes. Spur 11–14 mm long. Stigmatic arms 7–9 mm long.

HABITAT: In shade among boulders, in scrub, 60–1500 m (200–5000 ft.).

DISTRIBUTION: South Africa (Eastern Cape), Zimbabwe.

Bonatea polypodantha (Reichenbach f.) L. Bolus

DESCRIPTION: A slender species, 30–35 cm (12–14 in.) tall, forming clumps. Leaves borne towards the base of the stem, to 11 × 3.5 cm (4 × 1 in.), elliptic. Inflorescences laxly 2- to 9-flowered; flowers pale green and white. Sepals 9–13 mm long, the dorsal ovate, convex, the laterals spreading. Petal lobes linear; upper lobe 8–11 mm long, joined to the dorsal sepal; lower lobe 30–40 mm long, very slender, curved. Lip lobes narrowly linear, threadlike; midlobe 22 mm long, side lobes 30–35 mm long. Spur 4 cm (2 in.) long, slightly enlarged in the apical half.

HABITAT: In dryish grassland and thorn scrub, 700 m (2300 ft.).

DISTRIBUTION: South Africa (Eastern Cape, KwaZulu-Natal, Mpumalanga).

Bonatea porrecta (H. Bolus) Summerhayes

DESCRIPTION: A fairly robust species, 20–65 cm (8–26 in.) tall; stems leafy. Leaves 7–11 cm (3–4 in.) long, narrowly oblong, more or less withered by flowering time. Inflorescences several to many-flowered; flowers green and white. Pedicel and ovary 25–30 mm long; bracts to 30 mm long. Sepals 10–12 × 8–10 mm; dorsal erect, ovate, very convex; laterals obliquely elliptic. Petal lobes both linear; upper lobe 10–12 mm long, joined to dorsal sepal; lower lobe 20 mm long, curving up. Lip 25 mm long, with a claw 9 mm long,; midlobe to 20 mm long, linear, bent in the middle; side lobes to 22 mm long, narrowly linear, slightly curled near the apex. Spur 3–3.5 cm (1 in.) long, somewhat swollen towards the apex. Stigmatic arms 10 mm long.

HABITAT: Open grassland, 150–800 m (500–2600 ft.).

DISTRIBUTION: Mozambique, South Africa (Eastern Cape, KwaZulu-Natal, Transvaal).

Bonatea pulchella Summerhayes

DESCRIPTION: A slender species, 20–30 cm (8–12 in.) tall, with woolly, cylindrical tubers; stems with about three sheathing leaves. Leaves several, in a basal rosette, to 9 × 3 cm (4 × 1 in.), ovate, with a petiole-like base 2.5 cm (1 in.) long. Inflorescences 10–12 cm (4–5 in.) long, laxly 3- to 5-flowered. Flowers white and green. Sepals 11–13 × 6–8 mm, the dorsal erect, ovate, convex; laterals joined to the lip for 5 mm, obliquely ovate, with an apicule 3 mm long. Petal lobes threadlike, upper lobe 10–12 mm long, joined to the dorsal sepal; lower lobe to 47 mm long. Lip lobes all threadlike; basal claw to 6 mm long; midlobe 25–30 mm long; side lobes 45–55 mm long, spur 5–7 cm (2–3 in.) long, slender but slightly swollen near the apex. Stigmatic arms 8–10 mm long.

HABITAT: Dune forest and bush, in coarse, damp, basic, sandy soil, to 600 m (2000 ft.).

DISTRIBUTION: Mozambique, South Africa (KwaZulu-Natal, Mpumalanga).

Bonatea saundersioides (Kränzlin & Schlechter) Cortesi

DESCRIPTION: A slender species, 30–35 cm (12–14 in.) tall; stems leafy. Leaves to 14 × 2.5 cm (6 × 1 in.), narrowly elliptic, acute. Inflorescences laxly to 20-flowered; flowers green, the lower petal lobes and lip side lobes white. Petal lobes linear; upper lobe 8–12 mm long, joined to dorsal sepal; lower lobes 15–20 mm long, spreading, somewhat curved. Lip lobes all narrowly linear, midlobe 12–15 mm long, curving up; side lobes 15–23 mm long, curved. Spur 18–23 mm long.

HABITAT: In shade in forested ravines and in woodland, in dryish positions, 600–900 m (2000–3000 ft.).

DISTRIBUTION: South Africa (KwaZulu-Natal, Mpumalanga).

Bonatea speciosa (Linnaeus f.) Willdenow PLATE 29

DESCRIPTION: A robust species, 40–100 cm (16–40 in.) tall, arising from woolly, cylindrical tubers; stems leafy. Leaves 7–10 × 2–3 cm (3–4 × 1 in.), lanceolate or ovate, acute, clasping stem at base. Inflorescences fairly densely to 15-flowered. Flowers green and white, with a slight spicy scent. Pedicel and ovary 40–45 mm long; bracts 30–45 mm long. Dorsal sepal 18–20 × 12 mm, erect, ovate, acute, very convex; lateral sepals slightly longer, oblique, partly rolled up lengthwise. Upper petal lobe linear, 15–16 × 2–3 mm, joined to dorsal sepal; lower lobe 20–25 mm long, linear to oblanceolate. Lip 30 mm long, with a basal claw 10 mm long; all lobes linear, 20–23 × 1–2 mm, the midlobe bent back about the middle. Spur 3.5–4 cm (1–2 in.) long, slender, swollen at apex. Stigmatic arms to 16 mm long.

HABITAT: Coastal bush, open deciduous woodland, and forest edge, to 1200 m (4000 ft.).

DISTRIBUTION: South Africa (Eastern Cape, KwaZulu-Natal, Transvaal, Western Cape), Zimbabwe.

Bonatea steudneri (Reichenbach f.) T. Durand & Schinz

DESCRIPTION: A robust species, to 1 m (3 ft.) tall, or even more; stems leafy; roots fleshy, tuberous. Leaves 7–17 × 3–6 cm (3–7 × 1–2 in.), ovate, acute, clasping the stem at the base. Inflorescences to 30 cm (12 in.) long, rather laxly few- to many-flowered. Flowers mostly green, white in the center. Pedicel and ovary 5–6 cm (2 in.) long; bracts 4 cm (2 in.) long, rather papery. Sepals 25 × 15 mm, the dorsal erect, ovate, acute, very convex; laterals deflexed, lanceolate, apiculate. Petal lobes linear, upper lobe 24 × 1–2 mm, joined to the dorsal sepal; lower lobe 50–70 mm, curving downwards and outwards. Claw of lip 15–30 mm long; midlobe 20–37 × 1–3 mm, linear, decurved; side lobes 25–85 × 1–2 mm, spreading, narrowly linear. Spur 10–21 cm (4–8 in.) long, pendent, slender but slightly swollen at apex. Stigmatic arms 20–30 mm long.

HABITAT: Dry woodland and scrub, 900–1100 m (3000–3600 ft.).

CULTIVATION: When grown at Kew, this species flowered in July.

DISTRIBUTION: Ethiopia, Kenya, Rwanda, Somalia, Uganda, Tanzania, Zaire, Zambia, Zimbabwe. Also in Yemen and Saudi Arabia.

Brachycorythis Lindley

The genus *Brachycorythis,* established by John Lindley in 1838, is closely related to the European genera *Orchis* and *Dactylorhiza.* The name is derived from the Greek words *brachys* (short) and *korys* (helmet), referring presumably to the shape of the flowers. The genus is comprised of about 35 species in tropical and South Africa, Madagascar, and tropical Asia. About one third of these species are Asiatic. Many of the African species are very beautiful but only two are in cultivation.

DESCRIPTION: Predominantly terrestrial, with one epiphytic member. Roots fleshy, tuberous; stems leafy with a terminal, usually many-flowered inflorescence, the leaves grading into the floral bracts, which are sometimes longer than the flowers, at least at the base of the inflorescence. Flowers often very attractive, usually purple or mauve-pink, but in a few species yellow, white, or greenish. Petals usually joined to the dorsal sepal, forming a hood. Lip in two parts; the basal part, the hypochile, is boat-shaped and either saccate or spurred; the apical part, the epichile, is flat and either entire or lobed.

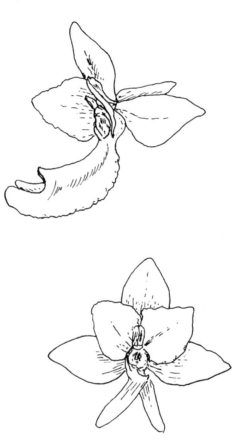

Figure 10-26. *Brachycorythis kalbreyeri*. Flower, ×1.5.

Brachycorythis kalbreyeri Reichenbach f. FIGURE 10-26

DESCRIPTION: Epiphytic or lithophytic herbs, 15–40 cm (6–16 in.) tall, often growing on mossy logs. Roots cylindrical, thick, fleshy and woolly. Leaves numerous, to 11 × 2.5 cm (4 × 1 in.), lanceolate, acute. Inflorescences rather laxly several-flowered.

Flowers 4–5 cm (2 in.) in diameter, white and mauve. Sepals 15–20 mm long, the dorsal elliptical, the laterals obliquely ovate. Petals 10–15 mm long, broadly ovate, erect or projecting forwards. Lip with a small hypochile 6 mm long, not spurred; epichile 15–20 mm long and wide, almost orbicular, trilobed towards the apex with the mid-lobe much smaller than the side lobes.

HABITAT: Rainforest and riverine forest, usually in deep shade, 1800–2350 m (6000–7800 ft.).

CULTIVATION: *Brachycorythis kalbreyeri* requires similar conditions in cultivation to species of *Stenoglottis*. It should be potted in a light, free-draining mixture, watered normally while growing, and when it starts to die back after flowering, it should be kept almost dry. If the pot is lightly sprinkled with water every few weeks, this helps to prevent the fleshy roots from shrivelling, but any excess of water is fatal. The temperature should be intermediate to cool.

DISTRIBUTION: Cameroon, Kenya, Liberia, Sierra Leone, Uganda, Zaire.

Brachycorythis macrantha (Lindley) Summerhayes

DESCRIPTION: A robust, leafy species, to 40 cm (16 in.) tall. Leaves to 13 × 5 cm (5 × 2 in.), broadly lanceolate, decreasing in size as they grade into the bracts. Flowers green with a mauve or lilac lip, all but the lowest much longer than the bracts. Pedicel and ovary 10–12 mm long. Sepals and petals all 10 mm long, the dorsal sepal forming a hood with the petals, the lateral sepals spreading. Lip 20 mm long, the hypochile bearing a conical spur 7–10 mm long; epichile fan-shaped, 16–20 mm wide, emarginate.

HABITAT: Shady places in forest, often on hillsides; occasionally in wet areas near a river, or on mossy rocks, 240–900 m (800–3000 ft.).

CULTIVATION: Potted, in a standard terrestrial mix. When the plant dies back after flowering, it should be kept almost dry until the spring; when new shoots start to appear, water can be given with care.

DISTRIBUTION: Cameroon, Central African Republic, Gabon, Guinea, Liberia, Nigeria, Sierra Leone.

Bulbophyllum Thouars

The genus *Bulbophyllum,* with around 1000 species, is one of the largest of all orchid genera. It occurs worldwide, with the largest number and greatest diversity of species in Southeast Asia. About 70 species are found on mainland Africa, which makes *Bulbophyllum* the second largest genus of African epiphytic orchids, *Polystachya* being comfortably the largest. The genus was established in 1822 by the French botanist A. du Petit Thouars, who in 1809 had used the name *Phyllorkis* for the same genus. As a rule, the valid name for any plant is the earliest one, but in this case the name *Bulbophyllum* was conserved over *Phyllorkis* as it had become widely accepted. The genus name is derived from the Greek words *bulbo* (bulb) and *phyllon* (leaf).

Species of *Bulbophyllum* form a prominent part of the African orchid flora, with at least some species occurring wherever any epiphyte orchids grow; they seem to be particularly frequent in West Africa. A few species have a relatively limited distribution but, unlike in *Polystachya* where there are many narrow endemics, most species are widespread on the continent. Only four African species, however, occur elsewhere, three in Madagascar and/or the Seychelles, and one, *B. longiflorum,* extending into Southeast Asia.

Species of *Bulbophyllum* are easily recognized. Few of the African species have beautiful flowers, but they are always interesting on close examination. The most recent revision of African species of *Bulbophyllum* was made in 1987 by J. J. Vermeulen, who decided against any formal division into sections because this could only be justified when a worldwide revision was undertaken. Vermeulen assembled the species in similar groups, one of which, the *Megaclinium* group, is particularly distinctive and apparently confined to Africa. In members of this group, the rachis is usually swollen or flattened, sometimes very long and colored purple or orange, with flowers arising along either side. In most species, only a few flowers are open at one time and the plant may continue in flower over a long period, the open flowers gradually getting nearer the end of the inflorescence. Several species are rather similar in appearance. At one time, these species were placed in a separate genus, *Megaclinium,* established by John Lindley in 1824, but as early as 1861, H. G. Reichenbach made *Megaclinium* a section of *Bulbophyllum.* Over the years some botanists have kept the genera separate, but it is now generally accepted that these species fall within *Bulbophyllum.* Members of the Megaclinium group include *B. colubrinum, B. falcatum, B. imbricatum, B. lizae, B. maximum, B. purpureorhachis, B. resupinatum,* and *B. sandersonii.*

DESCRIPTION: Pseudobulbs 1- to 2- leaved, rarely 3-leaved, set on a woody rhizome, either close together, forming clumps or mats, or well spaced, forming long, sometimes branching, chains; each pseudobulb with several wiry roots arising from the base. Leaves usually thick and leathery, narrowed at the base to form a short stalk. Inflorescences arising from the base of the pseudobulb, unlike in *Polystachya,* where they are terminal on the pseudobulb. Flowers of almost all African species rather small, dull-colored, often greenish-purple but sometimes white, yellow, reddish, or deep purple, Lip motile, in some species fringed with long hairs; in the wild, the lip constantly moves in the breeze and must be of significance in pollination, which in many cases may be carried out by flies.

CULTIVATION: In general, species of *Bulbophyllum* are easily grown. The main problem is that those with long, creeping rhizomes are difficult to contain in a pot. We grow most of our plants in a mix of medium bark, perlite, and charcoal in a shallow pot. Some people get good results using sphagnum as a growing medium, but we have not been very successful with that. Plants can be grown mounted on bark or fern blocks, which has advantages for these creeping species, but the wiry roots dry out very quickly. They do well in baskets, when they can just spill out and grow around the container. Most species of *Bulbophyllum* like fairly good light; in the wild, they are rarely to be found in heavy shade, even the forest species tend to grow on the higher branches. Many of the larger species are pretty drought- resistant, but like most orchids, they like a good supply of water and high humidity while actively growing. It is necessary, though, to water carefully when the new growths are just starting as at that stage, they are rather vulnerable to rot. Fortunately, they will usually develop a second growth later on. All our plants are grown at intermediate temperatures and are kept fairly dry in winter, or when the new growths have matured. Like all sympodial orchids, species of *Bulbophyllum* are easily divided, but several pseudobulbs are needed to make a good plant. Divisions with only one or two pseudobulbs, if they survive at all, take a long time to become established. These species look better as specimen plants and should not be divided unless it is necessary.

Bulbophyllum acutebracteatum De Wildeman

DESCRIPTION: Pseudobulbs 1–4 × 0.5–1 cm (0.5–2 × 0.25–0.5 in.), ovoid or ellipsoid, 4- to 6-angled, two-leaved, set 1–8 cm (0.5–3 in.) apart. Leaves 1–7 × 0.5–2 cm (0.5–3 × 0.25–1 in.), elliptic or lanceolate, obtuse and emarginate at the apex, thick and leathery. Inflorescences 5–16 cm (2–6 in.) long, few to many-flowered. Rachis 4-angled in cross-section, with the flowers set on two concave, opposite sides. Bracts 4–6 × 2–4 mm, recurved or spreading, ovate, acute or acuminate, yellow or dark red. Flowers distichous, yellow to orange-red, set 4–8 mm apart, not opening wide, several to many open at a time. Sepals 3.5–6 × 1.5–3 mm, ovate or triangular, the laterals wider than the dorsal, and slightly recurved. Petals 2–3 × 0.5 mm. Lip 1–2.5 × 1 mm, elliptic, obtuse, with a median ridge.

HABITAT: Epiphytic in lowland forest.

DISTRIBUTION: Gabon, Liberia, Sierra Leone, Zaire.

NOTE: Vermeulen (1987) recognized two varieties: var. *acutebracteatum,* with glabrous floral bracts and sepals, and var. *rubrobrunneopapillosum* (De Wildeman) J. J. Vermeulen, with coarsely papillose floral bracts and sepals.

Bulbophyllum barbigerum Lindley

DESCRIPTION: One of the most attractive and best known of the African species of *Bulbophyllum,* but not easy to obtain. Pseudobulbs 1.5–3.5 cm (1 in.) long and wide, orbicular or ovoid, rather flattened, with one leaf. Leaf 3–13 × 1.5–3 cm (1–5 × 1 in.), narrowly elliptic, the apex obtuse and slightly emarginate. Inflorescences 7–18 cm (3–7 in.) long, several- to many-flowered. Flowers distichous, opening wide, several opening together, greenish or yellowish, heavily marked with purple. Sepals 9–14 × 2–4 mm, lanceolate or ovate-lanceolate, acute. Petals less than 1 mm long. Lip 8–11 × 1–1.5 mm, densely fringed with long hairs, white towards the base of the lip and purple towards the tip.

HABITAT: Epiphytic both on trunks and in the crown of trees in evergreen and semideciduous forest, to 900 m (3000 ft.).

DISTRIBUTION: Cameroon, Central African Republic, Congo, Gabon, Ivory Coast, Liberia, Nigeria, Sierra Leone, Zaire.

Bulbophyllum cochleatum Lindley

DESCRIPTION: Pseudobulbs 2–11 cm (1–4 in.) × 4–13 mm, very narrowly conical or cylindrical, yellow-green with purple marks, with two leaves, set 1–7 cm (0.5–3 in.) apart on the rhizome. Leaves 3–23 × 0.5–2 mm, linear-lanceolate or linear. Inflorescences 8–55 cm (3–22 in.) long, many-flowered. Bracts 4.5–12 mm long, pale green, rather boat-shaped. Flowers distichous; sepals and petals green tinged with purple, sometimes light purple, with a deeper purple lip. Sepals 3–8 × 1–4 mm, ovate, acute. Petals 1–2.5 × 1 mm. Lip 2–6 × 0.5–1.5 mm, oblong, the edges with fine hairs.

Var. *bequaertii* (De Wildeman) J. J. Vermeulen
SYNONYM: *Bulbophyllum bequaertii* De Wildeman
DESCRIPTION: Similar to var. *cochleatum,* but the pseudobulbs tend to be rather stouter, and the lip is not fringed with hairs.
HABITAT: Epiphytic at high level in submontane and montane forest, 900–2400 m (3000–8000 ft.).
DISTRIBUTION: Cameroon, Rwanda, Tanzania, Uganda, Zaire.

Var. *cochleatum*
HABITAT: Epiphytic in submontane and montane forest, occasionally lithophytic, 900–2000 m (3000–6600 ft.).
DISTRIBUTION: Cameroon, Congo, Equatorial Guinea (Bioko), Gabon, Guinea, Ivory Coast, Kenya, Liberia, Malawi, Nigeria, Rwanda, São Tomé, Sierra Leone, Sudan, Tanzania, Uganda, Zambia.

Var. *gravidum* (Lindley) J. J. Vermeulen
SYNONYM: *Bulbophyllum gravidum* Lindley
DESCRIPTION: Pseudobulbs 3–4 × 1 cm (1–2 × 0.5 in.), ovoid, 4- to 5-angled with very knobby edges, with two leaves, set 3–10 cm (1–4 in.) apart on the rhizome. Flowers similar to those of var. *cochleatum,* but the flowers are usually mustard-yellow with a purple-red lip.
HABITAT: Submontane or riverine forest, occasionally in woodland, not infrequently lithophytic, 900–1260 m (3000–4100 ft.).
DISTRIBUTION: Cameroon, Equatorial Guinea (Bioko), Malawi, Tanzania, Zaire, Zambia.
NOTE: The appearance of var. *gravidum* is very different from that of var. *cochleatum,* and in *Orchids of Malawi* (la Croix et al. 1991) it is kept as a separate species. Although the details of the flowers of the two varieties are similar, we are not 100 percent convinced they should be treated together.

Bulbophyllum cocoinum Lindley

DESCRIPTION: Pseudobulbs 2–5 × 1–3 cm (1–2 × 0.5–1 in.), ovoid, 3- to 4-angled, with one leaf, set 3–6 cm (1–2 in.) apart on the rhizome. Leaf 9–25 × 1–3.5 cm (4–10 × 0.5–1 in.), lanceolate. Inflorescences 10–40 cm long (4–16 in.), many-flowered, erect to pendent. Flowers scented, not opening wide, white, the sepals often pink-tipped, many open together. Dorsal sepal 7–12 × 1–2 mm, linear-lanceolate, acute; lateral sepals similar but slightly larger. Petals 2–3 mm long, lanceolate. Lip recurved, 1.5–3 × 1 mm, ovate, obtuse, with two knobs on the upper side just above the base.

HABITAT: Epiphytic at high levels in lowland and submontane forest, to 1200 m (4000 ft.), rarely to 2000 m (6600 ft.).

DISTRIBUTION: Angola, Gabon, Ghana, Ivory Coast, Liberia, Sierra Leone, Uganda, Zaire.

Bulbophyllum colubrinum (Reichenbach f.) Reichenbach f.

DESCRIPTION: Pseudobulbs 2.5–6 × 1–2 cm (1–2 × 0.5–1 in.), ellipsoid, somewhat flattened, 2- to 4-angled, with one leaf, set 3–6 cm (1–2 in.) apart on the rhizome. Leaf 10–20 × 1.5–3.5 cm (4–8 × 1 in.), lanceolate, very thick and leathery, almost fleshy. Inflorescences 15–50 cm (6–20 in.) long, many-flowered. Rachis swollen and flattened, to 2.5 cm (1 in.) wide, the edge smooth or indented, yellowish-green spotted with purple, or all purple. Flowers set alternately on each side of the rachis, 15 mm apart on each side, yellow, tinged with purple on the outside, occasionally all purple, not opening wide. Bracts to 6 × 3 mm, spreading or reflexed. Dorsal sepal 6–11 × 2 mm, lanceolate, cuspidate, concave; lateral sepals 5–9 × 4 mm, ovate, curved, cuspidate. Petals 3–5 × 1–2 mm. Lip recurved, 3 × 1.5 mm, elliptic, obtuse, not hairy.

HABITAT: Epiphytic in lowland and submontane forest, 100–1000 m (330–3300 ft.).

CULTIVATION: In our greenhouse, it flowers in spring and summer (May and June).

DISTRIBUTION: Angola, Cameroon, Congo, Gabon, Ghana, Ivory Coast, Nigeria, Sierra Leone, Zaire.

Bulbophyllum encephalodes Summerhayes   FIGURE 10-27

DESCRIPTION: Pseudobulbs 2–4 × 1–1.5 cm (1–2 × 0.5–1 in.), ellipsoid but 4-angled, yellow-green with purple marks between the angles, with one leaf, set 2–8 cm (1–3 in.) apart on the rhizome. Leaf erect, 6–12 × 1.5–3 cm (2–5 × 1 in.), elliptic, rounded at the tip, thick and leathery or somewhat fleshy. Inflorescences to 35 cm (14 in.) long, erect but bent down quite sharply where the rachis joins the peduncle. Rachis rather fleshy, many-flowered. Flowers distichous, greenish marked with purple, the lip purple. Dorsal sepal 4–5 × 2.5–3 mm, ovate, acute, concave; laterals slightly longer. Petals 2.5–3 × 0.5–1 mm, oblong. Lip 2.5 × 1.5 mm, very fleshy, with two ridges in the basal half and with a brainlike surface (hence the name *encephalodes*).

HABITAT: Evergreen forest, particularly riverine forest, and high rainfall woodland, usually epiphytic on the trunks of large trees where it forms long, ascending chains, 800–1500 m (2600–5000 ft.). In Malawi, this species is local in its occurrence, being absent from many apparently suitable areas.

DISTRIBUTION: Burundi, Cameroon, Kenya, Malawi, Tanzania, Uganda, Zaire, Zambia, Zimbabwe.

← Figure 10-27. *Bulbophyllum encephalodes.* Plant, ×0.7.

Bulbophyllum expallidum J. J. Vermeulen PLATE 30

DESCRIPTION: Pseudobulbs to 4 × 2.5 cm (2 × 1 in.), ovoid to pear-shaped, slightly bilaterally flattened, glossy yellow, with one leaf, set close together and forming large clumps. Leaf erect, 6–12 × 1.5–3 cm (2–5 × 1 in.), oblong-elliptic, obtuse, bright green. Inflorescences to 35 cm (14 in.) long, many-flowered. Flowers secund, slightly scented, creamy-white, not opening wide, many open at one time. Sepals 10–11 × 2 mm, lanceolate, acuminate. Petals 2.5 × 1.5 mm, ovate. Lip 2–4 × 1 mm, fleshy, channelled, recurved at the tip.

HABITAT: Epiphytic on trunks and lower branches of trees in high rainfall woodland, rarely lithophytic, 800–2100 m (2600–7000 ft.).

DISTRIBUTION: Malawi, Rwanda, Tanzania, Zaire, Zambia.

Bulbophyllum falcatum (Lindley) Reichenbach f. PLATE 31

DESCRIPTION: Pseudobulbs 1–7 × 0.5–2 cm (0.5–3 × 0.25–1 in.), broadly to narrowly ovoid, usually 2- to 4-angled, with two leaves, set 0.5–5 cm (0.25 × 2 in.) apart on the rhizome. Leaves 2–20 × 0.5–3 cm (1–8 × 0.25 × 1 in.), lanceolate or linear. Inflorescences 3–40 cm (1–16 in.) long, several- to many-flowered. Rachis swollen, flattened, to 18 mm wide, or not swollen or flattened at all. Flowers distichous, yellowish or greenish marked with purple-red, or all purple-red or all yellow, set 2–20 mm apart. Dorsal sepal 2–9 × 1–4 mm, obovate; lateral sepals 2–9 × 1–7 mm, obliquely ovate or triangular, acute. Petals 1.5–3 × 1 mm. Lip recurved in the lower half, 1–4 × 0.5–3 mm, broadly ovate, obtuse.

HABITAT: Epiphytic in lowland and submontane forest, to 1800 m (6000 ft.).

DISTRIBUTION: Cameroon, Congo, Equatorial Guinea (Bioko), Gabon, Ghana, Guinea, Ivory Coast, Liberia, Nigeria, São Tomé e Príncipe, Sierra Leone, Zaire.

NOTE: Vermeulen (1987) recognized three varieties of this variable species, which he separated mainly on the shape of the petals, although they have more easily recognizable differences.

Var. *bufo* (Lindley) J. J. Vermeulen

DESCRIPTION: Rachis flattened, to 28 cm (11 in.) × 2–18 mm; petals ovate, not thickened at the tip; flowers whitish or yellowish, with red-purple spots, opening a few at a time.

Var. *falcatum*

SYNONYM: *Bulbophyllum ugandae* (Rolfe) De Wildeman

DESCRIPTION: Rachis flattened, to 23 cm (9 in.) × 4–13 mm; petals thickened at the tip.

Var. *velutinum* (Lindley) J. J. Vermeulen

DESCRIPTION: Rachis may be widened and flattened, to 20 cm (8 in.) × 5–10 mm, or may not be flattened at all; flowers dark red with a yellow base to the lip, or all yellow, most opening at the same time, set closely together, facing the same way. This is by far the most attractive variety. The yellow form is sometimes known as var. *flavum*, but it has not been botanically described as such.

Bulbophyllum fuscum Lindley

DESCRIPTION: Pseudobulbs 1–5 × 0.5–1.5 cm (0.5–2 × 0.25–1 in.), ovoid or ellipsoid, sometimes rather obscurely 4-angled, light green, with two leaves, set 2–13 cm (1–5 in.) apart on the rhizome. Leaves 3–6 × 1–1.5 cm (1–2 × 0.5–1 in.), narrowly elliptic, pale green, stiff and coriaceous. Inflorescences erect, usually 8–10 cm (3–4 in.) long, the rachis wider than the peduncle with 10 to many flowers borne in channels on opposite sides, set 3–9 mm apart. Flowers yellow or orange, the lip orange or vermilion red, not opening wide, and many open together. Pedicel and ovary 1–2 mm long; bracts 2–6 × 1.5–4 mm, partially enclosing the flowers. Dorsal sepal 2–5 × 1–2 mm, ovate, acute; lateral sepals 2–6 × 1.5–2.5 mm, obliquely ovate. Petals 1.5–4 × 0.5 mm. Lip 1–3 × 0.5–1.5, elliptic, rounded, fleshy, channelled at the base.

HABITAT: In eastern Africa, woodland, sometimes riverine forest, not infrequently lithophytic on lichen-covered rocks. In western Africa, lowland and submontane forest. Altitude 600–2100 m (2000–7000 ft.).

CULTIVATION: This is an attractive and easily grown species. In our greenhouse, it flowers in winter (November and December).

DISTRIBUTION: Angola, Cameroon, Central African Republic, Equatorial Guinea (Bioko), Gabon, Guinea, Ivory Coast, Kenya, Liberia, Malawi, Mozambique, Nigeria, Sierra Leone, Tanzania, Uganda, Zaire, Zambia, Zimbabwe.

NOTE: Vermeulen (1987) distinguished two varieties, var. *fuscum* and var. *melinostachyum* (Schlechter) J. J. Vermeulen, but the differences are small and of little significance to a grower. The former is confined to the west side of Africa, while the latter occurs there and in the east. In eastern Africa, it has been confused in the past with *B. oreonastes*.

Bulbophyllum imbricatum Lindley

DESCRIPTION: Pseudobulbs 2–7 × 1–4 cm (1–3 × 0.5–2 in.), narrowly ovoid or ovoid, rather flattened, 3- to 4-angled, green, with one to two leaves. Leaves 6–25 × 1–4 cm (2–10 × 0.5–2 in.), linear or lanceolate, thick and fleshy. Inflorescences to 60 cm (24 in.) long, many-flowered, erect or arching, the rachis swollen and moderately flattened, to 13 mm wide, the edges wavy, yellowish-white, greenish, or purple. Bracts spreading or reflexed, to 7 × 8 mm. Flowers cream, greenish-yellow, or orange-yellow, often with large dark purple blotches, or all dark purple, set 6 mm apart on either side of the rachis. Dorsal sepal 6–11 × 1.5–3 mm, ovate-lanceolate, acute; lateral sepals 3–7 × 2–5 mm, recurved, obliquely triangular. Petals 4–9 × 1 mm. Lip recurved,

1–3 × 0.5–2 mm, triangular, obtuse, not hairy but deeply toothed towards the base.

HABITAT: Epiphytic at high levels in lowland forest, to 800 m (2600 ft.), occasionally in coastal forest.

DISTRIBUTION: Cameroon, Central African Republic, Congo, Equatorial Guinea (Pagalu Island), Gabon, Ghana, Ivory Coast, Liberia, Nigeria, São Tomé, Sierra Leone, Zaire.

Figure 10-28. *Bulbophyllum intertextum.* Plant (left), ×1; flower (right), ×4.

Bulbophyllum intertextum Lindley   FIGURE 10-28

DESCRIPTION: Pseudobulbs 0.5–1 cm (0.25–0.5 in.) long and wide, ovoid or orbicular, glossy green, sometimes reddish-tinged, with one leaf, set close together and forming clumps. Leaf 1–10 × 0.5–1 cm (0.5–4 × 0.25–0.5 in.), elliptic, obtuse. Inflorescences 5–8 cm (2–3 in.) long, rarely to 20 cm (8 in.), rather laxly several-flowered, the peduncle and rachis both thin and wiry. Flowers greenish-white, the sepals sometimes purple-tipped, sometimes opening wide and sometimes not, several open together. Vermeulen (1987) remarked that the flowers can be entirely purple. Sepals 3–6 × 1–3 mm, ovate, acute. Petals 1–3 × 1 mm. Lip fleshy, recurved, with two basal ridges, 1–4 × 1–2 mm, triangular, elliptic or ovate, the margins sometimes hairy.

HABITAT: Epiphytic on mossy branches of trees in evergreen forest, rarely in high rainfall woodland, 300–1900 m (1000–6300 ft.).

CULTIVATION: This pretty little species is not difficult to grow, treated as described for the genus, except that it seems particularly prone to infection with red spider mite, even managing to acquire it when placed in front of a humidifier. This can easily be treated when necessary, but one must watch out for it.

DISTRIBUTION: Angola, Cameroon, Equatorial Guinea (Bioko), Ethiopia, Gabon, Guinea, Ivory Coast, Kenya, Liberia, Malawi, Nigeria, São Tomé e Príncipe, Sierra Leone, Tanzania, Zaire, Zambia, Zimbabwe.

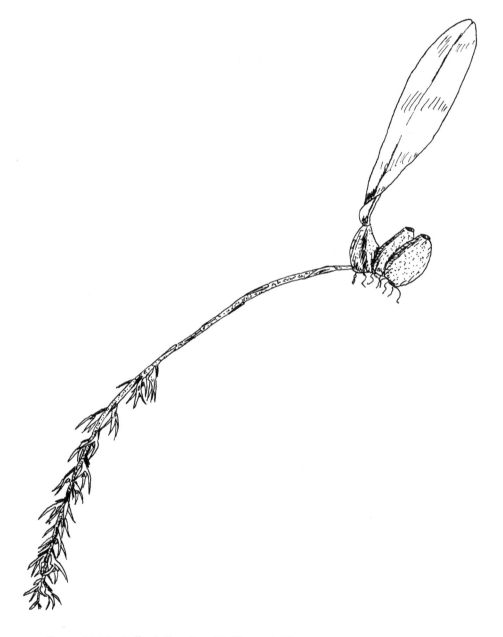

Figure 10-29. *Bulbophyllum josephii.* Plant, ×0.75.

Bulbophyllum josephii (Kuntze) Summerhayes PLATE 32, FIGURE 10-29
SYNONYM: *Bulbophyllum mahonii* Rolfe

DESCRIPTION: Pseudobulbs 1.5–4 × 1–2.5 cm (1–2 × 0.5–1 in.), ovoid, slightly flattened bilaterally, dark maroon-red or greenish-brown with a pitted surface like orange peel, with one leaf, set close together forming clumps. Leaves erect, 5–25 × 1–3 cm (2–10 × 0.5-1 in.), elliptic or lanceolate, obtuse and minutely bilobed at the tip. Inflorescences 10–40 cm (4–16 in.) long, arching or pendent, many-flowered, the flowers sometimes, but not always, secund. Flowers often with a strong, fruity scent, creamy white, the sepals sometimes tipped with purple or vermilion-orange, the lip white or yellowish, not opening wide, many open at once. Sepals 5–12 × 1–3 mm, narrowly lanceolate, acuminate, the laterals slightly longer and wider than the dorsal and somewhat oblique. Petals 2–5 × 1 mm. Lip recurved, 2–3 × 1–1.5 mm, fleshy, ovate, sometimes papillose towards the tip and round the margin.

HABITAT: High rainfall woodland, sometimes evergreen forest, to 2000 m (6600 ft.) in West Africa, and 850–2400 m (2800–8000 ft.) in eastern Africa.

DISTRIBUTION: Burundi, Cameroon, Equatorial Guinea (Bioko), Ethiopia, Guinea, Ivory Coast, Kenya, Liberia, Malawi, Mozambique, Nigeria, Rwanda, Tanzania, Uganda, Zaire, Zambia, Zimbabwe.

NOTE: Plants with maroon-red pseudobulbs and strongly scented, purple-tipped flowers are among the most attractive of all *Bulbophyllum* species. In northern Malawi they grew in woodland with *B. expallidum,* the deep red and glossy yellow pseudobulbs making a pleasant contrast.

Bulbophyllum lizae J. J. Vermeulen

DESCRIPTION: Pseudobulbs 4–7 × 1.5–2 cm (2–3 × 1 in.), ovoid, yellow-green, 4- to 6-angled, with two leaves, set 5–8 cm (2–3 in.) apart on a woody rhizome. Leaves 10–23 × 1–2.5 cm (4–9 × 0.5–1 in.), narrowly lanceolate, with a petiole 5–15 mm long. Inflorescences to 25 cm (10 in.) long, 10- to 12-flowered. Rachis slightly swollen and flattened, 5–7 mm wide, with the flowers distichous, set along the midline of the flat side, 12–30 mm apart on each side. Flowers greenish-cream. Pedicel and ovary 7–10 mm long; bracts to 9 mm long, reflexed, rather membranous. Dorsal sepal curving back, 29 × 6 mm, lanceolate, acute; lateral sepals 17 × 13 mm, broadly ovate, oblique, somewhat concave. Petals 23 long, spreading, linear, the top club-shaped and antenna-like. Lip 7 × 8 mm, recurved, broadly ovate, fleshy.

HABITAT: Evergreen forest, 1350–1400 m (4450–4600 ft.).

DISTRIBUTION: São Tomé.

NOTE: This species is not yet in cultivation, but it is to be hoped that it will become available as, apart from *Bulbophyllum longiflorum,* the flowers are so much larger than those of any other African species of *Bulbophyllum,* approaching those of some Asiatic species in size. It is rather like an outsize *B. sandersonii,* but it is improbable that it is just a polyploid form of this, as there are various differences, including the color. We have seen plants of *B. sandersonii* with yellow flowers, but never with cream or greenish-white.

Bulbophyllum longiflorum Thouars

SYNONYMS: *Cirrhopetalum africanum* Schlechter, *Cirrhopetalum umbellatum* (Forster) Hooker & Arnold

DESCRIPTION: Pseudobulbs 1.5–3 × 1 cm (1 × 0.5 in.), obliquely conical, with one leaf, set 2–6 cm (1–2 in.) apart on a stout woody rhizome. Leaf erect, 8–20 × 1.5–4 cm (3–8 × 1–2 in.), oblong, with a petiole 1–1.5 cm (0.5–1 in.) long. Inflorescences to 20 cm (8 in.) long, 2- to 7-flowered, the flowers set very close together. Flowers light purple or bronze with darker blotches, or clear yellow. Dorsal sepal 9–10 × 5–9 mm, concave, elliptic, with a filiform tip 1 cm (0.5 in.) long. Lateral sepals 22–38 × 4–7 mm, lanceolate, acute, twisted so that the outer edges are joined, but with the tips free. Petals 5–9 × 2–3 mm, lanceolate, with a filiform tip 6 mm long. Lip 6–7.5 × 1.5–2.5 mm, fleshy, recurved, oblong.

HABITAT: Epiphytic in riverine and submontane forest, usually growing on vertical trunks, in fairly deep shade, 500–1700 m (1650–5600 ft.).

DISTRIBUTION: Malawi, Tanzania, Uganda, Zaire, Zimbabwe. Also Madagascar, Mascarene Islands, Seychelles, and east to the Pacific Islands.

NOTE: The genus *Cirrhopetalum* was established by John Lindley in 1824, but H. G. Reichenbach merged it with *Bulbophyllum* in 1861, as he did with *Megaclinium*. The species described above is the only African one that falls into the *Cirrhopetalum* group, but there are many similar Asiatic species. Garay et al. (1994) have resurrected *Cirrhopetalum* as a genus, but this is not yet universally accepted.

Bulbophyllum maximum (Lindley) Reichenbach f.   FIGURE 10-30

SYNONYMS: *Bulbophyllum oxypterum* (Lindley) Reichenbach f., *Bulbophyllum platyrhachis* (Rolfe) Schlechter

DESCRIPTION: A robust species. Pseudobulbs 3–15 × 1–3 cm (1–6 × 1 in.), oblong to ovoid, yellowish, 3- to 5-angled, the edges sometimes knobby, with two leaves, set 2–10 cm (1–4 in.) apart on a stout, woody rhizome. Leaves 3–20 × 3.5–5.5 cm (1–8 × 1–2 in.), oblong, the apex rounded and slightly emarginate, very thick and leathery. Inflorescences to 50 cm (20 in.) long, occasionally even longer, many-flowered. Rachis either swollen and somewhat flattened, or completely flat and almost leaflike, then to 5 cm (2 in.) wide, in either case, the edges usually dentate. Plants with the very flat rachis have been known as *Bulbophyllum platyrhachis* and the rachis then is almost orange in color; the color in plants with the swollen and fleshy rachis is usually purple. Although the two types of plants have a different appearance, the flowers are identical, and there are so many intermediate forms that it is difficult to separate the two types. Flowers yellow or green, spotted with purple, set 1 cm (0.5 in.) apart, opening in succession. Dorsal sepal 5–7 × 1.5 mm, lanceolate, acute; laterals recurved, 4–6 × 3–3.5 mm, ovate, acuminate. Petals 3 × 1 mm. Lip recurved, 3 × 1.5 mm, oblong, fleshy, not hairy.

HABITAT: Epiphytic in open woodland and riverine forest, sometimes lithophytic, to 1500 m (5000 ft.).

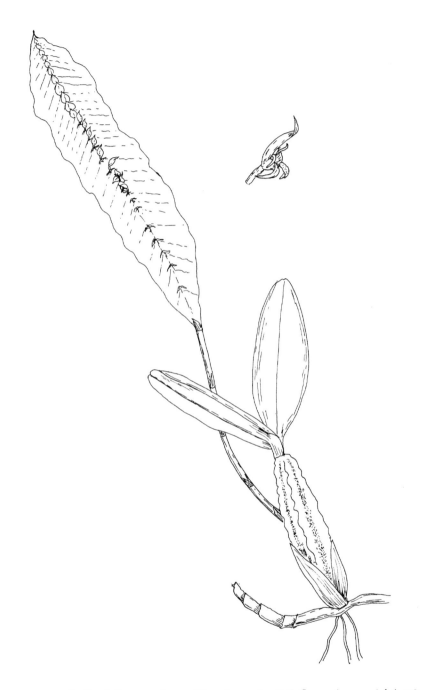

Figure 10-30. *Bulbophyllum maximum*. Plant (center), ×0.6; flower (upper right), ×3.

DISTRIBUTION: Angola, Cameroon, Central African Republic, Congo, Equatorial Guinea (Pagalu Island), Gabon, Ghana, Guinea, Ivory Coast, Kenya, Liberia, Malawi, Mozambique, Nigeria, São Tomé e Príncipe, Sierra Leone, Tanzania, Uganda, Zaire, Zambia, Zimbabwe.

Bulbophyllum nigericum Summerhayes   PLATE 33

DESCRIPTION: A very attractive species, with flowers opening wide, many opening together, all facing the same way, and with a fairly neat growth habit. Pseudobulbs 1.5–3 × 1–1.5 cm (1 × 0.5–1 in.), ovoid or oblong, obtusely 4-angled, with two leaves, set 1–3 cm (0.5–2 in.) apart on the woody rhizome. Leaves 3–7 × 0.5–1 cm (1–3 × 0.25–0.5 in.), narrowly lanceolate. Inflorescences 8–25 cm (3–10 in.) long, to 30-flowered. Flowers distichous, borne in channels on opposite sides of the rachis, purplish, opening wide, many open together. Dorsal sepal to 7 × 4 mm, ovate, acuminate; lateral sepals to 9 mm long, spreading or reflexed. Petals to 4 × 3 mm. Lip recurved, to 4 × 3 mm, rather fiddle-shaped, the margins not hairy.

HABITAT: Usually lithophytic, at the edge of riverine forest, 1000–2050 m (3300–6800 ft.).

CULTIVATION: In our greenhouse, it usually flowers in autumn (September and October).

DISTRIBUTION: Cameroon, Nigeria.

Bulbophyllum oreonastes Reichenbach f.

SYNONYM: *Bulbophyllum zenkerianum* Kränzlin

DESCRIPTION: Vegetatively, very similar to *Bulbophyllum fuscum,* with flowers borne in channels on either side of the rachis and floral bracts 3–7 × 2–3.5 mm, spreading. Whether it is because the pedicel and ovary at 2–3 mm long are slightly longer than those of *B. fuscum,* or whether the rachis is not so deeply channelled, in this species the flowers stand out farther and are not so enclosed in the bracts. The size and coloring of the flowers of *B. fuscum* and *B. oreonastes* are similar, but the sepals of the latter are usually striped with deep purple-red or red-brown; on occasion they can be entirely purple-red.

HABITAT: Woodland and lowland, submontane and montane forest, sometimes lithophytic, to 2300 m (7600 ft.).

DISTRIBUTION: Cameroon, Central African Republic, Equatorial Guinea (Bioko), Gabon, Ghana, Guinea, Ivory Coast, Liberia, Malawi, Mozambique, Nigeria, Rwanda, Sierra Leone, Uganda, Zaire, Zambia.

Bulbophyllum porphyrostachys Summerhayes   PLATE 34

DESCRIPTION: Pseudobulbs 3–6 × 1–2 cm (1–2 × 0.5–2 in.), ellipsoid, slightly flattened, 4- to 5-angled, with one to two leaves, set 3–7 cm (1–3 in.) apart on the rhizome. Leaves 10–20 × 1.5–3 cm (4–8 × 1 in.), lanceolate, thick and leathery. Inflorescences arching, to 20 cm (8 in.) long, many-flowered. Flowers distichous; bracts large, 7–12 × 7–12 mm, ovate, concave, dark purple, completely concealing the flowers. Flowers yellow-green, marked with red. Sepals 3–4 × 2–3 mm, ovate. Petals 2 × 0.5 mm. Lip 1.5–2 × 1–1.5 mm, ovate, thick.

HABITAT: Epiphytic in rainforest, 600 m (2000 ft.).

CULTIVATION: In our greenhouse, it flowers in summer (July and August).

DISTRIBUTION: Cameroon, Congo, Nigeria.

NOTE: The showy part of this species is the purple bracts, arranged along either side of the rachis like ears of wheat and persisting for months, after the flowers have faded.

Bulbophyllum pumilum (Swartz) Lindley

SYNONYMS: *Bulbophyllum flavidum* Lindley, *Bulbophyllum nanum* De Wildeman, *Bulbophyllum winklerii* Schlechter

DESCRIPTION: An attractive species but very variable; Vermeulen (1987) gave 18 synonyms. Pseudobulbs 0.5–4 × 0.5–2 cm (0.25–2 × 0.25–1 in.), orbicular or ovoid, obscurely 2- to 4-angled, with one leaf, set 2–30 mm apart on the rhizome. Leaves 1–23 × 0.5–4 cm (0.5–9 × 0.25–2 in.), almost round to linear, sometimes tinged with purple. Inflorescences 2–30 cm (1–12 in.) long, erect or pendent, few- to many-flowered, with many flowers open together. Flowers white or cream, flushed with purple-red, sometimes entirely purple-red; lip white, yellow or red. Sepals usually recurved to some extent, 2.5–8 × 1–3 mm, ovate-lanceolate, acute. Petals 1–3 × 0.5–1 mm, elliptic. Lip 1–2.5 × 0.5–1 mm, recurved, ovate, fleshy, tonguelike.

HABITAT: Epiphytic in lowland to montane forest, rarely lithophytic, to 1900 m (6300 ft.).

DISTRIBUTION: Cameroon, Congo, Equatorial Guinea (Bioko), Gabon, Ghana, Guinea, Ivory Coast, Liberia, Nigeria, Sierra Leone, Zaire.

Bulbophyllum purpureorhachis (De Wildeman) Schlechter

DESCRIPTION: Pseudobulbs 5–12 × 2–5.5 cm (2–5 × 1–2 in.), ovoid to almost rectangular, rather flattened, 2- to 3-angled, olive green or yellowish-brown, with two leaves, set 4–8 cm (2–3 in.) apart on the rhizome. Leaves 12–30 × 3–8 cm (5–12 × 1–3 in.), lanceolate, thick and coriaceous. Inflorescences to 95 cm (38 in.) long, many-flowered. Rachis flattened and bladelike, to 4.5 cm (2 in.) wide, pale green spotted with purple. Flowers pale green or white, streaked, spotted and flushed with purple, set 1–2 cm (0.5–1 in.) apart on each side of the rachis. Dorsal sepals 7–14 × 2–4 mm, narrowly triangular; lateral sepals 6–13 × 4–7 mm, obliquely triangular, sometimes recurved, with dark hairs on the outer side. Petals 5–9 × 1–2 mm. Lip 3–6 × 3–4 mm, slightly recurved, ovate, the tip rounded.

HABITAT: Epiphytic in lowland forest.

DISTRIBUTION: Cameroon, Congo, Gabon, Ivory Coast, Zaire.

Bulbophyllum resupinatum Ridley

DESCRIPTION: A neat little species. Pseudobulbs 1–5 × 0.5–1.5 cm (0.5–2 × 0.25–1 in.), ovoid or ellipsoid, sometimes 2- to 4-angled, with two leaves, set 0.5–3.5 cm (0.25–1 in.) apart. Leaves 1.5–5 × 0.5–1.5 cm (1–2 × 0.25–1 in.), oblong or lanceolate, leathery. Inflorescences 2–40 cm (1–16 in.) long, several- to many-flowered; rachis erect or pendent, sometimes slightly flattened below each flower and slightly zigzag, but sometimes not. Flowers distichous, dark red, or yellow-green with purple-brown marks, set 2–11 mm apart. Dorsal sepal 2–5 × 1 mm, ovate, acute; lateral sepals 2–4 × 1–3 mm, sometimes recurved, obliquely triangular. Petals 1.5–3 × 1 mm. Lip recurved, 1–1.5 × 1 mm, ovate, the tip rounded.

HABITAT: Epiphytic in lowland and submontane forest.

DISTRIBUTION: Cameroon, Gabon, Ghana, Ivory Coast, Liberia, Nigeria, São Tomé, Sierra Leone, Zaire.

NOTE: Vermeulen (1987) distinguished two varieties, var. *resupinatum,* with dark red flowers set rather close together, and var. *filiforme* (Kränzlin) J. J. Vermeulen with yellow-green flowers marked with purple, covered with fine, dark hairs on the outer surface, and set farther apart on a long rachis. The latter variety has a long, straggling inflorescence with only a few flowers open at a time, although plants remain in flower for several months.

Bulbophyllum rugosibulbum Summerhayes

DESCRIPTION: Pseudobulbs 1–1.5 cm (1 in.) long, rarely to 2 cm (1 in.) × 8–15 mm, ovoid or almost round, sometimes slightly flattened, purple-red, wrinkled, set close together forming large clumps or mats. Leaves 3.5–5 × 0.5 cm (1–2 × 0.25 in.), linear or narrowly oblong. Inflorescences 5 cm (2 in.) long, semi-erect, to 20-flowered. Bracts 2 mm long, papery, completely covering the ovary. Flowers distichous, deep maroon-purple, paler in the center, most open together. Dorsal sepal 3–4.5 × 1.5–2 mm, ovate, acute; lateral sepals 2–4 × 1–2 mm, recurved and deflexed. Petals 1–1.5 mm long, linear. Lip 3–4 × 0.5 mm, projecting forwards, linear, fringed with hairs in the apical half, hinged so that it moves in the breeze.

HABITAT: Epiphytic on trunks and lower branches of trees in high rainfall areas, but very local in its occurrence, 1200–1800 m (4000–6000 ft.).

DISTRIBUTION: Malawi, Tanzania, Zambia.

NOTE: Vermeulen (1987) included this attractive little species in *Bulbophyllum cochleatum* var. *gravidum,* but when seen in the wild, it is very distinctive, and would be a very desirable plant to grow.

Bulbophyllum saltatorium Lindley   PLATE 35, FIGURE 10-31

DESCRIPTION: Pseudobulbs 1–5 × 0.5–3.5 cm (0.5–2 × 0.25–1 in.), orbicular to ovoid, with one leaf. Leaf 1.5–21 × 1–5.5 cm (1–8 × 0.5–2 in.), elliptic to lanceolate, thick and leathery. Inflorescences 3–84 cm (1–33 in.) long, few- to many-flowered.

Figure 10-31. *Bulbophyllum saltatorium* var. *albociliatum*. Plant (left), ×1; flower (right), ×2.

Sepals 6–15 × 2–4 mm, ovate, acute. Petals 2–6 × 1 mm. Lip recurved, 4–12 × 1–2 mm, ovate-oblong, the margins fringed with hairs.

Var. *albociliatum* (Finet) J. J. Vermeulen

SYNONYM: *Bulbophyllum distans* Lindley

DESCRIPTION: Plant larger than var. *saltatorium,* with size of leaves, inflorescence, and flowers at the upper end of the range; flowers yellowish or greenish, flushed with red-purple or sometimes entirely red-purple; lip edged with either purple or white hairs.

HABITAT: Lowland and coastal forest, to 750 m (2500 ft.).

DISTRIBUTION: Cameroon, Central African Republic, Congo, Equatorial Guinea (Bioko), Gabon, Ghana, Ivory Coast, Liberia, Nigeria, Uganda, Zaire.

Var. *calamarium* (Lindley) J. J. Vermeulen

SYNONYM: *Bulbophyllum calamarium* Lindley

DESCRIPTION: Like var. *albociliatum,* but the long deep purple hairs of the lip go right round the lip apex, whereas in the other two varieties, they stop just short of it.

HABITAT: Epiphytic in primary forest, to 900 m (3000 ft.).

DISTRIBUTION: Cameroon, Congo, Equatorial Guinea, Gabon, Ghana, Ivory Coast, Liberia, Sierra Leone, Zaire.

Var. *saltatorium*

DESCRIPTION: A small, neat plant with leaves to 10 cm (4 in.) long and often shorter and arching or almost pendent inflorescences to 8 cm (3 in.) long; flowers at the smaller end of the size range, dark purple, most opening together.

HABITAT: Epiphytic in primary forest, to 600 m (2000 ft.).

DISTRIBUTION: Congo, Equatorial Guinea, Ghana, Ivory Coast, Liberia, Nigeria, Sierra Leone, Nigeria.

Bulbophyllum sandersonii (Hooker f.) Reichenbach f.

SYNONYM: *Bulbophyllum tentaculigerum* Reichenbach f.

DESCRIPTION: A striking species with a deep purple rachis. Pseudobulbs 2–5 × 1–1.5 cm (1–2 × 0.5–1 in.), ovoid or conical, 4- to 5-angled, sometimes with knobby edges, yellow-green, with two leaves, set 2–6 cm (1–2 in.) apart on the rhizome. Leaves 3–9 × 1–2 cm (1–4 × 0.5–1 in.), elliptic or narrowly oblong, thick and leathery. Inflorescences 7–20 cm (3–8 in.), many-flowered, the rachis fleshy and somewhat bilaterally flattened, to 7 mm wide, usually purple but sometimes greenish marked with purple, many-flowered. Flowers distichous, green, so heavily marked with purple as to look purple, or rarely, clear yellow, set to 10 mm apart, only a few opening at a time. Dorsal sepal 7–10 × 1–2 mm, linear-lanceolate; lateral sepals to 5 × 3 mm, ovate, subacute, the apex decurved. Petals 5–6 mm long, linear, clubbed at the tip like a butterfly's antennae. Lip 2 × 1–2 mm, fleshy, tonguelike.

HABITAT: Epiphytic in woodland and riverine forest, occasionally submontane forest; rarely lithophytic on large rocks in montane grassland, 200–2200 m (660–7300 ft.).

DISTRIBUTION: Cameroon, Congo, Gabon, Kenya, Malawi, Mozambique, South Africa (KwaZulu-Natal, Mpumalanga, Northern Province), Tanzania, Uganda, Zaire, Zambia, Zimbabwe.

Bulbophyllum scaberulum (Rolfe) Bolus   FIGURE 10-32
SYNONYM: *Bulbophyllum congolanum* Schlechter

DESCRIPTION: Vegetatively, a variable species. Pseudobulbs 2–9 × 1–3 cm (1–4 × 0.5–1 in.), ovoid or ellipsoid, green, yellow-green, or brownish, 3- to 5-angled, the edges sometimes undulate or knobby, with two leaves, set 2.5–13 cm (1–5 in.) apart on the rhizome. Leaves 3–28 × 1–6 cm (1–11 × 0.5–2 in.), linear or elliptic, leathery or fleshy. Inflorescences 6–55 cm (2–22 in.) long, many-flowered. Rachis sometimes forming an angle with the stalk, fleshy, bilaterally flattened, to 15 mm wide, sometimes with scattered hairs, the edges undulate. Flowers fleshy, green with purple-brown mottling, set 3–18 mm apart on each side of the rachis, a few opening together. Dorsal sepal 6–10 × 1–2 mm, linear-lanceolate, acute or obtuse, concave; lateral sepals 4–8 × 2–4 mm, obliquely ovate, acute, the apex decurved. Petals 3–6 × 1 mm. Lip to 6 × 3 mm, ovate, rounded at the apex, fleshy, deflexed.

HABITAT: Epiphytic in woodland and forest, sometimes lithophytic, 100–2300 m (330–7600 ft.).

DISTRIBUTION: Cameroon, Central African Republic, Congo, Ethiopia, Gabon, Ghana, Guinea, Ivory Coast, Kenya, Malawi, Mozambique, Nigeria, Sierra Leone, South Africa (Eastern Cape, KwaZulu-Natal), Sudan, Tanzania, Uganda, Zaire, Zambia, Zimbabwe.

Bulbophyllum schimperianum Kränzlin
SYNONYM: *Bulbophyllum acutisepalum* De Wildeman

DESCRIPTION: Pseudobulbs 1–2.5 × 1–2 cm (0.5–1 × 0.5–1 in.), ovoid to orbicular, slightly flattened, glossy green, with one leaf, set 1–2.5 cm (0.5–1 in.) apart on the rhizome. Leaf 4–16 × 1–2.5 cm (2–6 × 0.5–1 in.), linear-lanceolate. Inflorescences 6–36 cm (2–15 in.) long, erect or somewhat arching, many-flowered. Flowers creamy white, the sepals sometimes pink-tipped, not opening wide, sometimes secund, many open at a time. Dorsal sepal 6–9 × 1–2 mm, linear-lanceolate, acute; lateral sepals 6–10 × 2–3.5 mm, narrowly triangular, acute. Petals 2.5–3 × 1 mm. Lip recurved, 2–3.5 × 1.5–2 mm, elliptic, without knobs at the base but with short, stiff hairs round the margin.

HABITAT: Epiphytic in lowland, submontane and montane forest, 600–2000 m (2000–6600 ft.).

CULTIVATION: This attractive species forms a neat clump in a pot. In our greenhouse, it flowers in early winter (November).

DISTRIBUTION: Cameroon, Central African Republic, Congo, Gabon, Nigeria, Uganda, Zaire.

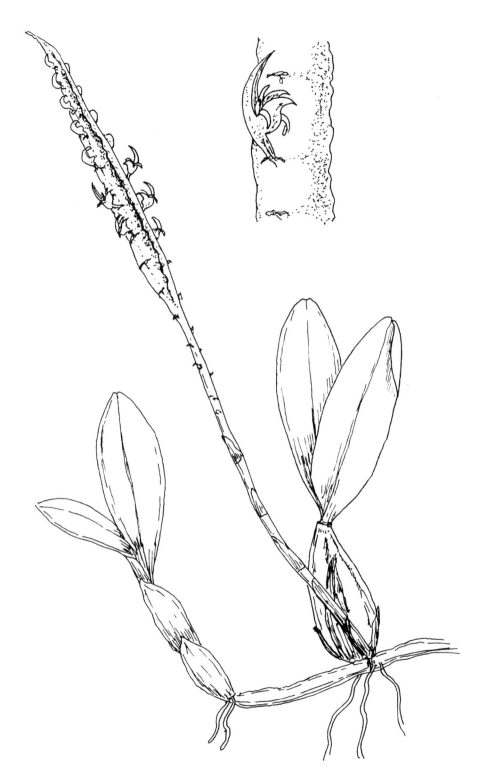

← Figure 10-32. *Bulbophyllum scaberulum.* Plant (lower), ×1; part of rachis with flower (upper), ×2.5.

Bulbophyllum schinzianum Kränzlin

DESCRIPTION: Pseudobulbs 1–6 × 1–3 cm (0.5–2 × 0.5–1 in.), orbicular to ovoid, somewhat flattened, with one leaf, set 1–7 cm (0.5–3 in.) apart on the rhizome. Leaf 7–30 × 1.5–6.5 cm (3–12 × 1–2 in.), oblong to linear-lanceolate. Inflorescences erect, 28–100 cm (12–40 in.) long, many-flowered. Bracts conspicuous, 16–30 mm long, yellowish or orange, spreading. Flowers yellowish or greenish flushed with purple, sometimes all purple, the hairs on the lip purple or brown, not opening wide, and not many open at one time. Petals and ovary 8–24 mm long. Sepals 6–14 × 1.5–5 mm, ovate or lanceolate, acute. Petals 2.5–8 × 1 mm. Lip slightly recurved, 5–11 × 1–3.5 mm, oblong, the margins densely fringed with hairs.

HABITAT: Epiphytic at high level in primary forest, to 800 m (2600 ft.).

DISTRIBUTION: Cameroon, Congo, Gabon, Ghana, Ivory Coast, Liberia, Nigeria, Zaire.

NOTE: Individually, the flowers of this species are attractive, but few are open together and the inflorescence is often very long.

Bulbophyllum stolzii Schlechter   FIGURE 10-33

DESCRIPTION: Pseudobulbs to 15 × 1 mm, round or ovoid, reddish, smooth and shiny when young but wrinkled when old, with two leaves, set 2–10 cm (1–4 in.) apart on a wiry rhizome. Leaves 2 × 0.8 cm (1 × 0.25 in.), elliptic, slightly bilobed at the tip. Inflorescences to 10 cm (4 in.) long, erect or arching, few to several-flowered, the peduncle very slender, the rachis slightly zigzag. Flowers distichous, more or less secund, most open together, the sepals and petals white flushed with purple, the lip yellow. Sepals 4–6 × 2–4 mm, ovate, acute. Petals 2 × 1 mm. Lip fleshy, 2–3.5 × 1–1.5 mm, oblong, recurved at about halfway.

HABITAT: Epiphytic in submontane and montane forest, usually sunk in moss and lichen and forming large colonies on trunks and lower branches, 1300–2500 m (4300–8250 ft.).

CULTIVATION: As given for the genus, but it likes temperatures on the cool side of intermediate.

DISTRIBUTION: Malawi, Tanzania.

Calanthe R. Brown

The large genus *Calanthe* includes around 150 species of terrestrial orchids, most of which are Asiatic; only one variable species is known from mainland Africa. The genus was established by R. Brown in 1821 and has been conserved over the earlier name *Alismorkis* Thouars. It is derived from the Greek words *kalos* (beautiful) and *anthe* (flower). Many of the Asiatic species are popular in cultivation, and the African species is equally well worth growing.

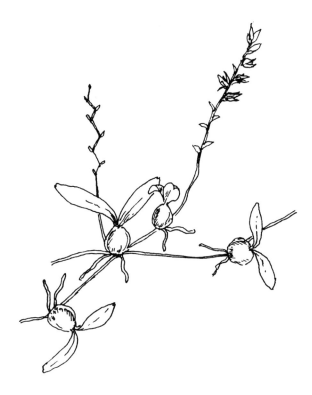

Figure 10-33. *Bulbophyllum stolzii.* Plant, ×1.

DESCRIPTION: Pseudobulbs above ground (in most species). Leaves large, fairly thin-textured, pleated, stalked. Inflorescences unbranched; flowers usually showy. Sepals and petals similar. Lip with three or four lobes and a basal spur.

Calanthe sylvatica (Thouars) Lindley   PLATE 36

SYNONYMS: *Calanthe corymbosa* Lindley, *Calanthe natalensis* Reichenbach f., *Calanthe volkensii* Rolfe

DESCRIPTION: Pseudobulbs to 5 cm (2 in.) long, partly above ground, ovoid, often rather obscure, being hidden by leaf bases; roots fleshy. Leaves several, forming a basal tuft, to 35 × 12 cm (14 × 5 in.), elliptic, ribbed, dark green and evergreen, with a stalk 10–20 cm (4–8 in.) long. Inflorescences 50–60 cm (20–24 in.) long, slightly pubescent, densely many-flowered. Flowers rather variable in size, purple or white, orange in the throat. Sepals 20–35 × 9–12 mm, lanceolate, acute. Petals 16–30 × 8–10 mm, elliptic, acute. Lip 15–20 mm long, trilobed at the base, with two crests between the basal, crescent-shaped side lobes; midlobe 14–20 mm wide, obovate, the apex emarginate with a small tooth in the middle. Spur S-shaped, 2–4 cm (1–2 in.) long.

HABITAT: Evergreen forest, in humus in deep shade, often near a stream and sometimes in very wet ground, 900–2700 m (3000–8900 ft.).

CULTIVATION: Although in the wild this species tends to grow in damp areas, it still needs a well-drained compost in cultivation as the fleshy roots rot easily. We use a mix of approximately equal parts of loam, peat, perlite, and fine bark, with some perlag mixed in. Plants should be kept drier in the resting season, but not be allowed to dry out completely. They seem to do well at intermediate temperatures, in moderate to heavy shade.

DISTRIBUTION: Angola, Burundi, Cameroon, Equatorial Guinea (Bioko and Pagalu Islands), Gabon, Guinea, Kenya, Malawi, Rwanda, São Tomé e Príncipe, Sierra Leone, South Africa (Eastern Cape, KwaZulu-Natal), Swaziland, Tanzania, Uganda, Zaire, Zambia, Zimbabwe. Also in Comoro Islands, Madagascar, Mascarene Islands.

Calyptrochilum Kränzlin

The genus *Calyptrochilum* was created by Fritz Kränzlin in 1895 to accommodate two species that had originally been described in *Angraecum,* but differ in the sharply recurved spur with a very swollen apex, and in the elongated rostellum. The genus name comes from the Greek words *kalyptra* (veil, covering) and *cheilos* (lip), but it is not known to what the name refers.

Calyptrochilum christyanum (Reichenbach f.) Summerhayes

FIGURE 10-34

DESCRIPTION: Stems woody, to 50 cm (20 in.) long, pendent or almost horizontal, usually unbranched; roots stout, to 7 mm in diameter, arising along the stem. Leaves numerous, distichous, usually 6–8 × 1.5–2.5 cm (2–3 × 1 in.), oblong or strap-shaped, unequally and obtusely bilobed at the apex, fleshy, olive green. Inflorescences 1.5–4 cm (1–2 in.) long, borne along underside of stem, densely 6- to 9-flowered. Flowers white, yellowish in the throat with a green spur, turning apricot as they fade, often lemon-scented. Sepals and petals ovate or elliptic, 5–10 × 2.5–4 mm, the petals slightly shorter than the sepals. Lip 7–12 × 7–10 mm, trilobed near the base, the side lobes rounded and erect, the midlobe 5–10 × 5–8 mm, oblong, emarginate. Spur 9–11 mm long, wide-mouthed, then narrowing and bending sharply down, inflated again at the apex. Column 1–2 mm long.

HABITAT: Riverine forest and woodland, occasionally growing on rocks, 900–1400 m (3000–4600 ft.).

CULTIVATION: Mounted on bark, in shade in intermediate temperatures.

DISTRIBUTION: Angola, Cameroon, Central African Republic, Congo, Eritrea, Gambia, Ghana, Guinea, Guinea Bissau, Ivory Coast, Kenya, Liberia, Malawi, Mali, Mozambique, Nigeria, Sierra Leone, Sudan, Tanzania, Uganda, Zaire, Zambia, Zimbabwe.

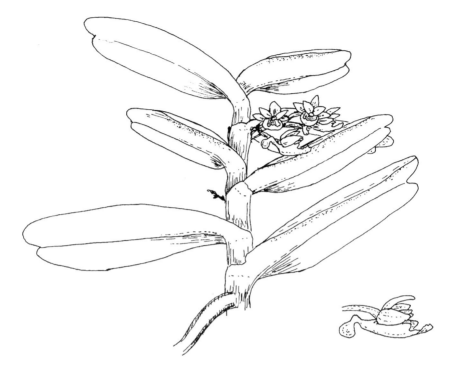

Figure 10-34. *Calyptrochilum christyanum*. Plant (left), ×0.75; flower (right), ×1.5.

Calyptrochilum emarginatum (Swartz) Schlechter

DESCRIPTION: Stems long, sometimes reaching as much as 3 m (9 ft.); roots arising along the stem. Leaves distichous, 8–18 × 2–5 cm (3–7 × 1–2 in.), ovate, leathery, unequally and obtusely bilobed at the apex. Inflorescences arising along the stem, densely many-flowered. Flowers strongly scented, white with a yellowish or yellow-green lip. Sepals and petals 10 × 3–5 mm, broadly ovate or obovate. Lip 10 mm long, obscurely trilobed in front, the side lobes broadly rounded, the midlobe smaller and acute; spur 10 mm long, much incurved, slightly swollen at the tip.

HABITAT: Forest.

CULTIVATION: Mounted on bark, in shade in intermediate temperatures.

DISTRIBUTION: Angola, Cameroon, Central African Republic, Equatorial Guinea (Bioko), Gabon, Ghana, Guinea, Ivory Coast, Liberia, Nigeria, Sierra Leone, Zaire.

Chamaeangis Schlechter

The genus *Chamaeangis* was established in 1915 by Rudolf Schlechter. Several species were already known, but had been placed in other genera such as *Angraecum* and *Listrostachys*. Schlechter divided the genus into two sections, *(Eu) Chamaeangis*, with two stipites and one viscidium, and *Microterangis,* with one stipes and one viscidium. Members of the latter section occur in Madagascar and have been placed in their own genus, *Microterangis.* This leaves seven species of tropical African orchid in *Chamaeangis.* The genus name is derived from the Greek words *chamai* (lowly) and *angos* (vessel), presumably referring to the small flowers with a spur that is usually globose at the apex.

DESCRIPTION: Epiphytic plants with slender roots. Flowers small, dull-colored, borne in dense, many-flowered inflorescences, usually in whorls of two to six at the nodes. Leaves often interesting, usually rather fleshy, linear, curved, with the apex very unequally bilobed.

CULTIVATION: Plants seem to be satisfactory either mounted on bark or in pots, but if pot-grown, the pots need to be suspended both because of the usually pendent inflorescences and because plants are apt to develop fungal blotching if they do not have good air movement around them. The slender roots indicate that these species do not like dry conditions.

Chamaeangis ichneumonea (Lindley) Schlechter   FIGURE 10-35

DESCRIPTION: Stems short, usually pendent; roots slender. Leaves several, to 25 × 3 cm (10 × 1 in.), occasionally longer, linear, curved, acutely bilobed at the apex, the shorter lobe usually almost absent, rather fleshy, olive green. Inflorescences pendent, 20–50 cm (8–20 in.) long, densely many-flowered, the flowers arranged spirally on the rachis, not in pairs or whorls. Flowers creamy yellow or yellow-green. Pedicel and ovary 5 mm long. Sepals 4–5 × 2–2.5 mm, oblong, obtuse, the laterals slightly longer and somewhat recurved. Petals 4 × 1 mm, linear, recurved. Lip 4.5–5 × 2.5–3 mm, oblong, shortly 3-toothed at the apex, but appearing emarginate as the midlobe curves back. Spur 12–13 mm long, C-shaped, the apical 5 mm very swollen and ellipsoid. The name *ichneumonea* refers to the supposed flylike appearance of the flowers.

HABITAT: High-level epiphyte in forest, in deep shade, 600 m (2000 ft.).

CULTIVATION: Does well at intermediate temperatures, in heavy shade, and with high humidity. It flowers regularly in spring (March to May).

DISTRIBUTION: Congo, Gabon, Ghana, Liberia, Nigeria, Sierra Leone.

NOTE: A related species, *Chamaeangis lanceolata* Summerhayes, also has flowers borne singly at the nodes. It is similar to *C. ichneumonea,* but has slightly smaller, greenish-orange flowers and a lanceolate to triangular lip with an acute apex. It is known only from southern Nigeria.

Chamaeangis odoratissima (Reichenbach f.) Schlechter

PLATE 37, FIGURE 10-36

DESCRIPTION: Stems woody, pendent, 20–50 cm (8–20 in.) long, leafy for much of the length. Leaves distichous, 10–24 × 2–3 cm (4–9 × 1 in.), narrowly oblanceolate, very unequally and acutely bilobed at the apex, the shorter lobe often almost absent, rather fleshy, olive green. Inflorescences several, to 25 cm (10 in.) long, densely many-flowered with the flowers in whorls of two to six, usually four, at the nodes. Flowers

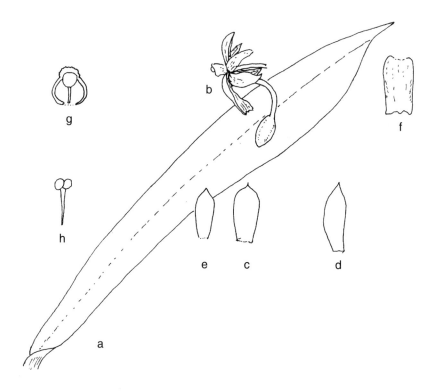

Figure 10-35. *Chamaeangis ichneumonea.* A: leaf, ×0.75. B: flower, ×2.25.
C: dorsal sepal, ×3.75. D: lateral sepal, ×3.75. E: petal, ×3.75. F: lip, ×3.
G: column from front, ×7.5. H: pollinia and stipes, ×11.25.

creamy yellow or yellow-green, strongly scented. Sepals 1–2 × 1–1.5 mm, elliptic, obtuse, the laterals slightly longer than the dorsal. Petals 1–1.5 × 1.5 mm, suborbicular, standing forward like ears on either side of the column. Lip 1.5–2 × 1–1.5 mm, ovate, concave, entire; spur 5–12 mm long, somewhat incurved, slender but very slightly inflated at the apex. Column less than 1 mm long.

HABITAT: Epiphytic at low levels, growing on tree trunks and branches in forest, usually riverine forest, 900–2100 m (3000–7000 ft.). We have seen this species growing terrestrially; a plant had obviously fallen from a tree and established itself on the river bank below.

CULTIVATION: We have grown this species in the tropics in a shade house. It is likely to require intermediate temperatures, heavy shade, and high humidity.

DISTRIBUTION: Widespread in West Africa from Sierra Leone to the Central African Republic, Angola, Kenya, Malawi, Rwanda, Tanzania, Uganda, Zaire.

Figure 10-36. *Chamaeangis odoratissima.* Plant, ×0.7. →

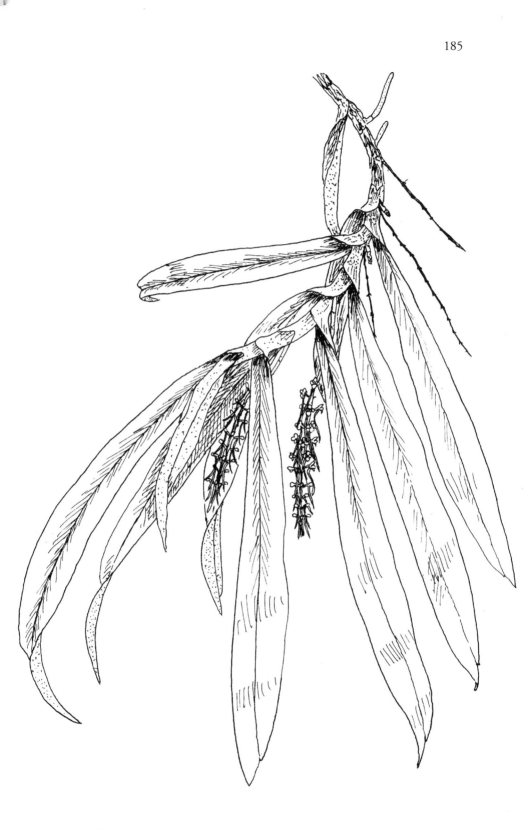

Chamaeangis sarcophylla Schlechter

SYNONYM: *Chamaeangis orientalis* Summerhayes

DESCRIPTION: Stems short, pendent; roots fine. Leaves 7–25 × 0.5–1.5 cm (3–10 × 0.25–1 in.), linear, curved, fleshy, very unequally bilobed at the apex, keeled on the underside, dark olive green sometimes tinged with orange. Inflorescences one to two, erect, densely many-flowered with three to four flowers at each node; because the inflorescence is erect, the flowers seem to be standing on their heads with the spurs pointing upwards. Flowers pinkish-orange to orange, faintly scented. Sepals 2–3.5 × 1–2 mm, oblong to ovate, the laterals slightly longer than the dorsal and recurved. Petals 2.5–3.5 × 2–3 mm, suborbicular, spreading or recurved. Lip 2.5–3.5 × 2–3 mm, suborbicular to oblong, obtuse or obscurely 3-toothed at the apex. Spur 1–2 cm (1 in.) long, slender, but slightly inflated in the apical half. Column 0.5 mm long.

HABITAT: Epiphytic at high levels in montane and submontane forest, 1500–2400 m (5000–8000 ft.).

CULTIVATION: This attractive species seems to be rare in cultivation. We find it very slow growing and reluctant to flower. We grow it on bark, in intermediate conditions, but it might well be happier kept slightly cooler. High humidity is essential; the fleshy leaves start to wrinkle if they are kept too dry.

DISTRIBUTION: Kenya, Malawi, Rwanda, Tanzania, Uganda, Zaire.

Chamaeangis vesicata (Lindley) Schlechter

DESCRIPTION: A pendent epiphyte; roots slender. Leaves 3 to 10, 20–40 × 1.5 cm (8–16 × 1 in.), linear, curved, leathery or fleshy, unequally and acutely bilobed at the apex. Inflorescences pendent, to 30 cm (12 in.) long, densely many-flowered, with the flowers at opposite pairs at the nodes. Flowers lime green, yellowish or orange, sweetly scented during the day. Pedicel and ovary 4–5 mm long. Sepals 2–4 × 1.5–2 mm, ovate, acute, the laterals slightly longer than the dorsal. Petals 2.5–3 × 1 mm, lanceolate. Lip 2.5–3 × 1 mm, deflexed, ovate, convex; spur 7–12 mm long, C-shaped, abruptly swollen at the apex.

HABITAT: Riverine and submontane forest, 1100–1800 m (3600–6000 ft.).

CULTIVATION: Intermediate temperatures, with shade and high humidity.

DISTRIBUTION: West Africa, from Guinea and Sierra Leone to Zaire, Kenya, Rwanda, Tanzania, Uganda.

Cribbia Senghas

SYNONYM: *Azadehdelia* Braem

The genus *Cribbia* was created by the German botanist Karl-Heinz Senghas in 1986 to accommodate the plant previously known as *Rangaeris brachyceras*. It was named in honor of the Kew orchidologist Phillip Cribb. For 10 years this was thought to be a monotypic genus, but three more members have been described. All four species occur in tropical Africa.

DESCRIPTION: Smallish, monopodial epiphytes. Leaves distichous. Inflorescences rather lax, arising from or near the base of the plant. Flowers translucent, with free sepals and petals, the lateral sepals longer than the dorsal. Lip entire, lacking a callus, spurred at the base. Rostellum trilobed, the midlobe slightly longer than the side lobes; pollinia two, stipites two, viscidia two, very small.

CULTIVATION: Easily grown in pots, in a standard bark mix, at intermediate temperatures and in moderate shade. They are not showy, but are neat, attractive plants, in flower over a long period.

Cribbia brachyceras (Summerhayes) Senghas

SYNONYMS: *Aerangis brachyceras* Summerhayes, *Azadehdelia brachyceras* (Summerhayes) Braem, *Rangaeris brachyceras* (Summerhayes) Summerhayes

DESCRIPTION: Stems erect, to 20 cm (8 in.) long, sometimes branching at the base; roots many, to 2 mm in diameter, arising on the lower part of the stem. Leaves several, distichous, 8–13 × 1 cm (3–5 × 0.5 in.), strap-shaped, unequally and obtusely bilobed at the apex. Inflorescences erect, 4–17 cm (2–7 in.) long, laxly to 15-flowered. Flowers translucent, pale yellow-green, sometimes tinged with orange towards the tips of the floral parts. Pedicel and ovary 3–5 mm long, bracts about the same length. Dorsal sepal 5–7 × 1.5–2 mm, oblong-lanceolate, acute; lateral sepals slightly longer and narrower, linear-oblanceolate. Petals 5 × 1.5–2 mm, oblong, rounded. Lip entire, 5 × 3 mm, lanceolate, acute, slightly recurved in the apical half; spur 5–6 mm long, very slightly swollen towards the apex. Column 2 mm long.

HABITAT: Epiphytic on mossy tree trunks, sometimes lithophytic on mossy rocks, in forest, 1500–2200 m (5000–7300 ft.).

DISTRIBUTION: Guinea, Kenya, Liberia, Nigeria, Rwanda, Sierra Leone, Uganda, Zaire, Zambia.

Cribbia confusa Cribb   FIGURE 10-37

DESCRIPTION: Stems to 10 cm (4 in.) long, sometimes branched at the base; roots numerous, 1–2 mm in diameter. Leaves distichous, 5–11 × 1–1.5 cm (2–4 × 0.5–1 in.), strap-shaped to linear-oblanceolate, unequally and obtusely bilobed at the apex, light green. Inflorescences several, erect, arising below the leaves, 9–17 cm (4–7 in.) long, very slender, rather laxly to 12-flowered. Flowers translucent yellow-green, turning orange towards the tips of the segments, very strongly honey-scented during the day. Pedicel and ovary to 12 mm long, the ovary arched. Sepals 7–11 × 1–2 mm, lanceolate, acuminate, the laterals slightly longer and narrower than the dorsal. Petals 6–8 × 1.5–2 mm, lanceolate, acuminate. Lip 11 × 3 mm, lanceolate, acuminate, with no callus; spur 5–10 mm long, slender, straight or slightly incurved. Column 1–2 mm long.

HABITAT: Epiphytic in secondary forest and in montane forest, 1300–2100 m (4300–7000 ft.).

DISTRIBUTION: Cameroon, Ivory Coast, Liberia, São Tomé.

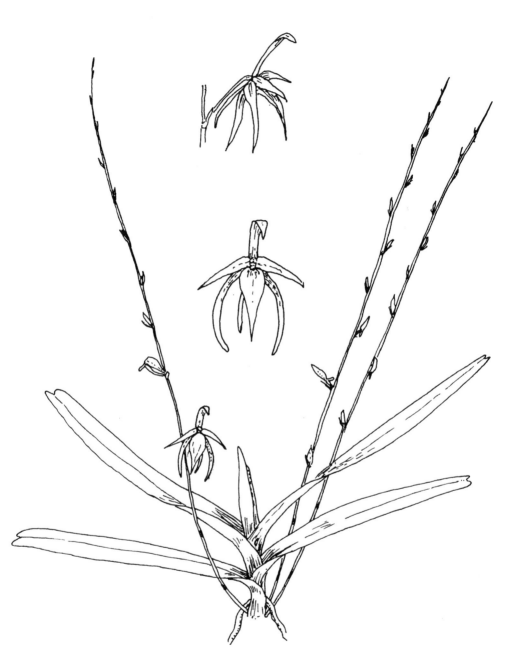

Figure 10-37. *Cribbia confusa.* Plant (center), ×1; flower (top), ×1.5; flower (middle), ×2.

Figure 10-38. *Cribbia thomensis.* Flower, ×3.

Cribbia thomensis Cribb

FIGURE 10-38

DESCRIPTION: Stems to 10 cm (4 in.) long, branched at the base. Leaves distichous, to 10 × 1.5 cm (4 × 1 in.), strap-shaped, unequally and roundly bilobed at the apex. Roots numerous, 2 mm in diameter. Inflorescences several, very slender, arising below the leaves, 8–11 cm (3–4 in.) long, to 12-flowered. Flowers pure white. Pedicel and ovary 10 mm long, white, slender, arched. Sepals 4 × 1.5 mm, lanceolate, acute. Petals 4 × 2 mm, triangular, somewhat reflexed. Lip 5 × 3.5 mm, entire, ovate, acute. Spur 8–9 mm long, incurved, rather thick. Column green, 1 mm long.

HABITAT: Epiphytic in montane forest, 1700–2025 m (5600–6700 ft.).

DISTRIBUTION: São Tomé.

Cynorkis Thouars

The large genus *Cynorkis* with about 125 species was first described by the French botanist A. du Petit Thouars in 1809. The genus name, sometimes incorrectly spelled *Cynorchis* or *Cynosorchis*, is derived from the Greek words *kynos* (dog) and *orchis* (testicle), in reference to the appearance of the usually paired tubers. In the wild, many species often form large colonies where they occur. Most species are native to Madagascar, but about 20 are known from tropical and South Africa.

DESCRIPTION: Mostly terrestrial species, many growing in leaf litter, on mossy rocks, and fallen logs, a few epiphytic. Leaves few, sometimes solitary, arising at the base of the plant, with a few sheathing leaves borne on the stem. Stem and parts of the flowers usually have scattered glandular hairs; some are very hairy, few if any have no hairs. Inflorescence terminal, few- to many-flowered. Flowers usually pink or mauve, occasionally white, although then usually spotted with purple. Dorsal sepal forming a hood with the petals; lateral sepals usually spreading. Lip usually with three or five lobes, sometimes unlobed. Stigma borne on two short processes.

CULTIVATION: All species, even the epiphytic ones, have a long resting season when they should be kept cooler and dry. They do well at intermediate temperatures and need a freely draining terrestrial mix. Most require shady, humid conditions while in active growth, but like most terrestrials need to be watered carefully in the early stages, or the shoots will rot at the base. Most species seem to self-pollinate, and capsules develop and quickly shed seed, which frequently germinates in pots of other orchids growing nearby. If left undisturbed for a couple of years, these will develop small tubers that will grow on when potted up.

Cynorkis compacta (Reichenbach f.) Rolfe

DESCRIPTION: Tubers ovoid or elongated. Leaf one, to 8 cm (3 in.) long, ovate-oblong, acute, erect or horizontal. Inflorescences to 20 cm (8 in.) high, several-flowered, lacking hairs. Flowers small, white, the lip with some purple-red spots. Dorsal sepal 4 × 2–3 mm, erect, ovate, convex; lateral sepals spreading, slightly longer. Petals 4 mm long, forming a hood with the dorsal sepal. Lip with three to five lobes, 9 × 9 mm across basal lobes. All lobes wider towards the apex, which is rounded; basal lobes much larger than apical lobes; spur 3 mm long, parallel to the ovary.

HABITAT: Terrestrial in rocky areas, 700 m (2300 ft.).

DISTRIBUTION: South Africa (only known from a few areas in KwaZulu-Natal).

Cynorkis hanningtonii Rolfe   PLATE 38, FIGURE 10-39

DESCRIPTION: Plants 20–30 cm (8–12 in.) high. Leaves usually two near base of plant, 6–15 × 1.5–5.5 cm (2–6 × 1–2 in.), elliptic or oblanceolate, glabrous, glossy gray-green. Inflorescences pubescent, fairly densely many-flowered. Flowers varying in color from white through pale to deep pink, always with purple spots on the lip. Pedicel and ovary with glandular hairs, 10–12 mm long. Dorsal sepal 4 × 4 mm, ovate, convex; lateral sepals spreading, 6–9 × 3–6 mm, obliquely ovate. Petals 4 mm long, forming a hood with the dorsal sepal. Lip 7–8 mm long, with five lobes, the basal pair of lobes 1 mm long, the pair nearer the apex 2 mm long; midlobe 1–2 mm wide. Spur 7–12 mm long, parallel to the ovary, slightly swollen at the apex.

HABITAT: Mainly woodland, occasionally evergreen forest, but then towards the edge, usually in lighter shade than *Cynorkis kassneriana*, 640–2200 m (2100–7300 ft.).

DISTRIBUTION: Angola, Malawi, Mozambique, Tanzania, Zaire, Zambia, Zimbabwe.

NOTE: Where it occurs, this species forms large colonies, carpeting the woodland floor, and is particularly attractive when the colors are mixed. According to Geerinck (1984), this species is synonymous with the West African *Cynorkis debilis* (Hooker f.) Summerhayes; if this were indeed so, *C. debilis* is the earlier name and would be correct.

Figure 10-39. *Cynorkis hanningtonii*. Plant (left) ×1; lip (right), ×2. →

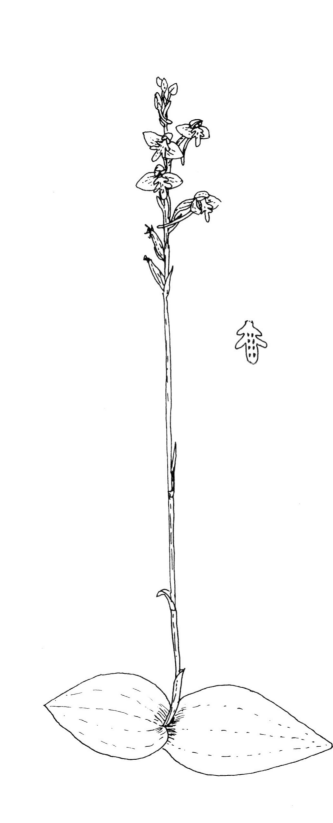

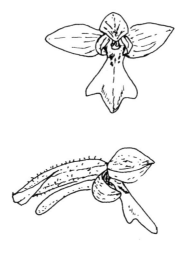

Figure 10-40. *Cynorkis kassneriana.* Flower (top and center), ×2; *Cynorkis kirkii,* lip (bottom), ×1.

Cynorkis kassneriana Kränzlin   PLATE 39, FIGURE 10-40

DESCRIPTION: Plants 20–30 cm (8–12 in.) tall. Basal leaves usually one but sometimes two, to 20 × 4 cm (8 × 2 in.), oblanceolate or elliptic, glabrous, dark, glossy green above, usually slightly mottled with paler green, and dark purple below. Inflorescences glandular hairy, with one or two sheathing leaves, fairly densely to 20-flowered. Flowers mauve-pink or purple-pink, usually with dark purple marks at the base of the lip. Pedicel and ovary 10–20 mm long, glandular-hairy. Dorsal sepal 5–8 mm long, ovate, convex; lateral sepals spreading, 6–8 × 4 mm, obliquely ovate; all sepals glandular-hairy on the outside. Petals 5–7 mm long, forming a hood with the dorsal sepal. Lip 8–10 × 5 mm, trilobed at about the middle, with the midlobe the largest; all lobes triangular. Spur 6–9 mm long, parallel to the ovary.

HABITAT: Evergreen forest, pine plantations; rarely woodland, sometimes among rocks or in moss on seepage slopes but almost always in deep shade; usually terrestrial in leaf litter, where it can carpet the ground like bluebells in a wood in Europe, but sometimes growing on rotting logs and mossy rocks, and occasionally epiphytic on tree trunks, usually at a fairly low level, 1300–2285 m (4300–7500 ft.).

DISTRIBUTION: Ethiopia, Kenya, Malawi, Mozambique, South Africa (Mpumalanga), Swaziland, Tanzania, Uganda, Zaire, Zambia, Zimbabwe.

Cynorkis kirkii Rolfe   FIGURE 10-40

DESCRIPTION: An attractive species, particularly when the inflorescence has several flowers. A slender plant, 10–30 cm (4–12 in.) high, with usually one but sometimes two basal leaves. Leaves 6–20 × 2–5 cm (2–8 × 1–2 in.), ovate or elliptic, gray-green, glabrous. Inflorescences glandular-hairy, 1- to 12-flowered. Flowers lilac-mauve, the lip yellowish at the base and with the lobes darker at the tips. Pedicel and ovary 25–35 mm long, slender. Dorsal sepal 5 × 5 mm, ovate, convex; lateral sepals spreading, 5–6 × 2–3 mm. Petals 5 × 2 mm, forming a hood with the dorsal sepal. Lip with four lobes, 15–20 × 15 mm, the lobes oblong. Spur 1–3 cm (0.5–1 in.) long, slender, pendent.

HABITAT: On seepage slopes or on mossy rocks, usually in light shade, but occasionally in the open, on seepage areas in montane grassland, 1200–1700 m (4000–5600 ft.).

DISTRIBUTION: Malawi, Mozambique, Tanzania, Zimbabwe.

Cynorkis symoensii Geerinck & Tournay   FIGURE 10-41

DESCRIPTION: Plants 15 cm (6 in.) tall. Leaves two, near the base, 8–10 × 1–3 cm (3–4 × 0.5–1 in.), elliptic, dark glossy green. Inflorescences glabrous, fairly densely to 12-flowered, the flowers secund. Sepals green, petals and lip bright magenta-pink. Pedicel and ovary 12 mm long, arching. Sepals 5 × 3 mm, ovate; petals 4 × 3 mm, forming a hood with the dorsal sepal. Lip by far the most prominent part of the flower, 10 × 12 mm, trilobed at the apex, the side lobes large and rounded, the midlobe represented by a small point. Spur 8 mm long, very swollen at the apex, parallel to the ovary.

HABITAT: Submontane and montane forest, sometimes on mossy rocks, and sometimes epiphytic on tree trunks and lianas, sunk in moss, at heights of to 6 m (20 ft.) above ground, 1750–2400 m (5800–8000 ft.).

DISTRIBUTION: Malawi, Rwanda.

NOTE: Although not known to be in cultivation, this species is exceptionally attractive, and one can always hope that one day it might be introduced. *Cynorkis summerhayesiana* Geerinck is a similar species with an even larger lip, 15–25 × 10–15 mm, known only from Zaire.

Cyrtorchis Schlechter

The genus *Cyrtorchis* includes about 15 species of epiphytic orchids confined to sub-Saharan Africa. It was created by Rudolf Schlechter in 1914, but many of the species had already been described in other genera, particularly *Angraecum*. The name is derived from the Greek words *kyrtos* (a swelling or curve) and *orchis* (orchids), most likely referring to the curved petals, or the curved spur, of these plants.

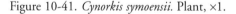

Figure 10-41. *Cynorkis symoensii.* Plant, ×1.

The flower pattern is very similar throughout the genus. Differences lie mainly in the size of flower and length of spur, and in the foliage and general size of the plant. Several species, in particular *Cyrtorchis chailluana* and *C. arcuata* can grow very large, with long, woody stems, while *C. crassifolia* is a dwarf plant, only a few inches across.

The genus was revised in 1960 by V. S. Summerhayes, who divided it into two sections depending on the character of the viscidium. This difference is of no relevance to the orchid grower, as both sections are similar in other ways. Few species are common in cultivation, but any is worth growing if it can be obtained.

DESCRIPTION: Flowers waxy white, turning apricot as they fade, starlike or rather bell-shaped, with a sweet, heavy scent particularly after dark, subtended by large, brown, rather loose bracts. Sepals and petals narrowly lanceolate, with tips usually recurved. Lip narrowly lanceolate, with a wide-mouthed, tapering spur.

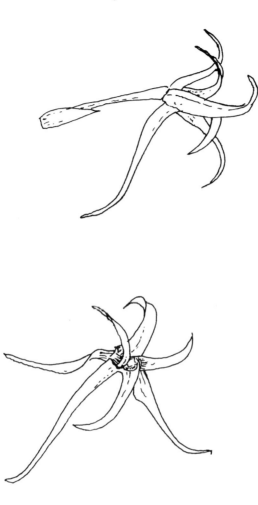

Figure 10-42. *Cyrtorchis arcuata* subsp. *arcuata.* Flower, ×1.

Cyrtorchis arcuata (Lindley) Schlechter subsp. *arcuata*

PLATE 40, FIGURE 10-42

SYNONYMS: *Cyrtorchis neglecta* Summerhayes, *Cyrtorchis sedenii* (Reichenbach f.) Schlechter

DESCRIPTION: A robust species; stems woody, to 30 cm (12 in.) long, often forming large clumps; roots stout, 5 mm in diameter. Leaves to 20 × 1–2.5 cm (8 × 0.5–1 in.), strap-shaped to elliptic, dull green. Inflorescences 6–20 cm (2–8 in.) long, fairly densely 5- to 14-flowered. Flowers waxy white, turning apricot as they fade, strongly scented in the evening. Pedicel and ovary 25 mm long; bracts 15–30 mm long. Sepals usually 20–30 × 6–8 mm, lanceolate, acuminate, recurved near the apex; petals and lip similar but slightly smaller. Spur 5–6 cm (2 in.) long, tapering, incurved or slightly S-shaped. Column short, 2 mm long.

HABITAT: Most often woodland, but sometimes riverine forest, 600–1600 m (2000–5300 ft.). We have seen plants in Swaziland growing on rocks and epiphytically on *Aloe arborescens* on an exposed hilltop, where they must have endured a long, hot dry season, although they would have received some protection by growing in a cleft of the rock.

CULTIVATION: Does well grown in a basket; it can also be mounted on bark. If grown in a pot, it needs to have a very coarse mix, otherwise the thick roots will start to rot. Even so, we find this species tends to be rather reluctant to flower—a feature it shares with most other species in the genus. Moderate to fairly bright light, intermediate temperatures, a cooler and drier rest in winter.

DISTRIBUTION: Throughout most of tropical Africa and as far south as the southern coast of South Africa.

NOTE: When Summerhayes revised *Cyrtorchis* in 1960, he divided *Cyrtorchis arcuata* into four subspecies, but subsequent work (Baker in press) has reduced these to two, subsp. *arcuata* and subsp. *whytei*. The former now includes plants that had been known as subsp. *variabilis* and subsp. *leonensis,* and what had been the species *C. neglecta.* Subsp. *arcuata,* as far as is known, is diploid or tetraploid.

Cyrtorchis arcuata subsp. *whytei* (Rolfe) Summerhayes

DESCRIPTION: Larger, more luxuriant than subsp. *arcuata.* Leaves glossy, dark green, to 20 × 5 cm (8 × 2 in.). Pedicel and ovary 4 cm (2 in.) long. Sepals 40–50 × 7–8 mm; petals and lip 25 × 5 mm. Spur to 9 cm (4 in.) long, S-shaped.

HABITAT: Usually riverine and submontane forest, sometimes in high-rainfall woodland, generally in more shade than the other subspecies and often at higher altitudes, 750–2000 m (2500–6600 ft.), although there is some overlap. In the northern region of Malawi, the two subspecies grew together. Normally, subspecies have to be geographically isolated, but there, these were able to preserve their identities by flowering at different times, subsp. *arcuata* in April to May, at the end of the rains, and subsp. *whytei* in November and December, in the early rains.

CULTIVATION: As for subsp. *arcuata,* but subsp. *whytei* needs more shade than does subsp. *arcuata.* Intermediate temperatures are satisfactory, but it benefits from a cooler and drier rest in winter.

DISTRIBUTION: Ghana, Ivory Coast, Liberia, Malawi, Sierra Leone, southern Tanzania, Togo. Possibly southeastern Zaire.

NOTE: Subsp. *whytei* has been found to be hexaploid (Baker, in press), with one plant sampled even being decaploid, which would account for the large size. It seems likely that West African and East African plants are of independent origin.

Cyrtorchis aschersonii (Kränzlin) Schlechter

DESCRIPTION: Stems to 30 cm (12 in.) long. Leaves 8–22 × 0.5–1.5 cm (3–9 × 0.25–0.5 in.), set closely together, linear to oblong, folded, often very fleshy, subequally bilobed at the apex. Inflorescences 4–15 cm (2–6 in.) long, 6- to 8-flowered. Flowers white, the spur greenish or brownish. All floral parts lanceolate, acuminate; sepals and petals 10–20 × 1.5–2 mm; lip 10–20 × 2–3 mm. Spur 1.5–4 cm (1–2 in.) long, S-shaped. Column very short.

HABITAT: Epiphytic in dense forest, to 1500 m (5000 ft.).

CULTIVATION: As for *Cyrtorchis arcuata* subsp. *whytei.*

DISTRIBUTION: Cameroon, Congo, Ghana, Nigeria, Sierra Leone, Zaire.

Cyrtorchis brownii (Rolfe) Schlechter

DESCRIPTION: Stems 8–20 cm (3–8 in.) long. Leaves 7–8.5 cm (3 in.) × 7–8 mm, linear, unequally bilobed at apex, leathery. Inflorescences to 9 cm (4 in.) long, densely to 12-flowered. Flowers white. Pedicel and ovary 3 mm long; bracts 6–8 mm long. Floral parts lanceolate, acuminate; sepals 10–14 × 2.5–3.5 mm; petals 8.5–9.5 × 2.5 mm. Lip 8.5–10.5 × 2.5–3 mm, recurved; spur 2–2.5 cm (1 in.) long, straight. Column short, 1.5 mm long.

HABITAT: Epiphytic in evergreen forest, to 1500 m (5000 ft.).

CULTIVATION: As for *Cyrtorchis arcuata* subsp. *whytei.*

DISTRIBUTION: Central African Republic, Congo, Ivory Coast, Sierra Leone, Tanzania, Uganda, Zaire.

Cyrtorchis chailluana (Hooker f.) Schlechter

DESCRIPTION: Largest of all the species of *Cyrtorchis.* Stems long, becoming pendent. Leaves to 25 × 3 cm (10 × 1 in.), ligulate to oblanceolate, sometimes with the edges undulate. Inflorescences to 25 cm (10 in.) long, 7- to 10-flowered. Flowers waxy white, turning apricot. Pedicel and ovary 4–4.5 cm (2 in.) long. Bracts loose, 18–23 mm long. Floral parts all linear-lanceolate, long acuminate, recurved towards the tips; sepals 45–50 × 6–9 mm; petals and lip 40 × 5 mm. Spur 9.5–16 cm (4–6 in.) long, curving forwards or S-shaped.

HABITAT: Epiphytic in forest, 1150–1250 m (3800–4100 ft.).

CULTIVATION: As for *Cyrtorchis arcuata* subsp. *whytei.*

DISTRIBUTION: Burundi, Cameroon, Central African Republic, Congo, Gabon, Nigeria, Sierra Leone, Uganda, Zaire.

Cyrtorchis crassifolia Schlechter   FIGURE 10-43

DESCRIPTION: A very attractive little species. The most distinctive species of *Cyrtorchis,* but possibly the trickiest to grow. A dwarf plant; stems short; roots stout, to 5 mm in diameter. Leaves two to six, 1.5–4, occasionally 6 cm (2 in.) long, 6–12 mm wide, gray-green, very fleshy, V-shaped in cross-section, recurved. Inflorescences 4 cm (2 in.) long, densely 3- to 8-flowered. Flowers creamy white, with a hyacinth-like scent in the evening. Peduncle very short, less than 1 cm (0.5 in.) long. Pedicel and ovary 10 mm long; bracts papery, 4 mm long. The flowers do not open wide and are rather bell-shaped; all floral parts are lanceolate, acuminate and recurved at the tips; sepals

Figure 10-43. *Cyrtorchis crassifolia.* Plant, ×1.

7–14 × 2–4 mm; petals slightly smaller. Lip to 11 × 5 mm, channelled towards the base, with a wide-mouthed, tapering, slightly incurved spur 2–3 cm (1 in.) long.

HABITAT: With its succulent appearance, *Cyrtorchis crassifolia* looks like a species of dry areas, but this is not the case. In the wild, it grows in high rainfall woodland, usually sunk in moss and lichen, at 1200–2000 m (4000–6600 ft.). It is very local in its occurrence, being absent from many places that would apparently be suitable. We have always found it growing on the large lower branches of trees growing on a ridge, or at least near the top of a slope, where there must be plenty of air movement, and frequent mist and drizzle even in the dry season.

CULTIVATION: Good ventilation seems to be the essential factor for successful cultivation; in stagnant conditions, it is sure to rot. We have been most successful growing it mounted, as rot is a problem when it is grown in a pot, but it needs high humidity. Intermediate conditions suit it well and reasonably good light.

DISTRIBUTION: Burundi, Malawi, Rwanda, southern Tanzania, Zaire, Zambia, Zimbabwe. Probably Mozambique.

Cyrtorchis hamata (Rolfe) Schlechter

DESCRIPTION: Leaves 9–24 × 1.5–4 cm (4–9 × 1–2 in.), linear, strap-shaped or elliptic. Inflorescences arching, 6–14 cm (2–6 in.) long, the lower bracts 1–2 cm (0.5–1 in.) long. Sepals, petals and lip lanceolate, acuminate, recurved; sepals 16–40 mm long; petals 16–20 mm long. Lip 13–30 mm long; spur 3.5–5 cm (1–2 in.) long, thickened and hooked at the tip. Column 1–2 mm long. This species is close to *Cyrtorchis arcuata;* further work may show that it is a form of that species—the spur with its hooked tip is the main difference.

HABITAT: Epiphytic at high level in forest.

CULTIVATION: We have never grown this species, but from its habitat, it would probably like similar conditions to *Cyrtorchis arcuata* subsp. *arcuata.* If it grows in the crowns of trees, it probably likes more light than *C. arcuata* subsp. *whytei.*

DISTRIBUTION: Ghana, Ivory Coast, southern Nigeria.

Cyrtorchis monteiroae (Reichenbach f.) Schlechter

DESCRIPTION: Does not look like other species of *Cyrtorchis* due to its long, pendent inflorescences. Stems woody, 30–80 cm (12–32 in.) long, becoming pendent, leafy towards the apex. Leaves 10–20 × 3–5 cm (4–8 × 1–2 in.), elliptic to oblanceolate, the edges slightly undulate. Inflorescences arising along the stem, pendent, 18–32 cm (7–13 in.) long, 10- to 20-flowered. Flowers white, the spur tinged with brownish-orange. Pedicel and ovary 13–15 mm long; bracts 5–8 mm long. Sepals, petals and lip all lanceolate, acuminate; sepals 15–18 × 4.5–5.5 mm; petals 14–15 × 4–4.5 mm. Lip 14–15 × 5 mm; spur 3.5–4.5 cm (1–2 in.) long, somewhat incurved. Column 2 mm long.

HABITAT: Epiphytic in evergreen forest, usually near a lake or river, 550–1300 m (1800–4300 ft.).

CULTIVATION: With its pendent growth habit and long inflorescences, this species should be mounted on bark or grown in a basket. Otherwise, it likes similar conditions to *Cyrtorchis arcuata* subsp. *whytei*. Uncommon in cultivation.

DISTRIBUTION: Angola, Cameroon, Gabon, Ghana, Nigeria, São Tomé e Príncipe, Sierra Leone, Uganda, Zaire.

Cyrtorchis praetermissa Summerhayes subsp. *praetermissa*   PLATE 41

DESCRIPTION: Stems short and erect when young, but in older plants becoming somewhat pendent, to 25 cm (10 in.) long; roots fairly stout, 3–4 mm in diameter. Leaves distichous, usually four to six pairs, 6–10 × 1 cm (2–4 × 0.5 in.), linear, recurved, V-shaped in cross-section, thick-textured but not fleshy like those of *Cyrtorchis crassifolia*. Inflorescences 2–4, arching, arising below the leaves, to 10 cm (4 in.) long, fairly densely 12-flowered, the flowers arranged in two rows. Flowers waxy white, turning apricot as the age, with a scent like lily-of-the-valley. Pedicel and ovary 10–15 mm long; bracts 4–5 mm long, dark brown, sheathing. Sepals, petals, and lip lanceolate, acuminate, recurved at the tips; sepals 8–12 × 2.5–5 mm; petals and lip similar but slightly smaller. Spur 2–3 cm (1 in.) long, tapering, slightly incurved.

HABITAT: Woodland, occasionally riverine forest, 450–1850 m (1500–6100 ft.).

CULTIVATION: Intermediate temperatures, moderate light, and a drier rest in winter seem to suit this species. It grows well either mounted on bark or in a pot, but if potted, a coarse mix is necessary and it is important not to overwater.

DISTRIBUTION: Burundi, Kenya, Malawi, Rwanda, South Africa (Mpumalanga, Northern Province), Tanzania, Uganda, Zaire, Zambia, Zimbabwe.

NOTE: Specimens from the Ruo Gorge on the lower slopes of Mount Mulanje in Malawi, where the species grows in riverine forest, have longer and narrower leaves than normal—only 4 mm wide—but the flowers seem identical. This form of the species is not known to be in cultivation.

Cyrtorchis praetermissa subsp. *zuluensis* (Harrison) Linder

DESCRIPTION: The main difference from the typical form lies in the leaves, which are broader and flat, rather than keeled.

HABITAT: A wide range from hot, humid coastal forest to cool, temperate forest and hot, dryish woodland (Harrison 1981).

DISTRIBUTION: South Africa (KwaZulu-Natal).

Figure 10-44. *Cyrtorchis ringens.* Plant, ×1.

Cyrtorchis ringens (Reichenbach f.) Summerhayes

PLATE 42, FIGURE 10-44

DESCRIPTION: Stems woody, covered with old leaf bases, to 30 cm (12 in.) long in old plants; roots 2 mm in diameter. Leaves usually six to seven, 7–14 × 1–2.5 cm (3–6 × 0.5–1 in.), strap-shaped, thick and leathery, slightly wrinkled when dry. Inflorescences 4–7 cm (2–3 in.) long, densely to 12-flowered. Flowers creamy white, scented. Pedicel and ovary 10–15 mm long; bracts prominent, to 8 mm long, whitish in bud but turning brown. Sepals 9–12 × 2–4 mm, lanceolate, acute, the tips recurved; petals similar but slightly smaller. Lip 7–10 × 3–4.5 mm, lanceolate, acuminate, recurved; spur 2–3.5 cm (1 in.) long, tapering, straight or incurved.

HABITAT: Although widespread, this species is oddly local in its occurrence. It usually grows in submontane and riverine forest, but occasionally in high rainfall woodland, 1000–1900 m (3300–6300 ft.).

CULTIVATION: Intermediate temperatures and moderate shade. We grow our plants mounted on bark, but they should grow equally well in a pot.

DISTRIBUTION: Cameroon, Congo, Ghana, Ivory Coast, Liberia, Malawi, Nigeria, Senegal, Sierra Leone, Tanzania, Uganda, Zaire, Zambia, Zimbabwe.

Diaphananthe Schlechter

Perhaps rather surprisingly, *Diaphananthe* is the largest genus of African angraecoid orchid. With around 50 species, it has slightly more than *Angraecum,* although of course the latter is a much larger genus over all, with about 150 species on Madagascar and other Indian Ocean islands, where *Diaphananthe* is not represented. The genus was established by Rudolf Schlechter in 1914; in 1918, he described two other genera, *Rhipidoglossum* and *Sarcorhynchus,* both of which were included by V. S. Summerhayes in *Diaphananthe* in his revision of the genus in 1960. In *Diaphananthe* in its original sense, the two pollinia are each attached by a separate stipes to a common viscidium, the rostellum is bifid, and there is usually a toothlike callus in the mouth of the spur. In *Rhipidoglossum* and *Sarcorhynchus,* each pollinium is attached by a stipes to its viscidium, the rostellum is rather obscurely trilobed with a prominent midlobe, and the callus at the mouth of the spur is obscure or sometimes absent. However, Summerhayes (1960) pointed out that there are several intermediate species and most botanists have followed him in recognizing only *Diaphananthe* as a genus, as we do here. Garay (1973) and Senghas (1986), however, both recognize *Rhipidoglossum* as distinct, Senghas also recognizing *Sarcorhynchus,* so perhaps the last word has not yet been said. The genus name derives from the Greek words *diaphanes* (transparent) and *anthe* (flower), referring to the distinctive translucent quality of the flowers of almost all species.

For such a large genus, few species of *Diaphananthe* are common in cultivation. They may not be among the most showy of species, but most have a quiet charm and we would want to grow any that we could obtain.

DESCRIPTION: In its widest sense includes long and short-stemmed epiphytic plants. Roots when wet, often greenish-gray with noticeable white streaks. Leaves variable in shape, falcate, often twisted at the base to face the same way. Flowers small to medium-sized, white, greenish, pale yellow, or rarely pinkish, usually translucent. Sepals similar, the petals often slightly shorter and broader, usually with apices rounded rather than acute. Lip is unlobed, or very obscurely lobed, spurred at the base, usually broader than long.

Diaphananthe adoxa Rasmussen

DESCRIPTION: Probably one of the least showy species of *Diaphananthe,* but for some reason established in cultivation. Stems pendent, 5–25 cm (2–10 in.) long, often forming thick clumps, with many prominent roots. Leaves several, 4–12 cm (2–5 in.) × 5 mm, linear, falcate, unequally bilobed at the apex. Inflorescences 2–3.5 cm (1 in.) long, 3- to 8-flowered. Flowers green or pale yellow-green. Sepals 2–3 × 1 mm, lanceolate, acute, the laterals slightly longer than the dorsal. Petals 2 × 1 mm, ovate, rounded. Lip 2 × 2 mm, ovate, obtuse, with no callus; spur to 2 mm long, swollen at the apex.

HABITAT: Epiphytic in submontane forest, 1300–1500 m (4300–5000 ft.), rarely to 2300 m (7600 ft.).

CULTIVATION: It is likely to succeed in intermediate temperatures, with fairly high humidity and in shade. With its pendent stems, it is likely to do better mounted rather than in a pot.

DISTRIBUTION: Ethiopia, Kenya, Uganda.

Diaphananthe bidens (Swartz) Schlechter

DESCRIPTION: Stems pendent, to 50 cm (20 in.) long, leafy for most of their length. Leaves distichous, 5–17 × 1–4 cm (2–7 × 0.5–2 in.), ovate or elliptic, unequally and acutely bilobed at the apex. Inflorescences arising along the apical half of the stem, to 22 cm (9 in.) long, to 25-flowered. Flowers white, buff-pink, or salmon-pink. Sepals 3–7 × 1–3 mm, lanceolate or triangular; petals 3–6 × 1–2 mm, lanceolate. Lip 3–7 × 3–6, quadrate, slightly emarginate or apiculate, with a tooth in the mouth of the spur; spur 3–7 mm long, incurved, slightly swollen in the middle. Column 2 mm long.

HABITAT: Epiphytic in rainforest, 1100–1300 m (3600–4300 ft.).

CULTIVATION: Because of its pendent habit, this species does better when mounted, but needs high humidity, particularly when in active growth. Intermediate temperatures are satisfactory. In cultivation it flowers in autumn (October).

DISTRIBUTION: Angola, Cameroon, Central African Republic, Congo, Equatorial Guinea (Pagalu Island), Gabon, Ghana, Guinea, Guinea-Bissau, Ivory Coast, Liberia, Nigeria, Rwanda, Sierra Leone, Togo, Uganda, Zaire.

Diaphananthe fragrantissima (Reichenbach f.) Schlechter

DESCRIPTION: A robust species; stems pendent, to 50 cm (20 in.) long, the lower part covered in old leaf bases; roots relatively fine, to 3 mm in diameter. Leaves several, 10–40 × 1–3.5 cm (4–16 × 0.5–1 in.), pendent, fleshy, linear-oblanceolate, unequally and acutely bilobed at apex, dull green. Inflorescences pendent, 20–60 cm (8–24 in.) long, fairly densely many-flowered, the flowers borne in whorls of four or in opposite pairs. Flowers creamy yellow or greenish-yellow, scented during the day. Pedicel and ovary 1–2 mm long; bracts sheathing, 3–5 mm long. Dorsal sepal 7–10 × 2 mm, lanceolate, acute; lateral sepals 10–11 × 3 mm, linear, acute, slightly curved. Petals 8 × 2 mm, linear. Lip oblong, with a tooth in the mouth of the spur, 10–13 × 7 mm including an acumen 2 mm long, the margins erose and often reflexed so that the lip looks narrower; spur 6–9 mm long, inflated. Column 2 mm long.

HABITAT: Epiphytic on trunks and lower branches of trees in woodland or riverine forest, often in hot, low-lying areas, 150–1400 m (500–4600 ft.).

CULTIVATION: With the stem, leaves, and inflorescences all pendent, this striking species needs to be either mounted or in a basket. It requires intermediate to warm temperatures, light to moderate shade, and plenty of water while growing; it benefits from a drier rest, as many of the places where it grows have a long dry season.

DISTRIBUTION: Angola, Burundi, Cameroon, Ethiopia, Kenya, Malawi, Mozambique, Rwanda, South Africa (KwaZulu-Natal), Sudan, Tanzania, Uganda, Zaire, Zambia, Zimbabwe.

Diaphananthe kamerunensis (Schlechter) Schlechter

DESCRIPTION: A robust species; stems short, 6–8 cm (2–3 in.) long; roots stout, 4–5 mm in diameter. Leaves several, 20–35 × 3–5.5 cm (8–14 × 1–2 in.), oblanceolate, falcate, unequally and obtusely bilobed at the apex. Inflorescences pendent, 10–12 cm (4–5 in.) long, rather laxly 5- to 10-flowered, the peduncle covered with loose, papery bracts 10–15 mm long. Flowers translucent, pale green or creamy yellow. Pedicel and ovary 2–2.5 cm (1 in.) long. Dorsal sepal 10–15 × 8–10 mm, ovate, obtuse; lateral sepals 20–23 × 8–10 mm, obliquely lanceolate, obtuse. Petals 15–17 × 12–14 mm, suborbicular, the edges fringed. Lip 18–20 × 22–24 mm, fan-shaped, with a tooth in the mouth of the spur, trilobed near the apex, the side lobes more or less oblong, the midlobe small and triangular, the whole apical margin fringed; spur 12–14 mm long, pendent, incurved. Column 4 mm long. This species has the largest flowers in the genus, and it is a great pity that it is not readily available in cultivation. The leaves are very similar to those of *D. pellucida,* but even when not in flower, *D. kamerunensis* can be distinguished by its much thicker roots.

HABITAT: Epiphytic in evergreen forest and woodland, 1000–1800 m (3300–6600 ft.).

CULTIVATION: Intermediate to warm temperatures and high humidity, particularly while in growth, either mounted or in a pot with a fairly coarse mix, in fairly heavy shade.

DISTRIBUTION: Cameroon, Nigeria, Uganda, Zaire, Zambia.

Diaphananthe pellucida (Lindley) Schlechter FIGURE 10-45

DESCRIPTION: A robust species; stems short, eventually reaching 12 cm (5 in.) in length; roots fine, 2 mm in diameter, dark brown with green growing tips. Leaves several, pendent, 18–40 × 2–9 cm (7–16 × 1–4 in.), oblanceolate, unequally and obtusely bilobed at the apex, pale to dark green with noticeable reticulate venation, rather fleshy. Inflorescences pendent, arising below leaves, 20–50 cm (8–20 in.) long, densely many-flowered. Pedicel and ovary 2–3 mm long; bracts large, brown and papery when the flowers are open, 6–10 mm long and wide. Flowers translucent creamy yellow or pale green, not scented. Sepals and petals all lanceolate, subacute; dorsal sepal 8–16 × 3–6 mm; lateral sepals 8–18 × 3–7 mm. Petals 8–18 × 3–6 mm. Lip deflexed, 8–18 × 7–18 mm, quadrate, with a tooth in the mouth of the spur, the margins fringed. Spur 5–15 mm long, swollen in the middle. Column 3 mm long.

Figure 10-45. *Diaphananthe pellucida.* Flower, ×1.

HABITAT: Epiphytic in dense shade in evergreen forest, on trunks and lower branches, 600–1500 m (2000–5000 ft.). We have seen this species growing in forests in the Congo in shade so deep that no reading was recorded on a light meter.

CULTIVATION: This species grows well in cultivation, although the leaves are not so large and luxuriant as they are in the wild. It does well either mounted or in a pot that is hung up, in heavy shade and high humidity. In cultivation, it seems to flower more than once a year—we have recorded flowers in February, September, November, and December.

DISTRIBUTION: Cameroon, Congo, Equatorial Guinea (Bioko and Pagalu Islands), Gabon, Ghana, Guinea, Ivory Coast, Liberia, Nigeria, Sierra Leone, Togo, Uganda, Zaire.

Diaphananthe pulchella Summerhayes   PLATE 43

DESCRIPTION: A variable species, depending on habitat. In woodland, stems short, to 10 cm (4 in.) long; roots numerous, stout, 3–4 mm in diameter. Leaves several, to 12 × 1–2 cm (5 × 1 in.), strap-shaped, unequally and obtusely bilobed at the apex, pale green. Inflorescences arising from base of plant, 8–10 cm (3–4 in.) long, arching, densely many-flowered. Flowers translucent, pale yellow, occasionally white, 15 mm in diameter. Pedicel and ovary 4 mm long. Dorsal sepal 7–8 × 3 mm, obovate, obtuse; lateral sepals similar, but slightly oblique and narrower. Petals 7–8 × 4 mm, elliptic. Lip 10 × 8 mm, oblong, erose on the lower edge, with a tooth in the mouth of the spur; spur 10 mm long, sometimes slightly inflated in the middle. In riverine forest, plants more slender, roots and leaves narrower, inflorescences longer and more lax, but flowers the same, although sometimes white rather than yellow.

HABITAT: Fairly open woodland, but in high rainfall areas, often on rocky hillsides, growing on big, horizontal branches; occasionally in riverine forest, 700–2500 m (2300–8250 ft.).

CULTIVATION: This pretty and floriferous species is not common in cultivation and although we are familiar with it in the wild, we do not grow it. It should do well in a pot with a fairly coarse mix, in light shade, at intermediate temperatures, with water freely given while in growth, but kept drier in winter.

NOTE: Two varieties have been described: var. *geniculata* Summerhayes, with larger flowers than those of var. *pulchella,* and a longer inflorescence, distributed in Cameroon,

Uganda, and Zaire; and var. *pulchella,* distributed in Cameroon, Kenya, Malawi, Rwanda, Tanzania, Uganda, Zaire, Zambia.

Diaphananthe rutila (Reichenbach f.) Summerhayes   PLATE 44
SYNONYM: *Rhipidoglossum rutilum* (Reichenbach f.) Schlechter

DESCRIPTION: Not showy, but with an interesting and unusual appearance. Probably the most widespread species of *Diaphananthe.* Stems 3–40 cm (1–16 in.) long, usually pendent and often dangling by one or two roots; roots numerous, 2 mm in diameter, usually with bright purple growing tips. Leaves 5–12 × 0.5–2 cm (2–5 × 0.25–1 in.), rarely to 3.5 cm (1 in.) wide, linear, strap-shaped or oblanceolate, unequally and roundly bilobed at the apex, leathery or almost fleshy, dark olive green often tinged with purple. Inflorescences arising along the stem between the leaves, pendent, 5–20 cm (2–8 in.) long, densely many-flowered. Flowers an odd purple-khaki color, occasionally creamy white. Pedicel and ovary 1–2 mm long; bracts 1–2 mm long. Dorsal sepal 2–3 × 1–2 mm, broadly elliptic; lateral sepals 2–4 × 1–2 mm, obliquely lanceolate, spreading. Petals 2–3 × 2–3 mm, almost orbicular. Lip 2–4 × 3–5 mm, fan-shaped; spur 4–8 mm long, slender, incurved. Column 1 mm long.

HABITAT: Epiphytic in evergreen forest, particularly riverine, often at a low level on trunks and branches, sometimes forming dense tangles that may fall off and continue to grow on the undergrowth, 550–2200 m (1800–7300 ft.).

CULTIVATION: This species should be mounted. It needs heavy shade and high humidity, at intermediate temperatures.

DISTRIBUTION: Angola, Burundi, Cameroon, Central African Republic, Congo, Gabon, Ghana, Guinea, Ivory Coast, Kenya, Liberia, Malawi, Mozambique, Nigeria, Rwanda, São Tomé, Sierra Leone, Sudan, Tanzania, Togo, Uganda, Zaire, Zambia, Zimbabwe.

Diaphananthe stolzii Schlechter   PLATE 45, FIGURE 10-46

DESCRIPTION: Stems long, pendent, sometimes branched, to 150 cm (60 in.) long, although usually less; roots numerous, to 3 mm in diameter, arising along the basal part of the stem and opposite leaf axils, many hanging freely. Leaves many, distichous, along the apical part of the stem, 5–7 × 1–2.5 cm (2–3 × 0.5–1 in.), rarely as much as 10 cm (4 in.) long, oblong, obtusely bilobed at the apex, dark green. Inflorescences arising along the stem, 4–5 cm (2 in.) long, densely several-flowered. Flowers white, greenish-white, or pale yellow (per *Flora of Tropical East Africa*), sweetly scented, particularly in the evening, 20 mm in diameter. Dorsal sepal 8–9 × 3–4 mm, erect, ovate; lateral sepals 9–14 × 2–3 mm, lanceolate, falcate. Petals 7–9 × 4–7 mm, broadly ovate, apiculate. Lip 11–12 × 10–17 mm, fan-shaped, the apical margin erose, with a tooth 1 mm long in the mouth of the spur. Spur 15–25 mm long, incurved. Column 3 mm long; stipites two and viscidia two.

HABITAT: Epiphytic at low levels in submontane and riverine forest, sometimes in wet woodland, occasionally lithophytic, 200–1900 m (660–6300 ft.).

Figure 10-46. *Diaphananthe stolzii*. Flower, ×2.

CULTIVATION: *Diaphananthe stolzii* is a very attractive species, well worth growing if it can be obtained. It should be mounted, and does well at intermediate temperatures, in deep shade, and with high humidity.

DISTRIBUTION: Malawi, Tanzania, Zimbabwe.

Diaphananthe tenuicalcar Summerhayes

DESCRIPTION: A rather straggly species. Stems 10–25 cm (4–10 in.) long, often forming large clumps. Leaves several, in the apical part of the stem, 1–6 cm (0.5–2 in.) × 7–13 mm, linear-lanceolate, falcate, unequally and acutely bilobed at the apex, twisted at the base to face the same way. Inflorescences 1–3 cm (0.5–1 in.) long, to 7-flowered. Flowers white, scented. Pedicel and ovary 4–12 mm long. Sepals 4–5 × 2–3 mm, elliptic, obtuse, the laterals slightly longer than the dorsal and oblique. Petals 4–5 × 2.5 mm, ovate. Lip 4.5–6.5 × 4–7.5 mm, fan-shaped, the apical margin obscurely 2- or 4-lobed, with a tooth in the mouth of the spur. Spur 15–25 mm long, slender from a wide mouth. Column 2 mm long; stipites two, viscidia two.

HABITAT: Montane forest, both inside it and at the edge, and in woodland near the forest edge, 2100–2700 m (7000–8900 ft.).

CULTIVATION: Mounted, in intermediate to cool temperatures, in moderate shade.

DISTRIBUTION: Ethiopia, Kenya, Uganda.

Diaphananthe xanthopollinia (Reichenbach f.) Summerhayes

PLATE 46

SYNONYM: *Rhipidoglossum xanthopollinium* (Reichenbach f.) Schlechter

DESCRIPTION: Vegetatively, a very variable species. Stems usually long, erect or trailing, to 30 cm (12 in.) long; roots many, stout, 4–5 mm in diameter, arising along the stem. Leaves several to many, on upper part of stem, 5–15 × 0.5–1.5 cm (2–6 ×

0.25–1 in.), distichous, linear to oblanceolate, unequally and roundly bilobed at the apex, rather leathery and slightly V-shaped in cross-section. Inflorescences arising along the stem, 3–9 cm (1–4 in.) long, densely many-flowered. Flowers lilac-scented, 8 mm in diameter, translucent creamy-yellow, sometimes tinged with orange. Sepals 3–5 × 2–3 mm, elliptic, obtuse, the laterals slightly longer than the dorsal. Petals 2.5–3.5 × 2–3 mm, suborbicular. Lip 3–5 × 3–6 mm, fan-shaped or transversely oblong, the apical margin lightly reflexed and with no tooth in the mouth of the spur but only an obscure, transverse callus. Spur 5–7 mm long, incurved. Column 1–2 mm long; stipites two, viscidia two. Anther cap bright yellow.

HABITAT: Submontane and riverine forest and woodland, usually epiphytic on the main branches, 600–1800 m (2000–6000 ft.), but lower in South Africa.

CULTIVATION: The long-stemmed plants do well in a basket, at intermediate temperatures, and in moderate to light shade. The short-stemmed form should be grown in a pot.

DISTRIBUTION: Angola, Kenya, Malawi, Mozambique, South Africa (Eastern Cape, KwaZulu-Natal), Tanzania, Uganda, Zaire, Zambia, Zimbabwe.

NOTE: Plants from the central and northern regions of Malawi are short-stemmed with fleshy, strap-shaped leaves markedly V-shaped in cross-section, 4–8 × 1.5–2.5 cm (2–3 × 1 in.). The flowers are, however, apparently identical except for a slight orange tinge. Such South African plants as we have seen have been long-stemmed, but tend to be somewhat smaller and finer than tropical African specimens.

Disa Bergius

The genus *Disa* was established in 1767 by the Swedish botanist and physician Peter Jonas Bergius. There have been many suggestions as to the origin of the name. Börge Pettersson (1985) concluded that the genus was named for Queen Disa, a figure in Swedish mythology or legend, who was ordered to appear before the king neither clothed nor naked. She solved this problem by wearing a fishing net, and Pettersson believes that the net veining on the sepals of *Disa uniflora* (the type species of the genus) made Bergius think of the tale.

The most recent revision of the genus was by H. P. Linder (1981b, 1981c), who recognized five subgenera divided into 15 sections. The genus, which contains about 130 species, is widespread in tropical and South Africa, with a few species occurring in Madagascar and Réunion, and one extending into Arabia. The most widely grown species of *Disa* belong to series *Racemosae* of section *Disa,* one of four series into which Linder divided that section (Linder 1981b). Members of this series have resupinate flowers and a racemose inflorescence, and are associated with permanent water. The seven species of series *Racemosae* described here are placed by Linder into two ecological groups: *D. aurata, D. cardinalis, D. caulescens, D. tripetaloides,* and *D. uniflora* grow, in the wild, along permanent streams, while *D. racemosa* and *D. venosa* grow in swampy and marshy places. In cultivation, all seven species can be grown in the same way as *D. uniflora,* as can their hybrids.

DESCRIPTION: Terrestrial (rarely lithophytic), growing from an underground tuber that is renewed each year; in a few species, stolons are produced that develop tubers at the ends so that the plants increase vegetatively. Most species are deciduous, disappearing underground in the resting season, but a few are evergreen. Stems usually leafy; separate sterile shoots with foliage leaves are produced in two sections and occasionally in a third. Inflorescence terminal, one- to many-flowered. Flowers often very showy—white, yellow, orange, pink, red, or purple, sometimes spotted—and usually resupinate. Dorsal sepal spurred, forming a deep or a shallow hood; lateral sepals usually spreading; petals small, often inside the hood. Lip small, narrow. Column short; anther erect, horizontal, or reflexed. Rostellum small, trilobed, lying between the anther and the cushionlike stigma. Pollinia two, caudicles two, viscidia two.

CULTIVATION: *Disa* includes some of the most beautiful of African orchids—indeed of all orchids—but relatively few are in cultivation; this is probably due to a mixture of being difficult to obtain, and difficult to grow. *Disa uniflora* and a few of its relatives are now widely grown and have been hybridized, particularly in South Africa. A few other species are also cultivated in South Africa and, as the techniques of their cultivation become established, they will become more widely grown elsewhere in the world. In more pessimistic moments, we sometimes feel that the ability to grow *Disa* species is a gift that you either have or have not, like perfect pitch. However, the techniques for growing at least *Disa uniflora* and its allies and hybrids are well known.

Disa aurata (H. Bolus) Linder

SYNONYM: *Disa tripetaloides* subsp. *aurata* (H. Bolus) Linder

DESCRIPTION: Similar to *Disa tripetaloides* but differing in the color, which is bright yellow, and in having a shallower hood, longer lateral sepals (14–16 mm long), and a shorter spur (0.5–2.5 mm long).

HABITAT: Wet mountain slopes.

DISTRIBUTION: South Africa (Langeberg Mountains in the Swellendam area of Western Cape).

Disa bivalvata (Linnaeus f.) Durand & Schinz

SYNONYMS: *Orthopenthea bivalvata* (Linnaeus f.) Rolfe, *Penthea melaleuca* (Thunberg) Lindley

DESCRIPTION: Plants 10–45 cm (4–18 in.) tall, with leafy stems. Leaves numerous and of similar length up the stem, to 8 cm (3 in.) long, linear-lanceolate, acute. Inflorescences corymbose, to 5 cm (2 in.) diameter, densely to 30-flowered. Sepals white, petals and lip pale to deep red. Dorsal sepal reflexed, 9–13 × 3–6 mm, forming a hood 2–4 mm deep, with the spur obsolete. Lateral sepals spreading, 10–15 mm long, obliquely oblong. Petals 5–7 mm long, standing beside the anther and curving over it. Lip projecting, 5–10 mm long.

HABITAT: Usually in swampy areas, but also on well-drained, sandy slopes, to 2000 m (6600 ft.), growing both in the winter rainfall area and in places where there is rain all year round. It is sometimes locally abundant and seems to flower freely after a fire.

CULTIVATION: As for *Disa uniflora.*

DISTRIBUTION: South Africa (Western Cape).

NOTE: This species belongs to section *Disa,* but it has been placed by Linder (1981b) in series *Complanae,* characterized by having an almost flat dorsal sepal and a corymbose inflorescence—that is, the flowers are held at more or less the same level.

Disa cardinalis Linder

DESCRIPTION: A beautiful species not described until 1980. Plants slender, evergreen, 30–60 cm (12–24 in.) tall, often spreading by underground stolons. Basal leaves 6 to 10, 5–10 cm (2–4 in.) long, elliptical; stem leaves sheathing. Inflorescences fairly densely to 20-flowered. Flowers bright red. Dorsal sepal 10–15 × 8–10 mm, forming a hood 6–8 mm deep, with a conical spur 4 mm long. Lateral sepals spreading and projecting, 18–28 mm long, elliptical. Petals 6–7 × 2 mm, oblong, standing inside the hood and curving over the anther. Lip projecting, 6–7 × 1–2 mm, rhomboid.

HABITAT: Banks of perennial streams in full sunlight, forming clumps, 600 m (2000 ft.).

CULTIVATION: As for *Disa uniflora.*

DISTRIBUTION: South Africa (extremely local in the Langeberg Mountains in Western Cape).

Disa caulescens Lindley

DESCRIPTION: Closely related to *Disa tripetaloides.* A slender species, 10–40 cm (4–16 in.) tall. Stems leafy. Inflorescences laxly few-flowered. Flowers white, the petals with maroon-purple bars. Dorsal sepal 6–8 mm long, forming a shallow hood 2 mm deep; spur 2–3 mm long, becoming slender from a conical base. Lateral sepals 7–11 mm long, projecting, elliptic. Petals 3–5 mm long, obovate, held inside the hood. Lip projecting, 4–5 mm long, linear.

HABITAT: Banks of perennial mountain streams in winter rainfall areas, usually as scattered plants rather than in colonies, in full sunlight, semishade, or even full shade, 600–1000 m (2000–3300 ft.).

CULTIVATION: As for *Disa uniflora.*

DISTRIBUTION: South Africa (Western Cape).

Disa cornuta (Linnaeus) Swartz

DESCRIPTION: A robust species, to 1 m (3 ft.) tall, but usually about 50 cm (20 in.). Stems leafy. Leaves overlapping, lanceolate or ovate. Inflorescences densely many-flowered; flowers purplish on the outside, greenish-white or yellow-green inside, the lip often purple. Dorsal sepal 12–18 mm long, forming a hood 8–12 mm deep, the entrance almost round, tapering into a cylindrical spur, horizontal at first, then decurved. Lateral sepals spreading, 12–16 mm long, oblong. Petals 8–10 mm long, curving over the anther inside the hood. Lip 5–10 mm long, linear to obovate.

HABITAT: *Disa cornuta* occurs in both summer and winter rainfall areas, and grows in a variety of habitats, from grassland to fynbos, but usually in well-drained areas in full sunlight, to 2500 m (8250 ft.).

CULTIVATION: Intermediate to cool temperatures and light shade, in a well-drained terrestrial compost. Water well while growing, then keep dry after flowering is finished and repot while dormant—it seems to be beneficial to repot every year. Start watering carefully when the new shoot appears.

DISTRIBUTION: Lesotho, South Africa (Eastern Cape, KwaZulu-Natal, Western Cape), Zimbabwe.

NOTE: This species belongs to the small section *Repandra* Lindley. It has been in cultivation at Kew off and on since the early nineteenth century—it is recorded in Aiton's *Hortus Kewensis* (1810–1813)—and may still be grown outside South Africa.

Disa crassicornis Lindley

DESCRIPTION: A robust species, to 1 m (3 ft.) tall, sometimes with a sterile shoot; stems with sheathing leaves. Leaves three to four, to 40 × 5 cm (16 × 2 in.), narrowly lanceolate, acute. Inflorescences 10–30 cm (4–12 in.) long, several to many-flowered. Flowers scented, large, 5 cm (2 in.) diameter, white or cream mottled with pink or purple. Dorsal sepal 20–40 × 15–30 mm, forming a hood 10–15 mm deep, tapering into a cylindrical spur 30–40 mm long, decurved, sometimes slightly swollen at the apex. Lateral sepals spreading, 20–30 × 10–20 mm, lanceolate or ovate, acute or rounded, with small apicules. Petals 20–30 × 10–15 mm, obliquely ovate, erect inside the hood. Lip projecting, then decurved, 20–25 × 4–15 mm.

HABITAT: Varied habitats including grassland, riverine forest, rock ledges, and swamp, 600–2700 m (2000–8900 ft.), usually 600–1000 m (2000–3300 ft.). It grows in summer rainfall areas, although usually in places where there will be at least some rain in winter, and at the higher altitudes, where snow and frost occur.

CULTIVATION: Reputed to be difficult. We have not grown this species, but it is most likely to be successful in a free-draining terrestrial mix, in intermediate to cool temperatures, with light shade. It should be kept almost dry in winter when the leaves have died back.

DISTRIBUTION: Lesotho, South Africa (Eastern Cape, KwaZulu-Natal).

NOTE: This striking species belongs to section *Hircicornes* Kränzlin, which contains 14 species in tropical and South Africa and Madagascar. It includes some outstandingly beautiful tropical African species, such as *Disa hircicornis, D. walleri,* and *D. robusta* (for photographs of these and other tropical *Disa* species see la Croix et al. 1991).

Disa marlothii H. Bolus

DESCRIPTION: Plants 15–35 cm (6–14 in.) tall. Stems leafy, the lowest 3 to 10 leaves in a cluster near the base, the remainder sheathing. Basal leaves to 5 cm (2 in.)

long, elliptic. Inflorescences 1- to 6-flowered, corymbose. Ovary 15–35 mm long; bracts much shorter, 10 mm long. Flowers purple-red, with darker speckling. Dorsal sepal forming a shallow hood, 10–14 × 8 mm; spur 15–20 mm long, very slender from a conical base, horizontal, but sometimes curved up at the apex. Lateral sepals spreading, 10–15 mm long, oblong, obtuse. Petals 8 mm long, erect, curving over and around the anther. Lip 8 mm long, narrowly elliptic.

HABITAT: Grows in rock crevices by streams. In one location it grows at altitudes of 1000–1300 m (3300–4300 ft.) in an area with 1000–1200 mm (40–50 in.) of winter rain per year and hot, dry summers. In another site it grows at 600 m (2000 ft.), with rainfall distributed round the year.

DISTRIBUTION: South Africa (Western Cape).

Disa racemosa Linnaeus f.

DESCRIPTION: A slender species, 30–100 cm (12–40 in.) tall. Leaves 3 to 10 at the base, narrowly lanceolate, to 10 cm (4 in.) long, with more leaves along the stem, gradually decreasing in size and grading into bracts. Inflorescences laxly 2- to 8-flowered, rarely with more. Flowers pink with darker veins. Dorsal sepal erect, 17–24 × 13–20 mm, forming a shallow hood 5–8 mm deep, with an almost obsolete spur. Lateral sepals spreading, 15–25 mm long, oblong or elliptic, apiculate. Petals 10–15 mm long, obliquely obovate, the apex curving over the anther. Lip projecting, 10 mm long, linear.

HABITAT: Swampy areas, often by streams, to 1500 m (5000 ft.). This species is quite widespread in the Western Cape, occurring both in the winter rainfall area and in areas of year-round rainfall. It flowers particularly well after a fire, perhaps because it gets more light after the dense surrounding vegetation has been burnt off. This is quite a common phenomenon, particularly in South African terrestrial orchids.

CULTIVATION: As for *Disa uniflora*.

DISTRIBUTION: South Africa (Eastern Cape, Western Cape).

Disa sagittalis (Linnaeus f.) Swartz

DESCRIPTION: Plants 7–30 cm (3–12 in.) tall; tubers unusually large, to 6 cm (2 in.) long. Basal leaves 5 to 10, to 9 cm (4 in.) long, narrowly elliptical; stem leaves sheathing, becoming dry by flowering time. Inflorescences 2–12 cm (1–5 in.) long, few to many-flowered. Flowers white or mauve, the petals usually darker. Dorsal sepal 6–13 × 8–20 mm, forming a shallow hood; spur 2–7 mm long, slender from a conical base, pendent. Lateral sepals projecting, 5–10 mm long, oblong, obtuse. Petals 7–12 mm long, narrowly lanceolate from a broad base, with a basal lobe 3–6 mm wide, papillose inside, beside the stigma. Lip projecting, 5–10 mm long, oblanceolate.

HABITAT: Usually grows on rocks or in rock crevices, often by streams and usually in semishade, to 1000 m (3300 ft.), both in areas of summer rainfall and year-round rainfall.

CULTIVATION: Very good drainage is essential. Keep dry when leaves die back after flowering. Intermediate temperatures and light shade.

DISTRIBUTION: South Africa (southern and eastern Cape and Natal Provinces).

NOTE: This species is in the section *Coryphaea* Lindley, which includes seven species.

Figure 10-47. *Disa saxicola.* Plant, ×1.

Disa saxicola Schlechter

PLATE 47, FIGURE 10-47

DESCRIPTION: A slender species, 10–40 cm (4–16 in.) tall. Leaves several, 7–20 × 0.5–1.5 cm (3–8 × 0.25–1 in.), linear-lanceolate, acute. Inflorescences 5–15 cm (2–6 in.) long, rather laxly several to many-flowered. Flowers white or pale pink, spotted with red-purple; spur red-purple. Dorsal sepal 5–8 × 3 mm, forming a deep hood, tapering into a slender spur 4–10 mm long, straight or slightly decurved. Lateral sepals spreading, 6 × 3 mm, oblong. Petals 4 × 2 mm, oblong, standing inside the hood. Lip projecting, 3–5 × 1 mm, linear-spathulate.

HABITAT: Among and on rocks (hence the name *saxicola,* which means "rock-dwelling") and in rock crevices on seepage slopes in montane grassland, 1000–2800 m

(3300–9200 ft.), sometimes in the open and sometimes in the shade of boulders or shrubs.

CULTIVATION: Intermediate temperatures and light shade. Free drainage and good ventilation are essential; keep dry in the resting season (that is, in winter), as it grows in areas with summer rainfall.

DISTRIBUTION: Malawi, Tanzania, South Africa (Mpumalanga, Northern Province), Swaziland, Zambia, Zimbabwe.

NOTE: This pretty little species belongs to section *Stenocarpa* Lindley, a section of about 15 species, most of which are confined to South Africa.

Disa tripetaloides (Linnaeus f.) N. E. Brown

DESCRIPTION: A slender, evergreen species, 10–60 cm (4–24 in.) tall, increasing vegetatively by stolons. Basal leaves 10–14 cm (4–6 in.) long, narrowly oblanceolate or elliptic, with smaller stem leaves. Inflorescences 15 cm (6 in.) long, laxly several to many-flowered. Flowers white to pink. Dorsal sepal erect, 5–12 mm long, forming a shallow hood 3–5 mm deep; spur to 3 mm long, conical or cylindrical, laterally flattened, horizontal or pendent. Lateral sepals spreading, 7–15 mm long, broadly obovate or elliptical. Petals 4–5 mm long, obliquely oblong, the apices curved over the anther. Lip 3–4 mm long, projecting, linear, the apex upcurved.

HABITAT: Wet areas on stream banks and mountain seepage slopes, to 1000 m (3300 ft.), usually in full sun, but sometimes under dense vegetation beside streams. *Disa tripetaloides* is unusual in occurring in areas of winter, summer, and year-round rainfall.

CULTIVATION: As for *Disa uniflora*.

DISTRIBUTION: South Africa (Eastern Cape, KwaZulu-Natal, Western Cape).

Disa uniflora Bergius
SYNONYM: *Disa grandiflora* Linnaeus f.

PLATES 48, 49

DESCRIPTION: Plants 15–60 cm (6–24 in.) tall; tuber renewed annually, but also reproducing vegetatively by stolons and so forming dense clumps. Leaves several, to 25 cm (10 in.) long, narrowly lanceolate, decreasing in size up the stem and grading into bracts. Inflorescences 1- to 3-flowered, rarely to 10-flowered. Several color forms are known, but the commonest is carmine-red, with pink occasional, and pure yellow very rare. Ovary 3–4 cm (1–2 in.) long, enclosed in the bracts, which are slightly longer. Dorsal sepal 20–60 × 15–20 mm, forming a fairly shallow hood; spur 10–15 mm long, conical but laterally flattened, pendent. Lateral sepals spreading, 35–65 mm long, ovate, acute, the apex sometimes reflexed. Petals 20–25 mm long, obovate, standing inside the hood. Lip 20–25 mm long, linear, projecting, with the apex reflexed.

HABITAT: Always associated with permanent but fast-flowing water; usually found growing along streams, or by waterfalls or on seepage rocks, growing both in deep sand by streams and in rock crevices, usually, although not always, in full sunlight.

CULTIVATION: *Disa uniflora* and its allies differ from most terrestrial orchids in never going completely dormant, so that plants should never be completely dried off.

In their native habitat, they grow throughout the rainy winter and flower in summer (January to March in South Africa). After flowering, growth slows down, but does not completely stop. Plants are intolerant of rich soil, need acid conditions with pH of 5–6, and require pure water of low conductivity (concentration of salts should not be more than 200 ppm). Some growers grow these species in a sterile medium, providing *weak* nutrients with every watering in spring and autumn. At one time, hydroculture was popular, with the plants in pots of coarse, sharp well-washed sand on top of gravel, and set in slowly moving water; this practice has now largely been discontinued, and plants are watered from above, although the inert medium is still used by many growers. *Disa uniflora* can also be grown in sphagnum moss, or in a mixture of sphagnum, fibrous peat, and chopped dead bracken. It seems necessary to experiment to find out which method (if any) suits the grower best. Cool to intermediate temperatures and relatively low humidity are necessary. The main difficulty with growing *Disa* species seems to be that they are very intolerant of conditions that are not exactly as they like—too hot, too dry, too rich, and so on—and unlike most orchids, which react to adverse conditions by looking unhealthy, and thus usually giving time to rescue them, *Disa* species react by dying without warning. If they can be grown successfully, the rewards are great. *Disa uniflora* and its hybrids are grown all over the world but are particularly popular in South Africa.

DISTRIBUTION: South Africa (Western Cape).

NOTE: This species has probably had more written about it than any other African orchid, and it seems likely that more is known about its biology. It is known to be pollinated by the butterfly *Meneris tulbaghia* (Vogelpoel 1994a).

Disa venosa Swartz

DESCRIPTION: Apparently rare and probably only flowering freely after a fire. A slender species, 30–50 cm (12–20 in.) tall. Basal leaves to 6 cm (2 in.) long, narrowly lanceolate, acute; stem leaves sheathing. Inflorescences to 15 cm (6 in.) long, laxly 2- to 6-flowered. Flowers pale pink with darker veins. Dorsal sepal erect, 12–18 mm long, narrowly obovate, forming a shallow hood; spur conical, laterally flattened, very short. Lateral sepals spreading, 12–23 mm long, narrowly oblong, obtuse, the apices somewhat reflexed. Petals 8 mm long, obliquely obovate, the apex curved over the anther. Lip 7 mm long, linear.

HABITAT: Swampy places, usually in hilly areas, to 1200 m (4000 ft.), but usually 600–1200 m (2000–4000 ft.).

CULTIVATION: As for *Disa uniflora*.

DISTRIBUTION: South Africa (Western Cape).

Disa woodii Schlechter

DESCRIPTION: A robust species, 15–70 cm (6–28 in.) tall. Leaves numerous, to 25, most clustered at the base of the stem, to 25 × 4 cm (10 × 2 in.), linear or narrowly lanceolate, acute, with the leaves becoming smaller and eventually bractlike farther up the stem. Rarely, sterile shoots with three to four leaves are present, in which case the stem leaves are all sheathlike. Inflorescences 3–17 cm (1–7 in.) long, densely many-flowered. Flowers small, less than 1 cm (0.5 in.) in diameter, bright yellow, sometimes tinged with orange at the tips. Dorsal sepal 5–7 × 3–4 mm, forming a shallow hood only 1 mm deep; spur 1–2 cm (0.5–1 in.) long, pendent, slightly swollen at the tip, arising just above the base of the dorsal sepal. Lateral sepals spreading, 6–7 × 3 mm, narrowly oblong. Petals 4–6 × 2–3 mm, narrowly obovate, curving over the anther. Lip 6 × 1 mm, linear.

HABITAT: Varied habitats, from grassland to swampy areas, and on roadsides where it seems to appreciate the disturbed conditions, to 1500 m (5000 ft.). Over most of its range, it receives summer rainfall, with about five dry winter months, but it extends into the area of the eastern Cape, which has rainfall year round.

CULTIVATION: Intermediate conditions and light shade in a standard, free-draining terrestrial mix, with high humidity and good ventilation during the growing season. It should be kept dry in winter, but not so dry that the tubers shrivel. It flowers in spring.

DISTRIBUTION: South Africa (Eastern Cape, KwaZulu-Natal, Mpumalanga, Northern Province), Zimbabwe.

NOTE: *Disa woodii* belongs to section *Micranthae* Lindley, which contains about 22 species, many of which occur in tropical Africa and, like section *Hircicornes,* also include some of the most beautiful of all *Disa* species. Again, sadly, these are not in cultivation. The smaller flowered species, such as *D. woodii* and the crimson *D. welwitschii,* make up for the lack of size of individual flowers by the brilliance of their colors and the density of the inflorescence. Others, such as *D. erubescens* and *D. ornithantha,* have fewer but larger flowers. These last two species grow mostly in montane bog, a notoriously difficult habitat to reproduce, but other species from drier areas, such as *D. engleriana* and *D. zombica,* should be possible to grow if they could be obtained.

Disperis Swartz

The genus *Disperis* was established by Olof Swartz in 1800. The name comes from the Greek words *dis* (two) and *pera* (wallet, pouch), referring to the saclike spurs on the lateral sepals of most species. There are about 80 species, most occurring in tropical and South Africa, with some in the Mascarene Islands, India, and New Guinea. Although not showy, they are appealing little plants and are attractive when several plants are grown together in a pan. Only a few seem to be in cultivation, although many others would be well worth growing, particularly those with attractive leaves.

DESCRIPTION: Slender, usually terrestrial, but a few epiphytic, arising from small, ovoid to round tubers. Leaves one to several (rarely absent), opposite or alternate, sometimes with attractive white or silvery veining. Inflorescences one- to several-flowered. Flowers white, yellow, green, pink, or magenta, fairly small. Dorsal sepal joined to the petals to form a hood, either flat and open, or deep and spurred. Lateral sepals spreading or deflexed, usually each with a saclike spur. Lip very complex, with a claw joined to the face of the column, and a strangely shaped appendage attached to it above that. Pollinia two, granular, arranged in a double row along the edge of a flattened caudicle; viscidia two.

CULTIVATION: All species of *Disperis* are deciduous, dying back below ground during the resting season—usually the winter, except for species from the winter rainfall area of South Africa. They like a free-draining but humus-rich terrestrial mix in a shallow pan as their root system is not extensive. Intermediate temperatures suit most species. The tropical African species are almost all forest or woodland plants, growing in heavy shade, but some of the South African species grow in open grassland. Humidity should be high during the growing season, and an occasional watering should be given even in the resting season, as the small tubers can easily dry out too much and shrivel.

Disperis capensis (Linnaeus f.) Swartz

DESCRIPTION: A slender species, 15–40 cm (6–16 in.) tall. Leaves two, alternate, to 9 × 1 cm (4 × 0.5 in.), narrowly lanceolate. Inflorescences 1- to 2-flowered. Flowers green-purple with magenta-purple petals, or green with yellow-green petals. Dorsal sepal to 30 mm long, with a long acumen, forming a hood with the petals. Lateral sepals somewhat reflexed, 12–35 mm long, narrowly lanceolate, long acuminate, each with a saclike spur 2–3 mm long in the basal half. Lip narrowly spathulate, hidden inside the hood.

HABITAT: Terrestrial in fynbos and in restio-veld, to 1000 m (3300 ft.).

CULTIVATION: As for the genus, but in light shade. This species comes from the winter rainfall area and thus needs a dry rest in summer.

DISTRIBUTION: South Africa (Western Cape).

NOTE: Two varieties have been described: var. *capensis,* with acumen of the dorsal sepal as long as the hood, and var. *brevicaudata* Rolfe, with acumen of the dorsal sepal much shorter than the hood.

Disperis fanniniae Harvey   PLATE 50
COMMON NAME: Granny's Bonnet

DESCRIPTION: A slender, terrestrial species, 15–45 cm (6–18 in.) tall. Leaves three, alternate, 2–8 × 1–3 cm (1–3 × 0.5–1 in.), lanceolate or ovate, clasping the stem at the base, dark, glossy green above, purple below. Inflorescences several-flowered. Flowers white, tinged with green or pink. Pedicel and ovary 13–18 mm long; bracts leafy. Dorsal sepal 12–20 mm long, forming a deep, blunt hood with the petals. Lateral sepals deflexed, 12–14 mm long, lanceolate, acuminate, with a saclike spur about halfway along. Lip 15 mm long, linear, folded back over the column and hidden in the hood.

HABITAT: In deep shade in leaf litter on forest floor, and in pine plantations, 1200–2000 m (4000–6600 ft.).

CULTIVATION: *Disperis fanniniae* comes from the summer rainfall area and has a winter rest.

DISTRIBUTION: Lesotho, South Africa (Eastern Cape, KwaZulu-Natal, Mpumalanga), Swaziland.

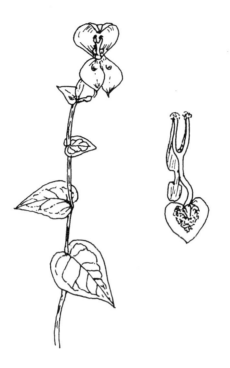

Figure 10-48. *Disperis johnstonii.* Plant (left), ×1; lip (right), ×6.

Disperis johnstonii Rolfe
FIGURE 10-48

DESCRIPTION: A small, slender species, 4–15 cm (2–6 in.) tall. Leaves two to three, alternate, 2–3 × 1.5–2 cm (1 in. long and wide), ovate, acute, clasping the stem at the base, dark green with white veins above, purple below. Inflorescences 1- to 5-flowered. Hood bright yellow, sometimes light mauve-purple; lateral sepals white or very pale mauve. Pedicel and ovary 10–12 mm long; bracts leafy. Dorsal sepal 8–11 × 1 mm, joined to the petals to form a shallow, open hood 9–10 mm deep. Lateral sepals 10–12 × 5–7 mm, almost semicircular, projecting forwards, joined to each other at the base for about a third of their length, each with a small, saclike spur 1 mm long. Lip 4–6 mm long, with a bilobed, papillose appendage, bent back to lie inside the hood.

HABITAT: In leaf litter in woodland or forest, often beside rocks, from near sea level in South Africa to 1350 m (4450 ft.), but usually over 1000 m (3300 ft.).

DISTRIBUTION: Cameroon, Malawi, Nigeria, South Africa (KwaZulu-Natal), Tanzania, Zambia, Zimbabwe.

Eggelingia Summerhayes

The genus *Eggelingia* was established by V. S. Summerhayes in 1951 and named in honor of J. Eggeling, a forestry officer who collected the type species of the genus in Uganda. Species of *Eggelingia* are quite closely related to *Tridactyle.* They are among the least showy of the African epiphytes, but we have seen one species advertised for sale and thus it is included here. Three species are known from tropical Africa.

DESCRIPTION: Slender, monopodial epiphytes with long, leafy stems. Leaves distichous, linear to strap-shaped, with a hairlike ligule at the apex of the leaf sheath, opposite a leaf. Inflorescences axillary, short, few-flowered. Flowers small, white. Sepals and petals similar. Lip entire or very obscurely trilobed. Column short; rostellum deeply bifid; pollinia two, stipes one, sometimes Y-shaped; viscidium one, large.

Eggelingia ligulifolia Summerhayes

DESCRIPTION: Stems to 45 cm (18 in.) long, pendent, occasionally branched, leafy towards the apex. Leaves 2–7 × 0.5–1 cm (1–3 × 0.25–0.5 in.), narrowly oblong-lanceolate, unequally and obtusely bilobed at the apex, twisted at the base to lie in one plane, jointed to a 6- to 8-mm-long sheath at the base, with a hairlike ligule 4–5 mm long at the apex of the sheath. Inflorescences 4–6 mm long, 2- to 3-flowered. Flowers white. Pedicel and ovary 5 mm long, slightly scurfy; bracts 1 mm long. Sepals 5–7 × 2–2.5 mm, lanceolate, acute. Petals 4.5–6 × 2 mm, oblong, obtuse. Lip 4.5–6 × 1.5–3.5 mm, entire, concave, oblong-ovate, acute; spur 4–5 mm long, straight, slender. Column 1–1.5 mm long.

HABITAT: Epiphytic in evergreen forest, rarely lithophytic on lava flows, 1300–2350 m (4300–7750 ft.).

CULTIVATION: We have not grown this species, but from its habit and habitat, it should grow better mounted, at intermediate temperatures, in moderate to heavy shade.

DISTRIBUTION: Rwanda, Uganda, Zaire.

NOTE: *Eggelingia clavata* Summerhayes, from West Africa and Malawi, is similar but with flowers little more than half the size, and with a bulbous spur only 2 mm long.

Eulophia R. Brown ex Lindley
SYNONYM: *Lissochilus* R. Brown

The genus *Eulophia* was established by John Lindley in 1823, but the name had to be conserved against a genus of alga by the same name that was described in the previous year. The name derives from the Greek words *eu* (well) and *lophos* (plume), referring to the crests on the lip of many species. *Lissochilus* was used for those species with sepals differing from the petals, usually being smaller and green, but as more species became known, it was evident that so many were intermediate that the two genera could not be kept separate. *Eulophia* is a large genus containing more than 250 species throughout the tropics, with most in Africa. Only a few are in cultivation, although many more would be well worth growing.

DESCRIPTION: Terrestrial, with fleshy roots, pseudobulbs, or underground tubers. Leaves, if present, lanceolate or linear, sometimes pleated, sometimes fleshy. There are a few saprophytic species with only scale leaves, where the whole plant is pale yellow or purplish, but none of these is in cultivation. Inflorescence appears with or before the leaves, arising beside them, few- to many-flowered, usually but not always unbranched. Flowers small or large, often very showy, in almost every color except blue. Sepals and petals different or similar. Lip spurred or at least saccate, usually trilobed but sometimes entire, usually with crests or papillae inside. Column long or short, often somewhat winged, with a short column foot; anther terminal, with an anther cap; pollinia two.

CULTIVATION: Many species are not too difficult, providing plants are allowed to follow their own rhythm and are kept dry while resting. Those with pseudobulbs partly above ground, such as *Eulophia guineensis* and *E. streptopetala,* tend to be the easiest— it always seems to help when at least something is visible in the resting season! Most species are suited by a well-drained mixture of fine bark, loam, perlag, and sand, good light, and intermediate temperatures.

Eulophia alta (Linnaeus) Fawcett & Rendle

DESCRIPTION: A robust species, 1–2 m (3–6 ft.) tall, with a long, fleshy underground rhizome 1 cm (0.5 in.) in diameter. Leaves four to six, to 120 × 5–10 cm (48 × 2–4 in.), lanceolate, plicate, with a long petiole. Inflorescences many-flowered; flowers with olive green sepals and purple-red petals and lip. Pedicel and ovary 15–25 mm long; bracts reflexed, to 30 mm long or more. Sepals 18–22 × 4–6 mm, oblong or oblanceolate. Petals 15–20 × 3–5 mm, oblong. Lip 14–20 × 8–12 mm, with a callus of two ridges in the middle, saccate at the base, trilobed in the apical half; midlobe 5–6 × 8 mm, almost orbicular, the edges undulate with papillae on the five central veins; side lobes rounded. Column 7–10 mm long.

HABITAT: In swamps and wet grassland, 1150–1300 m (3800–4300 ft.).

DISTRIBUTION: Angola, Cameroon, Central African Republic, Ethiopia, Gabon, Ghana, Guinea, Ivory Coast, Liberia, Nigeria, Sierra Leone, Sudan, Uganda, Zaire, Zambia, Zimbabwe. Also in tropical America, Florida, and the West Indies. This and *Eulophia pulchra* must be the two most widely distributed species of *Eulophia.*

Eulophia calanthoides Schlechter

DESCRIPTION: Plants 30–75 cm (12–30 in.) tall, usually rather slender, arising from a chain of tubers. Leaves fully developed at flowering time, to 70 × 6 cm (28 × 2 in.). Inflorescences 7- to 25-flowered, dense at first but becoming lax and elongated as more flowers open. Sepals brownish-purple outside, brownish-green inside; petals and lip pale yellow speckled with tiny blue dots. Sepals spreading, 20–33 mm long, narrowly lanceolate, acute or acuminate. Petals of similar length, but wider. Lip obscurely trilobed, with low, pubescent ridges in the basal third, and a sac 3 mm deep below the column apex. Spur 4–5 mm long, narrowly cylindrical. Column 4–5 mm long.

HABITAT: In bush and tall grass near the forest edge, to 3000 m (9900 ft.); in areas with a fairly high rainfall, usually 1000–1500 mm (40–60 in.) a year, with some frost in winter.

DISTRIBUTION: South Africa (Eastern Cape, KwaZulu-Natal).

Eulophia cristata (Swartz) Steudel

DESCRIPTION: A terrestrial herb, 60–150 cm (24–60 in.) tall, arising from an underground chain of potato-like tubers. Leaves four to six, 40–70 × 1–4 cm (16–28 × 0.5–2 in.), lanceolate, plicate, petiolate. Inflorescences appearing before the leaves, 10- to 30-flowered. Flowers lilac-pink, the lip purple. Pedicel and ovary 15–25 mm long; bracts 10–30 mm long, acuminate with a hairlike tip. Sepals 14–24 × 3–6 mm, oblanceolate or elliptic, the laterals slightly larger than the dorsal. Petals 12–20 × 6–10 mm, elliptic, obtuse. Lip 12–22 × 10–14 mm, with a callus of two rounded ridges at the base, trilobed, the side lobes erect and recurved, the midlobe deflexed, elliptic, with five to nine ridges and the edges crisped. Spur 2.5–5 mm long, conical, upcurved.

HABITAT: Grassland, scrub and woodland, 1100–1700 m (3300–5600 ft.).

DISTRIBUTION: Benin, Ethiopia, Gambia, Ghana, Ivory Coast, Nigeria, Senegal, Sierra Leone, Sudan, Togo, Uganda, Zaire.

Eulophia cucullata (Swartz) Steudel   PLATE 51

DESCRIPTION: A robust species, to 1 m (3 ft.) tall, arising from an underground chain of whitish, knobby tubers. Leaves three to four, just starting to develop at flowering time, eventually 20–70 × 0.5–1.5 cm (8–28 × 0.25–1 in.), linear, plicate, acuminate. Inflorescences rather laxly 2- to 9-flowered. Flowers showy, varying in color from pale pink, almost white, to rich purple, the lip white and yellow in the throat and spotted with purple. Sepals green, tinged with purple. Pedicel and ovary purple, 20–25 mm long; bracts purplish, acuminate, 25–35 mm long. Sepals reflexed, 25–30 × 10–12 mm, ovate, acuminate. Petals 20–25 × 15–25 mm, ovate to orbicular, lying over the column. Lip 30 × 40 mm, with two projections 6 mm long in the throat, obscurely trilobed, the midlobe transversely oblong, slightly emarginate. Spur broadly saccate, 10 mm long. Column 13–15 mm long. Rarely, plants are found with flowers only about half the size of those described, but otherwise the same.

HABITAT: Woodland, scrub, rough grassland, drier parts of marshes, 200–2300 m (660–7600 ft.). This is one of the most common and attractive African orchids, particularly in the deeper colored forms. We have seen bunches of the flowers on sale in cities all over Africa—Brazzaville, Nairobi, Mombasa, and Blantyre—which would all have been picked in the wild. It is a pity that this species could not be cultivated for the cut flower trade.

DISTRIBUTION: Throughout tropical Africa, from Senegal to Ethiopia, and south to South Africa (KwaZulu-Natal). Also in Madagascar.

Eulophia euglossa (Reichenbach f.) Reichenbach f.

DESCRIPTION: Plants 60–150 cm (24–60 in.) tall. Pseudobulbs 16–25 × 1–1.5 cm (6–10 in. × 0.5–1 in.), narrowly conical, mostly above ground, with 5 to 10 nodes. Leaves 5 to 10, 16–40 × 2–6 cm (6–16 × 1–2 in.), ovate or lanceolate, acuminate, plicate, petiolate. Inflorescences laxly many-flowered. Flowers rather nodding, greenish, the lip white with pink or purple marks. Pedicel and ovary 20 mm long; bracts spreading, 15–35 mm long. Sepals and petals all lanceolate, acuminate; sepals 18–24 × 3 mm, petals 15–18 × 3 mm. Lip 13–14 × 7–9 mm, trilobed; side lobes small, triangular; midlobe 8 × 6.5 mm, elliptic, the edges undulate, with two to three low ridges. Spur 5–7 mm long, slightly decurved, club-shaped. Column 5 mm long.

HABITAT: Dense forest on sandy loam, riverine forest, 1200–1300 m (4000–4300 ft.).

CULTIVATION: From the habitat and altitude, it seems this species would appreciate intermediate conditions and more shade than most species of *Eulophia*.

DISTRIBUTION: Cameroon, Ethiopia, Gabon, Ghana, Ivory Coast, Liberia, Nigeria, Sierra Leone, Togo, Uganda, Zaire.

Eulophia gracilis Lindley

DESCRIPTION: Plants to 120 cm (48 in.) tall, with pseudobulbs at the base. Leaves to six, with long petioles, 20–45 × 1–5 cm (8–18 × 0.5–2 in.), narrowly elliptic, acute. Inflorescences laxly 20-flowered. Flowers greenish, yellowish or mauve with a white lip. Pedicel and ovary 12–18 mm long; bracts slightly shorter. Sepals and petals 8–12 × 2–5 mm, lanceolate, acute. Lip 7–8 × 5–6 mm, obovate, truncate, fringed, with a toothlike callus near the tip; spur 4–8 mm long, slender but swollen at the apex. Column 4–6 mm long.

HABITAT: Riverine forest, in heavy shade. Altitude not known.

DISTRIBUTION: Cameroon, Ivory Coast, Gabon, Liberia, Zaire.

Eulophia guineensis Lindley   PLATE 52

SYNONYMS: *Eulophia guineensis* var. *purpurata* Kotschy, *Eulophia quartiniana* A. Richard

DESCRIPTION: One of the most attractive species of *Eulophia*, without the very long inflorescence of many of the other showy species. Plants 30–65 cm (12–26 in.) tall. Pseudobulbs conical, above ground, 3 × 2 cm (1 in. long and wide), forming clumps or chains. Leaves three to four, 10–35 × 3–10 cm (4–14 × 1–4 in.), ovate or elliptic, acute, pleated, with a short petiole. Inflorescences rather laxly to 12-flowered. Flowers large and showy; sepals and petals purple or green tinged with purple; lip purple-pink, sometimes paler at the base and sometimes with a magenta blotch. Pedicel and ovary 20 mm long, arched, purple. Bracts 10–30 mm long, rather papery. Sepals and petals lanceolate-linear, acuminate, erect with the tips reflexed, 15–30 × 4–7 mm, the petals very slightly shorter and broader. Lip 20–35 × 13–32 mm, trilobed near the base; side lobes erect, obtuse; midlobe 20–26 mm long and wide, orbicular or obovate, with a frilly edge. Spur 10–25 mm long, straight, tapering from a conical mouth. Column 5–7 mm long, anther cap winged.

HABITAT: In scrub and woodland, on poor rocky soil, in shade or semi-shade of rocks, or in dense forest, 600–2000 m (2000–6600 ft.).

DISTRIBUTION: Angola, Cameroon, Central African Republic, Ethiopia, Gambia, Ghana, Guinea, Ivory Coast, Kenya, Malawi, Mali, Nigeria, Sierra Leone, Sudan, Tanzania, Togo, Uganda, Zaire.

NOTE: This species was once divided into two varieties, var. *guineensis,* which flowers with the leaves and is more or less evergreen, and var. *purpurata,* which is definitely deciduous and flowers as the leaves are just starting to develop. This division, however, is not now usually recognized.

Eulophia horsfallii (Bateman) Summerhayes　　　　　　　　PLATE 53

SYNONYMS: *Eulophia porphyroglossa* (Reichenbach f.) Bolus, *Eulophia sandersonii* (Reichenbach f.) A. D. Hawkes, *Lissochilus sandersonii* Reichenbach f.

DESCRIPTION: A robust species, 1–3 m (3–9 ft.) tall. Pseudobulbs ovoid, mostly underground; roots thick, fleshy. Leaves evergreen, 30–250 cm (12–80 in.) long, including the petiole, 2–15 cm (1–6 in.) wide, lanceolate or oblanceolate, ribbed, dark green. Scape stout, to 3.5 cm (1 in.) in diameter. Inflorescences laxly or fairly densely many-flowered. Sepals shiny olive-green, purplish at the base; petals pink; midlobe of lip purple with cream ridges, side lobes green with purple veins. Pedicel and ovary 4 cm (2 in.) long; bracts 2 cm (1 in.) long, brown and papery by flowering time. Sepals 25 × 10 mm, erect, oblanceolate, acute. Petals 30 × 22 mm, ovate, lying over the column. Lip 45 mm long, trilobed, with a callus of three fringed ridges in the basal two-thirds; side lobes erect, rounded; midlobe 20 × 13 mm, oblong, obtuse; spur conical, 4–10 mm long. Column 10 mm long, arched; anther cap purple, shaped like a butterfly.

HABITAT: Riverine forest, usually near the edge, in swampy ground, usually but not always in heavy shade, to 2500 m (8250 ft.).

DISTRIBUTION: Angola, Benin, Burundi, Cameroon, Equatorial Guinea (Bioko), Gabon, Ghana, Guinea-Bissau, Ivory Coast, Kenya, Liberia, Malawi, Nigeria, Rwanda, Senegal, South Africa (KwaZulu-Natal, Mpumalanga), Swaziland, Tanzania, Togo, Uganda, Zambia, Zaire.

Eulophia leachii Greatrex ex A. V. Hall

DESCRIPTION: A slender species, 45–60 cm (18–24 in.) tall. Pseudobulbs 7–14 cm (3–6 in.) long, 1.5–2 cm (1 in.) in diameter near the base, cylindrical to conical, mostly above ground. Leaves several, 20–30 × 1–1.5 cm (8–12 × 0.5–1 in.), leathery, the margins rough. Inflorescences few to many-flowered. Flowers yellow-green with purple veining, with crests on the lip made up of thick white hairs. Sepals and petals 14–22 mm long, oblong to lanceolate, the petals slightly broader than the sepals. Lip with rounded side lobes gradually tapering into an elliptic midlobe, the margins wavy.

Spur 3–5 mm long, conical, tapering. Column 9–11 mm long, with a purple papilla 1 mm long on either side of the apex.

HABITAT: Among bushes under trees in hot, dry areas with a rainfall of only 375–750 mm (15–30 in.) per year. It tends to form large colonies where it occurs.

CULTIVATION: Intermediate to warm temperatures; moderate shade. Keep reasonably dry in winter. *Eulophia leachii* is summer-flowering. The potting compost should be sandy and free-draining. It is a good idea to use clay, rather than plastic, pots.

DISTRIBUTION: South Africa (KwaZulu-Natal, Northern Province), Zimbabwe.

NOTE: When in flower, this species is easily identifiable by the papillae near the apex of the column. When not flowering, it resembles the more widespread *Eulophia petersii*, but *E. leachii* has more leaves, which are not quite so stiff and rigid as those of *E. petersii*.

Eulophia petersii Reichenbach f.

DESCRIPTION: A robust species, 1–3 m (3–10 ft.) tall. Pseudobulbs mostly above ground, varying in shape from ovoid to cylindrical, 6–30 × 2–5 cm (2–12 × 1–2 in.), with four to six nodes, yellowish, ribbed. Leaves two to three, 14–80 × 1.5–6 cm (6–32 × 1–2 in.), linear to elliptic, stiffly succulent, gray-green, with a finely but sharply serrated margin. Inflorescences branched, rather laxly many-flowered. Flowers green tinged with purple-brown, the lip white with purple crests. Pedicel and ovary 2–4 cm (1–2 in.) long. Sepals 30 × 6 mm, narrowly lanceolate, acute, erect, curling back at the tips. Petals 22 × 8 mm, lying over the column, lanceolate, obtuse, the apex recurved. Lip 15–27 mm long, trilobed, with three longitudinal ridges turning to papillae near the apex; side lobes erect, rounded, 14–17 mm wide when flattened; midlobe orbicular, 12–14 mm wide; spur 4–6 mm long, cylindrical. Column 8–9 mm long.

HABITAT: In sandy soil in thickets, usually among rocks, in hot, dry areas often near a river, to 1800 m (6000 ft.), usually forming large colonies where it occurs. *Eulophia petersii* often grows with species of *Sanseveria* and other succulents; in fact, the leaves, at first glance, look more like those of an aloe than an orchid.

CULTIVATION: Intermediate to warm temperatures; light to moderate shade. In the wild it usually grows in thickets, where the shade might be fairly dense, but this is in areas much hotter than the average greenhouse. The compost should be sandy and free-draining; it is a good idea to use clay, rather than plastic, pots. Plants should be kept almost dry while not in growth.

DISTRIBUTION: Burundi, Ethiopia, Kenya, Malawi, Mozambique, Somalia, South Africa (KwaZulu-Natal, Mpumalanga, Northern Province), Sudan, Swaziland, Tanzania, Uganda, Zaire, Zambia, Zimbabwe. Also in Arabia.

Eulophia pulchra (Thouars) Lindley

SYNONYMS: *Eulophidium pulchrum* (Thouars) Summerhayes, *Oeceoclades pulchra* (Thouars) Clements & Cribb

DESCRIPTION: Pseudobulbs 10–14 × 1 cm (4–6 × 0.5 in.), cylindrical. Leaves two to four, 30–80 × 1–9 cm (12–32 × 0.5–4 in.), long-petiolate, lanceolate, acute, pleated.

Inflorescences 60–70 cm (24–28 in.) tall, densely many-flowered. Flowers yellow or pale green with an orange callus, the side lobes of the lip tinged with purple. Pedicel and ovary to 20 mm long; bracts 10–25 mm long, linear, acuminate. Sepals 12–15 × 3 mm; petals 11–13 × 5–6 mm, oblong. Lip 7 × 15 mm, trilobed, with a fleshy, bilobed callus at the mouth of the spur; side lobes large, rounded; midlobe transversely oblong, emarginate, recurved, narrowly elliptic, apiculate. Spur 3–4 mm long, globose. Column 5 mm long.

HABITAT: In riverine and submontane forest, in deep shade, 700–1400 m (2300–4600 ft.).

DISTRIBUTION: Mozambique, Tanzania, Zimbabwe. Also in Australia, Madagascar, Pacific Islands.

NOTE: There is some confusion whether this species belongs to *Eulophia* or *Oeceoclades*. The emarginate lip appears 4-lobed when flattened, which agrees with the latter, but the pleated leaves are typical of species of *Eulophia* such as *E. streptopetala,* and it seems to us to fit better in that genus.

Eulophia speciosa (Lindley) Bolus   PLATE 54

SYNONYMS: *Eulophia brevisepala* (Rendle) Summerhayes, *Eulophia wakefieldii* (Reichenbach f. & S. Moore) Summerhayes

DESCRIPTION: A robust species, 1–1.5 m (3–5 ft.) tall, arising from an underground chain of tubers. Leaves to 50 × 2 cm (20 × 1 in.), fleshy, stiff, narrowly lanceolate, absent at flowering time. Inflorescences laxly many-flowered; flowers bright yellow, the sepals green, the lip usually with faint red lines radiating from the mouth of the spur. Pedicel and ovary 20–25 mm long; bracts 10 mm long. Sepals 7–10 × 3–5 mm, reflexed, elliptic, apiculate. Petals 16–20 × 16–22 mm, spreading, suborbicular. Lip to 25 mm long, trilobed, difficult to flatten; side lobes erect, midlobe 12–17 mm wide, convex, elliptic, with three to five fleshy ridges. Spur conical, 3–8 mm long. Column short and stout, 4–6 mm long.

HABITAT: Very varied, but mainly grassland, bush and woodland, often persisting even in gum plantations, to 2000 m (6600 ft.).

DISTRIBUTION: Angola, Botswana, Burundi, Ethiopia, Kenya, Malawi, Mozambique, South Africa (Eastern Cape, KwaZulu-Natal, Mpumalanga, Northern Province), Sudan, Swaziland, Tanzania, Uganda, Zaire, Zambia, Zimbabwe. Also in Arabia.

NOTE: As in *Eulophia cucullata,* the occasional plant of *E. speciosa* occurs with flowers very much smaller than usual. Again, like *E. cucullata, E. speciosa* is one of the most common African terrestrial orchids and one of the most brightly colored, a cheerful sight at the beginning of the rains.

Eulophia streptopetala Lindley

SYNONYMS: *Eulophia krebsii* (Reichenbach f.) Bolus, *Eulophia paiveana* (Reichenbach f.) Summerhayes

DESCRIPTION: A robust species, to 1.5 m (5 ft.) tall. Pseudobulbs conical to ovoid, to 10 × 3 cm (4 × 1 in.), above ground.. Leaves four to nine, fairly well developed at flowering time, to 50 × 8 cm (20 × 3 in.), lanceolate, pleated. Inflorescences laxly many-flowered. Sepals greenish, blotched with purple-brown; petals bright yellow outside, creamy-yellow inside; lip yellow, the side lobes and spur purple-red. Pedicel and ovary 20 mm long, arched, so that the flowers face down; bracts 10 mm long. Sepals 16–18 × 8–9 mm, oblanceolate, spreading or slightly reflexed. Petals 17–18 × 17–20 mm, horizontal, suborbicular. Lip 12–20 mm long, difficult to flatten, trilobed, the side lobes erect, the midlobe projecting, 12 × 12 mm, with the sides deflexed, and with a callus of three to five fleshy ridges. Spur 2–4 mm long, conical, tapering, pointing backwards. Column 5–8 mm long.

HABITAT: Varied, including woodland, gum plantations, long grass at the edge of thicket, rocks in montane grassland, and occasionally forest, 1100–2550 m (3600–8400 ft.).

CULTIVATION: This is one of the easiest species of *Eulophia* to grow successfully— the varied habitat reflects its adaptability. It needs a free-draining compost and, if dried off after flowering when the leaves have died back, should flower regularly in spring (April). Intermediate temperatures and light shade seem to suit it.

DISTRIBUTION: Angola, Burundi, Ethiopia, Kenya, Malawi, Mozambique, Rwanda, South Africa (Eastern Cape, KwaZulu-Natal, Mpumalanga, Northern Province, North West Province), Sudan, Swaziland, Tanzania, Uganda, Zaire, Zambia, Zimbabwe.

Eulophia taitensis Cribb & Pfennig

DESCRIPTION: Plants 60–110 cm (24–44 in.) tall. Pseudobulbs 7–22 × 1.5–3 cm (3–9 × 1 in.), mostly above ground, cylindrical, narrowly conical or spindle-shaped. Leaves 6 to 14, 10–50 × 1.5–3 cm (4–20 × 1 in.), fleshy, linear, the edges finely serrate. Inflorescences laxly 5- to 15-flowered. Sepals and petals yellow-green, flushed with purple-brown at the tips; lip white with a yellow callus and veined with red. Pedicel and ovary 15–25 mm long; bracts 10 mm long. Sepals to 25 × 6–8 mm, spreading, lanceolate or oblanceolate, acute or apiculate, the laterals slightly shorter than the dorsal; petals 20 × 8 mm, oblong. Lip 18–20 × 15–17 mm, obscurely trilobed, with a callus of three warty ridges; side lobes erect, midlobe subquadrate, the edges undulate; spur 3 mm long. Column 11 mm long.

HABITAT: In thickets on sandy soil, in coastal bush or woodland, to 1300 m (4300 ft.).

CULTIVATION: Intermediate to warm temperatures; light to moderate shade. In the wild it usually grows in thicket, where the shade might be fairly dense, but this is in areas much hotter than the average greenhouse. The compost should be sandy and free

226

Figure 10-49. *Eulophia streptopetala*. Plant, ×0.75.

draining; it is a good idea to use clay, rather than plastic, pots. Plants should be kept almost dry while not in growth.

DISTRIBUTION: Kenya, Tanzania, Uganda.

Eulophia zeyheri Hooker f. PLATE 56

DESCRIPTION: A robust species, 30–50 cm (12–20 in.) tall, arising from a chain of rather flattened, knobby tubers. Leaves two to three, to 60 × 5 cm (24 × 2 in.), lanceolate, acute, ribbed, only just starting to develop at flowering time. Inflorescences very densely many-flowered. Flowers primrose-yellow, the lip with a central orange blotch and large purple marks on the side lobes. Pedicel and ovary 10 mm long; bracts 15–20 mm long, lanceolate, acuminate. Sepals and petals all projecting forwards so that the flowers do not open wide, all elliptic, acuminate, 28–40 × 10–16 mm, the lateral sepals slightly longer than the dorsal sepal and petals. Lip trilobed, to 30 mm long with a callus of two ridges running from the base to the junction of the lobes; side lobes erect, obtuse, 22 mm across when flattened; midlobe 15 mm wide, ovate to orbicular, obtuse, with some papillae on the orange area. Spur 4–5 mm long, cylindrical. Column stout, 6–7 mm long.

HABITAT: Grassland, often with scattered shrubs, 1000–2135 m (3300–7000 ft.).

DISTRIBUTION: Angola, Kenya, Malawi, Mozambique, Nigeria, Rwanda, South Africa, Sudan, Tanzania, Uganda, Zaire, Zambia, Zimbabwe.

NOTE: If this species is not in cultivation outside Africa, it certainly deserves to be, as its compact habit and dense head make it one of the most attractive species. In South Africa, it is usually known as *Eulophia welwitschii* (Reichenbach f.) Rolfe, but it is not yet certain that the two names are synonymous. If they are, *E. welwitschii* will be the correct name.

Eurychone Schlechter

The genus *Eurychone,* with only two members, was separated from *Angraecum* by Rudolf Schlechter in 1918. The name is derived from the Greek words *eurys* (broad) and *stylis* (style), referring to the broad column. This seems to be a strange feature to pick out for distinguishing these plants, but the name is euphonious. Both species, among the most beautiful of African orchids, are much sought after by growers and have been used in hybridization (see Chapter 9).

DESCRIPTION: Short-stemmed plants with pendent inflorescences and large, showy, rather thin-textured flowers. Sepals and petals similar. Lip large, funnel-shaped, tapering gradually into a broad spur. Pollinia two, stipes one, viscidium one.

Eurychone galeandrae (Reichenbach f.) Schlechter FIGURE 10-50

DESCRIPTION: Stems short; roots 3–3.5 mm in diameter. Leaves several, 6–20 × 1–2 cm (2–8 × 0.5–1 in.), ligulate or narrowly elliptical or oblanceolate, unequally and

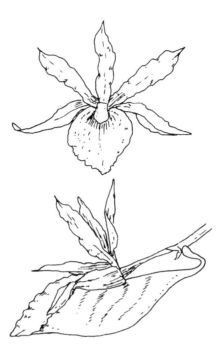

Figure 10-50. *Eurychone galeandrae.* Flower, ×1.

obtusely bilobed at the apex, thick-textured, dull olive green. Inflorescences pendent, 8–15 cm (3–6 in.) long, occasionally more, 3- to 12-flowered. Flowers rich salmon-pink with darker veins on the spur. Pedicel and ovary 12 mm long; bracts 3 mm long. Sepals and petals spreading, all lanceolate, acute, 15–18 × 4–5 mm, sepals slightly keeled on outside, the laterals slightly longer than the dorsal sepal and the petals. Lip 15–25 mm long, funnel-shaped, the margins erose and undulate, tapering into a broad spur 25 mm long, the last 10 mm or so much narrower, the apical 5 mm doubled back and inflated again at the tip. Column 6 mm long.

HABITAT: Forest and woodland.

CULTIVATION: This beautiful species needs intermediate to warm temperatures. It grows well in a pot, but is better mounted because of the pendent inflorescence with a short peduncle; the first flower is borne close to the base of the plant and thus tends to lie on the compost. It needs humid conditions and should not be allowed to dry out for long. It needs careful watching since pests of all kinds home in on it. We have had problems with aphids on the new growth, and buds just about to open were all eaten by a slug. The species is not common in cultivation.

DISTRIBUTION: Angola, Central African Republic, Gabon, Ivory Coast, Zaire.

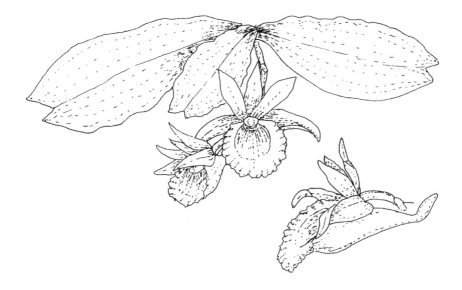

Figure 10-51. *Eurychone rothschildiana*. Plant (left) and flower (lower right), ×0.75.

Eurychone rothschildiana (O'Brien) Schlechter   PLATE 57, FIGURE 10-51

DESCRIPTION: Stems short; roots 3–4 mm in diameter. Leaves three to eight, 6–20 × 1.5–7 cm (2–6 × 1–3 in.), broadly ovate-elliptic or oblanceolate, unequally bilobed at the apex, leathery, dark green, the margins undulate. Non-flowering plants look very much like *Aerangis kotschyana*. Inflorescences pendent, 3–9 cm (1–4 in.) long, usually 2- to 6-flowered, rarely to 12-flowered. Flowers scented, sepals and petals white; lip white with a green and a purple-brown blotch. Sepals 20–25 × 6–7 mm, oblong-elliptic, acute, the laterals slightly longer than the dorsal; petals slightly shorter and broader. Lip 20–27 × 20-25 mm, very concave, the edge undulate and erose, tapering into a conical spur 20–25 mm long, constricted in the middle, then the apical part swollen again and bent downwards.

HABITAT: Evergreen forest, in shade, 1100–1200 m (3600–4000 ft.).

CULTIVATION: As for *Eurychone galeandrae*. This species may be habitually short-lived; we have had an apparently healthy mature plant die without warning and have heard other people say that plants have died suddenly.

DISTRIBUTION: Equatorial Guinea (Bioko), Ghana, Guinea, Ivory Coast, Liberia, Nigeria, Sierra Leone, Uganda, Zaire.

Genyorchis Schlechter

The genus *Genyorchis* was established in 1901 by Rudolf Schlechter. The name derives from the Greek words *genys* (jaw) and *orchis* (orchid); the flower from the side is, rather fancifully, thought to resemble an open jaw. There are about six species of *Genyorchis* in tropical Africa. Vegetatively, they look like small species of *Bulbophyllum* with the flowers of *Polystachya,* but according to Dressler (1981, 1993), they are not closely related to either of those genera. Only one species is known in cultivation, and it is not common.

DESCRIPTION: Small, sympodial epiphytes. Pseudobulbs, with one or two leaves each, well spaced on a creeping rhizome. Inflorescence arising from the base of the pseudobulb, laxly few-flowered. Flowers small, nonresupinate, not opening wide. Dorsal sepal free; lateral sepals form a conical mentum with the column foot. Petals much smaller than the sepals, or absent. Lip small, trilobed. Column short, with a long foot; pollinia two or four, stipes one, viscidium one.

Genyorchis apetala (Lindley) J. J. Vermeulen
SYNONYM: *Genyorchis pumila* (Swartz) Schlechter

DESCRIPTION: Pseudobulbs 6–15 × 4–5 mm, ovoid or oblong, 4-angled, set 1–2.5 cm (0.5–1 in.) apart on a woody rhizome. Leaves two, spreading, 7–25 × 4–7 mm, oblong-elliptic, bilobed at the apex, the lobes rounded, fleshy or leathery. Inflorescences 4–6 cm (2 in.) long, rarely more, several-flowered. Flowers white, with yellow patches on the lip; column with purple wings near the apex. Dorsal sepal 2.5–3 × 1–2 mm, lanceolate; lateral sepals 4–4.5 mm long, 1.5–2 mm wide near the base, obliquely triangular, forming a mentum 2 mm high with the column foot. Petals absent. Lip 2.5–3.5 mm long, fleshy and tonguelike, obscurely trilobed with small, erect side lobes; midlobe papillose and recurved near the apex. Column 1–2 mm long.

HABITAT: Rainforest, 1100–1400 m (3600–4600 ft.).

CULTIVATION: Intermediate temperatures and moderate shade; either mounted or in bark mix in a pan. The humidity should be high throughout the year.

DISTRIBUTION: Cameroon, Congo, Equatorial Guinea (Bioko), Ghana, Ivory Coast, Liberia, Nigeria, Príncipe, Sierra Leone, Uganda, Zaire.

Graphorkis Thouars
SYNONYM: *Eulophiopsis* Pfitzer

The genus *Graphorkis* was established by the French botanist A. du Petit Thouars in 1809. Because the flowers are similar to those of *Eulophia,* at one time the genus was known as *Eulophiopsis.* It includes five species of epiphytic, sympodial orchids, of which one species occurs on mainland Africa and the other four are found in Madagascar and the Mascarene Islands. The genus name is derived from the Greek words *graphe* (writing) and *orchis* (orchid), but nobody seems to know why it should have been applied to these plants.

Graphorkis lurida (Swartz) O. Kuntze FIGURE 10-52
SYNONYMS: *Eulophia lurida* (Swartz) Lindley, *Eulophiopsis lurida* (Swartz) Schlechter

DESCRIPTION: A robust species. Pseudobulbs ovoid, 3–9 × 1–3 cm (1–4 × 0.5–1 in.), yellowish and ribbed, forming big clumps, supposedly developing erect feeding roots, like *Ansellia,* but we have not noticed this either in the wild or in cultivation. Leaves four to nine, to 40 × 4 cm (16 × 2 in.), rather thin-textured, pleated, deciduous in the dry season. Inflorescences appear before the new leaves, 15–50 cm (6–20 in.) tall, usually branched, with many flowers. Flowers seem small for the size of plant, yellowish, flushed with purple or brown. Sepals and petals spreading; sepals 6–7 × 2 mm, oblanceolate; petals 5–6 × 2.5 mm, elliptic. Lip 4–6 × 3–3.5 mm, trilobed, with two fleshy keels at the base; the small side lobes are erect and the midlobe is notched at the apex. Spur 4–6 mm long, bent quite sharply forwards and often bifid at the tip.

HABITAT: Low- to mid-altitude forest, 300–1300 m (1000–4300 ft.), sometimes growing on *Hyphaene* palms. We saw it on several occasions in Congo Republic, not on palms but usually forming large clumps in the lower forks of trees; it even grew on street trees in the center of Brazzaville.

CULTIVATION: We have found this plant quite tricky, only having any success when it is grown in a basket in a coarse bark mix. The biggest problem is the propensity of the new growth to turn black and rot; obviously very careful watering is essential. It seems to like intermediate to warm temperatures and fairly good light, and needs a dry spell in winter. In our greenhouse, it flowers in spring, before the new growth starts.

DISTRIBUTION: Burundi, Cameroon, Congo, Equatorial Guinea (Bioko), Gabon, Ghana, Guinea, Guinea-Bissau, Ivory Coast, Liberia, Nigeria, Senegal, Sierra Leone, Tanzania, Togo, Uganda, Zaire.

Habenaria Willdenow

The genus *Habenaria* was established by Carl Ludwig von Willdenow in 1805. The name derives from the Latin *habena* (reins), presumably referring to the straplike petal and lip lobes, and long, slender spur, found in many species. It is one of the largest terrestrial genera, with about 600 species found in tropical, subtropical, and warm temperate areas around the world. About 200 species occur in tropical and South Africa, with the greatest number in central and southern central Africa. For example, of the approximately 400 species of orchid in Malawi, one-fifth are species of *Habenaria*.

The genus has been divided into a number of sections, depending on both vegetative and floral characters, but as so few species are in general cultivation, it is not worth going into detail about these here. A few enthusiasts in South Africa grow quite a range of the local species, but many of these are, as the expression goes, "of botanical interest only," and certainly are not widely grown.

DESCRIPTION: Variable, from slender plants with small green flowers (the majority) to robust species with large and striking, sometimes spectacular, flowers. Plants with

← Figure 10-52. *Graphorkis lurida*. Plant (left) and dehisced capsule (lower right), ×1; flower (upper and center right), ×3.

either ovoid or ellipsoid tubers or thick, fleshy roots. Stem sometimes leafy, sometimes with one or two fleshy leaves pressed tightly to the ground, with a few bracts scattered up the flowering stem. Inflorescence always terminal on the stem, usually several- to many-flowered. Flowers green, yellow-green, or green and white (three rare species have bright yellow flowers); flowers intricate in plan, confusing at first sight, many with bilobed petals, the upper lobe sometimes joined lightly to the dorsal sepal. Lip usually trilobed, spurred. Stigma in the form of two processes projecting from the front of the column, long or short, club-shaped or with enlarged, truncate tips.

CULTIVATION: Plants should be grown in a standard terrestrial mix. As with almost all terrestrial orchids, good drainage is essential. When species die back after flowering, they should be kept virtually dry during their resting period, although a light sprinkling of water can be given, perhaps once a month, to prevent shrivelling of the tubers. This is the time to repot; old dead roots can be pulled away, but it is not necessary to repot every year, as long as the compost is still open. When new shoots start to appear, careful watering can start, although it is best to wait until the shoots are 2.5 cm (1 in.) tall. Once the plant is growing strongly, water can be given more freely, although the compost should never be allowed to become soggy. In common with most terrestrial orchids, it is best to avoid getting water on the leaves.

Habenaria macrandra Lindley

DESCRIPTION: A terrestrial species, 15–55 cm (6–22 in.) tall. Roots fleshy, cylindrical, woolly; stem with a cluster of large leaves at the base and a few smaller ones up the length. The basal leaves have a stalk to 7 cm (3 in.) long, with a lanceolate, somewhat pleated dark green blade to 24 × 6 cm (9 × 2 in.). Inflorescences 4–20 cm (2–8 in.) long, rather loosely 2- to 11-flowered. Flowers white or green and white. Sepals 15–30 × 3–5 mm, lanceolate, acute, the dorsal erect and the laterals deflexed. Petals unlobed, 15–35 mm long, narrowly linear, erect. Lip trilobed almost to the base, all the lobes more or less threadlike, but the middle one slightly wider; midlobe 20–45 mm long; side lobes slightly longer, 30–55 mm long. Spur pendent, 5–7.5 cm (2–3 in.) long, slightly curved, swollen near the apex. Anther very tall and slender, 13–22 mm long.

HABITAT: Forest floor, growing in leaf litter in deep shade, 900–1500 m (3000–5000 ft.).

CULTIVATION: As given for the genus, in fairly heavy shade.

DISTRIBUTION: Throughout much of tropical Africa.

Habenaria praestans Rendle PLATE 58, FIGURE 10-53

DESCRIPTION: A robust species, to 1 m (3 ft.) tall but usually shorter; tubers ovoid or ellipsoid; stems leafy, the largest leaves near the base, usually 15 × 5 cm (6 × 2 in.), prominently five-veined, broadly lanceolate, acute, then decreasing in size up the stem. Inflorescences 10–20 cm (4–8 in.) long, densely 4- to 30-flowered. Flowers green, the lip white or greenish-white. Pedicel and ovary 20–25 mm long; bracts leafy, the lower

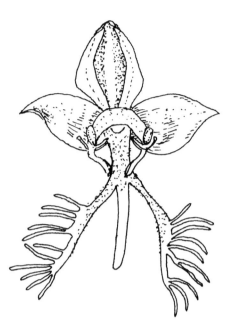

Figure 10-53. *Habenaria praestans.* Flower, ×2.

ones usually longer than the flowers. Sepals 20 × 12 mm, lanceolate, acute, the dorsal erect, the laterals spreading. Petals entire, 20 × 5 mm, lightly joined to the dorsal sepal. Lip trilobed to 4 mm from the base, the basal part very finely pubescent; midlobe 22 × 1 mm, linear; side lobes diverging, slightly longer, divided on the outer side into comblike segments. Spur 2 cm (1 in.) long, pendent, slightly curved and swollen at the apex. Anther connective horseshoe-shaped, 18 mm wide; stigmatic arms 10–18 mm long.

HABITAT: Montane grassland, bracken and briar, edge of forest, 1200–2440 m (4000–8000 ft.).

CULTIVATION: As described for the genus, with no more than light shade.

DISTRIBUTION: Kenya, Malawi, Rwanda, Tanzania, Uganda, Zaire, Zambia, Zimbabwe.

NOTE: This species belongs to section *Multipartitae,* where the side lobes of the lip are divided into comblike segments; all are striking looking plants. In this section the anther connective is horseshoe-shaped and wide.

Habenaria procera (Swartz) Lindley   PLATE 59, FIGURE 10-54

DESCRIPTION: Plants 60 cm (24 in.) tall; tubers elongate, woolly; stems leafy. Leaves to 30 × 2–7 cm (12 × 1–3 in.), broadly oblanceolate, light, glossy green. Inflorescences to 15 cm (6 in.) long, fairly densely 10- to 30-flowered. Flowers white. Pedicel and ovary arched, 20 mm long; bracts 3–5 cm (1–2 in.) long. Sepals 12 × 7 mm,

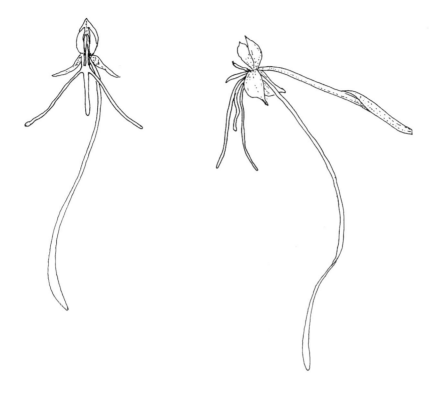

Figure 10-54. *Habenaria procera* var. *gabonensis.* Flower, ×0.75.

the dorsal erect, ovate, concave, forming a hood; the laterals obliquely ovate and deflexed. Petals 10 × 5 mm, ovate. Lip trilobed with a short undivided base; midlobe to 18 × 2 mm, linear; side lobes to 27 mm long, narrowly linear, almost threadlike. Spur 6–11 cm (2–4 in.) long, pendent, slender but inflated at the apex. Stigmatic arms to 5 mm long, club-shaped.

CULTIVATION: Plants should be potted in fine to medium bark, in moderate shade, in intermediate temperatures. After flowering, the leaves die back and plants should then be kept dry as described for terrestrial members of the genus. The species flowers in spring or summer.

Var. *gabonensis* (Reichenbach f.) Geerinck

SYNONYM: *Habenaria gabonensis* Reichenbach f.

DESCRIPTION: Differs from var. *procera* in being consistently terrestrial; leaves generally narrower, 1–4 cm (0.5–2 in.) broad; inflorescence laxer, with fewer flowers, rarely more than 12; spur 5–12 cm (2–5 in.) long.

HABITAT: In humus, or grassy places among rocks.

DISTRIBUTION: Cameroon, Congo, Equatorial Guinea (Bioko), Gabon, Ivory Coast, Liberia, Nigeria, Príncipe, Sierra Leone, Zaire.

NOTE: In the *Flora of West Tropical Africa,* var. *gabonensis* is treated as a separate species, *Habenaria gabonensis,* but there is so much overlap between it and *H. procera* that it can be difficult to distinguish them.

Var. *procera*

DESCRIPTION: Very unusual in the genus as it is usually epiphytic.

HABITAT: Mainly on tree trunks, to 6 m (20 ft.) above ground, usually among mosses and ferns; occasionally in leaf litter on the ground or on rotting logs. It is usually found at fairly low altitudes, but can grow to 1250 m (4100 ft.) altitude.

DISTRIBUTION: Cameroon, Congo, Gabon, Ghana, Ivory Coast, Nigeria, Sierra Leone, Uganda.

Habenaria splendens Rendle   PLATE 60, FIGURE 10-55

DESCRIPTION: A robust species, to 70 cm (28 in.) tall; stems leafy, the largest leaves in the middle, to 16 × 6 cm (6–2 in.), ovate-lanceolate, acute, dark green with three prominent veins, the upper ones getting smaller and grading into the bracts. Inflorescences to 20 cm (8 in.) long, rather loosely to 20-flowered. Flowers green and white, the sepals green and the petals and lip white, the lip greenish towards the tip. Pedicel and ovary 3–3.5 cm (1 in.) long; bracts 4 cm (2 in.) long. Sepals 25 × 10–13 mm, ovate, acute, the dorsal erect and the laterals spreading. Petals entire, 25 mm long, joined to the dorsal sepal and angled on the outer side. Lip trilobed to 7 mm from the base, the basal part finely and densely pubescent; midlobe 20 × 1 mm, linear; side lobes slightly shorter, divided on the outer edge into fine, comblike segments. Spur 5 cm (2 in.) long, pendent, S-shaped, swollen towards the apex. Anther connective 12 mm wide; stigmatic arms 9 mm long.

HABITAT: In long grass at the edge of forest, 1270–2200 m (4200–7300 ft.).

CULTIVATION: As described for the genus, with no more than light shade.

DISTRIBUTION: Ethiopia, Kenya, Malawi, Tanzania, Uganda, Zambia.

NOTE: This species, like *Habenaria praestans,* belongs to section *Multipartitae.*

Herschelianthe Rauschert

The genus *Herschelia* was established by John Lindley in 1838 and named in honor of the astronomer Sir John Herschel (1792–1871), who spent some years in South Africa, at the Cape. The genus is closely related to *Disa,* and its taxonomic history is complicated. At various times it has been considered to be a section of *Disa,* and some authorities still believe that it is better placed there. In 1983 the German botanist Rauschert published the name *Herschelianthe,* on the grounds that *Herschelia* was invalid because the name *Herschellea* had already been applied (although it was not in use) to a genus in the Solanaceae. Currently, 17 species of *Herschelianthe* are recognized: 4 are narrow endemics from tropical Africa, 12 are confined to the Western Cape in South Africa— some of these are very rare if not extinct—and one, *H. baurii,* is widespread, occurring

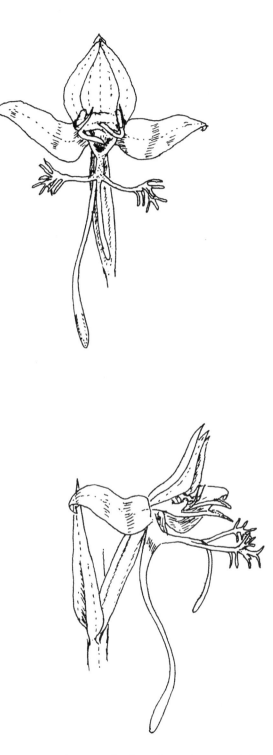

Figure 10-55. *Habenaria splendens.* Flower (upper and lower left) and petal (right), ×1.

in summer rainfall areas of South Africa and through eastern tropical Africa as far north as the southern highlands of Tanzania.

Although some of the species of *Herschelianthe* are outstandingly beautiful, they have proved to be difficult to cultivate, at least to keep going for any length of time. However, plants have been grown at times in Europe since the last century. *Herschelianthe spathulata* subsp. *spathulata* is illustrated as *Disa atropurpurea* in *Curtis's Botanical Magazine*, t. 6891 (Hooker 1886), followed by *H. hians* as *Disa lacera* in the same journal, t. 7066 (Hooker 1889). In 1905, three species were in cultivation, *H. graminifolia, H. spathulata,* and an unknown species (Linder 1981d).

DESCRIPTION: Slender, with linear, grasslike basal leaves and brown, sheathing stem leaves. Floral bracts dry and papery by flowering time. Tubers often large, to 6 cm (2 in.) long. Inflorescences laxly few- to many-flowered. Flowers usually blue, but sometimes purplish-red or greenish. Dorsal sepal forming a hood, spurred; lateral sepals spreading. Petals lobed, standing in the hood beside the anther. Lip usually fringed or dissected in some way, rarely entire. Anther horizontal or pendent.

CULTIVATION: Water quality seems to be of great importance, one grower recommends de-ionized tap water with a pH of about 5.5 (Vogelpoel 1994b). Plants should be kept cool and dry when dormant, and given good light while in growth. Rolfe (1912) mentioned *Herschelianthe lugens* as being grown and commented that it was not easy to keep going. In South Africa, efforts are being made to maintain *Herschelianthe* species in cultivation, and some growers are successful in growing and flowering them over a period of years (Vogelpoel 1994b). Successful growers use at least some soil from the original site, and when the plant is repotted, some of that soil is incorporated in the new mix, which suggests that these plants are particularly dependent on mycorrhizal fungi. This practice is obviously not possible for growers elsewhere, and before plants of this genus can be said to be truly "in cultivation," it should be possible to grow them from seed and establish them in compost afterwards. Many South African growers are very skilled with their native terrestrials, and in the hope that a technique can be developed which is applicable elsewhere, we have decided to include some species. Flasks of *Herschelianthe graminifolia* have been offered in Britain, but there are no records yet of anyone growing these on.

Herschelianthe baurii (H. Bolus) Rauschert   PLATE 61, FIGURE 10=56
SYNONYM: *Disa hamatopetala* Rendle

DESCRIPTION: A slender species, 20–40 cm (8–16 in.) tall, leafless at flowering time, but with remains of old leaves at the base of the stem. Leaves appearing after flowering, to 30 cm (12 in.) × 1–2 mm, stiff, linear and grasslike. Inflorescences laxly 2- to 14-flowered. Flowers pale to deep sky blue, sometimes violet-tinged, the lip usually darker. Petals green. Dorsal sepal 16–20 × 6–12 mm, forming a hood 5–10 mm deep with an upcurved, cylindrical spur 5–8 mm long. Lateral sepals deflexed, 10–20 × 9 mm, oblong, apiculate. Petals 8 mm long, lying inside the hood, shaped rather like a spanner, with a basal lobe, then a narrow middle part, and then expanded again and bilobed at the tip. Lip projecting, 10–25 × 10–20 mm, the margins deeply fringed.

Figure 10-56. *Herschelianthe baurii*. Plant, ×1.

HABITAT: Montane grassland in well-drained areas, sometimes on roadside cuttings in gravelly soil, 1000–2400 m (3300–8000 ft.), but usually over 1800 m (6000 ft.). In places where this beautiful species grows, the grass is often burnt in the dry season; even when it has not been burnt, there is little if any growth before the first rains come, which is when *Herschelianthe baurii* flowers. It is difficult to know what the stimulus to flowering must be. On the Nyika plateau in Malawi, there are one or two odd populations that consistently flower at the end of the rains, rather than before they start.

DISTRIBUTION: Burundi, Lesotho, Malawi, Mozambique, Rwanda, South Africa (Eastern Cape, KwaZulu-Natal, Mpumalanga, Northern Province), Swaziland, Tanzania, Zaire, Zambia, Zimbabwe.

Herschelianthe graminifolia (Sprengel) Rauschert

DESCRIPTION: A slender species, 50–100 cm (20–40 in.) tall. Basal leaves about five, 20–50 cm (8–20 in.) × 5 mm, often rolled lengthwise. Inflorescences laxly 2- to 6-flowered. Flowers blue to violet-purple, the lip deeper purple, the tips of the petals green. Dorsal sepal 15–20 tall, forming a hood 5–10 mm deep; spur 2–4 mm long, straight, swollen at the tip. Lateral sepals projecting, 13–18 × 6–10 mm, oblong, obtuse, apiculate. Petals 11–16 mm long, expanded at the tips to a fanlike structure 4–6 mm across, standing erect behind the anther. Lip 11–16 mm long, elliptical, the margins usually finely toothed or wavy, but not fringed.

HABITAT: Dry mountain slopes, usually on rocky soil, in full sunlight but often in dense vegetation, 300–1500 m (1000–5000 ft.). Rainfall is usually more than 1000 mm (40 in.) per year, and there is no long dry season.

DISTRIBUTION: South Africa (Western Cape).

Herschelianthe hians (Linnaeus f.) Rauschert

SYNONYM: *Disa lacera* Swartz

DESCRIPTION: A slender species, 40–60 cm (16–24 in.) tall. Basal leaves 8 to 13, shorter than the inflorescence, only 2 mm wide, stiff and erect. Inflorescences to 20 cm (8 in.) long, laxly 3- to 16-flowered. Flowers pale blue to purple-blue, the lip often darker purple. Dorsal sepal 8–15 mm long, forming a hood 8–10 mm deep, with a conical, tapering spur 4–6 mm long arising from the base of the hood. Lateral sepals projecting, 8–12 mm long, oblong. Petals 7–12 mm long, curving up behind the anther. Lip 7–12 mm long, oblong, the edge wavy or occasionally fringed.

HABITAT: Well-drained, often stony soil, 80–1000 m (260–3300 ft.), with year-round rainfall averaging 600–1000 mm (24–40 in.) per year.

DISTRIBUTION: South Africa (Western Cape).

Herschelianthe lugens (H. Bolus) Rauschert

DESCRIPTION: A slender species, 45–100 cm (18–40 in.) tall; tubers large, 5 × 2 cm (2 × 1 in.). Basal leaves to 15, grasslike, shorter than the flowering shoot. Inflorescences laxly 5- to 25-flowered. Flowers creamy-green to gray-green with darker veins. Dorsal sepal 12–16 mm tall, forming a hood 10 mm deep, with a slender, cylindrical spur 1–5 mm long arising from the base of the hood. Lateral sepals projecting, 8–13 mm long, oblong. Petals 10–15 mm long, with a right angle bend near the middle. Lip 13–19 mm long, ovate, the edges deeply dissected.

HABITAT: Most often on coastal flats, in deep sand, usually growing in tussocks of Restionaceae (sedgelike plants), but occasionally on well-drained hillsides, in scrub, from areas with 500–1000 mm (20–40 in.) of winter rain or year-round rain annually.

DISTRIBUTION: South Africa (Western Cape).

NOTE: Two varieties are recognized: var. *lugens,* with lateral sepals mainly mauve in color, and var. *nigrescens* Linder, with deep purplish-black lateral sepals. The latter is known from only one locality.

Herschelianthe purpurascens (H. Bolus) Rauschert

DESCRIPTION: Plants 25–50 cm (10–20 in.) tall; tubers 3 cm (1 in.) long. Basal leaves about 10, stiff and erect, shorter than, or as long as, the flowering stem but only 1 mm wide. Inflorescences laxly 1- to 7-flowered. Flowers blue, the lip more purplish; the tips of the petals yellow or green. Dorsal sepal 15–25 mm tall, forming a hood 10–15 mm deep, the spur arising from the base of the hood, 1–4 mm long, conical, obtuse, straight or curving up. Lateral sepals projecting, 15–18 mm long, oblong, obtuse. Petals 8–10 mm long, expanded at the top into a fanlike structure 4–5 mm wide. Lip 12–18 mm long, elliptical, the edges wavy and curving up.

HABITAT: Dry, rocky or stony areas in full sunlight, to 100 m (300 ft.), in areas of 800–1200 mm (30–50 in.) of winter rainfall annually.

DISTRIBUTION: South Africa (southern Cape Province).

Herschelianthe spathulata (Linnaeus f.) Rauschert

SYNONYM: *Disa atropurpurea* Sonder

DESCRIPTION: A slender species, 12–30 cm (5–12 in.) tall. Basal leaves 5 to 20, 5–15 cm (2–6 in.) × 2–4 mm, linear and grasslike. Inflorescences to 10 cm (4 in.) long, laxly 1- to 5-flowered. Flowers very variable in color, pale green, blue, or maroon, with darker veining. Dorsal sepal 9–20 mm long × 5 mm, forming a fairly deep or shallow hood; spur to 3 mm long, cylindrical or club-shaped. Lateral sepals projecting or curving up, 6–16 mm long, obliquely ovate. Petals 7–12 mm long, the apex enlarged and bilobed, to 4 mm wide. Lip with a long, linear claw 5–35 × 1–2 mm, then expanded into a blade that may be obscurely or deeply trilobed, with the margin undulate, midlobe of lip 5–22 mm long.

Subsp. *spathulata*

DESCRIPTION: Lip midlobe 5–14 mm long; inflorescence 1- to 5-flowered.

HABITAT: In damp and well-drained situations, in full sunlight, 150–1200 m (500–4000 ft.), in areas with 200–800 mm (8–32 in.) of winter rainfall annually.

DISTRIBUTION: South Africa (widespread in Western Cape).

Subsp. *tripartita* (Lindley) Linder
DESCRIPTION: Lip midlobe 16–22 mm long; inflorescence 1- to 2-flowered.
HABITAT: In scrub on shaley soil, 1000 m (3300 ft.), in areas with 600 mm (24 in.) of year-round rainfall.
DISTRIBUTION: South Africa (very local in Western Cape).

Jumellea Schlechter

The genus *Jumellea* was created by Rudolf Schlechter in 1914 and named in honor of French botanist Henri Jumel, who studied Madagascan plants. It is related to *Angraecum,* but is quite distinctive. There are about 45 species, most in Madagascar, the Comoro Islands, and the Mascarene Islands; only 2 occur on mainland Africa, of which one species, *J. filicornoides,* is in cultivation. The other species, *J. usambarensis* J. J. Wood, was described in 1982, and is known only from a few areas of montane and submontane forest in Kenya, southern Malawi, and Tanzania.

DESCRIPTION: Stems long or short. Leaves usually distichous, linear or strap-shaped, obtusely bilobed at the apex. Inflorescence one-flowered. Flowers white, usually scented, with narrow segments and a long, slender spur. Lip does not envelop the base of the column, as in *Angraecum.* Lateral sepals usually more or less joined under the spur. Column short, with a short foot, and with two parallel arms joined on the inner side to the lateral sepals and petals, giving them a characteristic twist. Capsule narrow, usually cylindrical, opening by a single slit.

Jumellea filicornoides (De Wildeman) Schlechter

PLATE 62, FIGURE 10-57

DESCRIPTION: Stems woody, 20–40 cm (8–16 in.) long, usually erect, forming large clumps; roots long and numerous, 3–4 mm in diameter. Leaves to about 16, distichous, 4–11 × 1–1.5 cm (2–4 × 0.5–1 in.), strap-shaped, slightly folded, thick and leathery, obtusely bilobed at the apex, dark green, held at an angle of 45° to the stem. Inflorescences axillary, 1-flowered. Flowers violet-scented, glistening white, turning apricot as they fade. Pedicel and ovary 4 cm (2 in.) long, usually S-shaped. Sepals 13–22 × 3–4 mm, lanceolate, the dorsal erect or recurved, the laterals deflexed. Petals 12–20 × 2–3 mm, narrowly lanceolate, angled so that they are more or less edge on when viewed from the front. Lip 16–25 × 5–7 mm, rhombic from a narrow base, somewhat channelled, keeled towards the base. Spur 2–3 cm (1 in.) long, very slender, gently curved. Column 2 mm long.

HABITAT: Riverine forest and high rainfall woodland, usually forming large clumps on big, horizontal branches, but occasionally growing on rocks, 350–1700 m (1150–5600 ft.).

CULTIVATION: This attractive species gives growers no problems. We find it does well either mounted on bark or in pot, in intermediate temperatures and moderate shade. If mounted, the humidity must be high, particularly in the growing season. In our greenhouse, it flowers in summer and early autumn (July to September).

Figure 10-57. *Jumellea filicornoides.* Plant (left), ×0.75; flower (right), ×0.9.

DISTRIBUTION: Kenya, Malawi, Mozambique, South Africa (KwaZulu-Natal, Northern Province), Tanzania, Zimbabwe.

Liparis L. Richard

The genus *Liparis* was created in 1818 by the French botanist L. C. Richard. The name derives from the Greek word *liparos* (shiny, greasy), referring to the smooth, glossy texture of the leaves of many species. *Liparis* is a large genus of about 250 species, found in the tropics throughout the world, and in temperate areas, including Europe and North America.

DESCRIPTION: Sympodial; most species terrestrial, some consistently epiphytic, others terrestrial, lithophytic, or epiphytic. Stems usually swollen at the base to form pseudobulbs. Leaves thin-textured and pleated to smooth and thick-textured. Inflorescences terminal, few- to many-flowered; flowers usually smallish, yellow-green or purplish. Dorsal sepal usually erect; lateral sepals often lying below the lip and sometimes partially joined. Petals often narrowly linear. Lip usually rather fleshy, entire or bilobed, with two calli at the base. Column long, curved; pollinia four, in two pairs.

Figure 10-58. *Liparis bowkeri.* Plant (lower right), ×1; flower (upper left), ×2.5.

Liparis bowkeri Harvey   PLATE 63, FIGURE 10-58
   SYNONYM: *Liparis neglecta* Schlechter

DESCRIPTION: A terrestrial or sometimes epiphytic species, variable in size. Pseudobulbs to 7 × 1.5 cm (2 × 1 in.), conical. Leaves two to five, usually deciduous, 6–12 × 3–6 cm (2–5 × 1–2 in.), ovate, acute, ribbed, the edge often undulate, with a petiole to 7 cm (3 in.) long, but usually shorter. Inflorescences terminal, to 20 cm (8 in.) long, rather laxly 2- to 25-flowered. Flowers green, yellow-green, or occasionally yellow, turning orange as they age, the lip with a metallic gray line down the center. Pedicel and ovary 7–11 mm long; bracts 10–15 mm long. Dorsal sepal erect, 10 × 2 mm, narrowly lanceolate; laterals 9 × 3 mm, obliquely elliptic, lying side by side below the lip, but not joined. Petals 11 × 0.5 mm, linear, fleshy, deflexed or spreading. Lip deflexed, 6 × 6 mm, orbicular, with a small, slightly bifid, callus near the base. Column 3–4 mm long, bent over at almost a right angle.

HABITAT: Evergreen forest and high rainfall woodland, in fairly heavy shade, growing terrestrially in leaf litter, or epiphytically at a low level on trunks and branches, or frequently on rotting logs or mossy rocks, 1200–2700 m (4000–8900 ft.).

Cultivation: Potted in a fairly fine bark mix (to which extra leaf mold can be added but the drainage must be free), at intermediate temperatures, in moderate to heavy shade. Water well while growing, but keep almost dry when resting.

Distribution: Burundi, Ethiopia, Kenya, Malawi, Rwanda, South Africa (Eastern Cape, KwaZulu-Natal, Transvaal), Swaziland, Tanzania, Uganda, Zaire, Zambia, Zimbabwe.

Liparis cespitosa (Lamarck) Lindley

Synonym: *Liparis caespitosa* (Thouars) Lindley

Description: An epiphyte. Pseudobulbs smooth, green, ovoid, 13×10 mm, set close together, forming large clumps, sometimes encircling a trunk or branch. Leaf one, $8–10 \times 1–1.5$ cm ($3–4 \times 0.5–1$ in.), oblanceolate, stiff-textured, smooth, glossy green, jointed at the base. Inflorescences terminal, 10–18 cm (4–7 in.) long, densely many-flowered. Flowers very small, greenish-yellow, nonresupinate. Pedicel and ovary 5 mm long; bracts 3 mm long. Sepals reflexed, the dorsal 2.5×1 mm, ovate, the laterals similar but very slightly broader. Petals 2.5×0.5 mm, linear. Lip 2.5×2 mm, oblong, apiculate or obscurely 4-lobed, with two small calli near the base. Column curved, 1.5 mm long.

Habitat: Epiphytic on trunks and lower branches of trees in evergreen forest, 425–1900 m (1400–6300 ft.). For a plant with such an extensive distribution world-wide, it is very local where it grows in Africa.

Cultivation: Intermediate conditions and heavy shade with high humidity, either in a pot with a bark mix, or mounted, if the humidity can be kept up. Reduce watering when plants are not in active growth, but do not allow them to dry out completely.

Distribution: Malawi, Tanzania, Uganda. Also Madagascar, Réunion, Sri Lanka, northeastern India to the Philippines, New Guinea, Solomon Islands, and Fiji.

Liparis nervosa (Thunberg) Lindley

Synonyms: *Liparis guineensis* Lindley, *Liparis rufina* (Ridley) Rolfe

Description: A terrestrial species. Pseudobulbs $2–4 \times 1.5–2.5$ cm ($1–2 \times 1$ in.), ovoid, only partly above ground, covered with papery sheaths. Leaves two to three, petiolate, to 35×9 cm (14×4 in.), ovate, acute, pleated. Inflorescences to 60 cm (24 in.) tall, densely many-flowered. Flowers small, greenish, the lip deep maroon-purple or greenish-purple. Pedicel and ovary more or less erect, 10 mm long; bracts to 7 mm long. Dorsal sepal $5–6 \times 1–2$ mm, erect or reflexed, linear; lateral sepals 4×2 mm, often rolled up under the lip. Petals 5–6 mm long, narrowly linear, almost threadlike. Lip recurved, $3–4 \times 2.5–4.5$ mm, orbicular, somewhat bilobed, with two toothlike calli at the base. Column 3 mm long, curved, winged near the apex.

Habitat: Usually in woodland, but sometimes in wet open grassland, in shade or in full sun, 500–1800 m (1650–6000 ft.).

Cultivation: Potted, in a standard terrestrial mix, at intermediate temperatures, with light to moderate shade. Keep dry when the leaves die back after flowering.

Liparis

DISTRIBUTION: Angola, Benin, Burundi, Cameroon, Central African Republic, Equatorial Guinea (Bioko and Pagalu Islands), Gabon, Ghana, Guinea, Guinea-Bissau, Ivory Coast, Liberia, Malawi, Nigeria, Rwanda, Senegal, São Tomé, Sierra Leone, Tanzania, Uganda, Zaire, Zambia, Zimbabwe. Possibly South Africa. Also India to Japan and the Philippines, West Indies, Central and South America.

Liparis platyglossa Schlechter

DESCRIPTION: An epiphyte. Pseudobulbs 2 × 1.5 mm, ovoid, forming clumps. Leaves two to four, 6–8 × 2–3 cm (2–3 × 1 in.), elliptic or ovate, with a short, sheathing petiole. Inflorescences to 10 cm (4 in.) long, fairly densely 10-flowered. Flowers deep purple, or greenish-white, the lip with purple veins. Dorsal sepal 15 × 4 mm, erect; lateral sepals projecting forwards under the lip, joined for half to three-quarters of their length, 12–14 × 5–10 mm, obliquely ovate. Petals 13–15 mm long, narrowly linear. Lip 8–12 × 11–15 mm, transversely bilobed with an apicule between the lobes and a bifid callus at the base. Column arched, 5 mm long.

HABITAT: Epiphytic in rainforest, 600–1300 m (2000–4300 ft.).

CULTIVATION: Potted in a standard bark mix at intermediate to warm temperatures, moderate shade, high humidity while in growth, but much drier while resting. This species does not seem to like being divided.

DISTRIBUTION: Cameroon, Congo, Equatorial Guinea (Bioko), Ivory Coast, Nigeria, Uganda.

Liparis remota J. Stewart & E. A. Schelpe

DESCRIPTION: Appears to be very close to *Liparis bowkeri*. A terrestrial, epiphytic, or lithophytic species. Pseudobulbs conical or ovoid, 2–5 cm (1–2 in.) tall, set 3–5 cm (1–2 in.) apart on creeping stems. Leaves 4–7 × 2–3.5 cm (2–3 × 1 in.), elliptic, with a narrow sheathing base about as long again. Inflorescences terminal, 10–15 cm (4–6 in.) long, 3- to 8-flowered. Flowers pale green. Dorsal sepal 6 mm long, strap-shaped. Lateral sepals 5 × 3 mm, joined at the base and projecting forwards to lie below the lip. Petals 6 × 1 mm, linear, deflexed. Lip 4 × 4 mm, rhomboid to orbicular, acute, without a callus.

HABITAT: Forest, below 400 m (1300 ft.).

CULTIVATION: Potted in a fairly fine bark mix (extra leaf mold can be added, but the drainage must be free), at intermediate temperatures, in moderate to heavy shade. Water well while growing, but keep almost dry when the plant is resting.

DISTRIBUTION: South Africa (Eastern Cape, KwaZulu-Natal), Swaziland.

Liparis tridens Kränzlin

DESCRIPTION: A dwarf epiphyte. Pseudobulbs to 13 × 7 mm, ovoid, bright green. Leaves about seven, distichous, 6 × 1 cm (2 × 0.5 in.), occasionally slightly bigger, oblong-lanceolate, the edges undulate, thin-textured, the midvein prominent on the underside. Inflorescences terminal, 5–10 cm (2–4 in.) long, densely several-flowered. Flowers greenish-yellow. Dorsal sepal 3 × 1 mm, ovate, acute; laterals slightly longer and wider. Petals 3 × 0.5 mm, linear. Lip trilobed, with a bilobed callus at the base; side lobes triangular; midlobe 5 mm long, linear, acuminate, the margins curved up, the whole lobe sharply bent up about halfway. Column 1.5 mm long, winged at the base and the apex.

HABITAT: Sunk in moss on branches of trees in submontane forest, usually near a stream, 900–1800 m (3000–6000 ft.).

CULTIVATION: We have not grown this species, although we have seen it. High humidity appears to be essential, and so plants are likely to do better potted in a rather fine bark mix than mounted. Plants are deciduous in the dry season, so should be kept drier then. Otherwise, intermediate temperatures and heavy shade should be suitable.

DISTRIBUTION: Cameroon, Equatorial Guinea (Bioko), Ivory Coast, Malawi, Nigeria, Tanzania, Uganda.

Listrostachys Reichenbach f.

The genus *Listrostachys* was established by H. G. Reichenbach in 1832. The name is derived from the Greek words *listron* (a spade) and *stachys* (a spike or ear of corn), possibly in reference to the spade-shaped lips of the flowers, which are arranged on either side of the long inflorescence. Rolfe (1897–1898) listed 52 species of *Listrostachys,* but almost all of these have now been transferred to other angraecoid genera, leaving only one species in the genus *Listrostachys.*

Figure 10-59. *Listrostachys pertusa.* Flower, ×3.

Listrostachys pertusa (Lindley) Reichenbach f.   PLATE 64, FIGURE 10-59

DESCRIPTION: A robust epiphyte; on old plants, woody stem to 15 cm (6 in.) long; roots 2–3 mm in diameter, with golden-brown growing tips. Leaves 9 to 15, distichous, set close together, 10–35 × 1–2 cm (4–14 × 0.5–1 in.), linear, folded, very stiff-textured, almost equally and obtusely bilobed at the apex. Inflorescences arising from the axils of lower leaves, 30 cm (12 in.) long, densely many-flowered, the flowers arranged in two rows. Flowers white, with a green spot at the opening of the spur, sometimes spotted with red. Peduncle 5 cm (2 in.) long. Pedicel and ovary 1.5 mm long, papillose; bracts very short. Sepals 3 × 1.5 mm, ovate; petals slightly smaller. Lip 7–8 mm long, the mouth of the spur 3 mm from the base, the apical part 4 × 3 mm, rectangular, the apex with a suggestion of three teeth. Spur green or sometimes reddish, 4 mm long, the apical half swollen to 1.5 mm wide, the apex rounded. Column 1–2 mm long.

HABITAT: Evergreen forest, 500–600 m (1650–2000 ft.).

CULTIVATION: This is a very obliging plant, growing well either mounted or in a pot, and flowering regularly in summer (June). We grow it in intermediate temperatures (although it should also do well in warm), in moderate shade.

DISTRIBUTION: Cameroon, Congo, Gabon, Ghana, Ivory Coast, Liberia, Nigeria, Príncipe, Sierra Leone, Zaire.

NOTE: Although the flowers are small, they all open together and the effect is attractive and most unusual. If a finger is rubbed lightly along a row of flowers, many pollinia will stick (very firmly) to it.

Margelliantha Cribb

The genus *Margelliantha* was established in 1979 by the Kew botanist Phillip Cribb to accommodate four East African species related to *Diaphananthe* section *Rhipidoglossum* and to *Mystacidium*. The name is derived from the Greek words *margelis* (pearl) and *anthe* (flower), referring to the pearly white flowers of the type species, *Margelliantha leedalii*.

In 1985 Phillip Cribb and Joyce Stewart transferred the South African species *Mystacidium caffrum* to *Margelliantha*. It bears a striking resemblance to the type species of that genus, *Margelliantha leedalii,* and differs in several ways from other species of *Mystacidium*. The latter have starry white flowers with lanceolate, acute floral parts and a wide-mouthed spur tapering to a pointed apex; the side arms of the rostellum are minutely papillose.

Linder (1989) transferred both *Margelliantha caffra* and *Mystacidium millarii* to *Diaphananthe,* but we are not following that here. Undoubtedly, detailed work needs to be done on the affinities of *Angraecopsis, Diaphananthe, Margelliantha,* and *Mystacidium. Margelliantha caffra* seems to be the only species of the genus in cultivation.

DESCRIPTION: Small, short-stemmed epiphytic plants. Leaves distichous, twisted to lie in one plane, linear or narrowly oblanceolate. Inflorescences rather few-flowered, shorter than the leaves. Flowers more or less bell-shaped, white, pale yellow, or pale green. Lip entire, lacking a callus; spur narrow-mouthed, swollen at the apex. Column short; pollinia 2; stipites 2; viscidia 2.

Margelliantha caffra (H. Bolus) Cribb & Stewart

SYNONYMS: *Angraecum caffrum* H. Bolus, *Diaphananthe caffra* (H. Bolus) Linder, *Mystacidium caffrum* (H. Bolus) H. Bolus

DESCRIPTION: A dwarf species with a very short stem and numerous, fairly stout roots, gray-green flecked with white. Leaves to 6 cm (2 in.) × 8 mm, linear or strap-shaped, dark green. Inflorescences arising below leaves, densely 8- to 12-flowered. Flowers rather bell-shaped, about 12 mm in diameter, glistening white, the anther cap bright green. Sepals 5 × 2 mm, ovate, obtuse; petals similar but slightly longer. Lip 6 × 4 mm, broadly ovate, obtuse, slightly recurved; spur 9–10 mm long, with a narrow mouth, slightly inflated at the tip. Column very short.

HABITAT: Epiphytic at low level in cool forests, to 1800 m (6000 ft.).

CULTIVATION: Mounted, with high humidity and at intermediate to cool temperatures. In cultivation, it flowers in summer (June).

DISTRIBUTION: South Africa (Eastern Cape, KwaZulu-Natal, Northern Province).

Microcoelia Lindley

SYNONYM: *Encheiridion* Summerhayes

The genus *Microcoelia* was established by John Lindley in 1830. The name is derived from the Greek words *mikros* (small) and *koilia* (abdomen), referring to the globose spur of *M. exilis,* the type species of the genus. The genus was revised by V. S. Summerhayes in 1943; he removed some leafless species to other genera, leaving 25 species in *Microcoelia.* The most recent revision is by Lars Jonsson in 1981; he recognized 26 species in Africa and Madagascar; one more African species, *M. ornithocephala,* has been described since then by P. J. Cribb in 1985. Twenty species are now known from tropical Africa, with one extending into South Africa.

DESCRIPTION: Leafless epiphytic, occasionally lithophytic plants. Stems short, dying back successively from the base, although the dead basal part may persist. Apical bud protected by scale leaves. Roots usually numerous, long or short, sometimes branched, either clinging to the substrate or with most hanging loose; in some species, the roots are only lightly attached to the branch and twig, and plants frequently fall off, sometimes getting caught up in undergrowth where they continue to grow. When wet, the roots have a greenish tinge; in some species they have numerous white streaks. Inflorescences axillary, arising towards the apex of the stem. Flowers small, usually white. Sepals and petals similar, usually spreading; lip entire or trilobed, spurred at the base. Pollinia two, stipes one, viscidium one.

CULTIVATION: Species of *Microcoelia* are not common in cultivation, but they deserve to be grown much more frequently. Although the flowers are small, they are often densely packed together and many have a glistening texture. They are among our favorites. Because they photosynthesize through their roots, they must be mounted, rather than having the roots buried in compost. We find that they seem to prefer smooth pieces of wood instead of the usual slabs of cork or pine bark; freshwater driftwood, or bogwood seems to be ideal. Sea driftwood could be used, but it would need to be soaked for some time to get rid of the salt. We have also grown species of *Microcoelia* on branches of smooth-barked trees, such as silver birch. Plants can sometimes take a while to become established, but once they decide to grow, they do so well. Most species seem to do well in intermediate temperatures, in moderate to light shade. Humidity must be high, especially when the plants are growing actively, and plants should not be allowed to dry out too much.

Microcoelia bulbocalcarata L. Jonsson

DESCRIPTION: Stems short; roots few, to 50 cm (20 in.) long, 2 mm in diameter. Inflorescences 1.5 cm (1 in.) long, to 6-flowered. Flowers white, tipped with pale green, with a dark green patch on the lip. Pedicel 5 mm long, ovary 3 mm long; bracts sheathing, 1.5 mm long. Dorsal sepal 5–6 × 2.5–3.5 mm, elliptic, acute, forming a hood; lateral sepals 5–7 × 3 mm, elliptic, acute. Petals 4.5–6 × 3–4 mm, ovate or obovate, obtuse. Lip 4–5 × 2.5–3.5 mm, obscurely trilobed, oblong, obtuse, 7.5–10.5 mm long, very swollen in basal part, then tapering and inflated again to a bulbous, incurved apex.

HABITAT: Epiphytic on trees and shrubs in the understory of dense forest, 1680–1950 m (5540–6430 ft.).

DISTRIBUTION: Rwanda, Uganda.

Microcoelia corallina Summerhayes   PLATE 65

DESCRIPTION: Roots fairly short, radiating from the center of the plant to form a conical mound. Inflorescences several per plant, 2–3 cm (1 in.) long, densely to 15-flowered; the pedicels of the lower flowers are longer than those of the upper flowers, so that all are held at almost the same level. Flowers white, the sepals and petals with a salmon-pink midline; column and spur deep salmon-red; peduncle, ovary and pedicel salmon-pink. Sepals 5 × 2 mm, ovate, acute; petals slightly shorter, oblong. Lip 5 × 4 mm, almost orbicular; spur parallel to the ovary, 6 mm long, slender but inflated in the apical half, tapering to a point at the tip. Column 1 mm long.

HABITAT: Hot, dry open woodland, usually near a river, growing most often on smooth-barked trees such as baobab, which are avoided by most orchids, 200–670 m (660–2200 ft.).

CULTIVATION: This little species does well in cultivation. We have it hanging on the bright side of the greenhouse, in very little shade, where it flowers in autumn (September and October).

DISTRIBUTION: Kenya, Malawi, Mozambique, Tanzania.

NOTE: This is a spectacular little species, sharing with *Aerangis luteoalba* var. *rhodosticta* the combination of white flowers with a red column, although in *Microcoelia corallina* the sepals and petals are pink-tinged.

Microcoelia exilis Lindley

DESCRIPTION: Stems to 5 cm (2 in.) long; roots very numerous, 1–3 mm wide, silvery gray-green, long, often branched, forming a tangled mass. Inflorescences several, to 25 cm (10 in.) long, densely many-flowered. Flowers white, the spur greenish, rather bell-shaped, not opening wide. Sepals and petals 1–1.5 × 0.5–1 mm, obovate, the petals slightly shorter than the sepals. Lip 1 × 0.7 mm, almost round, with a globose spur 1 mm in diameter. Column 0.5 mm long. The capsules are orange, 3–4 × 2–3 mm, ellipsoid.

HABITAT: Most often in dry woodland and thicket, but also in woodland in higher rainfall areas, growing epiphytically at high and low levels on a wide variety of tree species, usually abundant where it grows, to 1800 m (6000 ft.).

CULTIVATION: No one could call this species showy, but a large plant with its mass of branching roots is always interesting. This species seems to flower off and on throughout the year. It likes only light shade and intermediate to warm conditions.

DISTRIBUTION: Kenya, Malawi, Mozambique, South Africa (KwaZulu-Natal), Tanzania, Uganda, Zaire, Zambia, Zimbabwe. Also Madagascar.

NOTE: In the wild, almost every flower seems to set seed, but it cannot be self-pollinating, as this does not happen in a greenhouse.

Microcoelia globulosa (Hochstetter) L. Jonsson   PLATE 66
SYNONYM: *Microcoelia guyoniana* (Reichenbach f.) Summerhayes

DESCRIPTION: Roots numerous, rarely branched, to 30 cm (12 in.) × 2 mm, firmly or loosely attached to the host tree. Inflorescences several, 3–4 cm (1–2 in.) long, laxly 8- to 15-flowered. Pedicel 3 mm long, ovary 2 mm long, set at a slight angle to the pedicel. Bracts 2 mm long, sheathing the stem. Flowers scented, white, the spur dull orange, the anther cap yellow. Sepals and petals 2–3 × 1 mm, ovate, acute. Lip 2–3 × 1.5 mm, obscurely trilobed, obovate. Spur 3 mm long, conical, tapering, straight or slightly incurved. Column 0.5 mm long.

HABITAT: Open woodland, occasionally riverine forest, epiphytic both on large branches and small twigs, 500–1950 m (1650–6430 ft.).

CULTIVATION: As given for the genus, with moderate shade. In our greenhouse, it flowers in summer (August).

DISTRIBUTION: Angola, Burundi, Cameroon, Central African Republic, Ethiopia, Kenya, Malawi, Nigeria, Rwanda, Sudan, Tanzania, Uganda, Zaire, Zambia, Zimbabwe.

NOTE: This species has been confused with *Microcoelia stolzii,* but the latter has a much denser inflorescence and does not have sheathing bracts.

Microcoelia koehleri (Schlechter) Summerhayes   FIGURE 10-60

DESCRIPTION: Stems to 4 cm (2 in.) long; roots numerous, mostly unbranched, to 20 cm (8 in.) × 1–2 mm, sometimes slightly flattened, gray-green with white flecks,

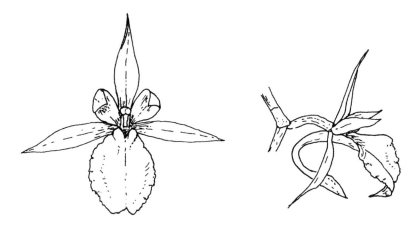

Figure 10-60. *Microcoelia koehleri.* Flower (left), ×3.5; flower (right), ×3.

particularly noticeable when the roots are wet. Inflorescences several, densely to 20-flowered. Flowers white, the sepals often with a salmon-pink midline; spur salmon-pink at the tip; anther cap orange. Pedicel and ovary 3 mm long, twisted, also salmon-pink. Dorsal sepal 6–7 × 2 mm, lanceolate, acuminate; laterals slightly longer and narrower. Petals 5–6 × 1.5–2 mm, ovate, acute. Lip 6–7 × 4–5 mm, obscurely trilobed, broadly ovate, apiculate; spur 6–7 mm long, straight or incurved, tapering to the apex, or sometimes slightly inflated at the tip. Column 2 mm long.

HABITAT: Difficult to characterize; epiphytic in riverine forest and on scattered trees on rocky hillsides and in dryish evergreen forest; occasionally on rocks; 200–1500 m (660–5000 ft.), usually more than 700 m (2300 ft.).

CULTIVATION: As given for the genus, in moderate shade. In our greenhouse, it flowers in late summer (August and September).

DISTRIBUTION: Kenya, Malawi, Nigeria, Rwanda, Tanzania, Uganda, Zaire, Zambia.

Microcoelia megalorrhiza (Reichenbach f.) Summerhayes

DESCRIPTION: An unmistakable plant. Roots stout, to 70 cm (28 in.) long, 4 mm in diameter, gray-brown, very warty. Inflorescences several, 8–10 cm (3–4 in.) long, densely to 20-flowered. Flowers glistening white, the spur brownish-orange at the tip; anther cap orange. Pedicel and ovary 3 mm long, pinkish-brown. Dorsal sepal 7 × 2 mm, elliptical, convex; lateral sepals 9 × 2, lanceolate. Petals similar to dorsal sepal. Lip 7–8 × 2–4 mm, trilobed, with thick, erect side lobes; midlobe broadly ovate; spur 8 mm long, tapering from a wide mouth, straight or slightly incurved. Column 3–4 mm long.

HABITAT: Epiphytic at high and low levels in hot, dry woodland and thicket, 10–550 m (33–1800 ft.). In cultivation, it flowers in summer (June to July).

CULTIVATION: As for the genus, in fairly good light, at intermediate to warm temperatures. Although this species is rare in the wild, it seems to grow well in cultivation.
DISTRIBUTION: Malawi, Tanzania.

Microcoelia obovata Summerhayes

DESCRIPTION: Stems to 3 cm (1 in.) long; roots smooth, to 35 cm (14 in.) long. Inflorescences several, erect or pendent, to 9 cm (4 in.) long, each to 20-flowered. Flowers white, rusty brown at the base of the sepals and petals. Pedicel and ovary each 3 mm long; bracts 2.5 mm long. Dorsal sepal 4–6 × 1–2 mm, oblong, apiculate; laterals similar but slightly longer and wider, reflexed at the tips. Petals 4–6.5 × 1.5 mm, oblong or obovate, apiculate, reflexed at the tips. Lip 5–7.5 × 3–5 mm, broadly obovate, thickened at the base on either side of the mouth of the spur. Spur to 5.5 mm long, conical, slender, incurved. Column 1–1.5 mm long.
HABITAT: Woodland, scattered trees in grassland, riverine forest, often in the crowns of the trees, to 1100 m (3600 ft.).
DISTRIBUTION: Kenya, Mozambique, South Africa (KwaZulu-Natal), Tanzania.

Microcoelia ornithocephala Cribb   PLATE 67, FIGURE 10-61

DESCRIPTION: Roots flattened, slightly keeled on top, clinging close to the bark of the host tree, 30–40 cm (12–16 in.) × 2–4 mm, unbranched, gray-green with white, longitudinal flecks. Inflorescences several, 3–7 cm (1–3 in.) long, to 20-flowered. Pedicel and ovary 6 cm (2 in.) long; bracts 1 mm long, black, sheathing. Sepals and petals pinkish-beige, lip white. Dorsal sepal 5 × 4 mm, ovate, convex; laterals spreading, slightly narrower. Petals spreading, 4 × 1.5 mm, oblong. Lip 6 × 3 mm, obovate, acute, with the apex slightly reflexed, and with two green tubercles at the mouth of the spur; spur 6 mm long, tapering from a wide mouth, then swollen again at the apex, C-shaped. Column 1.5 mm long, anther cap orange, beaked. Capsule to 24 × 2 mm, banana-shaped.
HABITAT: Dry deciduous forest and thicket, 600 m (2000 ft.).
DISTRIBUTION: Southern Malawi.
NOTE: This very distinctive species seems to be rare in the wild. It is to be hoped that it will become available in cultivation to safeguard its future.

Microcoelia smithii (Rolfe) Summerhayes

DESCRIPTION: A dwarf species; stems to 15 mm long, but usually shorter; roots to 12 cm (5 in.) × 2 mm, forming a low mound. Inflorescences to 3 cm (1 in.) long, fairly densely 4- to 10-flowered. Flowers white, the anther cap yellow. Pedicel and ovary 1.5 mm long; bracts 1 mm long, sheathing. Sepals and petals 2 mm long, less than 1 mm wide, ovate, acute. Lip similar but channelled; spur 1.5–2 mm long, straight, obtuse, at right angles to lip.
HABITAT: Dry deciduous forest and thicket, to 600 m (2000 ft.).
DISTRIBUTION: Kenya, Malawi, Tanzania.

Figure 10-61. *Microcoelia ornithocephala.* Plant, ×2.5.

Microcoelia stolzii (Schlechter) Summerhayes

DESCRIPTION: Roots to 30 cm (12 in.) × 0.5–3 mm, but usually 2 mm, silvery green. Inflorescences several, to 12 cm (5 in.) long, densely many-flowered. Flowers scented, glistening white; tip of spur and anther cap yellow. Pedicel and ovary 3 mm long; bracts 2 mm long, not sheathing. Sepals and petals 2–4 × 1–2 mm, ovate, acute, the petals slightly narrower. Lip 2–4 × 1–2 mm, ovate or obovate; spur conical, 1.5–3 mm, straight or slightly incurved. Column to 1 mm long.

HABITAT: Epiphytic in evergreen forest and high rainfall woodland, 800–2450 m (2600–8100 ft.).

CULTIVATION: As given for the genus, but in moderately heavy shade.

DISTRIBUTION: Kenya, Malawi, Mozambique, Tanzania, Zambia, Zimbabwe.

NOTE: This little species is quite showy. Although the flowers are small, they are numerous, and their crystalline texture is very attractive.

Mystacidium Lindley

The genus *Mystacidium* was established by John Lindley in 1836. The name is derived from the Greek word *mystax* (moustache), referring to the rostellum lobes that are hairy in some species. There are about 10 species confined to eastern and southern Africa, with 8 species occurring in South Africa. Although small, most species are very floriferous and are popular with growers.

DESCRIPTION: Small, monopodial epiphytes, many resembling small species of *Aerangis*. Flowers smallish, starry, white, greenish, or pale yellow. Sepals and petals similar, usually lanceolate and acute. Lip often similar, sometimes trilobed at the base, with a spur that tapers from a wide mouth. Rostellum trilobed, pendent, the lobes being papillose or hairy. Pollinia two, stipites two, viscidia two.

CULTIVATION: All the species of *Mystacidium* we have grown have disliked greatly, sometimes terminally, being in a pot. It seems to be necessary to grow them mounted on bark.

Mystacidium aliceae H. Bolus

DESCRIPTION: One of the smallest species. Roots fine, white-streaked, 1 mm in diameter. Leaves two to five, 2–6 cm (1–2 in.) × 4–6 mm, linear or strap-shaped. Inflorescences 1–1.5 cm (0.5–1 in.) long, densely 3- to 7-flowered. Flowers translucent yellowish-green, 6–7 mm in diameter. Sepals 3–4 × 1 mm, oblanceolate, acute; petals and lip 1–2 mm long, triangular, acute; spur 6–7 mm long, very slender from a wide mouth.

HABITAT: Epiphytic at a low level, growing on twigs and small branches in deep shade in forest and scrub, often near a river, to 500 m (1650 ft.).

CULTIVATION: Heavy shade with high humidity, in intermediate temperatures.

DISTRIBUTION: South Africa (known from a few localities in Eastern Cape, KwaZulu-Natal).

Mystacidium brayboniae Summerhayes

DESCRIPTION: Stems short; roots numerous, stout, 4–6 mm in diameter, gray-green with white streaks. Leaves two to five, 2–6 × 1–1.5 cm (1–2 × 0.5–1 in.), elliptic to strap-shaped, dark green. Inflorescences pendent, 2–5 cm (1–2 in.) long, 5- to 10-flowered. Flowers white, to 20 mm in diameter, slightly cup-shaped. Dorsal sepal and petals 6 × 2 mm, lanceolate, acute; lateral sepals 8 mm long. Lip 6–7 mm long, trilobed near the base, 4 mm wide across the lobes; midlobe ovate, obtuse. Spur 14–22 mm long, tapering from a wide mouth.

HABITAT: Epiphytic on *Ficus* species in shade in forest.

CULTIVATION: Intermediate temperatures, in moderate shade with high humidity while in growth; less water should be given while resting. It flowers in summer.

DISTRIBUTION: South Africa (known only from the Soutspansberg Mountains in Northern Province).

Mystacidium capense (Linnaeus f.) Schlechter

DESCRIPTION: Stems short; roots numerous, stout, gray-green with white streaks. Leaves 4 to 10, 3–13 × 1–1.5 cm (0.5–1 in.), strap-shaped or narrowly oblanceolate, unequally and obtusely bilobed at the apex, dark green. Inflorescences several, pendent, 6–10 cm (2–4 in.) long, with up to 14 flowers arranged in two rows. Flowers white, 2 cm (1 in.) in diameter. Pedicel and ovary arched, 7 mm long. Dorsal sepal 8–10 × 2–3 mm, lanceolate, acute; lateral sepals 12 × 3.5 mm, deflexed, obliquely lanceolate from a narrow base. Petals 8 × 2 mm, narrowly lanceolate, curving back. Lip 11 mm long, trilobed near the base, 3 mm wide across lobes; midlobe narrowly lanceolate, 2 mm wide; side lobes 1 mm long. Spur 4–6 cm (2–3 in.) long, straight, tapering to become slender from a wide mouth. Column very short.

HABITAT: This species grows in the hotter, drier areas, occurring in *Acacia* woodland and bush, a habitat where few, if any, other epiphytic orchids occur, and sometimes even on succulent candelabra *Euphorbia* trees, usually at low altitudes.

CULTIVATION: In spite of having what sounds like a fairly specialized habitat, *Mystacidium capense* is easily grown. It does well in intermediate conditions, but needs fairly good light and to be kept fairly dry in the resting period to stimulate flowering. It flowers in spring and summer (May and June).

DISTRIBUTION: South Africa (Eastern Cape, KwaZulu-Natal, Mpumalanga, Western Cape), Swaziland.

NOTE: This is the most widespread species in South Africa and the most common in cultivation. A well-grown plant or group of plants is a beautiful sight. This species won the award for Best Specimen Miniature Orchid at the 14th World Orchid Conference in Glasgow in 1993.

Mystacidium flanaganii (H. Bolus) H. Bolus

DESCRIPTION: A dwarf species. Roots fine, sometimes flexuous. Leaves two to five, to 3 cm (1 in.) × 4–7 mm, strap-shaped or elliptic. Inflorescences pendent, 5–6 cm (2 in.) long, rather laxly 5- to 10-flowered. Flowers pale green or yellowish-white, 8–10 mm in diameter, arranged in two rows. Dorsal sepal and petals 2 × 1 mm,; lateral sepals 4 × 1 mm, obliquely lanceolate from a narrow base. Lip 2 mm long, lanceolate, acute, recurved, with a slender spur 2–3 cm (1 in.) long tapering from a wide mouth.

HABITAT: Epiphytic on twigs and small branches in relatively cool, moist forests; sometimes in warmer scrub. Altitude not known.

CULTIVATION: We have not grown this species, but from habitat descriptions it should require moderate to heavy shade and high humidity, at intermediate temperatures.

DISTRIBUTION: South Africa (Eastern Cape, KwaZulu-Natal, Mpumalanga, Northern Province), Swaziland.

Plate 1. Mist over the Mayombe, at Dimonika, Congo, allows many epiphytic orchids to survive the dry season.

Plate 2. Tropical forest, on Mampong scarp, Ashanti, Ghana, in 1957. Once home to many epiphytic orchids, it is unlikely that much forest remains today.

Plate 3. Forest and stream, Congo Republic.

Plate 4. *Brachystegia* woodland, northern Malawi. The young growth comes in a variety of shades of red and pink.

Plate 5. Nyika plateau, Malawi. Montane grassland, which has many terrestrial orchids, with remnant patches of montane forest lying in the folds of the hills. *Aerangis montana* is one of the epiphytic species that grows there.

Plate 6. Malalotja, Swaziland, at the height of the dry season, looking towards the hills of Mpumalanga, South Africa. When the rains start, the montane grassland is covered with flowers, including terrestrial orchids.

Plate 7. *Acampe pachyglossa.* This large clump was flowering in a hot, dry area in Swaziland, although not far from a river; we got the scent of the colony well before we saw it.

Plate 8. *Aerangis arachnopus* from Congo, flowering in cultivation.

Plate 9. *Aerangis carnea,* known only from southern Tanzania and northern Malawi.

Plate 10. *Aerangis confusa* from Kenya, flowering in cultivation.

Plate 11. *Aerangis distincta,* a Malawi endemic, flowering in deep shade in riverine forest.

Plate 12. *Aerangis kirkii,* an East African species, flowering in cultivation.

Plate 13. *Aerangis luteoalba* var. *rhodosticta,* flowering in cultivation.

Plate 14. *Aerangis montana* grows in heavy shade in montane forest.

Plate 15. *Aerangis mystacidii,* flowering in Malawi.

Plate 16. *Aerangis oligantha* from southern Tanzania and northern Malawi.

Plate 17. *Aerangis splendida,* flowering in Malawi, is one of the finest *Aerangis* species.

Plate 18. *Aerangis ugandensis,* flowering in cultivation.

Plate 19. *Aerangis verdickii,* flowering in Malawi.

Plate 20. *Ancistrochilus rothschildianus.* Photo by Joyce Stewart.

Plate 21. *Ancistrorhynchus capitatus* from Congo, flowering in cultivation.

Plate 22. *Angraecopsis amaniensis,* flowering in Malawi. This little species produces a mass of scented flowers.

Plate 23. *Angraecum conchiferum* from Zomba plateau, Malawi.

Plate 24. *Angraecum pusillum* from South Africa.

Plate 25. *Angraecum stella-africae,* growing wild in Malawi.

Plate 26. *Ansellia africana,* a well-marked form from northern Malawi.

Plate 27. *Bolusiella maudiae* from Malawi, flowering in cultivation.

Plate 28. *Bonatea bracteata* from South Africa. Photo by Joyce Stewart.

Plate 29. *Bonatea speciosa,* flowering at Kirstenbosch, South Africa. Photo by Joyce Stewart.

Plate 30. *Bulbophyllum expallidum,* flowering in northern Malawi.

Plate 31. *Bulbophyllum falcatum* var. *velutinum* from Congo, flowering in cultivation.

Plate 32. *Bulbophyllum josephii,* flowering in northern Malawi.

Plate 33. *Bulbophyllum nigericum,* flowering in cultivation.

Plate 34. *Bulbophyllum porphyrostachys* from Congo, flowering in cultivation.

Plate 35. *Bulbophyllum saltatorium* var. *albociliatum* from Congo, flowering in cultivation.

Plate 36. *Calanthe sylvatica,* white-flowered form from southern Malawi; in northern Malawi, the flowers are purple.

Plate 37. *Chamaeangis odoratissima,* flowering on riverine trees in Malawi.

Plate 38. *Cynorkis hanningtonii,* growing in a pine plantation, Zomba plateau, Malawi.

Plate 39. *Cynorkis kassneriana,* growing under pines, Zomba plateau, Malawi.

Plate 40. *Cyrtorchis arcuata* subsp. *arcuata*, growing in full exposure on rocks in the Lebombo Mountains, Swaziland. The white flowers are just visible between the plants of the succulent *Aloe arborescens*.

Plate 41. *Cyrtorchis praetermissa* var. *praetermissa*, flowering in Malawi.

Plate 42. *Cyrtorchis ringens,* widespread in Africa, here flowering in Malawi.

Plate 43. *Diaphananthe pulchella* var. *pulchella,* flowering in riverine forest in Malawi.

Plate 44. *Diaphananthe rutila,* flowering in Malawi.

Plate 45. *Diaphananthe stolzii,* a large colony flowering in riverine forest in southern Malawi.

Plate 46. *Diaphananthe xanthopollinia,* flowering on a tree stump in northern Malawi.

Plate 47. *Disa saxicola,* flowering on Zomba plateau, Malawi.

Plate 48. *Disa uniflora,* showing different color forms. Grown and photographed by L. Vogelpoel.

Plate 49. *Disa* 'Foam' (*D.* 'Betty's Bay' × *D. uniflora*). Grown by S. and M. Cywes. Photo by L. Vogelpoel.

Plate 50. *Disperis fanniniae*, growing in heavy shade in forest, Natal, South Africa.

Plate 51. *Eulophia cucullata*, flowering in northern Malawi.

Plate 52. *Eulophia guineensis,* Malawi.

Plate 53. *Eulophia horsfallii*, Malawi.

Plate 54. *Eulophia speciosa*, Malawi.

Plate 55. *Eulophia streptopetala*, Malawi.

Plate 56. *Eulophia zeyheri*, Malawi.

Plate 57. *Eurychone rothschildiana,* flowering in cultivation.

Plate 58. *Habenaria praestans,* flowering on Zomba plateau, in southern Malawi.

Plate 59. *Habenaria procera* var. *gabonensis* from Congo, flowering in cultivation.

Plate 60. *Habenaria splendens,* flowering near Mzuzu, in northern Malawi.

Plate 61. *Herschelianthe baurii,* on the Nyika plateau, Malawi, flowering in the montane grassland before the first rains.

Plate 62. *Jumellea filicornoides,* flowering in Malawi.

Plate 63. *Liparis bowkeri,* growing on the forest floor, Mount Chiradzulu, Malawi.

Plate 64. *Listrostachys pertusa* from Congo, flowering in cultivation.

Plate 65. *Microcoelia corallina,* flowering in dry woodland, Malawi.

Plate 66. *Microcoelia globulosa,* flowering in Malawi.

Plate 67. *Microcoelia ornithocephala,* known from only two sites in southern Malawi, flowering in the wild.

Plate 68. *Mystacidium venosum* from Swaziland.

Plate 69. *Oberonia disticha,* Malawi.

Plate 70. *Polystachya adansoniae,* widespread in Africa, here flowering in Malawi.

Plate 71. *Polystachya affinis* from Congo, flowering in cultivation.

Plate 72. *Polystachya bella* from Kenya, flowering in cultivation.

Plate 73. *Polystachya bennettiana* from Nigeria.

Plate 74. *Polystachya brassii,* flowering on a lichen-covered branch in Malawi.

Plate 75. *Polystachya cultriformis,* flowering in cultivation.

Plate 76. *Polystachya dendrobiiflora,* flowering by the roadside in Malawi.

Plate 77. *Polystachya golungensis* from Congo, flowering in cultivation.

Plate 78. *Polystachya greatrexii,* flowering in Malawi.

Plate 79. *Polystachya johnstonii* from Malawi, flowering on *Xerophyta* sp. on Zomba plateau, Malawi.

Plate 80. *Polystachya lawrenceana* from Malawi, flowering in cultivation.

Plate 81. *Polystachya longiscapa,* a Tanzanian endemic, flowering in cultivation.

Plate 82. *Polystachya minima,* native to a small area in southern Malawi.

Plate 83. *Polystachya odorata,* flowering in cultivation. This species can have white or yellow flowers.

Plate 84. *Polystachya pubescens* from South Africa, on display at the 14th World Orchid Conference in Glasgow in 1993.

Plate 85. *Polystachya spatella* from Uganda.

Plate 86. *Polystachya tessellata.* This striking pink form comes from Congo; usually the flowers are yellow.

Plate 87. *Polystachya transvaalensis,* flowering on Dedza Mountain, Malawi.

Plate 88. *Polystachya villosa,* flowering in Malawi on a remnant tree.

Plate 89. *Polystachya woosnamii* from Nigeria.

Plate 90. *Polystachya zambesiaca,* flowering in Malawi.

Plate 91. *Rangaeris amaniensis,* flowering in cultivation.

Plate 92. *Rangaeris muscicola,* widespread in Africa, here flowering in Malawi.

Plate 93. *Rangaeris rhipsalisocia* from Congo, flowering in cultivation.

Plate 94. *Satyrium coriifolium,* Cape
Province, South Africa.

Plate 95. *Stenoglottis longifolia* from South
Africa, growing in cultivation.

Plate 96. *Stolzia repens* from Mount Mulanje in Malawi.

Plate 97. *Tridactyle anthomaniaca,* flowering in Malawi.

Plate 98. *Tridactyle bicaudata,* widespread in Africa, here flowering in Malawi.

Plate 99. *Tridactyle tricuspis,* flowering in Malawi.

Plate 100. *Tridactyle tridentata,* flowering in Malawi.

Plate 101. *Tridactyle truncatiloba* from Congo, flowering in cultivation. This handsome species has the largest flowers of any species of *Tridactyle.*

Plate 102. *Vanilla polylepis,* flowering in riverine fringe trees, northern Malawi.

Plate 103. *Ypsilopus erectus,* flowering in Malawi.

Mystacidium gracile (Reichenbach f.) Harvey

DESCRIPTION: A very slender species. Roots very fine, 1 mm in diameter, in a clump. Leaves usually absent (and then the plant looks like a species of *Microcoelia*), but a few are sometimes produced, more often in cultivation than in the wild; these are to 3 cm (1 in.) × 3 mm, elliptic or linear. Inflorescences 4–10 cm (2–4 in.) long, 4- to 12-flowered in two rows. Flowers greenish-white, fragile-looking, 14 mm in diameter. Dorsal sepal 5 × 1.5 mm, ovate, acute; lateral sepals spreading, 6 × 2, obliquely lanceolate from a narrow base. Petals 4 × 1 mm, linear. Lip 4 × 1.5 mm, obscurely trilobed at the base, the midlobe tapering, acute; spur 2–2.5 cm (1 in.) long, slender, tapering from a wide mouth.

HABITAT: Epiphytic on trunks and main branches of forest trees, to 1800 m (6000 ft.).

CULTIVATION: In heavy shade, with high humidity, at intermediate temperatures.

DISTRIBUTION: South Africa (Eastern Cape, KwaZulu-Natal, Mpumalanga), Zimbabwe.

Mystacidium millarii H. Bolus

SYNONYM: *Diaphananthe millarii* (H. Bolus) Linder

DESCRIPTION: Stems short; roots rather stout, gray with white streaks, 4 mm in diameter. Leaves 2 to 10, to 12 × 1.5 cm (5 × 1 in.), leathery, strap-shaped, unequally bilobed at the apex, dark green with raised reticulate venation and a rather velvety appearance. Inflorescences pendent, 2–5 cm (1–2 in.) long, fairly densely 7- to 12-flowered. Flowers rather bell-shaped, white with a green anther cap, to 12 mm in diameter. Pedicel and ovary 10 mm long. Dorsal sepal and petals 6–7 × 3 mm, obovate, obtuse; lateral sepals slightly longer, oblanceolate. Lip 5–6 mm long, oblong to obovate, subacute, recurved at the tip; spur 2 cm (1 in.) long, tapering to a slender apex from a wide, funnel-shaped mouth.

HABITAT: Epiphytic at low level in coastal bush.

CULTIVATION: Mounted, in intermediate temperatures and light to moderate shade, with plenty of water during the growing season, but much less in winter.

DISTRIBUTION: South Africa (Eastern Cape, KwaZulu-Natal). This species has always been local in its distribution and must be extinct in many of its original sites, mainly due to urban development; fortunately, however, it is well established in cultivation.

Mystacidium pusillum (Reichenbach f.) Harvey

DESCRIPTION: The smallest species of *Mystacidium,* virtually stemless; roots few, fine, 1 mm in diameter. Leaves two to five, 15–27 × 5–6 mm, elliptic. Inflorescences pendent, to 17 mm long, 2- to 5-flowered. Flowers pale green, 6–7 mm in diameter. Dorsal sepal 2 × 1 mm; laterals 3 mm long; petals slightly smaller than dorsal sepal. Lip 2 mm long, lanceolate, obtuse; spur 13–16 mm long, tapering from a wide mouth.

HABITAT: Epiphytic on bushes in scrub vegetation in light shade, 900–1200 m (3000–4000 ft.).

CULTIVATION: Not known to be in cultivation outside South Africa, where it is grown by some enthusiasts. Being so small, it would need fairly high humidity all year round, even though it might have to survive a long dry season in the wild.

DISTRIBUTION: South Africa (known only from a few localities in Eastern Cape, KwaZulu-Natal).

Mystacidium tanganyikense Summerhayes

DESCRIPTION: A dwarf species, virtually stemless; roots very fine, 1 mm in diameter. Leaves two to five, 1.5–5 × 0.5–1 cm (0.25–0.5 in.), oblanceolate, unequally and obtusely bilobed at the apex, dark green with raised, reticulate venation. Inflorescences to 6 cm (2 in.) long, rather laxly several-flowered. Flowers starry, translucent pale green or white, 10–15 mm in diameter. Pedicel and ovary 6–12 mm long, very slender. Sepals and petals lanceolate, acute, spreading; dorsal sepal 4–8 × 1–2 mm; laterals longer and rather oblique; petals slightly shorter. Lip 5–7 × 3 mm, lanceolate, acute, very obscurely trilobed at the base; spur 1–2 cm (0.5–1 in.) long, tapering from a wide mouth. Column 1 mm long.

HABITAT: Epiphytic in montane and submontane forest, growing on twigs, small branches, and lianas, usually sunk in moss and often abundant where it occurs, 1300–2500 m (4300–8250 ft.).

CULTIVATION: Intermediate to cool temperatures, heavy shade and high humidity.

DISTRIBUTION: Malawi, Tanzania, Zambia, Zimbabwe.

Mystacidium venosum Harvey ex Rolfe   PLATE 68, FIGURE 10-62

DESCRIPTION: Stems short; roots numerous, long, 3–6 mm in diameter, gray-green with white streaks. Leaves two to five, sometimes absent in the dry season, 1.5–6 cm (1–2 in.) × 7–11 mm, rather fleshy, elliptic to oblanceolate, unequally bilobed at the apex. Inflorescences several, 3–9 cm (1–4 in.) long, pendent, fairly densely to 12-flowered. Flowers white, 15–20 mm in diameter. Dorsal sepal 8 × 2.5 mm, lanceolate, acute; laterals spreading, 9 × 3 mm, obliquely lanceolate from a narrow base. Petals 5 × 1.5 mm, triangular. Lip 6 × 2 mm, trilobed, with toothlike lobes at the base, lanceolate, acute; spur 3–4.5 mm, tapering from a wide mouth.

HABITAT: Rather varied; epiphytic in bush and forest, sometimes in heavy shade and sometimes in exposed situations, often forming large colonies where it occurs.

CULTIVATION: We find this species is easily grown at intermediate temperatures, in moderate to light shade. In our greenhouse, it flowers in autumn and early winter (October and November).

DISTRIBUTION: South Africa (Eastern Cape, KwaZulu-Natal, Mpumalanga, Northern Province), Swaziland.

Figure 10-62. *Mystacidium venosum.* Plant, ×1.

Neobenthamia Rolfe

The genus *Neobenthamia* was created by Robert Rolfe in 1891 and named in honor of George Bentham (1800–1884), a friend and collaborator of Joseph Hooker, who worked for many years at the Royal Botanic Gardens, Kew. It is a monospecific genus, closely related to *Polystachya,* but differing mainly in the habit of growth and in having resupinate flowers without a distinct column foot.

Neobenthamia gracilis Rolfe

DESCRIPTION: Plants 90–200 cm (3–6 ft.) tall; stems branched, erect or straggling, leafy, often forming keikis at the nodes. Leaves 12–28 × 0.5–2 cm (5–11 × 0.25–1 in.), linear, distichous, unequally bilobed at the apex. Inflorescences terminal on the branches, to 6 cm (2 in.) long and wide, sometimes with up to seven branches, densely many-flowered. Flowers strongly scented, white, the lip with a yellow central area bordered by pink dots. Sepals 10–12 × 4 mm, oblong; petals 9 × 4 mm, oblong-spathulate, narrow at the base. Lip entire, 11 × 7 mm, oblong-obovate, truncate or rounded at the tip, narrower at the base, hairy in the center, with wavy margins. Column 2–3 mm long, white, the anther cap purple.

HABITAT: Terrestrial on dry, exposed, sloping rock faces, or on mossy ledges on precipices, 450–1800 m (1500–6000 ft.).

CULTIVATION: In a bark mix in a pot, at intermediate temperatures and with good light. Our plants are growing well but have not yet flowered; they are probably not large enough. Presumably, as they grow taller they might need to be staked. Although they are not epiphytic in the wild, we use an epiphytic mix as the places where they grow have extremely free drainage.

DISTRIBUTION: Tanzania (known only from the Nguru and Uluguru Mountains).

Nephrangis Summerhayes

The genus *Nephrangis* was created by V. S. Summerhayes in 1948 to accommodate a plant first described in 1895 by Fritz Kränzlin as *Listrostachys filiformis* and transferred in 1918 by Rudolf Schlechter to *Tridactyle.* The genus name is derived from the Greek words *nephro* (kidney) and *angos* (vessel), obviously referring to the kidney-shaped lamina of the lip.

Nephrangis filiformis (Kränzlin) Summerhayes

DESCRIPTION: Stems pendent, to 50 cm (20 in.) long but usually shorter, slender, usually branched. Leaves 1.5–9 cm (1–4 in.) × 1–2 mm, needlelike but slightly flattened, somewhat recurved. Inflorescences arising along the stem, 5–15 mm long, 1- to 4-flowered. Flowers translucent, light brown or brownish-green, the lip white. Pedicel and ovary 3–4 mm long; bracts to 1 mm long, papery. Sepals 1.5–2.5 × 1.5–2 mm, ovate to suborbicular, obtuse, the laterals joined at the base. Petals 1.5–2.5 × 0.5 mm, linear, acute. Lip 4–5 mm long, clawed and channelled at the base, then suddenly expanded into a bilobed lamina 3.5–5 mm wide; spur 4–9 mm long, conical, obtuse. Column 1 mm long.

HABITAT: Epiphytic in forest and woodland, 600–2000 m (2000–6600 ft.).

CULTIVATION: This species is not common in cultivation. We have not grown it, but have seen it offered. From the growth habit and habitat, it is likely to require being mounted or grown in a basket, at intermediate temperatures, in moderate shade.

DISTRIBUTION: Burundi, Kenya, Liberia, Rwanda, Tanzania, Uganda, Zaire, Zambia.

Oberonia Lindley

The genus *Oberonia* was created by John Lindley in 1830. The name refers to Oberon, the king of the fairies—perhaps because of the very small flowers? It is a big genus with more than 100 members, mostly in tropical Asia, but stretching to the Pacific Islands and Australia. One species is known from mainland Africa and Madagascar.

DESCRIPTION: Flowers tiny, nonresupinate, in a densely flowered, cylindrical, terminal spike. Leaves fleshy, distichous. Column very short. Pollinia four, pear-shaped.

Oberonia disticha (Lamarck) Schlechter   PLATE 69

DESCRIPTION: A small species, 2–15 cm (1–6 in.) long, flattened from side to side, sometimes forming clumps; roots very fine, less than 1 mm in diameter. Leaves usually seven to eight, to 5 × 1 cm (2–0.5 in.), distichous, overlapping, fleshy, bilaterally flattened, pale green, lanceolate, acute or acuminate, decreasing in size towards the top of the plant. Inflorescences terminal, 3–10 cm (1–4 in.) long, cylindrical and tapering, densely many-flowered. Flowers tiny, yellow-ocher to orange, less than 2 mm across. Sepals 0.7 × 0.5 mm, ovate, obtuse; petals 0.5 × 0.2 mm, elliptic, obtuse. Lip 1 × 0.7 mm, deflexed, somewhat fiddle-shaped, with no spur. Column very short.

HABITAT: Epiphytic in evergreen forest and high rainfall woodland, usually hanging downwards on trunks and lower branches, 470–1250 m (1500–4100 ft.). It tends to be very local in its distribution; in Malawi, for example, it is only found in one small area, although there are many other places where the habitat is apparently suitable.

CULTIVATION: Intermediate temperatures and moderate shade. This species can be either mounted, if the humidity is kept high, or grown in a pot, where it needs to be watered with care as too much moisture will cause the fleshy leaves to rot, although the fine roots do not like to be dried out too much.

DISTRIBUTION: Cameroon, Malawi, South Africa (Mpumalanga), Tanzania, Uganda, Zaire, Zimbabwe. Also in Comoro Islands, Madagascar, Mascarene Islands.

Oeceoclades Lindley
SYNONYM: *Eulophidium* Pfitzer

It is perhaps a pity that the name *Eulophidium*, which was in general use and reflected the close relationship between this genus and *Eulophia*, had to be replaced by the more difficult name *Oeceoclades*, which had been used some 50 years earlier, in 1832, by John Lindley. The name is derived from the Greek words *oikeos* (private) and *klados* (branch).

It has been suggested (Bechtel et al. 1992) that the name might refer to the separation of these species from *Angraecum* into a separate, or private, branch. The two genera, *Eulophia* and *Oeceoclades,* are similar in many ways; in fact Geerinck (1992) sank the latter into *Eulophia,* but this has not been generally accepted. *Oeceoclades* was revised by Garay and Taylor (1976).

Members of *Eulophia* section *Pulchrae,* which have aboveground pseudobulbs with several nodes and petiolate but plicate leaves have, at times, been placed in *Eulophidium* and *Oeceoclades.* By Lindley's original definition and its interpretation by Garay and Taylor, these would remain in *Eulophia,* which is where we have described the only species of relevance to this book, *E. pulchra.*

There are more than 30 species of *Oeceoclades* in tropical and South Africa, Madagascar, the Mascarene Islands, and the Seychelles, with one species, *Oeceoclades maculata,* also found in Central and South America and the West Indies. About 12 species are known to occur on mainland Africa. Many species are worth a place in a collection as foliage plants.

DESCRIPTION: Pseudobulbs with only one fully developed internode. Leaves thick, leathery, conduplicate, not pleated, one to three per pseudobulb, usually attractively mottled, almost always petiolate, and usually articulated some distance above the join of the petiole to the pseudobulb, so that when the leaves are shed, the lower part of the petiole remains attached to the pseudobulb. Inflorescence arises from the base of the pseudobulb and may be simple or branched. Flowers *Eulophia*-like. Lip 4-lobed, usually with two parallel calli at the mouth of the spur.

CULTIVATION: Species are usually terrestrial and should be grown in a very free-draining terrestrial mix, preferably in a clay pot. They have rather few, but very thick roots, which rot easily if kept too wet. Most species grow in dry areas, but the leaves usually persist for more than one season so that plants are never completely leafless. Accordingly, although they should be kept drier when not in growth, plants should not be kept totally dry for any length of time, unlike deciduous terrestrials. If possible, water should be kept from the leaves, which have a tendency to turn black. Temperatures should be intermediate to warm.

Oeceoclades decaryana (H. Perrier) Garay & Taylor

SYNONYMS: *Eulophia decaryana* Perrier, *Eulophidium decaryanum* (Perrier) Summerhayes

DESCRIPTION: A terrestrial species, usually 50–60 cm (20–24 in.) tall. Pseudobulbs ovoid, 2–4 cm (1–2 in.) long. Leaves two, 15–25 × 1–2 cm (6–10 × 0.5–1 in.), linear to lanceolate, narrowing to a petiolate base, leathery, gray-green with blue-gray and whitish-gray blotches. Inflorescences 20–40 cm (8–16 in.) tall, unbranched, rather loosely 10- to 20-flowered. Pedicel and ovary 22–25 mm long; bracts 5–10 mm long. Sepals and petals dark olive green with red or purple veins; lip yellow or cream, veined with red; spur green or orange. Sepals 12–20 × 3–4 mm, oblanceolate or spathulate; petals 7–10 × 4–7 mm, oblong, apiculate. Lip 12–16 × 13–18 mm, 4-lobed, the lobes rounded, with two calli at the base. Spur 3–6 mm long, stout, cylindrical. Column 4–5 mm long.

HABITAT: In humus among rocks in shade of riverine forest or thicket, to 900 m (3000 ft.).

CULTIVATION: As given for the genus.

DISTRIBUTION: Kenya, Madagascar, Mozambique, Zimbabwe.

Oeceoclades maculata (Lindley) Lindley   FIGURE 10-63

SYNONYMS: *Eulophia maculata* (Lindley) Reichenbach f., *Eulophidium maculatum* (Lindley) Pfitzer

DESCRIPTION: A terrestrial herb (very rarely a low-level epiphyte). Pseudobulbs ovoid, 2–4 cm (1–2 in.) long, eventually forming large clumps. Leaf one per pseudobulb, 10–30 × 2.5–5 cm (4–12 × 1–2 in.), oblong-elliptic, acute, with a petiolate base to 2 cm (1 in.) long, very stiff-textured, glossy gray-green with darker mottling. Inflorescences 20–30 cm (8–12 in.) tall, usually simple but sometimes with one to two short branches, laxly to 20-flowered. Sepals pinkish-brown, petals pink, or sometimes all straw-colored; lip greenish-white with two pink blotches in the middle, the side lobes with red-purple veins; spur usually brownish. Pedicel and ovary 10–15 mm long; bracts 10–20 mm long. Sepals 8–12 × 2–4 mm, narrowly oblanceolate; petals similar but slightly broader. Lip 7–10 mm long and broad when flattened; trilobed, the midlobe 3–4 × 7–8 mm, broadly obovate, emarginate; spur 4–5 mm long, straight, swollen at apex. Column 4–5 mm long.

HABITAT: In leaf litter in thicket, often on a slope, or in rocky scrub, to 1200 m (4000 ft.).

CULTIVATION: As given for the genus. This species is particularly prone to developing black spots on the leaf, which spread until the leaf falls off. This seems to be caused by water lying on the leaf, especially when temperatures are low, so particular care is needed when watering. The pot should be allowed to dry out between waterings.

DISTRIBUTION: Throughout tropical Africa. Also in Florida, Central and South America, and West Indies.

NOTE: *Oeceoclades mackenii* (Hemsley) Garay & Taylor, which is known from a few places in KwaZulu-Natal, South Africa, is very similar to *O. maculata,* and may be conspecific.

Oeceoclades saundersiana (Reichenbach f.) Garay & Taylor

SYNONYMS: *Eulophia saundersiana* Reichenbach f., *Eulophidium saundersianum* (Reichenbach f.) Summerhayes

DESCRIPTION: A terrestrial species, to 80 cm (32 in.) tall. Pseudobulbs narrowly ovoid, 8–15 cm (3–6 in.) long. Leaves two, with an elliptic blade 12–20 cm (5–8 in.) long, dark, glossy green, with petioles 6–17 cm (2–7 in.) long. Inflorescences to 30 cm (12 in.) long, simple or with one or two short branches, 15- to 30-flowered. Sepals and petals pale greenish-yellow with purple veins; lip pale yellow or greenish-cream with purple veins; spur reddish-brown. Pedicel and ovary 12–18 mm long; bracts 2–8 mm long, with an extrafloral nectary at the base that exudes a sweet, sticky fluid. Sepals

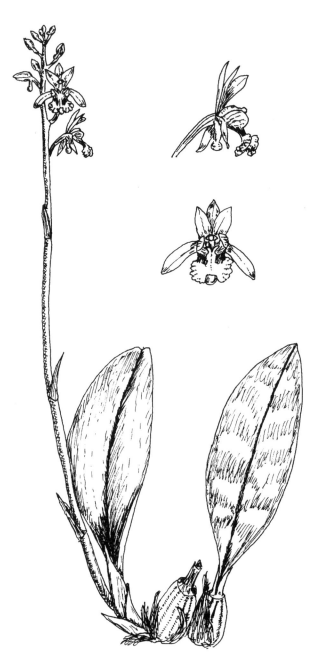

Figure 10-63. *Oeceoclades maculata.* Plant (center), ×0.75; flower (upper and middle right), ×1.5.

9–14 × 3–5 mm, narrowly oblong or obovate; petals 9–13 × 5–7 mm, ovate, obtuse. Lip 12–15 mm long, 4-lobed, the two lower lobes larger than the side lobes, 8–12 × 11–12 mm, suborbicular; callus with two parallel, fleshy keels. Spur 4–6 mm long, cylindrical, obtuse. Column 2.5–5 mm long.

HABITAT: In damp shade in forest and thicket, often in riverine forest, to 1200 m (4000 ft.).

CULTIVATION: Unlike many other species of *Oeceoclades* that are found in essentially dry areas, this species occurs in wetter areas and so should not be kept so dry.

DISTRIBUTION: Angola, Cameroon, Gabon, Ghana, Ivory Coast, Kenya, Liberia, Nigeria, Sierra Leone, Tanzania, Uganda, Zaire, Zambia.

Ossiculum Cribb & van der Laan

As far as we know, the genus *Ossiculum* is not in general cultivation, although it must have been grown in Holland as living material was used to prepare the illustration for the type description. However, it is so little known, so distinctive and potentially important, that it is worth including here. The genus *Ossiculum* was established in 1986 by P. J. Cribb and F. M. van der Laan to accommodate a plant collected by H. J. Beentjie in Cameroon. The name is given in his honor; *beentjie* is Dutch for "a small bone," and *ossiculum* is the Latin equivalent. The genus is monotypic; it does not seem to be very closely related to any other African representative of the tribe Vandeae, the nearest relative being *Calyptrochilum*. Its most striking feature is the color, bright orange. While several African angraecoid orchids have rather dull orange flowers, for example, some species of *Chamaeangis*, *Cribbia*, *Diaphananthe*, and *Tridactyle*, none has such brightly colored flowers. Bright orange flowers do occur, however, in two species of *Microcoelia* from Madagascar, *M. elliotii* and *M. gilpinae*. The column is distinctive, with an elongated, pincerlike rostellum; there are two pollinia, with one slender stipes and one large, semicircular viscidium.

Ossiculum aurantiacum Cribb & van der Laan

DESCRIPTION: An erect, monopodial epiphyte with a leafy stem, to 15 cm (6 in.) tall; roots arising from basal part of stem, to 12 cm (5 in.) long, 2 mm in diameter. Leaves distichous, 2–4.5 × 0.6–1 cm (1–2 × 0.25–0.5 in.), oblong-lanceolate, fleshy, obliquely bilobed at apex, V-shaped in cross-section, set 5–6 mm apart. Inflorescences axillary, to 18 mm long (or shorter than the leaves), densely 9- to 15-flowered. Flowers nonresupinate, fleshy; sepals and petals orange-red, lip yellow. Pedicel and ovary 2–2.5 mm long; bracts 1 mm long. Dorsal sepal 4 × 1.5 mm, elliptic, acuminate; lateral sepals slightly longer and broader, triangular. Petals 3.5 × 1 mm, oblanceolate, acuminate. Lip entire, 4.5–5 × 3 mm, oblong-obovate, apiculate, with a fleshy callus on each side of the mouth of the spur; spur 1.5–2 mm long, S-shaped, swollen to 1.5 mm in diameter at the apex. Column 0.5 mm long.

HABITAT: Epiphytic on lower branches of trees in primary forest. Altitude not known.

DISTRIBUTION: Cameroon.

NOTE: The chromosome number of this interesting species is $2n = 34$, a number that is more characteristic of subtribe Angraecinae than of subtribe Aerangidinae, into which it has been provisionally placed. The possibility of introducing the bright color to larger flowers by hybridization is an exciting one—if material of *Ossiculum aurantiacum* could be obtained.

Plectrelminthus Rafinesque

The monospecific genus *Plectrelminthus* was established by C. S. Rafinesque in 1838. The name is derived from the Greek words *plektron* (spur) and *helmins* (worm), referring to the stout, wormlike spur. A plant first flowered in England in 1835 and was described by John Lindley as *Angraecum caudatum* in 1936.

Plectrelminthus caudatus (Lindley) Summerhayes
SYNONYM: *Plectrelminthus bicolor* Rafinesque

DESCRIPTION: A robust epiphyte; stems leafy, to 15 cm (6 in.) long; roots long and stout, sometimes almost 10 mm in diameter. Leaves several, distichous, set close together, 10–30 × 1.5–3.5 cm (4–12 × 1 in.), broadly strap-shaped, unequally and obtusely bilobed at the apex. Inflorescences arising from axils of lower leaves, spreading or pendulous, 35–80 cm (14–32 in.) long, with 4 to 10 flowers on a zigzag rachis. Sepals and petals yellow-green, sometimes flushed with bronze; lip white. Pedicel and ovary twisted so that the lip of the flowers lies parallel to the rachis, with the tip pointing to the base of the plant. Sepals and petals all oblong, acuminate; dorsal sepal 30–50 × 5–7 mm; laterals slightly narrower and joined at the base under the spur. Petals 30–35 × 4–5 mm. Lip 35–50 mm × 10–25 mm, ovate with a wavy edge, caudate, with a long basal claw; claw with two projections about halfway along that almost meet to form a V. Spur 15–25 cm (6–10 in.) long, thick, pendent and flexuous.

HABITAT: Epiphytic in forest, but where it receives strong light.

CULTIVATION: This species will grow in intermediate temperatures, but is difficult to flower and is better in warm temperatures. Even then, it needs to be given good light and high humidity during the growing season. With the very long roots, it seems to do best grown in a basket. Although it was introduced to Europe long ago, it is still not common in cultivation, possibly because of its large size and the difficulty of getting it to flower. When it does flower, however, it is very spectacular, and it is well worth making an effort to satisfy it.

DISTRIBUTION: Cameroon, Central African Republic, Gabon, Ghana, Guinea, Ivory Coast, Liberia, Nigeria, Sierra Leone, Zaire.

Podangis Schlechter

The genus *Podangis* was established by Rudolf Schlechter in 1918 to accommodate a plant originally described by H. G. Reichenbach as *Listrostachys dactyloceras*. The one species in this genus has fleshy, bilaterally flattened leaves borne in a fan, rather like those of species of *Bolusiella,* but the flowers are quite distinct. The name is interesting. When Reichenbach described *L. dactyloceras,* he must have thought that the lobed tip of the spur resembled fingers, and used the Greek *dactyl* (fingers) and *ceros* (horn) to refer to the spur. When Schlechter created the genus *Podangis,* it presumably reminded him of toes, as the name is derived from the Greek words *podos* (foot) and *angos* (vessel), again referring to the spur.

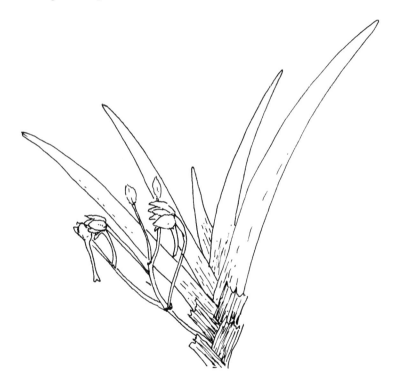

Figure 10-64. *Podangis dactyloceras.* Plant, ×1.

Podangis dactyloceras (Reichenbach f.) Schlechter   FIGURE 10-64

DESCRIPTION: An epiphyte; stems short, sometimes forming clumps; roots very fine, arising at the base. Leaves four to eight, borne in a fan, to 10 cm (4 in.) long, occasionally longer, and 5–10 mm wide, bilaterally flattened, linear, often curved, acute, fleshy. Inflorescences arising from the axils of the lower leaves and leaf bases, to

5 cm (2 in.) long, few- to 20-flowered. Flowers rather bell-shaped, translucent white with a crystalline texture, the anther cap dark green. Pedicel and ovary white, straight, 20–25 mm long, those at the base of the inflorescence being longer so that the flowers are held at almost the same level. Bracts 3 mm long. Sepals 4–7 × 3–4 mm, oblong, obtuse. Petals 4–5 × 3–5 mm, broadly obovate, acute. Lip 4–6 × 4–5 mm, entire, ovate, acute, very concave, the margin rather undulate; spur 9–11 mm long, tapering from a funnel-shaped mouth, then enlarged again into two lobules at the apex (the fingers or toes). Column 1–2 mm long.

HABITAT: Evergreen forest, 750–1590 m (2500–5250 ft.).

CULTIVATION: This unusual little species grows well at intermediate temperatures. The main problem is that the roots tend to rot if overwatered. We grow our plant in bark mix in a pot, which we allow to dry out before the plant is watered again. It might be better mounted, but the flowers turn brown if they get wet, and it is more difficult to prevent this with a mounted plant. As long as the grower is careful and uses a coarse mix, there should be no trouble. In our greenhouse, this species flowers in summer (July).

DISTRIBUTION: Angola, Cameroon, Ghana, Guinea, Ivory Coast, Nigeria, Sierra Leone, Tanzania, Uganda, Zaire.

Polystachya Hooker

Polystachya is by far the largest genus of epiphytic orchids found in Africa. Although it does not have as many species worldwide as does *Bulbophyllum, Polystachya* is predominantly an African genus: almost 200 species are found throughout the tropics, 160 of which occur in Africa. About 20 species are known from Madagascar and at least 2 of these, *P. cultriformis* and *P. fusiformis,* also occur in Africa. It is difficult to give exact figures, for while some species are widespread, others are narrow endemics. Whenever a part of Africa that is not too well known botanically is intensively collected, at least one new species of *Polystachya* is likely to turn up. It is safe to say that more new species are still being described in *Polystachya* than in any other genus of African orchid.

The genus *Polystachya* was established by Sir William Hooker in 1825. The name comes from the Greek words *polys* (many) and *stachys* (a spike or ear of grain), referring either to the clumps of many stems characteristic of most species, or to the appearance of an inflorescence in bud.

The last revision of the entire genus was made by the German botanist Fritz Kränzlin in 1926, when he divided it into a number of sections. Since then, many new species have been described, some sections have been revised, and some new sections have been created, notably by P. J. Cribb (1978), but a worldwide revision is much needed.

DESCRIPTION: Sympodial, usually epiphytic but several lithophytic, either occasionally or consistently; rarely terrestrial. Pseudobulbs usually well defined, set close together, forming clumps or chains, variable in shape from small and nutlike, to conical, spindle-shaped, and flat and coinlike, one-to several-leaved, often deciduous in the dry season. Plants in section *Caulescentes* have reedlike stems not swollen at the base.

Inflorescence terminal on the pseudobulb (unlike in *Bulbophyllum,* where it arises from the base), one- to many-flowered. Flowers small to medium-sized, commonly white, green, yellow, or yellow-green, but sometimes pink, mauve, purple, orange, or even red; flowers usually scented, most often with a primroselike perfume, but others with a strong, intensely sweet scent. Flowers nonresupinate; however, if a plant has an arching or pendent inflorescence, with the tip pointing down, the lip will seem to be at the bottom of the flower. Flowers usually rather bell-shaped, but in a few species they open widely to present an almost flat flower. Lateral sepals joined at the base to the column foot to form a chinlike structure called the *mentum.* The shape of the mentum is important in the identification of species; it is often low and rounded, but can be very prominent, occasionally forming a spurlike structure. Petals small. Lip usually trilobed, entire in some species, often recurved, sometimes very fleshy, usually with a callus at the junction of the lobes. Column usually short and stout, with a prominent foot; pollinia two, stipes one, viscidium one.

CULTIVATION: Many species of *Polystachya* are well worth growing, particularly the smaller ones. Most are compact plants that take up little space with long-lasting, scented flowers. Plants can be mounted on bark, but need high humidity and regular misting when in growth as the fine roots dry out quickly. We find these orchids are more successfully grown in pots in a medium bark mix that should not be allowed to remain wet. Deciduous species in particular should be kept pretty dry until new growth starts. Some species flower on an old pseudobulb after the leaves have fallen, while others flower on the newly developing shoots. Plants can easily be divided when they fill their pot, but this should only be done when necessary as they are all happier when in large clumps. Almost all species do well in intermediate temperatures and moderate shade, but lowland species should thrive at intermediate to warm temperatures, while those from montane areas prefer temperatures on the cool side of intermediate. In the descriptions that follow, all species are cultivated as described above, unless otherwise stated.

African Species of *Polystachya* included in this book, listed by sections

Polystachya Section *Affines* Kränzlin. One of the largest sections in the genus, with most species occurring in eastern Africa, although the type species of the section, *Polystachya affinis,* is West African. Section *Affines* is also one of the most confusing sections. It appears to be still evolving, as some species are variable, and it can be difficult to tell where one starts and another leaves off. The plants are small to medium-sized, rarely large, with well-developed pseudobulbs and lanceolate or elliptic leaves usually present at flowering time. The flowers come in a variety of colors. The lip is trilobed, fleshy, and recurved, difficult to flatten without breaking it.

Polystachya affinis Kränzlin
Polystachya bella Summerhayes
Polystachya campyloglossa Rolfe
Polystachya holmesiana Cribb

Polystachya johnstonii Rolfe
Polystachya laurentii De Wildeman
Polystachya lawrenceana Kränzlin
Polystachya leucosepala Cribb
Polystachya pubescens (Lindley) Reichenbach f.
Polystachya purpureobracteata Cribb & I. F. la Croix
Polystachya sandersonii Harvey
Polystachya valentina I. F. la Croix & Cribb
Polystachya villosa Rolfe
Polystachya zambesiaca Rolfe

Polystachya Section ***Aporoidea*** **Kränzlin.** Stems branched, dimorphic; pseudobulbs superposed, either narrowly cylindrical and canelike with many distichous leaves along their length, or swollen and with one terminal leaf; sometimes the lower part of a plant has leafy stems, while the upper branches take the latter form. This strange section has only one member.
Polystachya mystacioides De Wildeman

Polystachya Section ***Calluniflora*** **Kränzlin.** Plants small, with spindle-shaped, superposed pseudobulbs (that is, the new growth arises not from the woody rhizome but from one of the lower nodes of the previous year's pseudobulb), but forming tufts rather than long chains. Leaves linear and grasslike. Inflorescences unbranched, flowers small.
Polystachya anthoceros I. F. la Croix & Cribb
Polystachya calluniflora Kränzlin
Polystachya hastata Summerhayes

Polystachya Section ***Caulescentes*** **Kränzlin.** Stems cylindrical and canelike, not swollen at the base.
Polystachya albescens Ridley
Polystachya bennettiana Reichenbach f.
Polystachya bifida Lindley
Polystachya caloglossa Reichenbach f.
Polystachya paniculata (Swartz) Rolfe
Polystachya transvaalensis Schlechter

Polystachya Section ***Cultriformes*** **Kränzlin.** The largest section, with 40 species, several of which are narrow endemics and only one of which, *P. cultriformis,* could be called widespread. Members of this section are characterized by conical or cylindrical pseudobulbs, usually consisting of a single node, with one terminal leaf (although there may be additional bractlike leaves while the pseudobulb is developing). Inflorescences simple or branched.
Polystachya caespitifica Kränzlin ex Engler
Polystachya cultriformis (Thouars) Sprengel
Polystachya fallax Kränzlin

Polystachya galeata (Swartz) Reichenbach f.
Polystachya maculata Cribb
Polystachya melliodora Cribb
Polystachya poikilantha Kränzlin
Polystachya tenuissima Kränzlin
Polystachya undulata Cribb & Podzorski
Polystachya virginea Summerhayes
Polystachya vulcanica Kränzlin

Polystachya Section *Dendrobianthe* Schlechter. Plants lithophytic, terrestrial, or epiphytic on species of *Xerophyta* (family Velloziaceae). Pseudobulbs conical, with several nodes. Leaves linear, grasslike, deciduous in dry season. Flowers borne when the leaves are absent, white, mauve, or pink with an entire lip, flower stalk with dry sheaths.
Polystachya dendrobiiflora Reichenbach f.
Polystachya longiscapa Summerhayes
Polystachya zuluensis L. Bolus

Polystachya Section *Elasticae*. Plants very small, often with pink flowers, the lip more or less erect, projecting from the lateral sepals, and usually with a large, yellow callus. A small section confined to West Africa, except for the following species.
Polystachya songaniensis G. Williamson

Polystachya Section *Eurychilae* Summerhayes. Plants small; pseudobulbs round or ovoid. Leaves grasslike, deciduous in the dry season. Flowers large for the size of plant, borne on the new season's growth when the plants are still leafless.
Polystachya brassii Summerhayes
Polystachya greatrexii Summerhayes

Polystachya Section *Humiles* Summerhayes. Dwarf plants with well-developed pseudobulbs and few-flowered inflorescences with relatively large flowers. These are all attractive plants.
Polystachya confusa Rolfe
Polystachya disiformis Cribb
Polystachya heckmanniana Kränzlin
Polystachya ottoniana Reichenbach f.
Polystachya parva Summerhayes

Polystachya Section *Isochiloides* Summerhayes. Pseudobulbs obliquely conical, sometimes very small, often forming chains. Leaves linear, sometimes deciduous in the dry season. Flowers green, greenish-yellow, or yellow, usually with a white lip covered with club-shaped hairs. The free part of the column is relatively long. This section seems to be confined to eastern Africa, from Kenya to Zimbabwe.
Polystachya goetzeana Kränzlin
Polystachya minima Rendle

Polystachya Section *Kermesina* **Cribb.** Pseudobulbs slender, superposed. Flowers fleshy, opening flat. The section was created by P. J. Cribb (1978) to accommodate the following species, which did not fit into any other section.
Polystachya kermesina Kränzlin

Polystachya Section *Polychaete* **Cribb.** Plants with distinct pseudobulbs, forming clumps. Inflorescences usually simple with one or two compressed sheaths at the base, densely many-flowered. Flowers small, white, greenish-white, or yellow-green, sometimes marked with purple; bracts long, bristlelike. This section seems to be much better represented in West Africa than elsewhere on the continent.
Polystachya adansoniae Reichenbach f.
Polystachya coriscensis Reichenbach f.
Polystachya elegans Reichenbach f.
Polystachya polychaete Kränzlin
Polystachya seticaulis Rendle
Polystachya woosnamii Rendle

Polystachya Section *Polystachya.* Pseudobulbs usually well developed. Inflorescences many-flowered, often branched. Flowers small and fleshy.
Polystachya dolichophylla Schlechter
Polystachya golungensis Reichenbach f.
Polystachya leonensis Reichenbach f.
Polystachya modesta Reichenbach f.
Polystachya odorata Lindley
Polystachya tessellata Lindley

Polystachya Section *Superpositae* **Kränzlin.** Pseudobulbs elongated, with several nodes, either slender and cylindrical, or thicker and spindle-shaped, the new pseudobulbs growing from a node of an older pseudobulb and sometimes forming long chains. Flowers small to medium-sized, usually rather dull-colored.
Polystachya fusiformis (Thouars) Lindley
Polystachya spatella Kränzlin

Polystachya adansoniae Reichenbach f.   PLATE 70

DESCRIPTION: Pseudobulbs densely clustered, to 9 × 1 cm (4 × 0.5 in.), conical or oblong, slightly compressed, ribbed. Leaves two to three, to 16 × 1.5 cm (6 × 1 in.), linear or strap-shaped. Inflorescences 5–12 cm (2–5 in.) long, densely many-flowered. Flowers small, white or greenish-yellow with a purple column and anther cap, primrose-scented. Ovary with pedicel 4 mm long, arched, so that the flowers face down; bracts 8–9 mm long, bristlelike, reflexed. Sepals all acuminate, the dorsal 4 × 1.5, laterals 5 × 3 mm, obliquely triangular or ovate. Petals linear, 3 mm long. Lip recurved, 3–4 mm long, trilobed at about the middle with a fleshy, hairy callus between the lobes; side lobes erect, midlobe 2–4 × 1 mm, lanceolate, acute. Column 1.5 mm long.

HABITAT: Epiphytic in evergreen forest and in woodland in high rainfall areas, 1250–2000 m (4100–6600 ft.).

DISTRIBUTION: Angola, Cameroon, Equatorial Guinea (Bioko) Gabon, Guinea, Ivory Coast, Kenya, Liberia, Malawi, Nigeria, Sierra Leone, Tanzania, Uganda, Zaire, Zambia, Zimbabwe.

Polystachya affinis Kränzlin

PLATE 71

DESCRIPTION: Pseudobulbs almost round but compressed and coinlike, lying flat on the substrate, to 5 cm (2 in.) in diameter, with one node. Leaves two to three, 9–28 × 2.5–6 cm (4–11 × 1–2 in.), broadly oblanceolate or oblong, with a distinct stalk. Inflorescences arching or pendent, usually branched, to 40 cm (16 in.) long, many-flowered. Flowers scented, reddish-brown edged with mustard yellow, pubescent on the outside. Dorsal sepal 6–7 × 3–4 mm, elliptic; lateral sepals slightly longer and broader and oblique; mentum 5 mm high. Petals 6 × 2 mm, oblanceolate. Lip 6–7.5 × 5–6 mm, recurved, rather obscurely trilobed, with a central fleshy ridge between the lobes; side lobes erect, midlobe 2.5 × 3–3.5 mm, broadly ovate. Column short and stout, 1 mm long.

HABITAT: Epiphytic in evergreen forest, 600–1350 m (2000–4450 ft.).

CULTIVATION: Because the inflorescence is usually pendent, the pot needs to be suspended, or raised in some way, while the plant is flowering.

DISTRIBUTION: Angola, Cameroon, Central African Republic, Congo, Equatorial Guinea (Pagalu Island), Gabon, Ghana, Ivory Coast, Liberia, Nigeria, Sierra Leone, Togo, Uganda, Zaire.

NOTE: With its flat, coinlike pseudobulbs, this species attracts attention even when not in flower. The flowers are not brightly colored, but there are many of them.

Polystachya albescens Ridley

DESCRIPTION: Stems clustered, cylindrical, 10–20 cm (4–8 in.) long and 3–4 mm in diameter after the leaves have fallen, green or yellow-green with several nodes, covered with brown tubular sheaths when young. Leaves two to five, 10–20 × 1–2 cm (4–8 × 0.5–1 in.), linear or strap-shaped. Inflorescences to 20 cm (8 in.) long, the stalk covered with papery sheaths, simple or with some short branches; bracts usually over-lapping, 2–4 mm long. Flowers greenish-yellow, tinged with purple. Pedicel and ovary 5 mm long. Dorsal sepal 8 × 2.5 mm, ovate; laterals 10 × 7, obliquely triangular; mentum 6–9 mm high. Petals 7 × 1.5 mm, oblanceolate. Lip 6–9 × 5–7 mm with a short claw, trilobed at about halfway, with a glabrous, fleshy, yellow callus between the lobes; midlobe 2 × 2.5 mm, ovate, acute; side lobes erect. Column 1 mm long.

HABITAT: Epiphytic in riverine forest, often at the edge, and in woodland in high rainfall areas; occasionally lithophytic; 800–1850 m (2600–6100 ft.).

DISTRIBUTION: Angola, Cameroon, Kenya, Malawi, São Tomé, Tanzania, Uganda, Zaire, Zambia, Zimbabwe.

NOTE: This is one of the least exciting species of *Polystachya*. Four subspecies have been distinguished. The most widespread (and the most likely to be in cultivation) is subsp. *imbricata* (Rolfe) Summerhayes (synonym *P. imbricata* Rolfe).

Polystachya anthoceros I. F. la Croix & Cribb

DESCRIPTION: Pseudobulbs clustered or slightly superposed, 2–3 cm (1 in.) × 4 mm, spindle-shaped. Leaves two, 12–16 cm (5–6 in.) × 4–5 mm, linear, rather grasslike. Inflorescences 4–5 cm (2 in.) long, several-flowered. Flowers white, tipped with purple, smelling of creosote. Dorsal sepal 4 × 3 mm, ovate, acute; laterals 4 × 3 mm, obliquely ovate, but prolonged at the base and joined to the column foot to form a slender, bifid, spurlike mentum to 15 mm high. Petals 3 × 2 mm, ovate. Lip 12 × 3 mm, trilobed, with a slender, channelled claw 10 mm long; midlobe ovate, slightly emarginate; side lobes erect.

HABITAT: Epiphytic in submontane forest, 1500 m (5000 ft.).

CULTIVATION: Easily grown in cultivation, flowers in autumn (September and October).

DISTRIBUTION: Nigeria.

NOTE: This extraordinary species looks very much like the other members of section *Calluniflora* when not in flower, but the flowers, with the spurlike mentum, are quite unlike anything else in the genus. In all the specimens we have seen, the flowers have had three columns, which, according to Dressler (1993), is a not uncommon abnormality in the Orchidaceae. They seem, however, to be fertile as seed is set.

Polystachya bella Summerhayes   PLATE 72, FIGURE 10-65

DESCRIPTION: Pseudobulbs to 4 × 2.5 cm (2 × 1 in.), ellipsoid, somewhat bilaterally flattened, bright, glossy green, set close together on an ascending rhizome. Leaves one to four, 5–16 × 2–3 cm (2–6 × 1 in.), oblong or elliptical, slightly unequally bilobed at the apex, the lobes rounded, leathery, dark green. Inflorescences erect, 10–25 cm (4–10 in.) long, pubescent, simple or branched, densely many-flowered. Flowers primrose-scented, golden-yellow or orange, finely pubescent outside. Pedicel and ovary arched, 10–12 mm long, densely pubescent; bracts 10–15 mm long, narrowly triangular. Dorsal sepal 11–14 × 3 mm, lanceolate, acute; lateral sepals 14–17 × 4–5 mm, obliquely triangular-lanceolate; mentum 3 mm high. Petals 9–11 × 1.5 mm, oblanceolate. Lip 10–12 × 5–5.5 mm, trilobed at about halfway; side lobes erect, midlobe recurved, 5 × 2 mm, lanceolate, acute, fleshy, with a low, linear callus at the base. Column 3 mm long.

HABITAT: Epiphytic in forest, 1800–1950 m (6000–6430 ft.).

CULTIVATION: This is one of the most striking of all *Polystachya* species. Although it is confined to a limited area in the wild, it is well established in cultivation. It grows easily, as described for the genus. Because of its climbing rhizome, it is useful to place a slab of bark at the back of the pot so that new pseudobulbs can attach their roots to it. In cultivation, it usually flowers in winter.

DISTRIBUTION: Southwestern Kenya.

Figure 10-65. *Polystachya bella.* Plant, ×0.75.

Polystachya bennettiana Reichenbach f.

PLATE 73

SYNONYM: *Polystachya stricta* Rolfe

DESCRIPTION: Stems 9–24 cm (4–9 in.) tall, 3–5 mm in diameter, cylindrical, clustered, covered with loose, tubular leaf bases. Leaves 10–25 × 1–3.5 cm (4–10 × 0.5–1 in.), ligulate or narrowly elliptical. Inflorescences 10–30 cm (4–12 in.) long, with many secund, recurved branches, many-flowered. Flowers pubescent on the outside, greenish-yellow or cream, the lip usually marked with red or brown. Dorsal sepal 7–10 × 2–3.5 mm, lanceolate, acute; laterals 9–11 × 5.5–7 mm, obliquely triangular, with a conical mentum 6 mm high. Petals 6–8 × 2 mm, oblanceolate. Lip 7.5–10 × 6–7.5 mm, with a short claw, trilobed at about the middle, pubescent all over; midlobe 3–5 × 3 mm, ovate, recurved. Column 2 mm long.

HABITAT: Riverine forest or open woodland, 900–1900 m (3000–6300 ft.).

DISTRIBUTION: Cameroon, Ethiopia, Kenya, Nigeria, Tanzania, Uganda, Zaire, Zambia.

Polystachya bifida Lindley

FIGURE 10-66

DESCRIPTION: Stems clustered, cylindrical, 20 cm (8 in.) × 3 mm. Leaves three to six, 5–16 × 0.5–1.5 cm (2–6 × 0.25–1 in.), linear to strap-shaped, obtuse. Inflorescences 10–20 cm (4–8 in.) long, unbranched, 10- to 20-flowered. Flowers primrose-scented, greenish-yellow, the lip white, sometimes purple-tinged. Dorsal sepal 5 × 2 mm; laterals 7 × 6 mm, with a conical, obtuse mentum 5.5–8 mm high. Petals 5 × 0.5 mm, linear. Lip protruding from flower for the whole of its length, 6–9 mm long, trilobed, with a round, hairy callus at the base and a small tooth just in front of it; midlobe oblong.

HABITAT: Epiphytic in evergreen forest, to 2500 m (8250 ft.).

DISTRIBUTION: Cameroon, Equatorial Guinea (Bioko), Gabon, Nigeria, Rwanda, São Tomé, Zaire.

Polystachya brassii Summerhayes

PLATE 74

Descriptions: Pseudobulbs 1 cm (0.5 in.) long and wide, round or ovoid, green or purple, forming dense mats. Leaves two to three, 10–15 cm (4–6 in.) × 3–4 mm, linear, grasslike. Inflorescences 3–4 cm (1–2 in.) long, 5- to 6-flowered. Flowers primrose-scented, white or pale lilac, with a pale yellow line on the lip. Sepals ovate, slightly pubescent on the outside, 5 × 3 mm; mentum rounded, 3 mm high. Petals 5 × 1.5 mm, oblanceolate. Lip 6 × 7 mm, trilobed at about half way, pubescent inside near the base; side lobes erect; midlobe 2 × 3 mm, rounded at apex. Column slender, 3 mm long.

HABITAT: Usually epiphytic in woodland in high rainfall areas, forming large mats on trunks and lower branches; sometimes lithophytic; 1100–2000 m (3600–6600 ft.).

CULTIVATION: Although this pretty little species is deciduous in the resting season and must be kept fairly dry, it still needs regular misting to keep up the humidity, other-

Figure 10-66. *Polystachya bifida*. Plant (left), ×1; lip (right), ×6. →

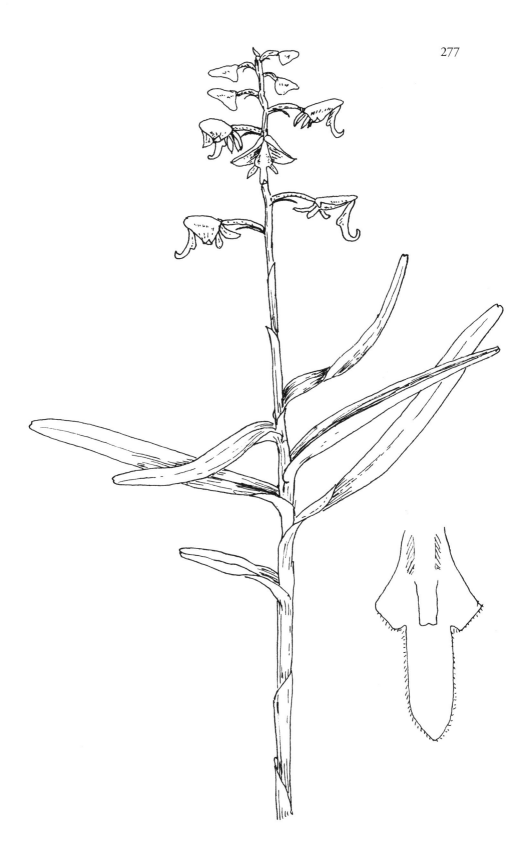

wise the pseudobulbs will shrivel. In the places where it grows in the wild, there is either frequent mist and occasional "out of season" drizzle.

DISTRIBUTION: Malawi, Zaire, Zambia.

Polystachya caespitifica Kränzlin ex Engler

DESCRIPTION: A small epiphyte, forming dense clumps; pseudobulbs to 6 cm (2 in.) tall, 0.5–2.5 mm wide, narrowly cylindrical. Leaf one, 4–15 cm (2–6 in.) × 1–10 mm, flat or terete and fleshy. Inflorescences shorter than leaf, unbranched, with to six flowers. Flowers white or yellow, tinged with lilac or purple; lip mauve at the base with a yellow or orange central line. Sepals 4–8 mm long, the dorsal 2–4 mm wide, ovate; the laterals 5–8 mm wide, triangular, with a conical mentum 5–6 mm high. Petals 4–7 × 1–3 mm, Lip recurved, lacking a callus, 4–8 × 7–11 mm, trilobed towards the apex, the midlobe rectangular, 1–4 × 2–4 mm.

NOTE: Podzorski and Cribb (1979) distinguished three geographically separated subspecies of *Polystachya caespitifica*, which differ vegetatively. The rather oddly shaped lip, lobed near the apex and without a callus, is similar in all the subspecies.

Subsp. *caespitifica*

DESCRIPTION: Plants 5–8 cm (2–3 in.) tall, with pseudobulbs less than 3.5 cm (1 in.) long and flat, strap-shaped leaves 3–5 cm (1–3 in.) × 4 mm.

HABITAT: Montane and submontane forest, 1500–2300 m (5000–7600 ft.).

DISTRIBUTION: Tanzania.

Subsp. *hollandii* (L. Bolus) Cribb & Podzorski

SYNONYM: *Polystachya hollandii* L. Bolus

DESCRIPTION: Plants 9–14 mm tall, with pseudobulbs to 5 cm (2 in.) long, very slender; leaves fleshy, terete, to 10 cm (4 in.) × 1–2 mm.

HABITAT: Montane and submontane forest, 1500–2300 m (5000–7600 ft.).

DISTRIBUTION: Tanzania, Zimbabwe.

Subsp. *latilabris* (Summerhayes) Cribb & Podzorski

SYNONYM: *Polystachya latilabris* Summerhayes

DESCRIPTION: Plants to 14 cm (6 in.) tall, with pseudobulbs less slender than those of the other subspecies, 1.5–2 mm in diameter; leaves 6–10 × 0.5–1 cm (2–4 × 0.25–0.5 in.), flat strap-shaped.

HABITAT: Montane and submontane forest, 1500–2300 m (5000–7600 ft.).

DISTRIBUTION: Kenya, northern Tanzania.

Polystachya calluniflora Kränzlin   FIGURE 10-67

DESCRIPTION: Pseudobulbs 5 cm (2 in.) × 4 mm, spindle-shaped, often purple, superposed, the new growth arising from the lower half of the old pseudobulb, forming dense mats. Leaves two, 5–17 cm (2–7 in.) × 5–6 mm, linear and grasslike. Inflorescences 4–10 cm (2–4 in.) long, fairly densely several-flowered. Pedicel and ovary

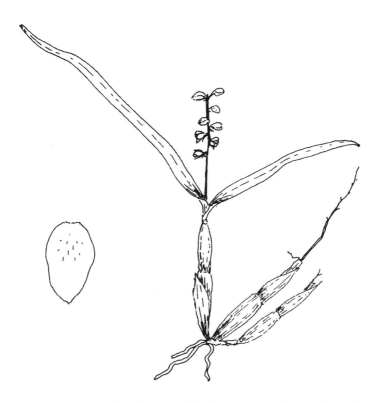

Figure 10-67. *Polystachya calluniflora* var. *hologlossa*. Plant (right), ×1; lip (left), ×6.

2 mm long; bracts 2–4 mm long, bristlelike. Flowers white. Dorsal sepal 2.5 × 1.5 mm, ovate, acuminate; laterals 3 × 2 mm, obliquely ovate, acute; mentum low and rounded. Petals 2.5 × 1.5, elliptic. Lip 3.5 × 1.5, trilobed near the base with a very short claw, spear-shaped, the side lobes small and triangular, the midlobe 3 × 1.5 mm, lanceolate, acute with a callus at its base consisting of two curved, fleshy ridges.

CULTIVATION: In our greenhouse, it flowers in early winter (November).

NOTE: The name *calluniflora* means heatherlike flowers, and this pretty little species when in flower is rather reminiscent of white heather.

Var. *calluniflora*

HABITAT: Epiphytic in montane and submontane forest, to 2200 m (7300 ft.).

DISTRIBUTION: Cameroon, Equatorial Guinea (Bioko), Nigeria, Rwanda, Uganda.

Var. *hologlossa* Cribb & I. F. la Croix

DESCRIPTION: Flowers smaller than those of var. *calluniflora;* lip unlobed.

HABITAT: Epiphytic in montane and submontane forest, or on relict trees in high grassland, 1300–2200 m (4300–7300 ft.).

DISTRIBUTION: Northern Malawi, southern Tanzania.

Polystachya caloglossa Reichenbach f.

DESCRIPTION: Stems clustered, erect or pendent, cylindrical, 5–40 cm (2–16 in.) × 2–7 mm, covered at the base with one to three tubular sheaths. Leaves four to five, 5–17 × 1.5–5 cm (2–7 × 1–2 in.), oblanceolate, the edges undulate. Inflorescences 4–12 cm (2–5 in.) long, simple or with to five short branches. Flowers yellow, apricot, or reddish-green, the ovary red or purple. Dorsal sepal 8 × 3 mm, elliptic; laterals 10–13 × 8–8.5 mm, obliquely triangular, acute, forming a conical mentum 8 mm high. Petals 9 × 4 mm, oblanceolate. Lip 9–11 × 10–12 mm, trilobed in the middle, with a short claw; midlobe ovate, acute; side lobes rounded, with a fleshy callus at the junction of the lobes. Column 2 mm long.

HABITAT: Epiphytic in forest, 900–1500 m (3000–5000 ft.).

DISTRIBUTION: Cameroon, Equatorial Guinea (Bioko), Uganda, Zaire.

Polystachya campyloglossa Rolfe

DESCRIPTION: A small, variable species, to 12 cm (5 in.) high. Pseudobulbs 1–2.5 × 0.5–1 cm (1 × 0.25–0.5 in.), ovoid or almost round, forming clumps. Leaves two to three, 5–10 × 1–2 cm (2–4 × 0.5–1 in.), narrowly oblong or oblanceolate, dark green, sometimes edged with purple, narrowed at the base to a short stalk 1 cm (0.5 in.) long. Inflorescences erect, longer than the leaves, 2- to 6-flowered. Flowers scented, very strongly so in some forms, pubescent on the outside, variable in color and size, the sepals and petals green, yellow-green or rarely yellow, the lip white, with purple veins on the side lobes. Dorsal sepal 8–13 × 5–7 mm, ovate, acute; lateral sepals 8–14 × 7–10 mm, obliquely triangular; mentum 7–10 mm high. Petals 7–10 × 2–3 mm, oblanceolate. Lip 8–11 × 6–10 mm, strongly recurved, trilobed, with a pubescent disc and a conical callus at the base of the midlobe; side lobes erect, densely pubescent; midlobe 4–5 × 2–5 mm, fleshy, ovate, glabrous. Column short and stout, 3 mm long.

HABITAT: Epiphytic in evergreen forest—riverine, montane and submontane—and occasionally in high rainfall woodland, 1100–2700 m (3600–8900 ft.).

CULTIVATION: This species flowers in our greenhouse in summer (August), but such a variable species might well have different flowering times.

DISTRIBUTION: Kenya, Malawi, Tanzania, Uganda.

Polystachya confusa Rolfe

SYNONYM: *Polystachya ottoniana* var. *confusa* (Rolfe) Kränzlin

DESCRIPTION: A dwarf, creeping species. Pseudobulbs 5–20 × 3–9 mm, ovoid, usually with two leaves. Leaves to 6 × 1 cm (2 × 0.5 in.), strap-shaped. Inflorescences 3–7 cm (1–3 in.) long, 2- to 4-flowered. Flowers pubescent on the outside, pink to mauve, with an orange mark on the lip. Pedicel and ovary 5–7 mm long, pubescent; bracts 3–4 mm long, acuminate. Dorsal sepal 7–9 × 3 mm, elliptic, apiculate; laterals 10–11 × 3–5 mm, obliquely triangular; mentum 3 mm high. Petals 6 × 1 mm, linear. Lip slightly recurved, 7–9 × 4.5 mm, with a long claw and rather obscurely trilobed about the middle; side lobes erect, midlobe oblong, fleshy. Column 1 mm long.

HABITAT: Epiphytic in montane forest, 1800–3200 m (6,000–10,500 ft.).

CULTIVATION: From the altitudes at which this species grows, it would need temperatures on the cool side of intermediate.

DISTRIBUTION: Kenya, northern Tanzania.

NOTE: This species bears little resemblance to the southern African *Polystachya ottoniana,* in spite of having been considered by Fritz Kränzlin to be a variety of it.

Figure 10-68. *Polystachya coriscensis.* Plant (left), ×1; lip (upper right), ×6; lateral sepal (lower right), ×4.

Polystachya coriscensis Reichenbach f. FIGURE 10-68

DESCRIPTION: A small species, to 10 cm (4 in.) tall. Pseudobulbs rather obscure, covered with chaffy sheaths. Leaves about three, to 4 × 1 cm (2 × 0.5 in.), oblanceolate, acute, light green. Inflorescences enclosed at base by one to two compressed sheaths, to 20-flowered. Flowers creamy-white, the sepals and petals edged with red-purple, with an odd, musky scent. Sepals all acuminate; dorsal 4.5 × 1.5 mm; laterals 7 × 4 mm, obliquely ovate. Petals 2–3 × 1 mm. Lip strongly reflexed, 5 mm long, with long papillae at the junction of the lobes; side lobes erect, purple-tipped; midlobe ovate, papillose. Column 2 mm long.

HABITAT: Growing in moss on branches of trees in evergreen forest, 600 m (2000 ft.).

CULTIVATION: This is an attractive species with flowers that are larger than is usual in this section and pleasant foliage. The leaves, however, seem prone to developing

black streaking, which suggests that plants need careful watering and good air circula-
tion. In our greenhouse, the species flowers in autumn and early winter (November and
December).

DISTRIBUTION: Cameroon, Congo, Gabon, Nigeria, Zaire.

Polystachya cultriformis (Thouars) Sprengel   PLATE 75
SYNONYM: *Polystachya gerrardii* Harvey

DESCRIPTION: A variable species. Pseudobulbs narrowly conical or cylindrical,
usually 7–10 (3–4 in.) long, 1 cm (0.5 in.) wide at the base, but they can be shorter
than 2 cm (1 in.) and up to 18 cm (7 in.) tall. Plants eventually form large clumps. Leaf
one, $3–36 \times 1–5.5$ cm ($1–15 \times 0.5–2$ in.), ovate or obovate, auriculate at the base, the
edge often undulate, dark green, leathery. Inflorescences usually somewhat longer than
the leaf, usually branched, many-flowered. Flowers variable in size and color—white,
yellow, green, pink, or purple. There seems to be some geographical link with color; all
plants we saw in Malawi had white flowers; in South Africa and Zimbabwe, they may
be white or yellow (the yellow-flowered forms were known as *P. gerrardii*), while in
Kenya, the full range of color can be found. Dorsal sepal $4–8 \times 2–4$ mm, ovate; lateral
sepals $5–8 \times 3–5$ mm, triangular, forming a conical mentum to 7 mm high. Petals
$3–7 \times 1$ mm, linear. Lip strongly recurved, trilobed with a yellowish central callus,
$4–8 \times 3–6$ mm; midlobe $1–4.5 \times 1.5–3.5$ mm, triangular or oblong, apiculate.

HABITAT: Epiphytic at high and low levels in evergreen forest, montane, submontane, and riverine, rarely lithophytic, 500–2900 m (1650–9600 ft.).

CULTIVATION: It flowers in summer (June and July).

DISTRIBUTION: Burundi, Cameroon, Equatorial Guinea (Bioko), Ethiopia, Gabon,
Kenya, Malawi, Mozambique, South Africa, Tanzania, Uganda, Zaire, Zimbabwe. Also
in Madagascar, Mascarene Islands, Seychelles.

Polystachya dendrobiiflora Reichenbach f.   PLATE 76
SYNONYM: *Polystachya tayloriana* Rendle

DESCRIPTION: Pseudobulbs $1.5–5 \times 0.5–1$ cm ($1–2 \times 0.25–0.5$ in.), clustered,
conical, yellowish, ridged. Leaves 5 to 10, to 18×1 cm (7×0.5 in.), linear, grasslike,
deciduous in dry season. Inflorescences to 80 cm (32 in.) long, although usually much
less, the stalk covered with papery sheaths, to 20-flowered, usually branched. Flowers
showy, opening wide, lilac-pink, occasionally almost white. Sepals to 12×4 mm,
oblong, obtuse, the laterals forming a mentum 4–5 mm high. Petals similar to sepals.
Lip 11×5 mm, entire, slightly recurved, ovate to oblong, obtuse, with a slightly pubescent yellow callus towards the base. Column 4 mm long, slightly winged; anther cap
deep violet.

HABITAT: Often epiphytic on species of *Xerophyta,* which are curious shrubs with
fibrous stems that grow in exposed, rocky areas. An epiphyte's roots do not just cling to
the outside, but penetrate the stem, sometimes even entering the soil. *Polystachya
dendrobiiflora* is sometimes lithophytic, but more often grows terrestrially, frequently in

rocky soil under woodland but sometimes in montane grassland or by the roadside, 400–2150 m (1300–7100 ft.).

CULTIVATION: This species can either be grown in a bark compost or in a free-draining terrestrial mix at intermediate temperatures. It needs good light and should be kept dry after the leaves fall. The inflorescence seems slow to develop; it looks like a dead stalk for a long time.

DISTRIBUTION: Angola, Burundi, Kenya, Malawi, Mozambique, Tanzania, Zaire, Zambia, Zimbabwe.

Polystachya disiformis Cribb

DESCRIPTION: A dwarf species, to 7 cm (3 in.) tall. Pseudobulbs clustered, 1 cm (0.5 in.) long and wide, ovoid, usually with three leaves. Leaves to 4 × 8 mm, narrowly lanceolate, sage green with purple marks. Inflorescences 5–6 cm (2 in.) tall, 3- to 9-flowered. Flowers yellow or pale green, the sepals with red lines; lip magenta with a yellow-green callus. Dorsal sepal 6 × 3 mm, ovate; lateral sepals 7–9 × 6–7 mm, obliquely triangular; mentum prominent, conical, 6 mm high. Petals 5 × 1 mm, linear. Lip 9–12 × 5 mm, with a claw of about half its length, then trilobed around the middle, with a fleshy, glabrous callus between the lobes; side lobes erect; midlobe 4 × 2.5 mm, oblong-lanceolate, fleshy, bullate. Column 1 mm long, crimson-spotted, with a patch of long bristles below the stigma.

HABITAT: Epiphytic in submontane and montane forest, 1000–1800 m (3300–6000 ft.).

DISTRIBUTION: Kenya, Tanzania.

Polystachya dolichophylla Schlechter

DESCRIPTION: Leaves 8–30 × 1–2 cm (3–12 × 0.5–1 in.), narrowly oblong, the apex obtusely bilobed, not fully developed at flowering time. Inflorescences branched, to 25 cm (10 in.) high, the branches erect or nearly so. Flowers yellow or cream. Dorsal sepal 3.5–6 mm long. Lip 5–7.5 × 3–4.5 mm, trilobed with a central callus; midlobe ovate, acute; side lobes rounded.

HABITAT: Sometimes terrestrial in mats of sedge.

DISTRIBUTION: Cameroon, Gabon, Ghana, Guinea, Nigeria, Sierra Leone.

Polystachya elegans Reichenbach f.   FIGURE 10-69

DESCRIPTION: Pseudobulbs rather spindle-shaped, superposed, but forming clumps and not chains, covered in dry brown sheaths. Leaves eight to nine, to 10 × 1 cm (4 × 0.5 in.), distichous, strap-shaped, glossy green, articulated to a sheathing base, the joint marked by a purple line. Inflorescences 9–10 cm (4 in.) long, enclosed at the base by a flattened sheath, usually with one to three branches, many-flowered. Flowers greenish-yellow, tipped with purple. Sepals all acuminate, dorsal 3 × 1.5 mm; laterals 6–7 × 2 mm, forming a rounded mentum 2 mm high. Petals 2 × 1 mm. Lip 4–5 mm

Figure 10-69. *Polystachya elegans.* Plant (left), ×1; lateral sepal (upper right), ×5; lip flattened (lower right), ×7.

long, trilobed near the apex, with a long claw 3–4 mm long, and a pubescent callus between the lobes. Side lobes earlike, purple; midlobe 1 × 1 mm, reflexed. Column purple, 2 mm long.

HABITAT: Epiphytic in evergreen forest, 500 m (1650 ft.).

CULTIVATION: In our greenhouse, it flowers in summer (June and July).

DISTRIBUTION: Cameroon, Congo, Equatorial Guinea (Bioko), Nigeria.

Figure 10-70. *Polystachya fallax.* Plant, ×1.

Polystachya fallax Kränzlin

FIGURE 10-70

DESCRIPTION: Pseudobulbs 2.5–4.5 × 5–9 mm, ovoid, glossy light green, set on an ascending rhizome. Leaf one, to 10 × 1 cm (4 × 0.5 in.), linear or strap-shaped, stiff and leathery. Inflorescences 4–5 cm (2 in.) long, to 5-flowered. Flowers scented, white with a yellow callus and a purple anther cap. Dorsal sepal 7.5–11.5 × 2.5–3 mm, ovate, acuminate; laterals 8–14 × 5–7 mm, triangular, acuminate, forming a conical mentum 5–6 mm high. Petals 7–8 × 1–2 mm, linear. Lip recurved, 10–12.5 × 4–6 mm, trilobed at about halfway; midlobe 5–7 × 1.5–3 mm, lanceolate, acuminate.

HABITAT: Rainforest, 1350–1600 m (4450–5300 ft.).

CULTIVATION: In our greenhouse, it flowers in summer (late May to July).

DISTRIBUTION: Burundi, Rwanda, Uganda, Zaire.

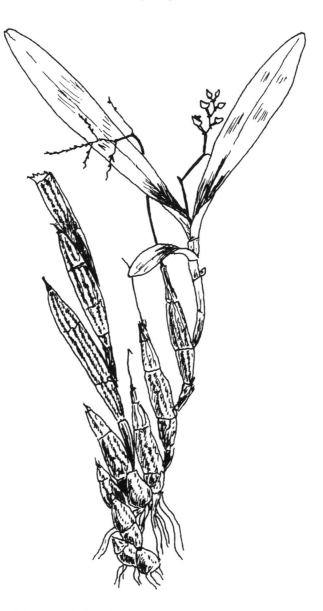

Figure 10-71. *Polystachya fusiformis.* Plant, ×1.

Polystachya fusiformis (Thouars) Lindley

FIGURE 10-71

DESCRIPTION: Not a showy species, but the pendulous habit is quite interesting. Pseudobulbs spindle-shaped, 5–20 cm (2–8 in.) × 3–6 mm, green or purple, with several nodes, the new growth arising about halfway along. In woodland, the pseudobulbs are short and stout and the plants are erect, while in forest, the plants form long, pendent chains. Leaves two to four, at the apex of the terminal pseudobulb, 5–15 × 0.5–3 cm (2–6 × 0.25–1 in.), lanceolate or oblanceolate. Inflorescences 4–8 cm (2–3 in.) long, many-flowered, usually much branched but occasionally simple. Flowers small, greenish-yellow marked with purple, or deep maroon-purple. Dorsal sepal 2 × 1.5 mm; laterals 3 × 2.5 mm; mentum rounded, 2 mm high. Petals 2 × 1 mm. Lip 2.5–3 × 2.5 mm, trilobed at about the middle; side lobes erect; midlobe almost round. Column 1 mm long. Sometimes the flowers do not open properly, but capsules develop.

HABITAT: Epiphytic at high and low levels in woodland in high rainfall areas, and in riverine and submontane forest, 900–2150 m (3000–7100 ft.).

DISTRIBUTION: Cameroon, Equatorial Guinea (Bioko), Ghana, Kenya, Malawi, Rwanda, South Africa, Tanzania, Uganda, Zaire, Zambia, Zimbabwe. Also in Madagascar, Mascarene Islands.

NOTE: *Polystachya simplex* Rendle looks almost identical to this species when not in flower, but has flowers about twice the size, which still does not make them very big.

Polystachya galeata (Swartz) Reichenbach f.

SYNONYM: *Polystachya grandiflora* Lindley ex Hooker

DESCRIPTION: Pseudobulbs 6–14 cm (2–6 in.) × 3–5 mm, cylindrical, forming clumps. Leaf one, 8–27 × 1–3.5 cm (3–11 × 0.5–1 in.), oblanceolate or strap-shaped, leathery. Inflorescences unbranched, usually shorter than the leaf, several-flowered. Flowers green, yellow-green, yellow, pink, or white, usually flushed with purple, pubescent on the outside, sometimes very strongly scented. Dorsal sepal 7–14 × 3–7 mm, ovate; laterals 10–22 × 6–18 mm, with a curved, conical mentum 10–20 mm high. Petals 5–11 mm long, linear. Lip recurved, clawed, trilobed towards the base, 10–21 × 5–14 mm; midlobe 3–7 × 2–8 mm, orbicular, apiculate; callus rather obscure. Column 1–3 mm long.

HABITAT: Epiphytic in lowland and submontane evergreen forest, 400–1000 m (1300–3300 ft.).

CULTIVATION: It flowers in autumn (October and November).

DISTRIBUTION: Angola, Cameroon, Congo, Gabon, Ghana, Guinea, Ivory Coast, Liberia, Nigeria, Sierra Leone, Zaire.

NOTE: This rather variable species can have larger flowers than any other species of *Polystachya,* but unfortunately, plants with the largest flowers are usually the dullest in color. There would seem to be scope for selecting and crossing the best forms of this species in an attempt to obtain large, scented flowers of an attractive color.

Polystachya goetzeana Kränzlin

DESCRIPTION: Pseudobulbs to 10 × 7 mm, obliquely conical. Leaves two to three, 8–20 × 0.8–1 cm (3–8 × 0.25–0.5 in.), linear, dark green often with purplish marks. Inflorescences shorter than leaves, 6–16 cm (2–6 in.) long, the stalk almost covered by papery sheaths, 3- to 5-flowered. Flowers relatively large, bright yellow-green with a white lip with a yellow central line, with a musty smell. Dorsal sepal 12 × 4 mm, lanceolate, acute; lateral sepals 13–14 × 7 mm, obliquely triangular, with a conical mentum 5–8 mm high. Petals 10 × 3.5 mm, oblanceolate. Lip recurved, trilobed at about the middle, 13–14 × 9–10 mm, with a yellow, pubescent, fleshy, central keel in the basal half; midlobe 8 × 9 mm, oblong, apiculate; side lobes erect, rounded. Column 4.5 mm long.

HABITAT: Sunk in moss on the trunks and branches of trees in montane and sub-montane forest, 1850–2300 m (6100–7600 ft.).

CULTIVATION: We have not found this pretty species too easy in cultivation. We suspect it needs temperatures on the cool side of intermediate. However, several times we have turned a plant that looked a bit feeble out of its pot and found the pot full of vigorous roots.

DISTRIBUTION: Northern Malawi, southern Tanzania.

Polystachya golungensis Reichenbach f.   PLATE 77

DESCRIPTION: Pseudobulbs narrowly conical to cylindrical, curved, 2–6 cm (1–2 in.) long, less than 1 cm wide, set close together. Leaves two to four, 5–17 × 0.5–2 cm (2–7 × 0.25–1 in.), fleshy, narrowly strap-shaped, folded, unequally and obtusely bilobed to the apex. Inflorescences to 40 cm (16 in.) long, with short, secund branches, many-flowered, the lower part completely covered by papery sheaths. Flowers bright yellow or yellow-green, rather fleshy. Dorsal sepal 1.5–2.5 × 1–1.5 mm, ovate; laterals 2–3.5 × 1–2.5 mm, obliquely ovate; mentum conical or rounded, 2 mm high. Petals 1–2.5 × 0.5 mm, oblanceolate. Lip 2–3 × 2.5–3.5 mm, trilobed about the middle, with a cushion of hairs at the junction of the lobes; midlobe 1.5 mm long and wide, more or less orbicular. Column less than 1 mm long.

HABITAT: With its succulent leaves, this species looks as if it should grow in rather dry, open situations; however, it is usually a forest plant, occurring as a high level epiphyte in lowland evergreen forest and riverine forest, occasionally in high rainfall woodland and in drier scrub, sometimes growing lithophytically, 200–1800 m (660–6000 ft.).

CULTIVATION: It flowers in summer (June and July).

DISTRIBUTION: Angola, Congo, Gabon, Ivory Coast, Kenya, Liberia, Mali, Mozambique, Nigeria, Tanzania, Togo, Uganda, Zaire, Zambia, Zimbabwe.

NOTE: Although the flowers are small, they are numerous and with their bright yellow color can be quite attractive.

Polystachya greatrexii Summerhayes   PLATE 78

DESCRIPTION: Vegetatively, almost identical to *Polystachya brassii;* the two species are virtually impossible to tell apart when not in flower. Inflorescences 3–4 cm (1–2 in.) high, densely to 10-flowered. Flowers primrose-scented, pale lilac, the lip white with a brownish central line. Dorsal sepal 4 × 2 mm, ovate; lateral sepals 5 × 3 mm, obliquely ovate; mentum 3 mm high; sepals all slightly pubescent outside. Petals 4 × 2 mm, oblanceolate. Lip 5 × 4 mm, unlobed, recurved, the edges undulate, with a pubescent line down the middle. Column short and stout, 1–2 mm long.

HABITAT: Woodland in high rainfall areas, occasionally in evergreen forest; sometimes lithophytic, 900–2100 m (3000–7000 ft.).

CULTIVATION: This attractive species is deciduous in the resting season and must be kept fairly dry, but it still needs regular misting to keep up the humidity, otherwise the pseudobulbs will shrivel. In the places where it grows in the wild, there is either frequent mist and occasional "out of season" drizzle.

DISTRIBUTION: Malawi, southern Tanzania, Zaire, Zimbabwe.

Polystachya hastata Summerhayes

DESCRIPTION: Pseudobulbs to 10 cm (4 in.) × 2–5 mm, the new growth arising below the middle of an old pseudobulb. Leaves two, 3–18 cm (1–7 in.) × 3–5 mm, linear, grasslike. Inflorescences 5 cm (2 in.) long, fairly densely many-flowered. Pedicel and ovary 3 mm long, bracts linear, slightly shorter. Flowers white or pale pink. Dorsal sepal 2–3 × 1.5–2 mm, ovate, apiculate; laterals 2–3 × 2 mm, obliquely ovate, forming a low, rounded mentum 1 mm high. Petals 1.5–2 × 1.5 mm, obovate. Lip 2.5–3.5 × 1–1.5 mm, spear-shaped with a long claw, the blade of the lip 1.5–2 mm long and wide, triangular, the callus a curved ridge above a central depression.

HABITAT: Evergreen forest, 600–1800 m (2000–6000 ft.).

CULTIVATION: In our greenhouse, it flowers in winter (November to February).

DISTRIBUTION: Congo, Nigeria, Uganda, Zaire.

Polystachya heckmanniana Kränzlin   FIGURE 10-72

DESCRIPTION: An exceptionally attractive little plant, particularly the form from northern Malawi, which seems to have very large flowers. A dwarf species, less than 5 cm (2 in.) high. Pseudobulbs 1–2 × 1 cm (0.5–1 × 0.5 in.), ovoid or conical, forming clumps or chains. Leaves three to four, to 5 × 2 cm (2 × 1 in.), elliptic, glaucous green, sometimes tinged with purple. Inflorescences 2 cm (1 in.) high, 1- to 3-flowered. Flowers glabrous outside, large for the size of plant, greenish-yellow or lime green, the lip white with a yellow or lime green midline. Dorsal sepal 9–13 × 5–7 mm, ovate; lateral sepals 10–20 × 7–9 mm, obliquely triangular; mentum conical, slightly bifid, 9 mm high. Petals 9–13 × 3 mm, oblanceolate. Lip recurved, 10–17 × 7–12 mm, with a short claw, trilobed, with a pubescent callus at the junction of the lobes; side lobes erect; midlobe 7–10 × 7–10 mm, quadrate, the edges undulate. Column 3 mm long, purple at base.

HABITAT: Epiphytic at high level in submontane forest, occasionally lithophytic on rocks outside the forest, 1750–2200 m (5800–7300 ft.).

CULTIVATION: In our greenhouse, it flowers in summer (June and July).

Figure 10-72. *Polystachya heckmanniana.* Plant (left) and flower (right), ×1.

DISTRIBUTION: Kenya, Malawi, Tanzania.

NOTE: What may be another form of this species grows on the slopes of Mount Mulanje in southern Malawi. The flowers are almost identical, although slightly smaller, but the inflorescence is consistently one-flowered and the leaves are dark green and linear, only 6–7 mm wide. This form grows in riverine forest and high-rainfall woodland, 1050–1500 m (3500–5000 ft.).

Polystachya holmesiana Cribb

DESCRIPTION: Flowers not as large as in some species in section *Affines,* but they have one of the most unusual color combinations in the genus. Pseudobulbs to 4.5 × 1.2 cm (2 × 0.5 in.), tightly clustered, oblong but slightly bilaterally flattened, yellow, ribbed, with two to three nodes; roots 2–3 mm in diameter, the growing tips purple. Leaves two to three, 8–17 × 1.5 cm (3–7 × 1 in.), lanceolate or elliptic, just starting to develop at flowering time. Inflorescences erect, to 30 cm (12 in.) high, laxly to 15-flowered. Flowers rather fleshy, orange, the petals with a red central line, the lip with a bright magenta tip. Ovary and pedicel 8 mm long, arched, so that the flowers face down; bracts to 6 mm long. Dorsal sepal 9 × 6 mm, ovate, acute; lateral sepals 12 × 8 mm, obliquely triangular, keeled on the outside; mentum rounded, 6 mm high. Petals 6 × 3 mm, oblanceolate. Lip 8 × 8 mm, trilobed, bent down at the junction of the lobes and with a yellow, pubescent callus just below the junction. Side lobes erect, earlike; midlobe 4 × 3 mm, ovate, acute, papillose. Column 1 mm long.

HABITAT: Woodland, 1600–1920 m (5300–6300 ft.). This is one of those species that is plentiful where it occurs but has a very restricted distribution although there are many other areas that are apparently equally suitable for it.

DISTRIBUTION: Northern Malawi, Zambia.

Polystachya johnstonii Rolfe

PLATE 79

DESCRIPTION: Pseudobulbs 1–1.5 × 1 cm (0.5–1 × 0.5 in.), ovoid, oblong or almost round but slightly bilaterally flattened, forming dense clumps. Leaves usually three, 3–7 × 1–1.5 cm (1–3 × 0.5–1 in.), lanceolate, dark glossy green, sometimes edged with purple, often deciduous in the dry season. Inflorescences to 5 cm (2 in.) high, 2- to 10-flowered, borne on new pseudobulbs as the leaves start to develop. Flowers usually pink, tinged with green, the lip deep purple-pink, but some plants from Mount Mulanje have flowers with no tinge of pink, with yellow-green sepals and a white lip with purple veins on the side lobes. Sepals thick-textured, dorsal sepal 13 × 4 mm, ovate, acute; lateral sepals 13 × 6 mm, obliquely ovate, acute, keeled on the outside; mentum 5 mm high. Petals 9 × 2.5 mm, oblanceolate. Lip 9–10 × 6 mm, fleshy, strongly recurved, trilobed, with a glabrous callus surrounded by a pubescent area at the junction of the lobes; side lobes erect and earlike; midlobe 4–5 × 3–4 mm, lanceolate or ovate. Column short and stout, 1–2 mm long.

HABITAT: Epiphytic on species of *Xerophyta,* growing on open, rocky hillsides and mountain tops, 1600–2000 m (5300–6600 ft.). As with *Polystachya dendrobiiflora,* the roots may run through the *Xerophyta* stems for a long way.

CULTIVATION: Potted in medium bark, as is usual for the genus. This species needs good light, it does not thrive in shade; if grown in a shade house in the tropics or sub-tropics it should be placed at the very edge. It likes intermediate to cool temperatures and should be kept dry in the resting season, although it should be sprayed periodically so that the pseudobulbs do not shrivel.

DISTRIBUTION: Southern Malawi.

NOTE: This is a variable species, the shape of the lip differing from one plant to the next. Plants from Zomba Plateau are the most desirable: they are the smallest plants with the largest and most strongly colored flowers. Eventually, these might be described as a different species from plants from Mount Mulanje (one of which was the type specimen). Although plants from these two mountains look dissimilar, it is not easy to pick out any consistent points of difference.

Polystachya kermesina Kränzlin

DESCRIPTION: A dwarf species, to 11 cm (4 in.) tall. Pseudobulbs 2 cm (1 in.) × 1–1.5 mm, arising from about the middle of the previous growth. Leaves two to five, 2–4 cm (1–2 in.) × 1.5–2.5 mm, linear, acute. Inflorescences 1–2.5 cm (0.5–1 in.) long, shorter than the leaves, 1- to 3-flowered. Flowers fleshy, orange or scarlet, opening wide, the tips of the sepals and petals recurved. Dorsal sepal 4 × 4 mm, ovate to orbicular; laterals 5 × 6.5 mm, obliquely ovate-orbicular; mentum 3 mm high. Petals 4 × 1.5 mm, oblong. Lip 8.5 × 4 mm, fleshy, recurved, with a long, hairy claw; obscurely trilobed, with a fleshy, toothlike callus between the side lobes. Midlobe 3.5 × 3.5 mm, orbicular, fleshy, rough-textured. Column 1 mm long.

HABITAT: Epiphytic in *Hagenia* and *Podocarpus* forest, 2000–3200 m (6,000–10,500 ft.).

CULTIVATION: Not known to be in cultivation. With its brightly colored, wide-opening flowers, it would be very well worth growing, and it is to be hoped that it might become available.

DISTRIBUTION: Rwanda, Uganda, Zaire.

Polystachya laurentii De Wildeman

DESCRIPTION: Pseudobulbs 5–8 × 1–2 cm (2–3 × 0.5–1 in.), ellipsoid. Leaves three to four, 6–25 × 2–2.5 cm (2–10 × 1 in.), oblong, obtuse. Inflorescences erect, to 20 cm (8 in.) long, sometimes simple but usually with one to five branches, rather laxly many-flowered. Flowers strongly scented, densely pubescent on the outside, creamy white with two orange marks on the lip. Dorsal sepal 10–13 × 2–3 mm, narrowly lanceolate, acuminate; lateral sepals 10–15 × 4–5 mm, obliquely lanceolate, acuminate; mentum rounded, 4 mm high. Petals 8–11 × 1–1.5 mm, oblanceolate. Lip 10–12 × 5–6 mm, rather obscurely trilobed with a short, fleshy callus at the base and another fleshy callus on the midlobe; side lobes rounded, midlobe narrowly triangular, acute. Column 2 mm long.

HABITAT: Epiphytic in rainforest, 1350 m (4450 ft.).

DISTRIBUTION: Rwanda, Uganda, Zaire.

Polystachya lawrenceana Kränzlin   PLATE 80, FIGURE 10-73

DESCRIPTION: Pseudobulbs 2.5–5.5 × 1–1.5 cm (1–2 × 0.5–1 in.), conical-elliptic, glossy green with two to three nodes, forming dense clumps. Leaves to 15 × 2 cm (6 × 1 in.), strap-shaped, slightly bilobed at the apex, rather floppy. Inflorescences 16 cm (6 in.) long, arching, laxly to 10-flowered. Flowers fleshy, pubescent on the outside, sepals and petals bronze-green flushed with maroon, lip pale to bright pink with a white callus. Dorsal sepal 9 × 4.5 mm, ovate, acute; lateral sepals 11 × 6.5 mm, obliquely ovate-triangular, acuminate; mentum 5–6 mm high, conical. Petals 8 × 2.5 mm, oblanceolate. Lip somewhat recurved, 9 × 8 mm, with a smooth, fleshy callus at the junction of the lobes; side lobes erect, oblong; midlobe 7 × 6 mm, broadly ovate, obtuse, very fleshy with a central groove. Column 2 mm long.

HABITAT: Lithophytic on exposed rock faces, 1350–1600 m (4450–5300 ft.).

CULTIVATION: In our greenhouse, it grows very well and flowers for a long period in summer (June to August).

DISTRIBUTION: Malawi (known from a few localities in the southern part of the country).

NOTE: This is an attractive and distinctive species. It is very rare in the wild, but must have been cultivated in the last century, as it was described in 1893. It was named in honor of Sir Trevor Lawrence, who had a famous collection of orchids at Burford Lodge near Dorking in Surrey, and was president of the Royal Horticultural Society from 1885 to 1913. Lawrence received plants from, among others, John Buchanan (1855–1896), who worked in Malawi for many years and collected a large number of plants, including orchids. After that, the species was "lost" for many years, but was illustrated as *Polystachya* sp. in Audrey Moriarty's *Wild Flowers of Malawi* (1975).

Figure 10-73. *Polystachya lawrenceana.* Plant, ×1.

Polystachya leonensis Reichenbach f.

DESCRIPTION: Pseudobulbs 1 cm (0.5 in.) long and wide, globose, set close together and forming clumps. Leaves three to six, 7–20 × 1–3 cm (0.5–1 in.), lanceolate or oblanceolate. Inflorescences usually unbranched, 9–30 cm (4–12 in.) long, several to many-flowered. Flowers yellow-green usually flushed with purple-brown, the lip white, the side lobes tinged with purple. Dorsal sepal 3–4 mm long, ovate, obtuse; lateral sepals 4–5 mm long, obliquely triangular; mentum conical, rounded, 5–6 mm high. Lip 5–7 mm long, trilobed near the apex, with a pubescent area between the lobes; midlobe ovate or obovate, obtuse.

HABITAT: 400–1500 m (1300–5000 ft.).

DISTRIBUTION: Cameroon, Guinea, Ivory Coast, Liberia, Sierra Leone.

Polystachya leucosepala Cribb

DESCRIPTION: Pseudobulbs to 3.5 × 1 cm (1–0.5 in.), narrowly conical, with two leaves. Leaves 6–15 × 1.5 cm (2–6 × 1 in.), elliptic, acute. Inflorescences borne on new growth before the pseudobulbs have fully developed, to 10 cm (4 in.) long, 2- to 3-flowered. Flowers large for the size of plant, 25 mm in diameter, scented, white, the lip with a yellow callus edged with crimson, the side lobes with a crimson margin. Dorsal sepal 13–14 × 7 mm, ovate, apiculate; lateral sepals to 16 × 12 mm, slightly keeled on outer surface. Petals 13 × 6 mm, obovate. Lip pubescent all over, 16 × 12 mm, trilobed; side lobes erect, midlobe recurved, 7 × 6.5 mm, oblong, obtuse, with a fleshy callus in the center.

HABITAT: Epiphytic, in moss, in montane forest, 2000–2200 m (6600–7300 ft.).

DISTRIBUTION: Northern Tanzania.

Polystachya longiscapa Summerhayes PLATE 81

DESCRIPTION: Pseudobulbs 1.5–10 × 1.5–3 cm (1–4 × 1 in.), conical, clustered, covered by old leaf bases. Leaves four to eight, 20–36 × 1.5–2.5 cm (8–15 × 1 in.), linear, acute, sometimes with purple blotches. Inflorescences to 90 cm (3 ft.) tall, the stalk covered with overlapping sheaths, with one to three arching branches, several-flowered. Flowers large, 4 cm (2 in.) in diameter, pale pink. Dorsal sepal 20 × 5 mm, oblong-lanceolate; laterals 18–20 × 5.5–6.5 mm, obliquely oblong-lanceolate; mentum 5 mm high. Petals very slightly shorter and narrower than dorsal sepal, oblanceolate. Lip 17–18 × 10 mm, entire, oblong-obovate, the apex rounded or emarginate. Column 5–6 mm long.

HABITAT: Growing on rocks on mountain slopes, 1100–1600 m (3600–5300 ft.).

CULTIVATION: This species can either be grown in a bark compost, or in a free-draining terrestrial mix at intermediate temperatures. It needs good light and should be kept dry after the leaves fall. It resembles a large version of *Polystachya dendrobiiflora*, and from its habitat it would seem that this species might prefer somewhat cooler temperatures, but we grow it and *Polystachya dendrobiiflora* together and they seem happy enough.

DISTRIBUTION: Tanzania (known only from the Uluguru Mountains).

Figure 10-74. *Polystachya maculata.* Plant, ×1.

Polystachya maculata Cribb

FIGURE 10-74

DESCRIPTION: A showy species only described in 1984, but already established in cultivation. Pseudobulbs 5–12 cm (2–5 in.) long, 1 cm in diameter at the base, ovoid or cylindrical. Leaf one, 10–15 × 2–4 cm (4–6 × 1–2 in.), oblong or obovate, acute. Inflorescences 10–18 cm (4–7 in.) long, arching, to 20-flowered, with only a few open together. Flowers 2–3 cm (1 in.) in diameter, yellow or greenish-yellow, the lip sometimes white, blotched and spotted all over with purple-red. Dorsal sepal 9–11 × 4–5 mm, ovate, apiculate; laterals spreading so the flower opens wide, 10–14 × 8 mm, ovate-triangular; petals 8–10 × 3 mm, oblanceolate. Lip 15 × 6–10 mm, rather fleshy, trilobed in the basal half, with a longitudinal ridge in the basal part; midlobe obovate, emarginate with an apicule in the center. Column 6 mm long.

HABITAT: Epiphytic in dense forest, 1500 m (5000 ft.).

CULTIVATION: It flowers mainly in autumn (October), but does flower off and on throughout the year.

DISTRIBUTION: Burundi.

Polystachya melliodora Cribb

DESCRIPTION: Pseudobulbs 3 × 2 cm (1 × 1 in.), oblong, bilaterally compressed, green, forming large clumps. Leaf one, to 15 × 3 cm (6 × 1 in.), elliptic, rounded at apex. Inflorescences 10 cm (4 in.) long, to 8-flowered. Flowers honey-scented, waxy, white, the lip with a purple margin and a yellow callus; anther cap pink. Dorsal sepal 12 × 7 mm, ovate, acuminate; lateral sepals 15 × 10 mm, obliquely triangular, acuminate, keeled on the outside; mentum 8 mm high, conical, bifid. Petals 11 × 5 mm, elliptic. Lip recurved, 11 × 9 mm, rather obscurely trilobed. Column 4 mm long.

HABITAT: Upland rainforest.

DISTRIBUTION: Tanzania.

Polystachya minima Rendle   PLATE 82

DESCRIPTION: A pretty species with a misleading name, as there are many species that are smaller both in growth and flower. Pseudobulbs 10–13 × 8–12 mm, green, slightly obliquely ovoid, forming chains; roots 2–2.5 mm in diameter, the growing tips bright purple. Leaves two to three, to 13 cm (5 in.) × 7 mm, linear, grasslike, deciduous in the dry season but almost fully developed at flowering time. Inflorescences 10–14 cm (4–6 in.) tall, to 10-flowered. Flowers with a spicy scent, bright yellow, the lip white with purple marks. Ovary with pedicel 6 mm long; bracts 3 mm long. Dorsal sepal 8 × 3 mm, lanceolate, acute; lateral sepals 9 × 6 mm, obliquely triangular, acute; mentum 5 mm high, cylindrical, bifid. Petals 7 × 1.5 mm, oblanceolate, acute. Lip much recurved, 9 × 6 mm, trilobed at about half way, with a longitudinal, glabrous callus running from the base of the lip to the junction of the lobes; midlobe 4–5 × 2.5 mm, lanceolate, acute, papillose. Column 2 mm long.

HABITAT: Epiphytic on trunks and main branches of trees in high rainfall woodland, occasionally lithophytic, 800–1400 m (2600–4600 ft.).

DISTRIBUTION: Southern Malawi, almost entirely within a 50-km (30-mi) radius of Blantyre. Where it grows, this little orchid is very plentiful; it is difficult to see why it should be absent from so many areas that are apparently suitable.

Polystachya modesta Reichenbach f.

DESCRIPTION: Pseudobulbs clustered, 1–10 × 0.5–1.5 cm (0.5-4 × 0.25–1 in.), conical or ovoid, often ribbed, with several nodes. Leaves three to five, 8–20 × 1–2 cm (3–8 × 0.5–1 in.), elliptic to oblanceolate, dark green edged with purple. Inflorescences borne on new pseudobulbs, of similar length to the leaves, simple or with a few short, secund branches; to 20-flowered. Flowers fleshy, usually yellow or yellow-green, often tinged with purple, the lip a deeper yellow; occasionally the flowers are pink or purplish with a yellow lip. Sometimes the flowers do not open, but seed is still set. Dorsal sepal 3 × 2 mm, ovate; laterals 5 × 3 mm, obliquely triangular; mentum conical, 3 mm high. Petals 3 × 1 mm, oblanceolate. Lip 3–5 × 2.5–3.5 mm, recurved, trilobed at about the middle, with no callus but with a pubescent cushion at the junction of the lobes; midlobe 2 × 2 mm, orbicular, bullate, apiculate. Column 1.5 mm long.

HABITAT: Epiphytic, rarely lithophytic, in open woodland usually in fairly hot, dry areas; occasionally on species of *Xerophyta* on rocky slopes at the edge of woodland, 500–1200 m (1650–4000 ft.), rarely to 1800 m (6000 ft.).

CULTIVATION: This species requires only light shade and should be kept drier in winter than most species of *Polystachya.*

DISTRIBUTION: Angola, Burundi, Central African Republic, Ghana, Ivory Coast, Kenya, Malawi, Mozambique, Nigeria, Rwanda, South Africa (KwaZulu-Natal) Tanzania, Togo, Uganda, Zaire, Zambia, Zimbabwe.

Polystachya mystacioides De Wildeman
SYNONYM: *Polystachya crassifolia* Schlechter

DESCRIPTION: Stems to 100 cm (40 in.) long, creeping or pendent. Leaves numerous, 2–15 × 0.5–1 cm (1–6 × 0.25–0.5 in.), fleshy, bilaterally flattened, ovate, acute. Inflorescences one-flowered. Flowers white marked with red or purple, or pinkish or purplish, relatively large, 10–15 mm in diameter. Dorsal sepal 7–8 × 5–6 mm, ovate, rounded; lateral sepals 10 × 7–8 mm, obliquely triangular, apiculate; all sepals pubescent. Petals 7–8 × 1–2 mm. Lip 10–12 × 4–6 mm, trilobed, with a longitudinal callus at the base; side lobes small; midlobe oblong, emarginate or apiculate. Column 4 mm long.

HABITAT: Epiphytic in dense forest. Altitude not known.

DISTRIBUTION: Cameroon, Ivory Coast, Zaire.

Polystachya odorata Lindley   PLATE 83

DESCRIPTION: An attractive and easily grown species with a mass of long-lasting flowers. Pseudobulbs 2–4.5 × 0.5–1.5 cm (1–2 × 0.25–1 in.), conical or almost round, forming dense clumps. Leaves 13–26 × 2–4 cm (5–10 × 1–2 in.), oblanceolate. Inflorescences erect, with several longish, spreading branches, many-flowered. Flowers slightly pubescent on outside, white or yellow, sometimes reddish-brown, scented, although less strongly so than many species. Dorsal sepal 5 × 3 mm, ovate; laterals 8–8.5 × 5–5.5 mm, obliquely ovate; mentum conical, 4–5.5 mm high. Petals 5 × 1.5 mm, oblanceolate. Lip 7–8 × 5–7.5 mm, recurved, trilobed at about the middle, with an elliptic, thickened callus between the lobes; midlobe 3 × 3.5 mm, suborbicular, the edges undulate, emarginate; side lobes erect. Column 2 mm long.

HABITAT: Epiphytic, occasionally lithophytic, in evergreen forest, sometimes riverine forest, 900–1350 m (3000–4450 ft.).

CULTIVATION: It flowers in autumn (September and October).

DISTRIBUTION: Angola, Burkina Faso, Cameroon, Central African Republic, Equatorial Guinea (Bioko), Gabon, Ghana, Ivory Coast, Nigeria, Rwanda, Tanzania, Uganda, Zaire.

Figure 10-75. *Polystachya ottoniana*. Plant, ×1.

Polystachya ottoniana Reichenbach f. FIGURE 10-75

DESCRIPTION: Pseudobulbs to 25 × 18 mm, ovoid, asymmetric, green, glossy, forming chains and eventually large clumps. Leaves two to three, to 13 × 1 cm (5 × 0.5 in.), linear, slightly bilobed at the apex. Inflorescences shorter than the leaves, 1- to 2-flowered. Pedicel and ovary slightly arched, 12 mm long. Flowers rather bell-shaped, usually white with a faint pink flush, but sometimes pink, green, or yellow, the lip with an orange or yellow midline. Dorsal sepal 10 × 3 mm, ovate, acute; lateral sepals 12 × 5 mm, obliquely ovate; mentum rounded, 4 mm high. Petals 9 × 3 mm, oblanceolate. Lip 10–12 mm long, trilobed at about halfway with a callus forming a low ridge between the lobes; side lobes erect, midlobe curving back, 5 mm wide.

HABITAT: Epiphytic, sometimes lithophytic, in forest and woodland, usually in cooler and moister areas.

CULTIVATION: It is easily grown and, in our greenhouse, it flowers in spring and early summer (May and June).

DISTRIBUTION: Mozambique, South Africa (Eastern Cape, KwaZulu-Natal, Mpumalanga, Northern Province), Swaziland.

Polystachya paniculata (Swartz) Rolfe

DESCRIPTION: A very desirable species, despite its small flowers, because of the number of flowers and their bright color. Stems erect, stout, cylindrical but compressed, 5–18 cm (2–7 in.) long, 1.5–2 cm (1 in.) in diameter, grooved when old, with three to four nodes. Leaves three to four, distichous, 10–30 × 2–3.5 cm (4–12 × 1 in.), strap-shaped. Inflorescences to 21 cm (8 in.) long, usually longer than the leaves, much branched and many-flowered. Flowers vermilion red or orange with red marks on the lip. Dorsal sepal 3 × 1 mm, lanceolate, acute; lateral sepals 4 × 2 mm, obliquely lanceolate, forming a mentum 1.5 mm high. Petals 3 × 0,5 mm, oblanceolate. Lip 3 × 2 mm, unlobed, ovate to elliptic, acute, with a small callus. Column 1 mm long.

HABITAT: Epiphytic in rainforest, 900–1150 m (3000–3800 ft.).

DISTRIBUTION: Cameroon, Congo, Gabon, Ghana, Ivory Coast, Liberia, Nigeria, Sierra Leone, Uganda, Zaire.

Polystachya parva Summerhayes   FIGURE 10-76

DESCRIPTION: Not one of the showier species, but nonetheless a neat little plant. Pseudobulbs to 20 × 8 mm, conical, forming clumps. Leaves three to four, to 5 × 1 cm (2 × 0.5 in.), ligulate. Inflorescences to 6 cm (2 in.) long, to 10-flowered. Flowers glabrous, scented, greenish-white, the lip a deeper yellow-green with two purple spots; column and anther cap purple. Pedicel and ovary arched, 5 mm long; bracts 3 mm long, acuminate. Dorsal sepal 5 × 1 mm, lanceolate, acute; lateral sepals 10 × 3 mm, very oblique; mentum cylindrical, bifid, 4–5 mm high. Petals 5 × 1 mm, oblanceolate. Lip 8 mm long with a claw 5 mm long, then trilobed, lacking a callus; side lobes erect, triangular; midlobe reflexed, 3 × 3 mm, ovate.

HABITAT: Riverine forest, 1600–1800 m (5300–6000 ft.).

CULTIVATION: It seems to flower off and on through the year; we have had it in flower in July and November.

DISTRIBUTION: Ghana, Nigeria, Zambia.

Polystachya poikilantha Kränzlin

DESCRIPTION: Pseudobulbs 8–18 × 1.5–4.5 cm (3–7 × 1–2 in.), cylindrical, tightly clustered. Leaf one, 12–22 cm (5–9 in) × 7–14 mm, linear, acute. Inflorescence usually longer than the leaf, with one to six branches, to 20 cm (8 in.) long, to 20-flowered, the flowers opening in succession. Flowers whitish, yellow, pale green, or yellow-green, often marked with purple. Dorsal sepal 6–8.5 × 2–3.5 mm, triangular, ovate; lateral sepals spreading, similar to the dorsal but broader, forming a conical mentum to 5 mm high. Petals 4.5–8 × 1.5–2.5 mm, elliptical or spathulate. Lip recurved, 5–6.5 × 3–5 mm, entire or obscurely trilobed. Column 1.5–2.5 mm long.

Figure 10-76. *Polystachya parva*. Plant, ×1.

Var. *leucorhoda* (Kränzlin) Cribb & Podzorski
DESCRIPTION: Flowers white, cream, or pale green, flushed with purple, lip obscurely trilobed.
HABITAT: Montane forest, 1900–2900 m (6300–9600 ft.).
DISTRIBUTION: Burundi, Rwanda, Uganda, Zaire.

Var. *poikilantha* Cribb & Podzorski
DESCRIPTION: Flowers green or yellow-green spotted with purple; lip entire, pubescent towards the base.
HABITAT: Montane forest, 1900–2400 m (6300–8000 ft.).
DISTRIBUTION: Rwanda, Uganda, Zaire.

Polystachya polychaete Kränzlin

DESCRIPTION: A fairly robust species, to 40 cm (16 in.) tall. Pseudobulbs 8–10 × 1 cm (3–4 × 0.5 in.), narrowly conical but sometimes rather obscure, forming large clumps. Leaves three to four, 12–18 × 1–2 cm (5–7 × 0.5–1 in.), strap-shaped, bright glossy green, bilobed at the tip, the lobes rounded. Inflorescences to 25 cm (10 in.) tall, with a compressed sheath at the base, densely many-flowered. Flowers very small, greenish-white or yellow-green with a brown anther cap and a slightly unpleasant scent. Sepals all ovate-triangular, acuminate; dorsal 2 × 1 mm; laterals 3 × 2 mm. Petals 1.5 × 1 mm.

HABITAT: Epiphytic in rainforest, 550–1200 m (1800–4000 ft.), rarely to 2200 m (7300 ft.).

CULTIVATION: The flowering time seems erratic in cultivation; we have had it in flower in winter (November and December) and in spring (March and April).

DISTRIBUTION: Cameroon, Equatorial Guinea (Bioko), Gabon, Ghana, Ivory Coast, Kenya, Liberia, Nigeria, São Tomé, Sierra Leone, Rwanda, Tanzania, Uganda, Zaire.

Polystachya pubescens (Lindley) Reichenbach f.   PLATE 84

DESCRIPTION: An attractive and easily grown species. Pseudobulbs 2–3 × 1–1.5 cm (1 × 0.5–1 in.), conical with two to three nodes, forming clumps. Leaves two to three, 5–10 × 1–1.5 cm (2–4 × 0.5–1 in.), dark green, elliptic. Inflorescences pubescent, to 12 cm (5 in.) tall, 7 to 12 flowered. Flowers opening wide, bright yellow, the lateral sepals with red-brown longitudinal lines on the upper half; lip also with red lines. Pedicel and ovary 10–15 mm long. Dorsal sepal 10–12 × 4 mm, lanceolate, acute; lateral sepals 14 × 7 mm, obliquely ovate, petals 11–12 × 4 mm, oblanceolate. Lip 9–12 mm long, trilobed; lateral lobes small, with long, white hairs; midlobe 5–6 mm long, ovate. Column very short.

HABITAT: Epiphytic in forest, also sometimes lithophytic, in light shade of bushes.

Cultivation. In our greenhouse, it flowers in autumn and early winter (October and November).

DISTRIBUTION: South Africa (Eastern Cape, KwaZulu-Natal, Mpumalanga), Swaziland.

Polystachya purpureobracteata Cribb & I. F. la Croix

DESCRIPTION: Pseudobulbs 1–2.5 × 0.5–1 cm (0.5–1 × 0.25–0.5 in.), ovoid or oblong, glossy, forming clumps. Leaves two to five, 6–9 × 1.5 cm (2–4 × 1 in.), ligulate or oblanceolate, bright green edged with purple, the underside paler and often with purple veins and a purple midrib. Inflorescences produced with developing leaves, pubescent, 6–15 cm (2–6 in.) long, densely 5- to 15-flowered, the flowers often secund. Pedicel and ovary arched so that the flowers are drooping, 6–8 mm long. Bracts 7 × 4 mm, deep purple. Flowers with a rather soapy scent, the sepals and petals yellow-green, turning mustard yellow as they age, veined with purple or red; lip white with purple veins and a yellow callus. Sepals slightly pubescent outside and inside; dorsal sepal 9–12 × 3–4 mm, lanceolate, acute; lateral sepals 10–14 × 4–5 mm, obliquely lanceolate, acuminate. Petals 8–10 × 2–3 mm, oblanceolate. Lip recurved, 7–9 × 5–6 mm, trilobed with a glabrous yellow callus at the junction of the lobes; side lobes erect, midlobe broadly ovate, acute. Column 1 mm long.

HABITAT: Epiphytic in submontane and riverine forest, occasionally lithophytic on rock faces, 1300–1550 m (4300–5100 ft.).

DISTRIBUTION: Southern Malawi.

Figure 10-77. *Polystachya sandersonii.* Plant, ×1.

Polystachya sandersonii Harvey

FIGURE 10-77

DESCRIPTION: Pseudobulbs 2–3 × 1–1.5 cm (1 × 0.5–1 in.), conical, yellowish, ribbed with usually two nodes, forming clumps. Leaves two to three, to 11 × 1.7 cm

(4 × 1 in.), ligulate, minutely bilobed at the apex. Inflorescences pubescent, to 10 cm (4 in.) long, rather laxly 6- to 10-flowered. Flowers greenish-yellow to mustard yellow. Pedicel and ovary 10 mm long, arched; bracts 4–5 mm long, ovate, acuminate. Sepals pubescent, dorsal sepal 8 × 4 mm, ovate, acute; lateral sepals 11–12 × 7 mm, keeled on the outside; mentum rounded, 5 mm high. Petals 8 × 2 mm, oblanceolate. Lip 7 mm long, trilobed at about halfway, with an oblong, pubescent callus on the basal half; midlobe recurved, 3 × 3 mm, with some purplish spots towards the base; side lobes erect, 1 mm long. Column 1–2 mm long.

HABITAT: Epiphytic in forest, sometimes riverine forest.

CULTIVATION: This species flowers over a long period in summer and autumn (August to October).

DISTRIBUTION: South Africa (Eastern Cape, KwaZulu-Natal), Swaziland.

Polystachya seticaulis Rendle   FIGURE 10-78

DESCRIPTION: A small species, less than 10 cm (4 in.) tall, usually 6 cm (2 in.); stems very slender, not at all swollen, forming dense clumps. Leaves four to six, distichous, 15 × 1.5 mm, linear. Flower stalk wiry, inflorescences several-flowered, the rachis zigzag. Flowers bell-shaped, creamy white, the sepals slightly keeled with a purple midvein. Dorsal sepal 1.5 × 1 mm; laterals 3 × 1.8 mm, obliquely ovate, acuminate, the tips slightly reflexed; mentum saccate. Petals less than 1 mm long. Lip 2 mm long, entire, fleshy, the tip recurved.

HABITAT: Evergreen forest, 500 m (1650 ft.). We found this species in Congo, where it formed grasslike mats over a fallen, mossy branch. It was not until we noticed the remains of terminal inflorescences that we realized it was a species of *Polystachya* and not some small angraecoid.

CULTIVATION: It flowers over a long period off and on throughout the year.

DISTRIBUTION: Cameroon, Congo, Gabon, Nigeria, Zaire.

NOTE: This tiny plant has great charm. It may not be correctly placed in section *Polychaete*, as it has a very different appearance from the other members of the section.

Polystachya songaniensis G. Williamson   FIGURE 10-79

DESCRIPTION: Pseudobulbs 10–12 × 12–13 mm, squat, rather onion-shaped, green or purple, wrinkled when old, forming dense mats. Leaves two to three, to 15 × 0.5 cm (6 × 0.25 in.), linear, grasslike, deciduous in the dry season. Flowers produced on the new growth while the plants are still leafless. Inflorescences usually 6–10 cm (2–4 in.) tall, but occasionally to 25 cm (10 in.), densely many-flowered, usually with a few short branches. Flowers pale to deep pink, occasionally white, the lip almost covered with a large, yellow callus. Any colony seems to show a variation in flower color from almost white to deep pink. Pedicel and ovary purple, 4–5 mm long; bracts very short, 1.5 mm long. Sepals 4–5 × 2 mm, elliptic, the laterals oblique and forming with the column foot a narrow, cylindrical, spurlike mentum 2 mm high. Petals similar to

Figure 10-78. *Polystachya seticaulis.* Plant (left), ×5; flower (right), ×10.

sepals. Lip erect, entire, 5 × 3–4 mm, oblong, acute, with a frilly edge, and a large, oblong callus in the center. Column 1 mm long.

HABITAT: Grows on rock faces, or terrestrially in tufts of sedge overlying seepage rocks, or on old stumps of *Xerophyta* species on exposed hillsides, 1200–2200 m (4000–7300 ft.). We have never seen this little species growing epiphytically on a living plant of any kind.

Figure 10-79. *Polystachya songaniensis.* Flower, ×3.

CULTIVATION: This species should be kept dry after the leaves have fallen, but it does need occasional misting as the pseudobulbs should not be allowed to shrivel. It needs a fairly open situation and intermediate to cool temperatures.

DISTRIBUTION: Malawi (known from several localities in the southern part of the country, possibly more widespread as, unless it is in flower, it is almost impossible to see, with the pseudobulbs sunk in tufts of sedge and the leaves looking like grass).

Figure 10-80. *Polystachya spatella.* Plant, ×1.

Polystachya spatella Kränzlin
PLATE 85, FIGURE 10-80

DESCRIPTION: An erect or pendent species, to 25 cm (10 in.) long. Pseudobulbs 2–10 cm (1–4 in.) × 1.5 mm, arising from older growth and with roots arising at the base of each pseudobulb. Leaves two, 3–7 cm (1–3 in.) × 3–8 mm, linear-lanceolate. Inflorescences 2- to 8-flowered, unbranched. Pedicel and ovary arched, 7–10 mm long; bracts linear, 3 mm long. Flowers yellow-green with a white lip, sometimes with two purple spots on top of the mentum. Dorsal sepal 5 × 2 mm; lateral sepals 6 × 4–5 mm, very obliquely ovate, somewhat spreading, the tips reflexed; mentum 5–6 mm high, cylindrical, slightly bifid. Petals 4 × 1 mm, oblanceolate. Lip 8–9 mm long with a claw 5 mm long, then trilobed, with a fleshy callus at the junction of the lobes; midlobe 3 × 5 mm, quadrate, apiculate; side lobes erect. Column 2.5 mm long.

HABITAT: Epiphytic in montane and submontane forest and woodland, 1600–2700 m (5300–8900 ft.).

DISTRIBUTION: Burundi, Kenya, Rwanda, Tanzania, Uganda, Zaire.

Polystachya tenuissima Kränzlin

SYNONYM: *Polystachya inconspicua* Rendle

DESCRIPTION: Not one of the showier species. Pseudobulbs 6 × 1 mm, very slender, cylindrical. Leaf one, 2–15 cm (1–6 in.) × 2–7 mm, linear, fleshy. Inflorescences to 15 cm (6 in.) long, with several secund branches, to 40-flowered. Flowers yellow, tinged with green and purple. Dorsal sepal 1.5–3.5 × 0.5–2 mm, ovate; laterals 2–5 × 4–6 mm, obliquely triangular, with a narrow, bifid mentum 4 mm high. Petals 3 × 1 mm. Lip to 6.5 × 4 mm, trilobed towards the apex; midlobe 0.5–2.5 × 1–2 mm, rectangular, very fleshy; callus obscure. Column to 1 mm long.

HABITAT: Rainforest and drier montane woodland, 300–2300 m (1000–7600 ft.).

CULTIVATION: It flowers in autumn and continues over a long period.

DISTRIBUTION: Cameroon, Congo, Ghana, Ivory Coast, Kenya, Uganda, Zaire.

Polystachya tessellata Lindley   PLATE 86

DESCRIPTION: A robust species, to 60 cm (24 in.) tall. Pseudobulbs 1–5 cm (0.5–2 in.) long, 1 cm (0.5 in.) wide at the base, conical or almost round. Leaves three to five, 15–30 × 1.5–6 cm (6–12 × 1–2 in.), oblanceolate, minutely bilobed at the apex, dark green, often with a purplish tinge. Inflorescences to 50 cm (20 in.) long, the stalk covered with papery bracts, the flowering part with several short, secund branches, many-flowered. Flowers slightly pubescent on the outside, variable in color—pale to bright yellow, green, pink, or dull red—the lip either white or pink. Dorsal sepal 3–4.5 × 2 mm, oblong, acute; lateral sepals 4–7 × 3 mm, obliquely ovate; mentum conical, 3.5 mm high. Petals 3 × 1 mm, spathulate. Lip 5 × 4 mm, trilobed at about halfway, with a densely pubescent, longitudinal callus running from the base to the junction of the lobes; midlobe 2.5 × 2.5 mm, orbicular, the edges undulate. Column 1.5 mm long.

HABITAT: Epiphytic or lithophytic in riverine forest or high rainfall woodland, to 1650 m (5500 ft.).

CULTIVATION: In our greenhouse, it flowers in autumn (September to November).

DISTRIBUTION: Angola, Burundi, Cameroon, Congo, Equatorial Guinea (Bioko and Pagalu Islands), Ethiopia, Ghana, Guinea, Sierra Leone, Ivory Coast, Kenya, Malawi, Mozambique, Nigeria, Rwanda, São Tomé, Sudan, Tanzania, Togo, Uganda, Zaire, Zambia, Zimbabwe.

NOTE: This can be an attractive species. We grow a form from Congo with relatively large, dusky pink, long-lasting flowers that is well worth space in the greenhouse. Garay and Sweet (1974) considered this species and *Polystachya modesta* to be conspecific with the very widespread *P. concreta* (Jacquin) Garay & Sweet, found in Central America and Asia. Cribb (1984), however, believes them to be distinct species, although he says that *P. tessellata* is certainly very close to *P. concreta.*

Polystachya transvaalensis Schlechter

PLATE 87

SYNONYM: *Polystachya nigrescens* Rendle

DESCRIPTION: Stems usually 8–20 cm (3–8 in.) long but occasionally longer, cylindrical, covered in black, tubular sheaths. Leaves two to five, 5–12 × 1–2 cm (2–5 × 0.5–1 in.), ligulate, obtuse, dark green often flushed with purple. Inflorescences 3–13 cm (1–5 in.) long, usually simple but occasionally with one to three branches, to 12-flowered. Flowers glabrous, green, yellow-green or bright yellow, sometimes purple-tinged; lip creamy white with purple veins. The whole plant turns black when dried. Dorsal sepal 5.5–8 × 2.5–4 mm, ovate, acute; laterals 8.5–11 × 6–9.5 mm, obliquely triangular; mentum conical, 5.5–9 mm high. Petals 5–6.5 × 1–2 mm, oblanceolate. Lip 6.5–10.5 × 6–8 mm, with a long claw, rather obscurely trilobed in the apical half; midlobe 2.5 × 3.5 mm, triangular; side lobes rounded. Column 2.5 mm long.

HABITAT: Usually epiphytic at low levels in montane and submontane forest, or on remnant trees in montane areas, occasionally lithophytic, 1200–2900 m (4000–9600 ft.).

DISTRIBUTION: Burundi, Kenya, Malawi, South Africa (Eastern Cape, KwaZulu-Natal, Mpumalanga, Northern Province), Tanzania, Uganda, Zaire, Zambia, Zimbabwe.

Polystachya undulata Cribb & Podzorski

DESCRIPTION: Pseudobulbs 4 × 1 cm (2 × 0.5 in.), oblong but rather compressed, forming clumps. Leaf one, 8–10 × 4 cm (3–4 × 2 in.), oblong or obovate, obtuse, glaucous green, auriculate at the base. Inflorescences 8–10 cm (3–4 in.) long, simple or with a few short branches, 15- to 20-flowered. Flowers fleshy, pink or whitish, the basal part of the lip orange. Dorsal sepal 5 × 4 mm, elliptic; laterals 6 × 5 mm, obliquely ovate, forming a mentum 3–4 mm high. Petals 4.5 × 3 mm, obovate. Lip 6 × 7 mm, trilobed towards the base; side lobes erect, midlobe obovate, strongly undulate, emarginate. Column 1.5 mm long, triangular in cross-section.

HABITAT: Not recorded.

DISTRIBUTION: Rwanda. Possibly Zaire and Burundi.

NOTE: This is an attractive species; although the flowers are not very large, they are well colored, and the glaucous, gray-green foliage looks good even when the plant is not in flower. It is apparently rare in the wild, but fortunately seems to have become established in cultivation.

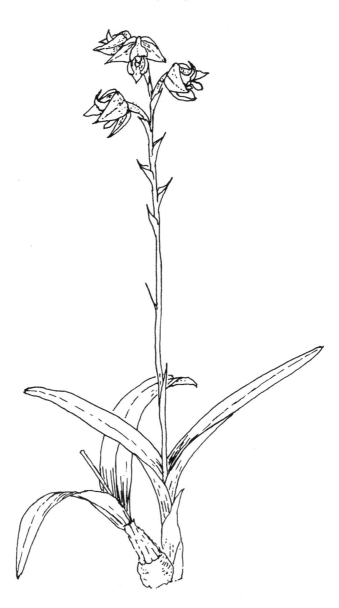

Figure 10-81. *Polystachya valentina*. Plant, ×1.

Polystachya valentina I. F. la Croix & Cribb   FIGURE 10-81

DESCRIPTION: Pseudobulbs 1.5 × 1 cm (1 × 0.5 in.), conical to pear-shaped, clustered, slightly ridged, with one node. Leaves four to five, 4–7 cm (2–3 in.) × 7–12 mm,

narrowly elliptic, dark green with a purple margin. Inflorescences to 12 cm (5 in.) tall, 6- to 10-flowered, the stems pubescent. Flowers pale to deep pink, the lip white with yellow, club-shaped hairs and a brown spot on the callus. Sepals pubescent on the outside; dorsal sepal 8–9 × 3 mm, lanceolate, acute; lateral sepals 9–10 × 5 mm, obliquely triangular, acute, keeled. Petals 8 × 1.5 mm, oblanceolate. Lip strongly recurved, 8–10 mm long, trilobed towards the base with a V-shaped or heart-shaped callus outlined by yellow hairs at the junction of the lobes; side lobes erect, earlike; midlobe 6 × 3 mm, ovate, acute, fleshy. Column 1–2 mm long.

HABITAT: Lithophytic on sandstone and granite rocks, 1220–1800 m (4000–6000 ft.).

CULTIVATION: In spite of its rather specialized habitat, this pretty little species seems to grow easily in cultivation when potted in a bark mix at intermediate temperatures. It flowers for a long time in summer.

DISTRIBUTION: Eastern Zimbabwe.

Polystachya villosa Rolfe   PLATE 88

DESCRIPTION: Pseudobulbs to 4 × 1.5 cm (2 × 1 in.), oblong or conical, somewhat bilaterally flattened, yellowish, ribbed with several nodes. Leaves three to four, to 18 × 2.5 cm (7 × 1 in.), oblanceolate or ligulate, minutely bilobed at the tip. Inflorescences densely hairy, 15–20 cm (6–8 in.) tall, densely many-flowered, usually simple but occasionally with one branch. Pedicel, ovary, bracts, and sepals all densely hairy. Ovary and pedicel 9 mm long; bracts to 12 × 7 mm, broadly ovate, acuminate, whitish-green. Flowers strongly primrose-scented, creamy white or greenish white, the lip white with purple spots on the side lobes and at the base of the midlobe. Dorsal sepal to 10 × 4 mm, ovate, acute; lateral sepals to 13 × 7 mm, obliquely triangular, acute, slightly keeled on outside. Petals 7 × 2 mm, oblanceolate. Lip recurved, fleshy, 8 mm long, trilobed with a rather obscure, glabrous callus at the junction of the lobes; side lobes erect, rounded; midlobe 5 × 4 mm, ovate, acute, bullate.

HABITAT: Riverine forest and high rainfall woodland, 1150–2000 m (3800–6600 ft.).

DISTRIBUTION: Malawi, Tanzania, Zambia.

Polystachya virginea Summerhayes

DESCRIPTION: Pseudobulbs 6–11 cm (2–4 in.) × 7–10 mm, cylindrical or narrowly conical, forming clumps. Leaf one, 12–25 × 1–3 cm (5–10 × 0.5–1 in.), lanceolate, obtuse, leathery. Inflorescences 4–9 cm (2–4 in.) long, shorter than the leaf, unbranched, to 10-flowered. Flowers white, scented. Sepals 8.5–12 × 4.5–10 mm, ovate-triangular; mentum 9 mm high, conical. Petals 8–13 × 3–4 mm, elliptical. Lip strongly recurved, 11–15 × 8–11 mm, trilobed towards the base; midlobe 4–6 × 4–6.5 mm, triangular to quadrate, with a recurved apicule; side lobes erect, with a callus at the junction of the lobes. Column 1–3 mm long.

HABITAT: Montane forest, 2200–2600 m (7300–8600 ft.).

DISTRIBUTION: Burundi, Rwanda, Uganda, Zaire.

NOTE: Podzorski and Cribb (1979) remarked that there seem to be two forms of this species, large and small, of which the smaller one is the one most frequently met with in cultivation.

Polystachya vulcanica Kränzlin

DESCRIPTION: Pseudobulbs to 9 cm (4 in.) × 1 mm, forming dense clumps. Leaf one, 11 × 1.4 mm, linear, fleshy, flat or terete. Inflorescences 2–8 cm (1–3 in.) long, shorter than the leaf, unbranched, to 5-flowered. Flowers creamy white, flushed with pink and violet; anther cap purple. Dorsal sepal 3–7 × 2–4 mm, ovate, apiculate; laterals 5–8 × 4–9 mm, obliquely triangular, apiculate; mentum to 8 mm high. Petals 3–6 × 1–2 mm, oblanceolate. Lip fleshy, 5–10 × 4–7 mm, trilobed towards the base; midlobe 1–4 × 1.5–6 mm, suborbicular, pubescent in the middle; side lobes erect, somewhat pubescent. Callus present or absent. Column 1–2 mm long.

HABITAT: Epiphytic on mossy branches in montane forest, sometimes lithophytic, 1650–3000 m (5500–9900 ft.).

CULTIVATION: It flowers off and on throughout the year.

DISTRIBUTION: Rwanda, Uganda, Zaire.

NOTE: Two varieties have been described: var. *aconitiflora* (Summerhayes) Cribb & Podzorski, synonym *Polystachya aconitiflora* Summerhayes, with pseudobulbs less than 5 cm (2 in.) long, a flat leaf, and flowers 6 mm in diameter, and var. *vulcanica,* with pseudobulbs over 4.3 cm long, a fleshy, almost terete leaf, flowers 10 mm in diameter, a dorsal sepal to 7 mm long, and a mentum more than 6 mm high.

Polystachya woosnamii Rendle   PLATE 89

DESCRIPTION: Pseudobulbs 6 cm (2 in.) × 8 mm, conical, with two nodes, partly covered by sheaths, set close together. Leaves two to three, 6–16 × 1 cm (2–6 × 0.5 in.), ligulate or linear-lanceolate, slightly bilobed at the apex. Inflorescences to 15 cm (6 in.) long, with one to two compressed sheaths at the base, fairly densely many-flowered. Flowers greenish-white or yellowish, the apex of the lip yellow or red. Pedicel and ovary arched, 3 mm long; bracts hairlike, to 8 mm long, reflexed at flowering time. Dorsal sepal 3–4 × 1–2 mm, concave, ovate, acuminate; laterals 7–11 × 2–4 mm, obliquely ovate, acuminate; mentum 7 mm high. Petals 2 × 1 mm. Lip to 7.5 × 4.5 mm with a long claw, trilobed in the apical half; side lobes erect; midlobe 3 × 2.5 mm, reflexed, ovate, the tip rounded and papillose. Column 2 mm long.

HABITAT: Epiphytic or lithophytic in riverine and montane forest, 1800–2700 m (6000–8900 ft.).

DISTRIBUTION: Burundi, Nigeria, Rwanda, Uganda, Zaire.

Polystachya zambesiaca Rolfe

PLATE 90

DESCRIPTION: Pseudobulbs 1–2 × 0.5–1 cm (0.5–1 × 0.25–0.5 in.), oblong or ovoid, somewhat compressed, often ribbed. Leaves two to three, 3–8 × 0.5–1.5 cm (1–3 × 0.25–1 in.), oblong or lanceolate, slightly folded, rather glaucous green, often purple-edged. Inflorescences pubescent, 5–8 cm (2–3 in.) long, fairly densely 3- to 20-flowered. Flowers pubescent outside, lemon yellow, buff yellow, or yellow-green, the lip white or pale yellow, purple-veined on the side lobes, with a brown spot at the base of the column foot. Pedicel and ovary 6–9 mm long; bracts 13 × 6 mm, ovate, acuminate, yellowish-white. Dorsal sepal 8–12 × 4–6 mm, ovate, acute; lateral sepals 9–12 × 4–6 mm, obliquely triangular, acuminate, slightly keeled; mentum rounded, 5 mm high. Petals 6–7 × 2 mm, oblanceolate. Lip 6–7 × 4–5 mm, strongly recurved, fleshy, with a hairy, fleshy callus at the base, trilobed; side lobes erect, rounded; midlobe 4 × 3 mm, ovate, acute. Column short and stout.

HABITAT: Rather varied; it often grows on rocks, sometimes on stunted trees, in exposed places on or near the tops of hills, but can also sometimes be found growing epiphytically in woodland, 900–2000 m (3000–6600 ft.).

CULTIVATION: As might be expected, *Polystachya zambesiaca* is fairly amenable, doing well either mounted or potted in a bark compost, at intermediate temperatures. It should have only light shade and is better with a cooler and drier rest in winter. It flowers in spring (April and May).

DISTRIBUTION: Malawi, Mozambique, South Africa (Mpumalanga, Northern Province), Tanzania, Zambia, Zimbabwe.

NOTE: This is a very variable species; some of the forms might yet be described as separate species, but often there are intermediate forms, which make it difficult to draw any sort of dividing line. The small plants with lemon yellow flowers from southern Malawi, which resemble the type specimen, are amongst the most attractive.

Polystachya zuluensis L. Bolus

DESCRIPTION: Very similar vegetatively to the more widespread *Polystachya dendrobiiflora*. Flowers often slightly smaller, although there is an overlap in size, and not opening as wide, pale lilac, with a yellow or orange central line on the lip. Sepals, petals, and lip acute rather than obtuse.

HABITAT: Usually epiphytic on species of *Xerophyta* on exposed hillsides, 1200 m (4000 ft.), occasionally lithophytic or terrestrial, growing in rock crevices. We have only seen it growing on *Xerophyta*, on rocky slopes where it can become very hot indeed. The dry season is long, but at the altitudes where it grows, there must be mist.

CULTIVATION: We grow this species in a bark compost, but it should also grow in a free-draining terrestrial mix, at intermediate temperatures. It needs good light and should be kept dry after the leaves fall.

DISTRIBUTION: South Africa (KwaZulu-Natal), Swaziland. In Stewart et al. (1982) this species is said to be confined to the Lebombo Mountains, but we have found it in Swaziland well away from the Lebombos.

Pterygodium Swartz

The genus *Pterygodium* was founded by the Swedish botanist Olof Swartz in 1800. The name derives from the Greek word *pterugos* (winged); it is difficult to see the allusion, but it may refer to the spreading hood. About 15 species are currently recognized, all but one (*Pterygodium ukingense* from southern Tanzania) known only from South Africa, most endemic to the winter rainfall area of the Western Cape but with a few species found in other parts of South Africa. No species are known to be cultivated in Europe, but at least one is grown in Australia and thus is included here. *Pterygodium cooperi, P. leucanthum,* and *P. magnum* (synonym *Corycium magnum*) occur in the summer rainfall areas of South Africa and are dormant in winter; the other South African species should be treated like *P. catholicum.*

DESCRIPTION: Terrestrial plants related to *Disperis.* Inflorescences several-flowered, lax or fairly dense. Flowers green, greenish-white, greenish-yellow, or yellow, sometimes flushed with dull red or purple. Petals joined to the dorsal sepal, forming a shallow hood; lateral sepals spreading or reflexed. Lip joined to the face of the column and above the joint has a complex, fleshy short or tall appendage.

Pterygodium catholicum (Linnaeus) Swartz

DESCRIPTION: A slender species, to 30 cm (12 in.) tall. New tubers formed annually at the end of underground stolons so that plants increase well vegetatively. Flowering stems leafy, with about four oblong leaves to 11 cm (4 in.) long. Inflorescences laxly to 5-flowered, the flowers with a pungent scent. Sepals and petals yellow-green, occasionally the hood flushed with reddish-brown. Dorsal sepal and petals 7–11 mm long. Lip 4–5 mm long, triangular; lip appendage 6–11 mm tall, toothed near the apex.

HABITAT: Terrestrial in short, open scrub, flowering particularly well after a fire, 50–1600 m (165–5300 ft.).

CULTIVATION: This is a winter-rainfall species and so is dormant in the summer months, when it should be kept dry—a sprinkling of water can be given every few weeks to prevent the tuber from shrivelling. The plant can be carefully watered when growth starts in autumn, but water should not be allowed to stand on the foliage, particularly when it is still developing. A standard free-draining terrestrial compost is suitable, at intermediate temperatures, and in no more than light shade.

DISTRIBUTION: South Africa (Western Cape).

Rangaeris Summerhayes

The genus *Rangaeris* was created by V. S. Summerhayes in 1936 to accommodate a small group of plants that were closely related to *Aerangis* but did not fit in with the genus in several ways. The main botanical differences are that *Rangaeris* has a bifid rostellum and a viscidium with two stipites instead of just one stipes as in *Aerangis.* The name is a near anagram of *Aerangis.* The genus does not, however, seem to reflect a natural grouping: there are six members, as there were about 10 years ago, but they are not the same six species. In 1986, *Rangaeris brachyceras,* which Summerhayes had put in a separate section, was transferred to a new genus and became *Cribbia brachyceras,* while in 1989, *Barombia schliebenii* became *Rangaeris schliebenii.*

Apart from the bifid rostellum, it is difficult to pick out just what distinguishes *Rangaeris.* Most species have long, slender spurs; all but one have white flowers that turn apricot with age (a characteristic they share with *Cyrtorchis* and *Jumellea,* but not with *Aerangis*). Four of the six species have linear or strap-shaped leaves folded in the middle, but one has fleshy, bilaterally flattened leaves, and the other has flat, broadly oblong leaves. Five species have an entire or obscurely trilobed lip, while one has a distinctly trilobed lip. Still, whatever they are called, they are attractive plants and any that can be obtained are worth growing. Although two of the six species are not known to be in cultivation, they are mentioned here as they sound attractive and might yet become available.

Rangaeris amaniensis (Kränzlin) Summerhayes   PLATE 91, FIGURE 10-82

DESCRIPTION: Stems woody, to 45 cm (19 in.) long, sometimes branched, the lower part covered with old leaf bases; roots stout, 3–5 mm in diameter. Leaves numerous, distichous, 4–12 × 1–2.5 cm (2–5 × 0.5–1 in.), narrowly oblong or strap-shaped, unequally and roundly bilobed at the apex, leathery, folded. Inflorescences spreading, 6–9 cm (2–4 in.) long, 5- to 13-flowered. Flowers scented, white, turning apricot with age, very variable in size. Pedicel and ovary 2–3 cm (1 in.) long; bracts 5–6.5 mm long. Sepals lanceolate, acuminate, spreading or recurved, 10–25 × 2.5–5.5 mm; petals similar but slightly smaller. Lip 10–25 × 5–11 mm, rather obscurely trilobed at about halfway, the side lobes rounded, the midlobe lanceolate, acuminate. Spur 7.5–16 cm (3–6 in.) long, pendent, slender. Column 5 mm long.

HABITAT: This species seems to occupy two very different habitats, montane forest and open woodland, where it can be epiphytic or lithophytic, at altitudes of 1060–2600 m (3500–8600 ft.). This may account for the variability in size of the flowers.

CULTIVATION: Plants do best in a basket, where the long roots can straggle out. They need fairly bright light and a drier period in winter if they are to flower. They seem to do well at intermediate temperatures. The species flowers in summer (August). Our plant has large flowers and is quite spectacular.

DISTRIBUTION: Eritrea, Ethiopia, Kenya, Tanzania, Uganda, Zimbabwe.

Rangaeris longicaudata (Rolfe) Summerhayes

DESCRIPTION: Stems long, slender. Leaves 6–12 × 1–1.5 cm (2–5 × 0.5–1 in.), narrowly oblong. Inflorescences 8–15 cm (3–6 in.) long, 3- to 4-flowered. Flowers white. Pedicel and ovary 5–6 mm long; bracts 12–14 mm long. Sepals, petals and lip all 20–35 mm long, lanceolate, acuminate, the edges of the lip curled back. Spur 15–19 cm (6–8 in.) long. Column 6 mm long.

DISTRIBUTION: Southern Nigeria.

314

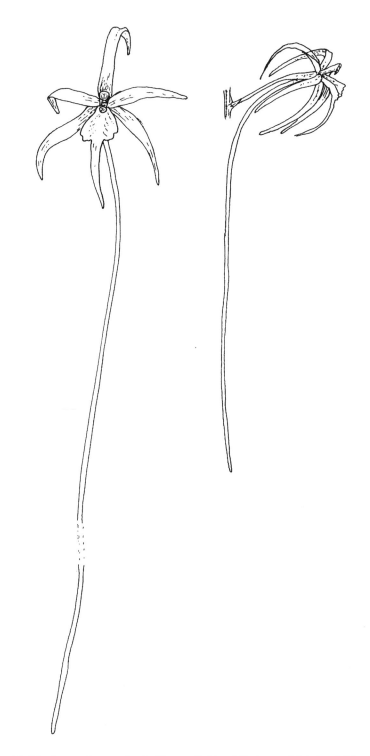

Figure 10-82. *Rangaeris amaniensis.* Flower (left), ×1.5; flower (right), ×0.75.

Rangaeris muscicola (Reichenbach f.) Summerhayes PLATE 92

DESCRIPTION: Stems short; roots stout, 3–5 mm in diameter. Leaves 5 to 11, borne in a fan, 6.5–20 × 0.5–1.8 cm (2–8 × 0.25–1 in.), linear, folded, stiff-textured, somewhat recurved, dark green. Inflorescences one to two, arising from lower leaf axils, 10–30 cm (4–12 in.) long, to 20-flowered or sometimes more. Flowers white, turning apricot with age, sweetly scented. Pedicel and ovary slender, 25 mm long; bracts 3–9 mm long, black, sheathing. Sepals 7–9.5 × 2.5–4 mm, lanceolate, acute, the laterals slightly longer and somewhat oblique. Petals 6.5–8 × 1.5–3 mm, elliptic, slightly reflexed. Lip 6.5–9 × 4–7 mm, entire, broadly ovate, acute; spur 5.5–8.5 cm (2–3 in.) long, very slender, pendent, straight or slightly S-shaped. Column 3–4.5 mm long.

HABITAT: Very varied, from evergreen forest to woodland, sometimes on rocks on hilltops, 600–2200 m (2000–7300 ft.).

CULTIVATION: This species will grow mounted, but growth is more vigorous in a pot. If pot-grown, a coarse mix is necessary, and plants should be kept drier in winter. It requires intermediate temperatures and moderate light. In our greenhouse, it flowers in winter (November and December).

DISTRIBUTION: Cameroon, Congo, Ghana, Guinea, Ivory Coast, Kenya, Liberia, Malawi, Mali, Mozambique, Nigeria, Sierra Leone, South Africa (Eastern Cape, KwaZulu-Natal, Mpumalanga), Tanzania, Uganda, Zaire, Zambia, Zimbabwe.

Rangaeris rhipsalisocia (Reichenbach f.) Summerhayes

PLATE 93, FIGURE 10-83

DESCRIPTION: Stems short, to 4 cm (2 in.) long; roots stout, 4–5 mm in diameter. Leaves four to six, borne in a fan, to 12 × 0.8 cm (5–0.5 in.), bilaterally flattened, linear, acute, fleshy. Inflorescences arising below leaves, 10 cm (4 in.) long, 9- to 10-flowered. Flowers bell-shaped, not opening wide; white, turning apricot as they age, the spur greenish. Pedicel and ovary 10–12 mm long; bracts 2 mm long. Sepals and petals all lanceolate, acute; dorsal sepal 9 × 3 mm; laterals 11 × 2 mm. Petals 8 × 2 mm. Lip entire, 10 mm long, 3 mm wide at the base, tapering rather abruptly in the apical half to an acute apex; spur to 15 mm long, tapering, the apical third hooked forwards. Column short and stout, 2 mm long.

HABITAT: Evergreen forest, 100–200 m (330–660 ft.).

CULTIVATION: This species can do well in cultivation, both mounted and in a pot, but can also be temperamental. If pot-grown, it needs a fairly coarse mix, which must not become too wet, or the roots rot. We grow it in moderate shade in intermediate temperatures, but it would probably be even better in warm temperatures. It flowers in spring and early summer (May and June)

DISTRIBUTION: Angola, Cameroon, Central African Republic, Congo, Ghana, Guinea, Ivory Coast, Liberia, Nigeria, Senegal, Sierra Leone, Zaire.

Rangaeris schliebenii (Mansfeld) Cribb FIGURE 10-84

SYNONYMS: *Barombia schliebenii* (Mansfeld) Cribb, *Leptocentrum schliebenii* Mansfeld

DESCRIPTION: Stems fairly short, to 10 cm (4 in.) long; roots long and stout, 4–5 mm in diameter. Leaves numerous, borne in a fan, 15–20 × 1–2.5 cm (6–8 ×

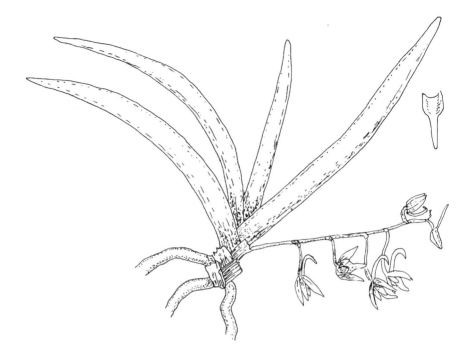

Figure 10-83. *Rangaeris rhipsalisocia.* Plant (left), ×0.75; lip (right), ×1.5.

0.5–1 in.), linear to strap-shaped, unequally and roundly bilobed at the apex, folded, stiff. Inflorescences spreading, 18–30 cm (7–12 in.) long, 4- to 8-flowered. Flowers white, the spur greenish-orange. Pedicel and ovary 6–9 cm (2–4 in.) long; bracts 1 cm (0.5 in.) long. Sepals and petals linear, acute, recurved, 35–40 × 3.5–4.5 mm. Lip 30–42 × 7–11 mm, recurved, narrowly elliptic, acuminate, the edges very finely toothed. Spur 16–19 cm (6–8 in.) long, tapering from a wide mouth to become very slender, pendent, straight. Column slender, 20–27 mm long.

HABITAT: Riverine and submontane forest, 400–1400 m (1300–4600 ft.).

CULTIVATION: This species has grown well for us in a pot with a coarse mix. The long roots wander about and try to bury themselves in other pots, so the plant might be even better in a basket. Furthermore, the flowers have long spurs and then a pot needs either to be suspended or stood on another upturned pot. Our plant is given intermediate temperatures, fairly good light and is kept drier in winter. In our greenhouse, it flowers in winter (December and January).

DISTRIBUTION: Tanzania.

NOTE: This strange-looking but beautiful species for a time shared the genus *Barombia* with the plant now known as *Aerangis gracillima,* which also has a very long, slender column.

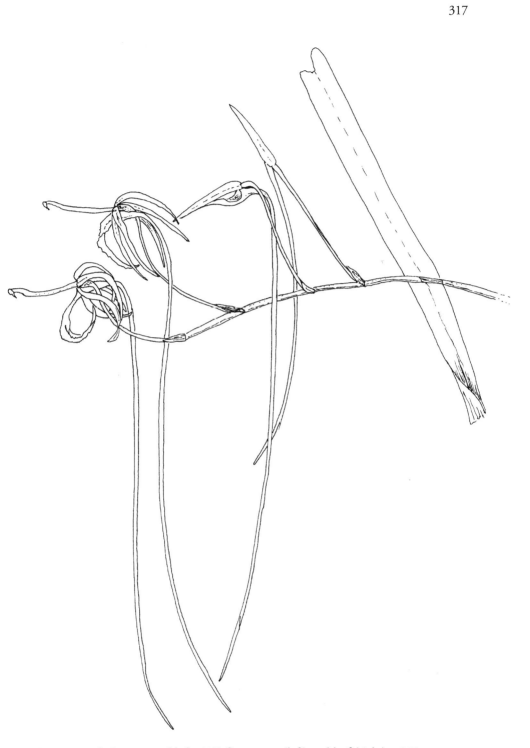

Figure 10-84. *Rangaeris schliebenii.* Inflorescence (left) and leaf (right), ×0.7.

Rangaeris trilobata Summerhayes

DESCRIPTION: Stems long, narrow; roots slender, along the stem. Leaves 4–8 × 1–2 cm (2–4 × 0.5–1 in.), narrowly oblong-lanceolate, acute, set along the stem 2–5 cm (1–2 in.) apart. Inflorescences 4–12 cm (2–5 in.) long, few-flowered. Sepals salmon pink, petals and lip white. Sepals and petals 6.5–8.5 mm long. Lip 5–9 mm long, trilobed, the midlobe linear or lanceolate, acuminate, the side lobes much shorter, suborbicular, with wavy edges.

DISTRIBUTION: Gabon, southern Nigeria.

NOTE: We have only seen this species as a herbarium specimen and in a photograph, and it looks more like a species of *Solenangis* than a *Rangaeris*. The flowers are rather small, but the coloring is attractive.

Satyrium Swartz

The genus *Satyrium* was established in 1800 by the Swedish botanist Olof Swartz (1760–1818). The name is derived from the word *satyr*; in Greek mythology, satyrs were woodland demigods, half man and half goat, lustful companions of Bacchus. The name may refer to the twin, goatlike horns borne on the lip of species of *Satyrium*. Bechtel et al. (1992) suggested that in the Greek herbals of Dioscorides and Pliny, the name *satyrion* referred to the European man orchid, *Aceras anthopophorum*, the tubers of which were believed to have aphrodisiac properties. Finally, A. V. Hall (1982) suggested that the name refers to the goatlike smell of the European lizard orchid, *Himantoglossum hircinum*, which was originally named by Linnaeus as *Satyrium hircinum*. Readers can take their choice. The genus was revised in 1901 by both Rudolf Schlechter and Fritz Kränzlin. The most recent revision was by A. V. Hall in 1982, but unfortunately this covers only the southern African species. There are about 100 species, more than 30 of them South African and many in tropical Africa. Five species are from Madagascar and two from Asia. The most distinctive feature is the lip, which is held at the top of the flower and bears twin spurs, varying from long and slender to short and saccate, even, in one tropical African species, completely absent. The only other orchid genus to have twin spurs borne on the lip is the South African *Satyridium*, which contains only one species, *S. rostratum* Lindley, endemic to the Western Cape.

DESCRIPTION: Terrestrial species, growing each year from ovoid tubers, occasionally increasing vegetatively by underground runners. In some species, the foliage leaves are borne on a separate sterile shoot, the flowering stem having only sheathing leaves, while in others, the foliage leaves arise on the flowering stem. There may be either one or two basal leaves tightly appressed to the ground, or several leaves arranged up the stem. Inflorescence usually a dense or fairly dense raceme, several- to many-flowered, often with large bracts, usually reflexed at flowering time. Flowers never very large but often extremely showy, white, green, yellow, orange, pink, red, or purple. Sepals and petals small, rather similar, usually joined at the base for part of their length. Lip the most noticeable part of the flower, forming a hood; column inside lip, with the stigma at the top, the anther loculi hanging below it, with the trilobed rostellum between them. Pollinia two, joined by caudicles to two viscidia.

CULTIVATION: Species of *Satyrium* have the reputation of being difficult in cultivation. Few species are grown outside South Africa, except for the Asiatic *S. nepalense,* which does well in an alpine house. Several South African growers have developed the technique for growing and propagating *Satyrium,* and it is hoped that enthusiasts in the rest of the world will be able to follow suit. South African growers are often able to use some of the original soil when growing species of *Satyrium,* and indeed other terrestrial orchids, which should supply the associated fungi that must be beneficial to growth. For orchid growers without access to the original soil, a standard, free-draining terrestrial compost should be used, in a shallow pot. As with all species of deciduous terrestrial orchids, it is essential to follow the plant's natural rhythm. Water can be applied freely while the plant is in growth, but one must be careful that water does not collect in the cups formed by the developing leaves as this is liable to cause rot, particularly if it has not dried off by nightfall. The pot should be allowed to dry out before watering again. A cool, dry rest is essential after the year's growth has died back.

Species that come from the winter rainfall area of South Africa are dormant during the hot, dry summer months. In autumn, the tubers start to sprout and careful watering can begin. The leaves and inflorescences develop through the winter, and the plants flower in spring. While the leaves are developing, so is the new tuber; after flowering, the old tuber withers away. It is not necessary to repot every year; instead, every other year should be enough. Repotting should be done in early autumn, just before growth starts.

Species that grow in summer rainfall areas of South and tropical Africa should be kept cooler and drier in winter than those that come from the winter rainfall area. New growth starts in spring (instead of autumn), and the plants flower in summer. Even when a species grows in an area of relatively high rainfall, drainage must be good.

Satyrium bicorne (Linnaeus) Thunberg

DESCRIPTION: A slender species, 10–60 cm (4–24 in.) tall, with two basal leaves appressed to the ground and sheathing leaves on the stem. Basal leaves 3–6 cm (1–2 in.) long, almost round. Inflorescences rather laxly 4- to 30-flowered; flowers dull yellow or greenish-yellow, tinged with purple-brown. Ovary 6–14 mm long; bracts about twice its length, reflexed. Sepals and petals 6–9 mm long, the petals slightly shorter. Lip 9 mm long, the mouth facing down; spurs 1–2 cm (0.5–1 in.) long, lying along the ovary.

HABITAT: Fynbos, sandy bush and grassland, in open or partly shaded places, to 1200 m (4000 ft.), but mostly 200–500 m (660–1650 ft.), in the winter rainfall area.

DISTRIBUTION: South Africa (Northern Cape, Western Cape).

Satyrium carneum (Dryander) Sims

DESCRIPTION: A robust species, 30–80 cm (12–32 in.) tall, with two broadly ovate basal leaves to 23 cm (9 in.) long, tightly appressed to the ground; flowering stem with sheathing leaves, the lower two sometimes slightly spreading at the tips. Inflorescences densely many-flowered; flowers pink, relatively large. Ovary 12–15 mm long; bracts about twice as long, reflexed at flowering time. Sepals and petals 15–18 mm long. Lip 15 mm long, with a prominent dorsal crest, the mouth 12–14 mm high, with the apical flap 2 mm long. Spurs 1.5–2 cm (1 in.) long, parallel to the ovary.

HABITAT: Coastal bush and fynbos, in moist or dry sand and limestone, 15–300 m (50–1000 ft.). This species is becoming rarer, because of urban development, invasion of alien species such as Australian acacias, and overcollecting.

CULTIVATION: Unlike *Satyrium bicorne, S. carneum* produces more than one new tuber each year and so is more easily increased. It comes from the winter rainfall area.

DISTRIBUTION: South Africa (Western Cape).

Satyrium coriifolium Swartz   PLATE 94

DESCRIPTION: A robust species, to 75 cm (30 in.) tall, with two to four spreading or semi-erect leaves on the lower part of the stem. Leaves to 15 cm (6 in.) long, elliptic or ovate, stiff and leathery, purple-spotted on the underside near the base. Inflorescences densely many-flowered. Flowers relatively large, bright orange or bright yellow, the lip often tinged with red. Ovary 10–14 mm long; bracts two to three times its length, reflexed at flowering time. Sepals and petals 7–13 mm long, oblong, reflexed, the petals slightly narrower. Lip bent forwards, 10–13 mm long, the mouth narrowly oblong, the apical flap 2 mm long, reflexed. Spurs 9–12 mm long, slender, lying along the ovary.

HABITAT: Coastal sandy flats, to 300 m (1000 ft.), rarely to 750 m (2500 ft.), often forming large colonies but becoming less frequent. It comes from the winter rainfall area.

DISTRIBUTION: South Africa (southwestern and eastern Cape Province).

Satyrium erectum Swartz

DESCRIPTION: A robust species, 10–50 cm (4–20 in.) tall, with two basal leaves appressed to the ground. Leaves 4–16 cm (2–6 in.) long, ovate to round, fleshy; flowering stem with sheathing leaves. Inflorescences several to many-flowered. Flowers pale to deep pink, flushed with darker pink and with darker spots on the petals and apex of lip, and with a strong, sweet scent. Ovary 6–14 mm long; bracts two or three times its length, reflexed at flowering time. Sepals and petals 10–15 mm long, obovate-oblong, curving down. Lip with a dorsal ridge, 10–15 mm long, the mouth obovate, 6–8 mm high; the apical flap 3–4 mm long, partly reflexed. Spurs 5–11 mm long, usually shorter than the ovary.

HABITAT: Dry sandy or clay soil, on slopes or flat areas in scrub and fynbos, 50–1500 m (165–5000 ft.), in the winter rainfall area.

DISTRIBUTION: South Africa (Northern Cape, Western Cape).

Satyrium longicauda Lindley

DESCRIPTION: A slender species, usually 30–60 cm (12–24 in.) tall, with two ovate foliage leaves 4–20 cm (2–8 in.) long on a separate sterile shoot, the flowering stem bearing sheathing leaves. Inflorescences rather loosely several- to many-flowered. Flowers white tinged with pink, or pale pink, sweetly scented. Ovary 8–15 mm long; bracts pinkish-brown, about twice its length, reflexed at flowering time. Sepals and petals 9–11 mm long, spreading, recurved at the tips, the petals slightly shorter than the sepals. Lip 8–12 mm long, with a wide mouth and a prominent apical flap. Spurs 2.5–4.5 mm long, slender, parallel to ovary and stem.

HABITAT: Open grassland and rocky slopes, usually 1200–2100 m (4000–7000 ft.), in summer rainfall areas.

DISTRIBUTION: Mozambique, South Africa (Eastern Cape, Free State, KwaZulu-Natal, Mpumalanga, Northern Province, Western Cape), Swaziland, Tanzania, Zimbabwe.

NOTE: Variety *jacottetianum* (Kränzlin) A. V. Hall has smaller flowers than typical individuals and shorter spurs (1.5–2.5 mm long).

Satyrium macrophyllum Lindley   FIGURE 10-85
SYNONYM: *Satyrium cheirophorum* Rolfe

DESCRIPTION: Plants 15–80 cm (6–32 in.) tall; stems leafy, with two or three large, spreading leaves near the base, 16–20 × 5–7 cm (6–8 × 2–3 in.), ovate; the rest sheathing, becoming bractlike. Inflorescences fairly densely many-flowered; flowers pale to deep pink, or cherry red. Ovary 10 mm long, green streaked with pink; bracts about twice as long, reflexed. Sepals and petals 7–15 mm long, spreading. Lip 10–12 mm long, wide-mouthed, with a small apical flap, tapering at the back into the spurs, 10–25 mm long, slender, parallel to the ovary.

HABITAT: Woodland or in long grass, also montane grassland, 350–2000 m (1150–6600 ft.), in summer rainfall areas.

DISTRIBUTION: Kenya, Malawi, Mozambique, South Africa (Eastern Cape, KwaZulu-Natal), Swaziland, Tanzania, Zimbabwe.

NOTE: In Malawi, plants growing at higher altitudes are smaller than typical individuals described above, with rich cherry-red flowers.

Satyrium membranaceum Swartz

DESCRIPTION: Plants 20–50 cm (8–20 in.) tall, with two basal leaves appressed to the ground and sheathing leaves on the flowering stem. Basal leaves to 12 cm (5 in.) long, broadly ovate, obtuse. Inflorescences several to many-flowered; flowers pale to deep pink, rarely almost white. Ovary 8–18 mm long, bracts to twice its length, becoming reflexed at flowering time, mostly dry and papery. Sepals and petals 9–11 mm long, the petals finely toothed and with a wavy edge. Lip 9–11 mm long, with an oblong mouth 5–9 mm high, the apical flap reflexed, 3 mm long, with a finely toothed and wavy edge. Spurs 2–3 cm (1 in.) long, arching away from the ovary.

Figure 10-85. *Satyrium macrophyllum*. Flower, ×2.

HABITAT: Open, grassy hillsides, 60–1600 m (200–5300 ft.), but usually 200–700 m (660–2300 ft.), mainly in the winter rainfall area. Flowering seems to be stimulated by veld fires.

DISTRIBUTION: South Africa (Eastern Cape, Western Cape).

Satyrium odorum Sonder

DESCRIPTION: A robust species, 20–50 cm (8–20 in.) tall; stems leafy. Leaves two to six, the largest 5–25 cm (2–10 in.) long, ovate, spreading, fleshy, grading into bracts. Inflorescences fairly densely few- to many-flowered. Flowers pale green or yellow-green tinged with purple-brown, pungently scented. Ovary 9–13 mm long; bracts about twice its length, reflexed at flowering time. Sepals deflexed, 4–8 mm long; petals about half their length. Lip 8–10 mm long, the mouth 4–6 mm high; the apical flap 2 mm long. Spurs 13–18 mm long, arched above the ovary, occasionally with additional spurs 3 mm long.

HABITAT: Locally common on sandy soil in shade of rocks and bushes, to 200 m (660 ft.), rarely to 650 m (2100 ft.), sometimes forming colonies. It grows in the winter rainfall area.

CULTIVATION: This is one of those species that forms runners, which develop a tuber at the tips, which then gives rise to a new plant.

DISTRIBUTION: South Africa (Western Cape).

Satyrium princeps H. Bolus

DESCRIPTION: A robust species, 30–80 cm (12–32 in.) tall, with two basal leaves appressed to ground. Basal leaves 8–23 cm (3–9 in.) long, broadly ovate, obtuse; stems with sheathing leaves that are usually dry and papery by flowering time. Inflorescences densely several to many-flowered; flowers relatively large, rose pink to carmine red. Ovary 8–17 mm long; bracts about twice that length, dry, papery and reflexed by flowering time. Sepals and petals deflexed, 11–14 mm long, the petals with a toothed, wavy edge. Mouth of lip obovate, 8–10 mm high, the apical flap 3–4 mm long, partly reflexed, with a toothed, wavy edge. Spurs 17–20 mm long, parallel to the ovary.

HABITAT: Sandy soil in coastal bush, mostly near sea but occasionally to 150 m (500 ft.), in the winter rainfall area.

DISTRIBUTION: South Africa (Western Cape).

Satyrium pumilum Thunberg

DESCRIPTION: A dwarf species, almost rosettelike, 1–3 cm (1 in.) high. Leaves three to five, the lowest spreading, 2–5.5 cm (1– 2 in.) long, ovate, the upper ones sheathing and bractlike. Inflorescences densely to 7-flowered. Flowers large for the size of plant, dull green on the outside, yellow-green inside banded with dark maroon, smelling of rotting meat. Ovary 5–11 mm long; bracts 3–8 times its length. Sepals and petals joined for most of their length, 8–11 mm long. Lip 9–12 mm long, the apex not reflexed; spurs saccate, rather flattened, 2–3 mm long.

HABITAT: Seepage areas in clay or sandy soils in lower rainfall areas, rather rare and local, usually 450–1200 m (1500–4000 ft.), in the winter rainfall area.

DISTRIBUTION: South Africa (Western Cape).

Solenangis Schlechter

The genus *Solenangis* was established by the German botanist Rudolf Schlechter in 1918 for a small group of long-stemmed, monopodial epiphytic plants, most of which had already been described under *Angraecum*. The name is derived from the Greek words *solen* (pipe, tube) and *angos* (vessel), a reference, perhaps, to the tubular spur that is the most prominent feature of the flower in some species. There are six species in tropical Africa and Madagascar. None is widely grown, but all are in cultivation. They are not showy, but interesting and unusual.

DESCRIPTION: Stems long, often scandent, with many long roots arising all along the stem. Leaves present or absent. Inflorescences axillary, one- to many-flowered. Flowers small, white, greenish-white, or yellow-green, sometimes tinged with rusty pink. Sepals and petals free, subsimilar. Lip unlobed or rather obscurely trilobed, often very small, with a tubular, funnel-shaped or club-shaped spur at the base. Column short, with no foot; rostellum bilobed. Pollinia two, stipes one, viscidium one.

Solenangis aphylla (Thouars) Summerhayes

DESCRIPTION: Stems scandent or pendent, leafless, to 90 cm (3 ft.) long; roots numerous, long, branched, 2 mm in diameter. Inflorescences arising along the stem, 1–2.5 cm (0.5–1 in.) long, densely 8- to 16-flowered. Pedicel and ovary 4–5 mm long; bracts 0.5 mm long. Peduncle and rachis brown. Flowers faintly scented, white, the sepals and petals tipped with reddish-pink. Sepals 2.5–3 × 1.5–2 mm, elliptic, obtuse. Petals 2.5–3 × 1 mm, linear, acute. Lip 2.5–3 × 2 mm, concave, obscurely trilobed, the side lobes erect and rounded, the midlobe ovate, obtuse; spur 4–5 mm long, incurved, swollen at the tip. Column 2 mm long.

HABITAT: Epiphytic at low levels in thicket and riverine forest, to 900 m (3000 ft.).

CULTIVATION: Mounted, in moderate shade at intermediate temperatures. Although the flowers are small, the numerous, dense inflorescences make this an attractive plant.

DISTRIBUTION: Kenya, Mozambique, Tanzania, Zimbabwe. Also in Madagascar, Mascarene Islands.

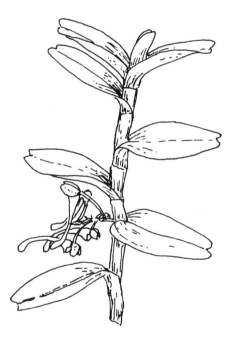
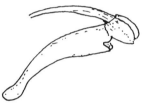

Figure 10-86. *Solenangis clavata.* Plant (left), ×1; flower (right), ×2.5.

Solenangis clavata (Rolfe) Schlechter FIGURE 10-86

DESCRIPTION: Stems elongated, sometimes branched, to 50 cm (20 in.) long or more; roots numerous, long, branching, 1–2 mm in diameter. Leaves numerous, distichous, 2–4 × 1–2 cm (1–2 × 0.5–1 in.), elliptic, unequally and obtusely bilobed at the apex. Inflorescences arising along the stem opposite the leaves, 6- to 10-flowered. Pedicel and ovary 6–8 mm long; bracts 1 mm long. Flowers greenish-white. Sepals and petals 3–4 × 1.5–2 mm, elliptic, rounded. Lip rather obscurely trilobed, barely 1 mm long, grading into a wide-mouthed spur 10–13 mm long, becoming narrow, then swollen at the apex. Capsule ellipsoidal, 20 × 6 mm.

HABITAT: Epiphytic, lithophytic, or terrestrial in forest and marshy areas, 1300–2000 m (4300–6600 ft.).

CULTIVATION: Scandent plants like this usually seem better mounted, but high humidity seems so essential to this species that we find it does better in a pot. Possibly as the plants grow larger, they would benefit from having a slab of bark or even a moss pole at the back of the pot for them to root into. Intermediate to warm temperatures and fairly heavy shade are best.

DISTRIBUTION: Cameroon, Congo, Ghana, Ivory Coast, Liberia, Nigeria, Rwanda, São Tomé, Zaire.

Figure 10-87. *Solenangis conica.* Plant (left), ×1; flower (right), ×3.

Solenangis conica (Schlechter) L. Jonsson   FIGURE 10-87
SYNONYM: *Solenangis angustifolia* Summerhayes

DESCRIPTION: A slender epiphyte; stems more or less erect, 4–20 cm (2–8 in.) long; roots numerous, 1 mm in diameter. Leaves borne towards the tip of the stem, needle-shaped but slightly flattened, to 15 × 1.5 mm. Inflorescences arising along the stem, 8–14 mm long, 2- to 4-flowered. Pedicel and ovary 2 mm long; bracts 0.5 mm long. Flowers white, bell-shaped, the spur tipped with green. Sepals 2–3 × 1–1.5 mm, elliptic, obtuse; petals similar but slightly smaller. Lip 3 × 1.5 mm, concave, oblong; spur 1–2 mm long, conical. Column 1 mm long.

HABITAT: Epiphytic on twigs and small branches in montane forest, usually sunk in moss and lichen, 1800–2250 m (6000–7400 ft.).

CULTIVATION: This little species grows surprisingly well, either mounted or in a pot, in shaded, humid conditions at intermediate temperatures.

DISTRIBUTION: Guinea Bissau, Kenya, Malawi, Tanzania, Zimbabwe.

Solenangis scandens (Schlechter) Schlechter

DESCRIPTION: Stems long, leafy, scandent; roots numerous. Leaves 3–5 × 1.5–2.5 cm (1–2 × 1 in.), distichous, ovate. Inflorescences arising along the stem, 2–10 cm (1–4 in.) long, 3- to 15-flowered. Flowers white, greenish, yellowish or pinkish. Sepals and petals 5–7 × 2–3 mm, ovate or elliptic, obtuse. Lip 6–8 × 2.5–4 mm, entire, ovate, obtuse; spur 2–2.5 cm (1 in.) long, with a wide mouth, then becoming narrow, and swollen again at the apex.

HABITAT: Dense forest.

CULTIVATION: As for *Solenangis clavata*.

DISTRIBUTION: Cameroon, Congo, Gabon, Ghana, Ivory Coast, Liberia, Nigeria, Sierra Leone, Zaire.

Solenangis wakefieldii (Rolfe) Cribb & J. Stewart

SYNONYM: *Tridactyle wakefieldii* (Rolfe) Summerhayes

DESCRIPTION: A scandent epiphyte, to 100 cm (40 in.) long, climbing by the roots; stems shiny brown, with many roots arising along the stem. Leaves numerous, 1.5–3 × 0.5–1.5 cm (1 × 0.25–1 in.), lanceolate, unequally and acutely bilobed at the apex. Inflorescences arising along the stem, 4–6 cm (2 in.) long, laxly 4- to 6- flowered. Pedicel and ovary 1–2 cm (0.5–1 in.) long; bracts 3–5 mm long. Flowers scented, white. Dorsal sepal 3 × 1.5–2 mm, oblong-elliptic, obtuse; lateral sepals similar but slightly longer. Petals 3.5 × 1.5 mm, lanceolate, obtuse. Lip trilobed in the apical half, 10 mm long and wide across the lobes; midlobe 3.5 × 1 mm, lanceolate, acute; side lobes 4.5–5 mm long, linear, spreading and reflexed. Spur 6–7 mm long, pendent, very slender. Column 1 mm long.

HABITAT: Epiphytic in coastal and lowland bush, to 300 m (1000 ft.).

CULTIVATION: As for *Solenangis clavata*.

DISTRIBUTION: Kenya, Tanzania (including Zanzibar).

Sphyrarhynchus Mansfeld

The genus *Sphyrarhynchus* was established by the German botanist R. Mansfeld in 1935. The unwieldy name comes from the Greek words *sphyra* (hammer) and *rhynchos* (beak), referring to the shape of the rostellum. Only one species is known.

Sphyrarhynchus schliebenii Mansfeld

DESCRIPTION: A dwarf, monopodial species; stems short; roots rather flattened, 2–3 mm wide. Leaves three to five, 2–3.5 cm (1 in.) × 5 mm, linear to elliptic, unequally and obtusely bilobed at apex, rather fleshy. Inflorescences usually to 3 cm (1 in.) long (occasionally longer), densely 6- to 10-flowered. Flowers rather variable in size, but usually large for the size of plant, glistening white with a green mark on the lip. Pedicel and ovary 5–6 mm long; bracts sheathing, 1 mm long. Sepals and petals to 14 × 4 mm, lanceolate, acute. Lip to 6 × 4 mm, entire, oblong or oblanceolate; spur to 8 mm long, swollen at the tip. Column less than 1 mm long. Pollinia and stipites two; viscidium one; rostellum hammer-shaped, bilobed.

HABITAT: Epiphytic in evergreen forest, 900–1600 m (3000–5300 ft.).

CULTIVATION: This little species is well known in cultivation, even though it is not always easy to obtain a specimen. It is best mounted, at intermediate temperatures, in moderate shade, with high humidity, and should not be allowed to become too dry. It flowers in spring (April).

DISTRIBUTION: Tanzania.

Stenoglottis Lindley

The genus *Stenoglottis* was established by John Lindley in 1837, based on a plant of *S. fimbriata* from Transkei in South Africa. The name is derived from the Greek words *stenos* (narrow) and *glossa* (tongue), referring to the shape of the free part of the lip. By the end of the nineteenth century, two more species had been described, but Fritz Kränzlin, revising the genus in 1901, considered that only one species should be recognized. Another species, *S. woodii*, was described in 1924. V. S. Summerhayes (1968) considered two or three species to belong to the genus, but Joyce Stewart (1989) recognized four species from southern and eastern tropical Africa. A fifth species has been transferred to the genus (McDonald 1995), and a sixth species from South Africa is soon to be described. The species are all rather similar.

DESCRIPTION: Terrestrial, epiphytic or lithophytic, with tuberous roots and a basal rosette of many leaves. Inflorescence tall, arising from the middle of the rosette. Flowers pink or white, sometimes spotted with purple. Sepals free or shortly joined to the base of the column, the dorsal erect and somewhat concave, the laterals spreading. Petals smaller than the sepals, projecting forwards and more or less concealing the column. Lip 3- or 5-lobed about half way along, with a short spur at the base or with no spur. Column short and broad; pollinia two, each with a short caudicle and a round viscidium; stigmatic arms short and erect, with staminodes behind them.

CULTIVATION: All species have a similar life cycle and can be treated in much the same way in cultivation. They do well at intermediate temperatures and moderate shade, with good air movement; if ventilation is poor, they develop black blotching on the leaves, or the leaves may die back completely. Plants should be potted in a free-draining terrestrial mix of bark, perlag, perlite, peat, and some loam. They die back after flowering—sometimes the leaves start to turn yellow before flowering is finished—and should then be kept dry and cooler until the new growth starts to show, usually after two or three months. Remove the old leaves when they have turned brown, as they may become a focus for rot. The best time to repot is when the new growth is just starting; repotting should be done every year or at least every other year. At this time, old dead roots can be easily pulled away. Plants are easily divided, usually one or two tubers will fall away and can be potted up separately. Once the new growth is clearly visible, careful watering can be started; the rosettes soon develop in spring and summer, and then the inflorescences start to elongate. According to Stewart (1989), the sequence of flowering is first, *Stenoglottis woodii*, followed by *S. fimbriata* and *S. zambesiaca*, with *S. longifolia* flowering last of all in autumn and early winter. Provided plants are kept dry while resting, species of *Stenoglottis* are easily grown and do well as house plants, preferably on a windowsill where they do not receive direct sunlight. The individual flowers are not large, but they are numerous, and a plant remains in flower for several weeks, if not months.

Stenoglottis fimbriata Lindley

DESCRIPTION: Leaves to 10 in a basal rosette, 2.5–15 × 0.5–1.5 cm (1–6 × 0.25–1 in.), lanceolate or oblong, the edge undulate, dark green, spotted with purplish-brown. Inflorescences 10–40 cm (4–16 in.) tall, several- to many-flowered, the scape with many bracts decreasing in size towards the top. Flowers rosy-mauve, the lip and sometimes the sepals and petals spotted with purple. Sepals 3–8 × 2–5 mm, ovate, obtuse. Petals 3–6 × 2–4 mm, ovate-oblong, pointing forwards, often fringed on the apical edge. Lip unspurred, 6–15 mm long, trilobed at about halfway, lobes acute, midlobe longer and narrower than side lobes, all lobes usually fringed. Staminodes small, sickle-shaped, obtuse, smooth, joined to the sides of the column.

HABITAT: Terrestrial in humus, or growing on mossy rocks or low down on tree trunks or on fallen logs, in shade in forest, to 2200 m (7300 ft.).

DISTRIBUTION: South Africa (Eastern Cape, KwaZulu-Natal, Mpumalanga, Northern Province), Swaziland.

Stenoglottis longifolia Hooker f.   PLATE 95

DESCRIPTION: Leaves numerous, in a basal rosette, 9–25 × 1–4 cm (4–10 × 0.5–2 in.), oblanceolate or narrowly oblong, acute, the edges undulate, light green, not spotted. Inflorescences 30–100 cm (12–40 in.) tall, densely many-flowered. Flowers pale to deep lilac-pink, rarely white, purple-spotted particularly on the lip. Sepals 7–10 mm long, oblong or ovate. Petals 4–6 mm long, ovate, acute, sometimes finely toothed at the apex, pointing forwards. Lip unspurred, 12–16 mm long, 5-lobed at about two-thirds of the way from the base, the lobes acute, the midlobe longer than the side lobes, all lobes usually fringed. Staminodes with swollen, lumpy tips.

HABITAT: Terrestrial in humus or on mossy rocks and banks, often associated with rock outcrops, to 1300 m (4300 ft.).

DISTRIBUTION: South Africa (KwaZulu-Natal, Northern Province).

Stenoglottis macloughlinii (L. Bolus) G. McDonald
SYNONYM: *Cynorchis macloughlinii* L. Bolus

DESCRIPTION: *Cynorchis* (= *Cynorkis*) *macloughlinii* was described in 1928 by the South African botanist Louisa Bolus. This was later considered to be synonymous with *C. compacta,* but in 1989, Joyce Stewart, in a revision of the genus *Stenoglottis,* reduced the name *Cynorchis macloughlinii* to synonymy with *S. woodii,* commenting that these plants differed from typical *S. woodii* in several ways, such as having narrower leaves and a longer spur. Gavin McDonald (1995) has now resurrected this entity to specific level, as *S. macloughlinii.* It differs from *S. woodii* in the side lobes of the lip being broader, and rounded or truncate rather than pointed. He also mentioned the longer spur, which often curves down at the apex. In the herbarium specimens, the dried leaves are yellowish and translucent, with distinct reticulate venation. The flowers are white with lilac spots, or rosy crimson.

HABITAT: In moss or humus-rich soil, in light dappled shade.

DISTRIBUTION: South Africa (KwaZulu-Natal).

Stenoglottis woodii Schlechter

DESCRIPTION: Leaves to 20 in a basal rosette, 5–15 × 1–3 cm (2–6 × 0.5–1 in.), linear to lanceolate, acute, the edges not undulate. Inflorescences to 40 cm (16 in.) high, to 40-flowered. Flowers white, pale pink or rosy red, the lip usually with a few purple spots. Sepals 4–6 mm long, ovate, obtuse. Petals 3–5 mm long, ovate, pointing forwards. Lip 10–14 mm long, 5-lobed in the apical half, midlobe linear, obtuse; side lobes wider and usually slightly longer than the midlobe, rounded or truncate at the apex; spur 1.5–3 mm long, narrow, acute, straight or slightly curved. Staminodes erect, narrow and club-shaped, obscurely lobed at the apex.

HABITAT: Very local, in rocky areas, to 500 m (1650 ft.).

DISTRIBUTION: South Africa (Eastern Cape, KwaZulu-Natal), Zimbabwe.

Stenoglottis zambesiaca Rolfe   FIGURE 10-88

DESCRIPTION: Leaves 6 to 12, in a basal rosette, 5–12 × 1–2 cm (2–5 × 0.5–1 in.), oblanceolate, acute, the edges undulate, dark green, sometimes spotted with dark brown. Inflorescences to 30 cm (12 in.) tall but usually less, secund, several to many-flowered. Flowers pale to deep pink, the lip with darker purple spots or streaks. Sepals 3–6 × 2–3 mm, the dorsal elliptic, the laterals obliquely ovate and slightly longer. Petals

Figure 10-88. *Stenoglottis zambesiaca*. Plant (left), ×1; flower (upper right), ×2.5.

5 × 3 mm, pointing forwards. Lip unspurred, 5–12 × 3–6 mm, trilobed in the apical third, the midlobe pointed and slightly longer and narrower than the side lobes, which are truncate at the apex. Staminodes fist-shaped with a rather warty apex.

HABITAT: Terrestrial in leaf litter, occasionally epiphytic on tree trunks, but most often growing lithophytically on mossy rocks, or on rotting logs; usually in forest but occasionally in woodland, but usually in deep shade, 1300–2150 m (4300–7100 ft.).

DISTRIBUTION: Malawi, Mozambique, South Africa (Northern Province), Tanzania, Zimbabwe.

NOTE: This is the most widespread species of the genus, but has been rather overlooked as Summerhayes (1968b) placed it in synonymy with *Stenoglottis fimbriata*. The species are very similar, but Stewart (1989) pointed out several differences, the most important being the shapes of the staminodes and of the side lobes of the lip.

Stolzia Schlechter

The genus *Stolzia* was established by the German botanist Rudolf Schlechter in 1915 and named in honor of Adolf Stolz, a German missionary based in southern Tanzania who made many important orchid collections. About 15 species are known, all from tropical Africa. Their closest relatives seem to be the Asiatic genera *Eria* and *Porpax*.

Species of *Stolzia* are uncommon in cultivation; they are not showy, but are neat plants with an interesting and unusual appearance.

DESCRIPTION: Dwarf, sympodial species, often forming large mats. Stems creeping. Pseudobulbs asymmetrical, with one to two leaves at the apex. Inflorescences terminal on the pseudobulb (in all but one species), one- to many-flowered. Flowers rather bell-shaped, more or less secund, green, yellow, brown, orange, or purple-red. Lateral sepals joined at the base, forming a mentum with the column foot, as in *Polystachya*. Petals smaller than the sepals. Lip recurved, entire, V-shaped in cross-section. Column short, the foot about three times the length of the free part; pollinia eight, four large and four small.

Figure 10-89. *Stolzia compacta* subsp. *purpurata*. Plant, ×1.

Stolzia compacta Cribb

FIGURE 10-89

DESCRIPTION: A dwarf species; pseudobulbs ovoid or pear-shaped, to 15 × 9 mm, forming chains, with one leaf at the apex. Leaves to 9 × 1 cm (4 × 0.5 in.), oblanceolate, rather thin in texture. Inflorescences one-flowered, very short. Flowers pale to deep yellow or purple-red. Dorsal sepal 7–10 × 2–3.5 mm, lanceolate, acuminate, the margins reflexed; lateral sepals of similar length, joined to each other and to the column foot in the basal half to form a saccate mentum 2 mm high. Petals 4–6 × 1 mm, linear-lanceolate, acute. Lip 4 × 2 mm, ovate, channelled in the basal half.

HABITAT: Epiphytic on mossy branches in montane forest, 1600–2350 m (5300–7750 ft.).

CULTIVATION: Potted in a standard bark mix, or mounted, but the humidity must be kept high, particularly in the growing season. Intermediate temperatures and heavy shade.

NOTE: This species is divided into three geographically separated subspecies that differ in size and color of flower. Subsp. *compacta* is the largest, has yellow flowers, and is distributed in northern Malawi. Subsp. *iringana* Cribb is the smallest, also has yellow flowers, and is distributed in southern Tanzania. Subsp. *purpurata* Cribb is intermediate in size, has purple-red flowers, and is distributed in southern Malawi and Zimbabwe.

Figure 10-90. *Stolzia repens.* Plant, ×1.

Stolzia repens (Rolfe) Summerhayes   PLATE 96, FIGURE 10-90
    SYNONYM: *Polystachya repens* Rolfe

DESCRIPTION: A dwarf, creeping species, only 1 cm (0.5 in.) high; pseudobulbs to 3 cm (1 in.) × 3 mm, rather club-shaped, with two leaves borne at the widest part of the pseudobulb, just before the start of the next pseudobulb. Leaves 9–14 × 5–7 mm, elliptic, obovate or almost round, rather fleshy. Inflorescences one-flowered, arising between the leaves, very short. Flowers yellowish, brownish, or reddish, striped with red or brown. Dorsal sepal to 7 × 3 mm, oblong, obtuse; lateral sepals similar but oblique and rather shorter, forming a saccate mentum with the column foot. Petals 5 × 1 mm, linear, curved, acute. Lip 2 × 1 mm, fleshy and tonguelike.

HABITAT: Epiphytic on mossy trunks and branches in evergreen forest and high rainfall woodland, 900–2200 m (3000–7300 ft.).

CULTIVATION: Potted in a standard bark mix, or mounted, but the humidity must be kept high, particularly in the growing season. Intermediate temperatures and heavy shade.

DISTRIBUTION: Burundi, Cameroon, Ethiopia, Ghana, Kenya, Malawi, Nigeria, Tanzania, Uganda, Zaire, Zambia, Zimbabwe.

Summerhayesia Cribb

The genus *Summerhayesia* was established by P. J. Cribb in 1977 and named in honor of V. S. Summerhayes, who was curator of the Orchid Herbarium at Kew from 1926 to 1968 and a great expert on African orchids. The type species of the genus, *S. laurentii,* was originally described in 1904 by De Wildeman as *Angraecum laurentii* and later put into *Aerangis* by Schlechter in 1918. The genus *Summerhayesia* differs from *Aerangis* in several ways: the leaves are linear, stiff and folded; the flowers are non-resupinate with a deeply concave, boat-shaped lip; the lateral sepals are joined at the base; and the viscidium is slipper-shaped rather than flat. When the new genus was created, another species was described, *S. zambesiaca*. Since then, a third species, *S. rwandensis* Geerinck, was described in 1988; it has the smallest flowers of the three species and is not in cultivation.

Summerhayesia laurentii (De Wildeman) Cribb

DESCRIPTION: Stems usually short, but sometimes to 18 cm (7 in.) long. Leaves several, distichous, 11–20 × 0.5–1 cm (4–8 × 0.25–0.5 in.), linear, folded, arching, borne in a fan. Inflorescences arched or spreading, 15–50 cm (6–20 in.) long, laxly to 20-flowered. Flowers creamy white, the spur greenish. Pedicel and ovary 10–13 mm long; bracts 2 mm long. Sepals 6–9 × 3–5 mm, elliptic, obtuse, the laterals slightly longer than the dorsal and joined at the base, surrounding the spur. Petals 5.5–8 × 2–3 mm, oblong, obtuse. Lip 5–8.5 × 3.5–6 mm, held uppermost, ovate, obtuse, very concave; spur 6–8 cm (2–3 in.) long, pendent, slender, straight. Column 1.5–2.5 mm long.

HABITAT: Epiphytic in rainforest, to 800 m (2600 ft.).

CULTIVATION: From its habitat and distribution, this species should like intermediate to warm temperatures, moderate shade, and high humidity.

DISTRIBUTION: Gabon, Ghana, Ivory Coast, Liberia, Zaire.

Summerhayesia zambesiaca Cribb FIGURE 10-91

DESCRIPTION: Stems short, 2.5 cm (1 in.) long; roots stout, to 6 mm in diameter, arising at base of stem. Leaves three to seven, to 14 × 1.5 cm (6 × 1 in.), distichous, linear, folded, recurved, thick-textured, rather yellowish-green, borne in a fan. Inflorescences arising from lower leaf axils, erect or arching downwards, 12–15 cm (5–6 in.) long, 4- to 5-flowered, the terminal flower opening first. Pedicel and ovary 2 cm (1 in.) long, twisted where it joins the rachis. Flowers fleshy, nonresupinate, set 2–4 cm (1–2 in.) apart, creamy yellow, the ovary and outside of sepals and petals scattered with short, sparse, rusty hairs. Dorsal sepal 13–14 × 6 mm, ovate; lateral sepals similar but slightly shorter and oblique, with an extension on the lower side at the base by which they are joined for 4 mm under the spur. Petals 11–12 × 5–5.5 mm, ovate, acute, spreading. Lip 11–12 × 5.5–6 mm, very concave, boat-shaped, acute, fleshy. Spur 16–20 cm (6–8 in.) long, pendent, straight, very slender. Column 3 mm long.

HABITAT: Usually epiphytic at high level in open woodland with high rainfall and a long dry season, sometimes also in rainforest, sometimes lithophytic, 600–700 m (2000–2300 ft.).

CULTIVATION: We grow this species mounted on bark, at intermediate temperatures, but it might do better slightly warmer. It needs high humidity in the growing season, but to be kept fairly dry in winter and in fairly bright light.

DISTRIBUTION: Malawi, Tanzania, Zaire, Zambia, Zimbabwe.

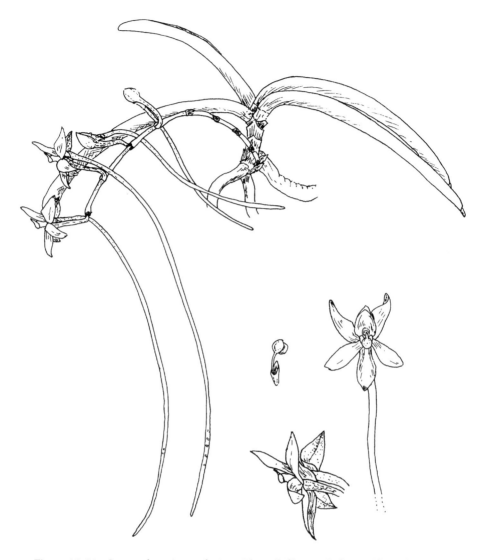

Figure 10-91. *Summerhayesia zambesiaca.* Plant (left), ×.0.6; flower (far right), ×0.9; flower (lower center), ×1; pollinarium (center), ×9.

Tridactyle Schlechter

This is one of the larger genera of African angraecoid orchids, with more than 40 species in tropical and South Africa. The genus *Tridactyle* was established in 1914 by the German botanist Rudolf Schlechter, although many species had already been described in *Angraecum*. *Tridactyle* seems to be a very natural grouping, as there is rarely any doubt as to the generic identity of its members. The genus name is derived from the Greek words *tri* (three) and *daktylos* (fingers), referring to the trilobed lip of many species. Some species of *Tridactyle* are among the most common African orchids, and at least one member of the genus seems to be present anywhere that any orchids grow. Many are rather unexciting plants, but a few are attractive, one quite spectacularly so.

DESCRIPTION: Stems long or short; roots usually fairly stout, sometimes warty. Leaves distichous, usually linear or strap-shaped. Flowers usually smallish, white, green, yellow, straw-colored, or brownish. Sepals and petals rather similar, usually spreading. Lip with earlike structures called auricles at the base, sometimes entire but usually trilobed in the apical half, the side lobes sometimes ending in comblike segments. Column short; pollinia two, joined to a single stipes and viscidium.

Tridactyle anthomaniaca (Reichenbach f.) Summerhayes   PLATE 97

DESCRIPTION: Stems pendent, long, leafy, often branched; roots warty, 2–3 mm in diameter. Leaves distichous, 4–8 × 1–2 cm (2–3 × 0.5–1 in.), linear to narrowly oblong, unequally and obtusely bilobed at the apex, rather fleshy, olive green, twisted at the base to face the same way. Inflorescences arising along the stem, 10–15 mm long, 2- to 4-flowered. Flowers dull orange or straw-colored. Pedicel and ovary 4 mm long, scaly; bracts brown, 1–2 mm long. Sepals 5 × 2–3 mm, oblong, acute, the laterals somewhat oblique. Petals 5 × 1 mm, lanceolate, acute. Lip 5–6 × 2 mm, entire, lanceolate, acute, with two fleshy auricles at the mouth of the spur; spur 10–15 mm long, slender, straight. Column 1–2 mm long; anther cap brown.

HABITAT: Epiphytic in high rainfall woodland and at the edge of evergreen forest, 640–1550 m (2100–5100 ft.).

CULTIVATION: With its pendent habit, this species needs to be mounted on bark. It does well at intermediate temperatures in moderate shade, with plenty of water while actively growing, but less in the resting season.

DISTRIBUTION: Cameroon, Central African Republic, Ivory Coast, Kenya, Liberia, Malawi, Mozambique, Nigeria, Rwanda, Sierra Leone, Sudan, Tanzania, Uganda, Zaire, Zambia, Zimbabwe.

Tridactyle bicaudata (Lindley) Schlechter   PLATE 98

DESCRIPTION: Stems woody, to 80 cm (32 in.) long, erect or pendent; roots 4–5 mm in diameter, smooth or very slightly warty. Leaves very variable in size and shape; in exposed situations they are usually 6 × 1 cm (2–× 0.5 in.), V-shaped in cross section and almost succulent, while in shade they are longer and laxer, and almost flat, to 14 × 1.5 cm (6 × 1 in.). Inflorescences borne along the stem, to 13 cm (5 in.) long, to 20-flowered, the flowers in two rows and all facing the same way. Flowers yellowish, 1 cm (0.5 in.) in diameter. Pedicel and ovary 2–3 cm (1 in.) long; bracts sheathing, 1–2 mm long. Dorsal sepal 4–6 × 2–3 mm, ovate, acute; lateral sepals 5–6 × 2.5–3.5 mm, obliquely ovate, acute. Petals 4–6 × 1–2 mm, linear. Lip 4–6 mm long with triangular auricles at the base, trilobed at about halfway; midlobe 2–2.5 mm long, narrowly triangular; side lobes 3–6 mm long, spreading, fringed at the apex. Spur 1–2 cm (0.5–1 in.) long, parallel to the ovary. Column 1 mm long.

HABITAT: Epiphytic or lithophytic inside or outside forest and woodland, to 2500 m (8250 ft.).

CULTIVATION: This species is best accommodated in a basket, in a coarse mix, in light to moderate shade, at intermediate temperatures.

DISTRIBUTION: Burundi, Ethiopia, Gabon, Ghana, Ivory Coast, Kenya, Liberia, Malawi, Mozambique, Nigeria, Rwanda, Sierra Leone, South Africa (Eastern Cape, KwaZulu-Natal, Western Cape), Swaziland, Tanzania, Togo, Uganda, Zaire, Zambia, Zimbabwe.

NOTE: H. P. Linder has separated a lithophytic form that grows along the South African coast as subsp. *rupestris* Linder, but similar forms occur in tropical Africa and seem to be ecological variants. We have seen erect, lithophytic plants with short, succulent leaves growing outside woodland, with longer, laxer plants growing in the woodland nearby.

Tridactyle citrina Cribb

DESCRIPTION: Stems to 6 cm (2 in.) long, erect, always growing singly and not forming clumps; roots stout, to 7 mm in diameter, clinging tightly to the bark. Leaves three to four, stiff, semierect, 7–15 × 1–1.5 cm (3–6 × 0.5–1 in.), linear, folded, rather gray-green. Inflorescences arising at base of stem, arching, 9–10 cm (4 in.) long, fairly densely to 10-flowered, the flowers arranged in two rows. Flowers creamy yellow or lime green, 15 mm across and 25 mm from top to bottom. Pedicel and ovary 6 mm long; bracts sheathing, 3 mm long. Dorsal sepal 10 × 2.5 mm, lanceolate, acute, the margins slightly erose; lateral sepals 10 × 3 mm, deflexed, the tips slightly reflexed, obliquely lanceolate, acute. Petals similar to lateral sepals. Lip 15 mm long, auriculate at the base, trilobed near the apex; midlobe 5 × 1 mm, narrowly triangular; side lobes spreading, about half the length of the midlobe, truncate at the tip. Spur 4–5 cm (2 in.) long, at first parallel to the ovary, then pendent. Column 4–5 mm long.

HABITAT: Epiphytic in woodland, usually on the lower branches of trees, 1350–2100 m (4450–7000 ft.).

CULTIVATION: Mounted, or in a pot with a coarse mix, at intermediate temperatures, in moderate to light shade.

DISTRIBUTION: Northern Malawi, Tanzania, Zambia.

NOTE: This is one of the most attractive species of *Tridactyle*, with a neat habit of growth and relatively large, well-colored flowers. We used to grow it in Malawi, but do not know if it is in cultivation in Europe or the United States; if not, we hope it will be introduced.

Tridactyle furcistipes Summerhayes

DESCRIPTION: Stems 7–18 cm (3–7 in.) long, usually erect; roots 2 mm in diameter. Leaves several, 11–18 cm (4–7 in.) × 7–13 mm, linear, unequally and roundly bilobed at the apex. Inflorescences to 11 cm (4 in.) long, densely several-flowered, the flowers in two rows. Flowers greenish-white or cream, turning ocher as they fade.

Sepals 9–12 × 2–4 mm, lanceolate, acute, the lateral sepals slightly longer and narrower than the dorsal. Petals 8–10 × 2–3 mm, lanceolate, acuminate. Lip auriculate at the base, 9–13 mm long, trilobed in the apical half; midlobe 4–6 × 1 mm, strap-shaped, acuminate; side lobes spreading, to 2 mm long, toothed at the tips. Spur 14–27 mm long, straight, very slender. Column 2–3 mm long.

HABITAT: Epiphytic in montane forest and scrub, 2500–2850 m (8250–9400 ft.).

CULTIVATION: In a pot with a coarse mix, at cool to intermediate temperatures, in moderate shade.

DISTRIBUTION: Kenya, Tanzania, Uganda.

NOTE: According to Cribb (1989), this species resembles a large-flowered form of the more widespread *Tridactyle tricuspis,* and the relationship between the two species needs further study.

Tridactyle gentilii (De Wildeman) Schlechter

DESCRIPTION: Stems long, to 80 cm (32 in.), becoming pendent with age and, in the wild, eventually forming large, tangled masses; roots smooth, 3–4 mm in diameter. Leaves numerous, 10–20 × 1–2 cm (4–8 × 0.5–1 in.), linear, unequally bilobed at the apex. Inflorescences arising along the stem, to 15 cm (6 in.) long, 7- to 15-flowered. Flowers scented, white, pale green or cream, sometimes with pinkish tips to the segments. Pedicel and ovary 6–7 mm long; bracts sheathing, 2 mm long. Sepals 7–9 × 3–5 mm, oblong or ovate, obtuse, the laterals rather oblique. Petals 7–9 × 2 mm, linear-lanceolate. Lip auriculate at the base, 9–10 mm long, 13–16 mm across at the widest point, trilobed in the middle; midlobe 2.5–4 × 2.5 mm, triangular; side lobes spreading, oblong, 6–8 mm long, deeply fringed at the tips. Spur 4–8 cm (2–3 in.) long. Column 2–3 mm long.

HABITAT: Epiphytic in forest and wet woodland, to 2200 m (7300 ft.).

CULTIVATION: With its growth habit, this species would best be accommodated in a basket, at intermediate to warm temperatures, with high humidity and fairly good light.

DISTRIBUTION: Angola, Cameroon, Ghana, Nigeria, South Africa (KwaZulu-Natal), Uganda, Zaire, Zambia.

Tridactyle tanneri Cribb

DESCRIPTION: Stems short, to 4 cm (2 in.) long; roots smooth, 2 mm in diameter. Leaves several, 6–11 × 0.5–1 cm (2–4 × 0.25–0.5 in.), linear, unequally and obtusely bilobed at the apex, pale green with dark green blotches, an unusual feature. Inflorescences 2–5 cm (1–2 in.) long, 2- to 8-flowered. Flowers green or greenish-yellow. Pedicel and ovary 6–8 mm long; bracts 3–4 mm long, ovate, reflexed. Sepals 7–9.5 × 2.5–3 mm, oblong, acute, the lateral sepals slightly longer than the dorsal, and acuminate. Petals 7 × 2 mm, lanceolate. Lip auriculate at the base, 8–9.5 × 3–3.5 mm, rather obscurely trilobed near the apex; midlobe 3.5 × 1.5 mm, narrowly triangular; side lobes toothlike, 1 mm long. Spur 2 cm (1 in.) long, pendent, slightly swollen and upcurved at the apex. Column 3 mm long.

HABITAT: Epiphytic on tree trunks in deep shade in submontane and dwarf ever-green forest, 1450–1600 m (4800–5300 ft.).

CULTIVATION: Intermediate temperatures, mounted or in a pot, in heavy shade with high humidity.

DISTRIBUTION: Kenya, Tanzania.

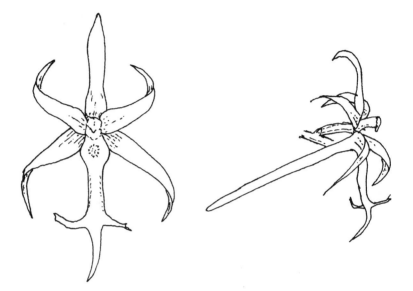

Figure 10-92. *Tridactyle tricuspis.* Flower (left), ×4; flower (right), ×3.

Tridactyle tricuspis (Bolus) Schlechter   PLATE 99, FIGURE 10-92
SYNONYM: *Tridactyle fragrans* Williamson

DESCRIPTION: Very widespread and common within its range. Variable in size. In its most common form, stems 20–25 cm (8–10 in.) long, erect; roots many, stout, to 5 mm in diameter, smooth or very slightly warty, often forming a large tangle. Leaves usually four to five near the apex of the stem, 7 × 1 cm (3 × 0.5 in.), strap-shaped, dark green. However, plants from montane forest are long-stemmed with narrower leaves, while others growing in exposed situations on high plateaus are consistently dwarf and almost stemless, with short, stiff leaves only 3 cm (1 in.) long. Inflorescences usually two, arising from base of stem, arching, 6–15 cm (2–6 in.) long, 12- to 13-flowered. Flowers greenish-white or yellow-green, turning yellower as they age, in two rows all facing the same way. Pedicel and ovary 3 mm long; bracts 1 mm long. Sepals 6–7 × 2 mm, lanceolate, acuminate, the laterals rather oblique. Petals 5–6 × 1–2 mm, lanceo-late acute, the tips curling back. Lip 6–8 mm long, auriculate at the base, trilobed in the apical third; midlobe 3 mm long, triangular; side lobes spreading or curving up, 1–2.5 mm long, sometimes slightly fringed at the tips. Spur 12–15 mm long, straight, very slender. Column 2 mm long.

HABITAT: Epiphytic at high and low levels in submontane and montane forest and high rainfall woodland, sometimes lithophytic at the edge of forest, 900–2600 m (3000–8600 ft.).

CULTIVATION: The dwarf form is well suited in a pot; otherwise this species with its long, tangled roots, many of which hang free, is better in a basket. Intermediate temperatures, moderate to light shade.

DISTRIBUTION: Burundi, Malawi, Mozambique, South Africa (Eastern Cape, KwaZulu-Natal, Mpumalanga, Northern Province), Swaziland, Tanzania, Zaire, Zambia, Zimbabwe.

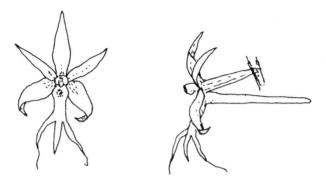

Figure 10-93. *Tridactyle tridactylites*. Flower, ×3.

Tridactyle tridactylites (Rolfe) Schlechter   FIGURE 10-93

DESCRIPTION: Stems to 1 m (3 ft.) long, usually trailing but sometimes erect; roots smooth, stout, 3–6 mm in diameter. Leaves distichous, on apical half or third of stem, 12–18 × 1–1.5 cm (5–7 × 0.5–1 in.), linear or strap-shaped, unequally bilobed at the apex, rather lax. Inflorescences arising along the stem, 3–6 cm (1–2 in.) long, 10- to 16-flowered. Flowers greenish-cream or yellow-green, 10 mm in diameter, arranged in two rows. Pedicel and ovary 6 mm long; bracts 1–2 mm long, reflexed. Sepals 3.5–5.5 × 1.5–2.5 mm, lanceolate, acute, the tips recurved; petals similar but slightly shorter and narrower. Lip auriculate at base, 4–5 mm long, trilobed at about half way; midlobe 2–3 mm long, triangular; side lobes longer, spreading, becoming almost threadlike. Spur 6–11 mm long, very slender, straight or incurved. Column 1.5–2 mm long.

HABITAT: Epiphytic on trunks and lower branches of tree in evergreen forest, usually riverine forest, forming large colonies; often growing very luxuriantly on rocks; 900–1800 m (3000–6000 ft.).

CULTIVATION: Potted in a coarse mix, in a basket, at intermediate temperatures, in moderate shade.

DISTRIBUTION: Angola, Burundi, Cameroon, Equatorial Guinea (Bioko),Guinea, Guinea Bissau, Ivory Coast, Malawi, Mozambique, Nigeria, São Tomé e Príncipe, Sierra Leone, Tanzania, Uganda, Zaire, Zambia, Zimbabwe.

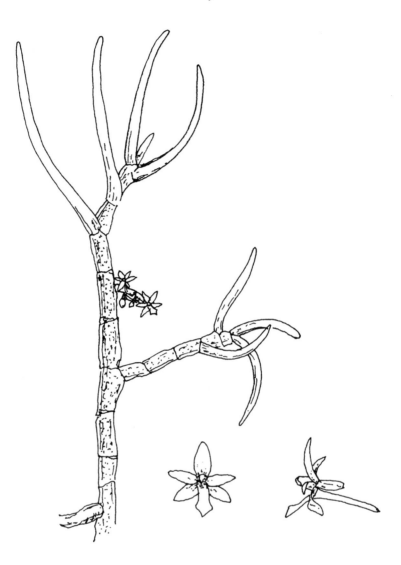

Figure 10-94. *Tridactyle tridentata*. Plant (left), ×1; flower (center and right), ×3.

Tridactyle tridentata (Harvey) Schlechter   PLATE 100, FIGURE 10-94
SYNONYMS: *Tridactyle bolusii* (Rolfe) Schlechter, *Tridactyle teretifolia* Schlechter

DESCRIPTION: Stems 10–50 cm (4–20 in.) long, erect or pendent, sometimes branched towards the base; roots 2–4 mm in diameter, smooth, arising at base of stem. Leaves several, borne on apical half of stem, 6–10 × 2–4 cm (2–4 × 1–2 in.), cylindrical, often, but not always, with a groove along the upper surface, dull olive green, the sheaths spotted with dark brown. Inflorescences borne along the stem,

1.5–2.5 cm (1 in.) long, densely 4- to 8-flowered. Flowers straw-yellow, the anther cap slightly darker, 6 mm in diameter. Pedicel and ovary 3–5 mm long, scaly; bracts less than 1 mm long. Sepals 3–5 × 2–3 mm, ovate, acute. Petals 3–5 × 1 mm, lanceolate, acute. Lip auriculate at base, 3–5 mm long, trilobed near the apex; midlobe 1–2 mm long, triangular, acute; side lobes from slightly shorter to slightly longer than the midlobe, very slender. Spur 6–18 mm long, straight, parallel to the ovary. Column 1 mm long.

HABITAT: Epiphytic in woodland, often but not always, in drier areas, occasionally lithophytic, 900–2250 m (3000–7400 ft.).

CULTIVATION: In a pot or basket at intermediate to warm temperatures, with fairly good light. Plants should be kept much drier in the resting season.

DISTRIBUTION: Angola, Burundi, Malawi, Mozambique, Rwanda, South Africa (Eastern Cape, KwaZulu-Natal), Tanzania, Uganda, Zaire, Zambia, Zimbabwe.

NOTE: This is a very variable species, and it is not impossible that some of the synonyms might yet be reinstated as species in their own right. However, it is difficult to pick out consistent features, and plants within the same colony may vary greatly, some being erect plants with rather thick, grooved leaves while others are pendent with fine, needlelike leaves.

Figure 10-95. *Tridactyle truncatiloba.* Flower, ×1.

Tridactyle truncatiloba Summerhayes PLATE 101, FIGURE 10-95

DESCRIPTION: Stems 25–100 cm (10–40 in.) long, erect or straggling, leafy towards the apex; roots smooth, 5 mm in diameter, to 100 cm (40 in.) long. Leaves to 15 × 2.5 cm (6 × 1 in.), strap-shaped, obtusely bilobed at the apex. Inflorescences borne along the stem, mostly below the leaves, 10–12 cm (4–5 in.) long, 7- to 10-flowered, the flowers in two rows, all open together. Flowers strongly and sweetly scented, glistening white, the lip with a green median streak, 5 cm (2 in.) long from tip of dorsal sepal to apex of lip. Pedicel and ovary 12 mm long; bracts 1 mm long, light brown. Sepals 20–21 × 6–7 mm, lanceolate, acute, the dorsal sepal with the edges slightly reflexed in the lower half. Lip 25 mm long, 5 mm wide at the base, trilobed at about halfway; midlobe 13 × 3 mm, lanceolate, acute; side lobes diverging, 8 mm long, widest (3 mm) at the apex, which is truncate and fringed. Basal auricles lobed, 3 mm long. Spur green, 6 mm long, slightly incurved, thickened to 3 mm in diameter in the apical half, then narrowing to a subacute apex. Column 6 mm long.

HABITAT: We first saw this species in Congo, growing on top of a brick pillar 6 m (20 ft.) tall, in full exposure, at an altitude of 350 m (1150 ft.). The pillar was all that remained of what was probably once a large packing shed. We could see other pillars in the middle of a dam, and they appeared also to have large plants of this species growing on them. Presumably these plants had originated in the surrounding forest, but we did not see any others growing there. A few days later we found *Tridactyle truncatiloba* again, growing in crumbling rock on a roadside cutting, at an altitude of 600 m (2000 ft.); these plants were 20–30 cm (8–12 in.) tall and were in full flower. The road ran through forest, but the plants received little shade.

CULTIVATION: We grow this species both in large pots and in baskets, in the warmest part of the intermediate house, and where they get fairly good light. In our greenhouse, it flowers in summer (June and July). So far, only one plant has flowered at a time, and evidently the plants are not self fertile, as when we have pollinated flowers, the ovary starts to swell, but drops off within a couple of weeks. At the last flowering, we saved pollen and hope that a different plant will flower in the coming year.

DISTRIBUTION: Gabon, Congo.

NOTE: This almost unknown species is by far the most striking member of the genus *Tridactyle*. We hope it will soon become available in cultivation.

Tridactyle verrucosa Cribb   FIGURE 10-96

DESCRIPTION: Stems 10–25 cm (4–10 in.) tall, erect, sometimes branched at the base, covered with old leaf bases with transverse wrinkles; roots arising at base of stem, 3–5 mm in diameter, markedly verrucose. Leaves usually six to seven, borne near apex of stem, to 7 × 1 cm (3 × 0.5 in.), stiff, strap-shaped, unequally and obtusely bilobed at the apex. Inflorescences arising on stem below leaves, 2–3 cm (1 in.) long, densely 4- to 6-flowered. Flowers straw yellow, 8 mm in diameter. Sepals 4–5 × 2 mm, lanceolate, acuminate; petals slightly shorter and narrower. Lip 4–5.5 mm long, trilobed at about halfway; midlobe 2 mm long, narrowly triangular; side lobes spreading, 3 mm long, entire or with threadlike processes at the apex. Spur 8–12 mm long, parallel to the ovary, slightly swollen at the apex. Column 1 mm long; anther cap orange-brown.

HABITAT: Lithophytic on exposed rocks in montane grassland or at the edge of forest, occasionally epiphytic on relict trees in montane areas, 1500–2200 m (5000–7300 ft.).

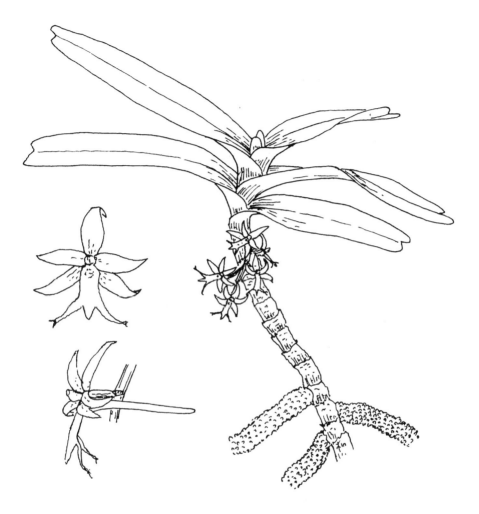

Figure 10-96. *Tridactyle verrucosa*. Plant (right), ×1; flower (upper and lower left), ×3.5.

CULTIVATION: This species is much more compact in its growth habit than many in the genus. It does well potted in a coarse mix, at intermediate temperatures, in fairly good light.

DISTRIBUTION: Malawi, Tanzania.

Vanilla Miller

The genus *Vanilla* was established by Philip Miller in 1754; the name comes from the Spanish word *vanilla* (a small pod). Although pods of this genus are particularly large, they are slender, and it is thought that it is to this that the name refers. There are almost 100 species of *Vanilla*, found in the tropics all around the world. *Vanilla planifolia*

G. Jackson is one of the few orchid species to be of economic importance other than in a horticultural sense; it is the source of vanilla flavoring, which is extracted from the fermented capsules. Native to Mexico, it has been widely cultivated elsewhere, particularly in Madagascar, but also in East Africa, and may be almost naturalized in some parts.

DESCRIPTION: Climbing and scrambling, vinelike, monopodial species with succulent green stems, sometimes channelled, with roots arising at the nodes. Leaves present or absent. Inflorescences axillary or rarely terminal, occasionally branched, few to many-flowered, but usually only with one or two flowers open at a time. Flowers large, often rather bell-shaped, white, yellowish, or green. Sepals and petals free, similar. Lip funnel-shaped, often with hairs and keels inside. Column long and curved. Capsules linear, often very long, with relatively large black seeds.

CULTIVATION: Although *Vanilla* species are often described as epiphytes, in our experience, plants are always rooted in the ground although they may scramble over trees and rocks for a considerable distance. They grow easily and rapidly in cultivation. We have them rooted in a large pot with bark mix, and then let them climb up poles; when they reach the roof of the greenhouse, they can be trained along horizontal poles; they will probably need to be tied to this at intervals, as the shoots always want to grow up rather than along. Species of *Vanilla* do not seem to flower until plants are of a considerable size; they also require light to flower. They are interesting to grow even if they do not flower, and grown as suggested, do not take up a great deal of space. They can easily be propagated from cuttings, since the adventitious roots that arise at the nodes become "normal" roots when planted in soil. For cuttings, we prefer to use side branches taken off at the junction, where there is usually a natural constriction of the stem, because the fleshy stems, like those of all succulents, rot easily. If it is necessary to cut through a stem to make a cutting, it should be left for a day or two so that the cut surface dries somewhat—it can also be dusted with something like flowers of sulfur. Intermediate temperatures seem to be satisfactory for most species.

Vanilla imperialis Kränzlin

DESCRIPTION: A long, leafy liana; stems green, succulent, channelled, to 2.5 cm (1 in.) wide. Leaves set about 15 cm (6 in.) apart, with one leaf and one root arising at each node. Leaves 15–25 × 8–12 cm (6–10 × 3–5 in.), ovate to oblong, apiculate, succulent, blue-green. Inflorescences axillary, to 15 cm (6 in.) long, erect, unbranched, densely many-flowered. Flowers creamy white or yellowish, the lip blotched with purple, usually opening singly and lasting for one or two days. Pedicel and ovary to 11 cm (4 in.) long; bracts to 3 cm (1 in.) long. Sepals and petals to 8 × 2 cm (3 × 1 in.), elliptic-lanceolate, acute. Lip to 6 cm (2 in.) long, joined to the column at the base, forming a funnel; obscurely trilobed; apical edge very wavy with long papillae at the tip and a dense tuft of hairs inside. Column to 4 cm (2 in.) long. Capsule to 25 × 1.5 cm (10 × 1 in.).

HABITAT: In forest, scrambling up trees in shade, 900–1200 m (3000–4000 ft.).

DISTRIBUTION: Angola, Cameroon, Ghana, Ivory Coast, Sierra Leone, Tanzania, Uganda, Zaire.

Vanilla polylepis Summerhayes

PLATE 102

DESCRIPTION: A climbing liana, reaching at least 8 m (26 ft.) in height. Stems green, succulent, channelled, 1.5 cm (1 in.) in diameter, with internodes 15 cm (6 in.) long and at each node one leaf and one root that clings to trees or rocks. Leaves 12–20 × 3–8 cm (5–8 × 1–3 in.), oblong, apiculate, bright, glossy green. Inflorescences axillary, unbranched, densely many-flowered, with only one to two flowers open at a time. Pedicel and ovary 6 cm (2 in.) long; bracts 1.5 cm (1 in.) long. Flowers large and showy, greenish-white, the lip usually purple towards the apex and yellow in the throat; occasionally the lip is lacking the purple blotch. Sepals and petals 6 × 1.8 cm (2 × 1 in.), oblanceolate or lanceolate, rather fleshy. Lip to 6 cm (2 in.) long, joined to the lip for the basal 3 cm (1 in), funnel-shaped, very obscurely trilobed, frilly edged, with a crest of to 12 transverse rows of branched scales. Column to 4.5 cm (2 in.) long, winged towards the apex. Capsule fleshy, 15 × 1.5 cm (6 × 1 in.).

HABITAT: Riverine trees and rocks, forming a tangled mass, at altitudes of 1200–1500 m (4000–5000 ft.). This species seems very local in distribution; it grew in only very few places in Malawi, and where it grew, formed large colonies, yet there were plenty of other sites which were apparently suitable. In one large colony, plants on the shaded side of the river grew high up the trees and looked very luxuriant, but had very few flowers. On the sunny side, plants were smaller and often yellow-green, but flowered freely. We never saw any fruit formed on the plants, which may explain why the species was not more widely distributed.

DISTRIBUTION: Angola, Kenya, Malawi, Zaire, Zambia, Zimbabwe.

Vanilla roscheri Reichenbach f.

DESCRIPTION: A leafless liana; stems brownish-green, channelled, 2 cm (1 in.) in diameter, with internodes 15 cm (6 in.) long and at each node a root and a brown, papery vestigial leaf to 3 cm (1 in.) long. Inflorescences axillary and terminal, unbranched, to 30 cm (12 in.) long, densely many-flowered, but only one or two opening at a time. Flowers opening pale pink, turning white, the lip salmon, coral pink or occasionally pale yellow in the throat. Sepals to 8 × 2.5 cm (3× 1 in.), lanceolate, obtuse; petals similar but broader. Lip funnel-shaped, entire, to 8 cm (3 in.) long, the basal 2 cm (1 in.) joined to the column, the margins undulate, with two rows of irregular crests from the base to about halfway. Column to 2.5 cm (1 in.) long. Capsule to 17.5 × 1 cm.

HABITAT: Coastal bush, coral rocks and mangrove swamps as well as open evergreen scrub inland, to 750 m (2500 ft.).

DISTRIBUTION: Kenya, Mozambique, South Africa (KwaZulu-Natal), Tanzania (including Zanzibar and Pemba).

NOTE: This species may be conspecific with *Vanilla phalaenopsis* Reichenbach f. from the Seychelles and with *V. madagascariensis* Rolfe from Madagascar. If so, *V. phalaenopsis* would be the correct name.

Ypsilopus Summerhayes

The small genus *Ypsilopus* was established by V. S. Summerhayes in 1949 for two species originally described in *Mystacidium*. The genus name is derived from the Greek words *upsilon* (the letter *Y*) and *pous* (foot), referring to the Y-shaped stipes of the pollinium. The genus seems to be most closely related to *Tridactyle*, but lacks the auricles at the base of the lip; the Y-shaped stipes can also be found in some species of *Tridactyle*, such as *T. furcistipes*. One of the two original species, *Ypsilopus graminifolius* (Kränzlin) Summerhayes, is now considered to be synonymous with the other, *Y. longifolius* (Kränzlin) Summerhayes. Four species are now known from East Africa, with one growing as far south as South Africa.

DESCRIPTION: A genus of monopodial epiphytes. Leaves linear, often arranged in a fan. Flowers white or pale green, with a few coarse hairs on the outside and on the ovary. Sepals and petals similar. Lip entire or obscurely trilobed, lacking a callus, spurred at the base.

CULTIVATION: Can be grown in a pot or mounted, provided the humidity is sufficiently high, at intermediate to cool temperatures. Should be kept somewhat cooler and drier in the resting period.

Ypsilopus erectus (Cribb) Cribb & J. Stewart   PLATE 103, FIGURE 10-97
SYNONYM: *Ypsilopus longifolius* var. *erectus* Cribb

DESCRIPTION: Stems short, usually 2–3 cm (1 in.) long but occasionally to 6 cm (2 in.), erect; roots 2–4 mm in diameter. Leaves usually four to five, borne in a fan, to 15 cm (6 in.) × 6 mm, linear, folded, somewhat recurved. Inflorescences arising at the base of the plant, arching, 5–20 cm (2–8 in.) long, 12- to 20-flowered. Flowers glistening white, spur greenish towards the tip; pedicel and ovary sometimes salmon pink. Pedicel and ovary 9–12 mm long, with scurfy hairs. Sepals 5–8 × 2–3 mm, ovate, acute, the laterals slightly longer than the dorsal, and oblique. Petals 5–7 × 2 mm, lanceolate, acuminate. Lip 5–7 × 3 mm, rather obscurely trilobed, rhombic; spur very slender, 4–6 cm (2 in.) long, slightly incurved. Column 2 mm long; anther cap brown.

HABITAT: Epiphytic in high rainfall woodland, 1000–2100 m (3300–7100 ft.), usually more than 1300 m (4300 ft.).

DISTRIBUTION: Malawi, Mozambique, South Africa (KwaZulu-Natal), Swaziland, Tanzania, Zambia, Zimbabwe.

Ypsilopus longifolius (Kränzlin) Summerhayes
SYNONYM: *Ypsilopus graminifolius* (Kränzlin) Summerhayes

DESCRIPTION: Stems to 4 cm (2 in.) long, pendent; roots 2 mm in diameter. Leaves 5–25 cm (2–10 in.) long, rarely to 50 cm (20 in.) × 2–3 mm, linear, acute, somewhat folded. Inflorescences pendent, 3–8 cm (1–3 in.) long, 2- to 9-flowered. Flowers white with greenish tips. Pedicel and ovary 9–12 mm long, covered with scurfy hairs; bracts 2 mm long. Sepals 6–9 × 2–4 mm, ovate, acute, the laterals slightly longer than the

Figure 10-97. *Ypsilopus erectus.* Plant (right), ×0.75; flower (left and center), ×1.5.

dorsal. Petals 5–7 × 2–3 mm, lanceolate, acute. Lip somewhat recurved, 6.5–7.5 × 2–4 mm, obscurely trilobed in the middle, rhombic, acute; spur 3.5–4 cm (1–2 in.) long, slender, pendent. Column 2 mm long.

Habitat: Epiphytic in submontane and montane forest, 1450–2400 m (4800–8000 ft.).

Distribution: Kenya, Tanzania.

Ypsilopus viridiflorus Cribb & J. Stewart

DESCRIPTION: Stems to 3 cm (1 in.) long, pendent. Leaves 4–25 cm (2–10 in.) ×
2–5 mm, linear, acuminate, bilaterally flattened and *Iris*-like, jointed at the base to
prominent leaf bases to 2 cm (1 in.) long. Inflorescences 2–6 cm (1–2 in.) long, 1- to
2-flowered. Flowers whitish-green or pale yellow-green, with scurfy hairs on the outer
surface. Pedicel and ovary 5–7 mm long; bracts 2–3 mm long. Sepals 7–9 × 1.5–2 mm,
lanceolate, acuminate, the laterals somewhat oblique. Petals 6–8 × 1.5–2 mm, linear-
lanceolate, acuminate. Lip deflexed, 7–8 × 2 mm, entire, lanceolate, acuminate; spur
15–18 mm long, slender, pendent. Column 1 mm long.

HABITAT: Epiphytic in montane forest, 2100–2350 m (7000–7750 ft.).

DISTRIBUTION: Northern Tanzania.

Appendix 1

Useful Addresses

Orchid Societies and Publications

The African Orchid Alliance
c/o Patrick Denissen
14, Speerstraat
2020 Antwerp
Belgium

American Orchid Society
6000 South Olive Avenue
West Palm Beach, Florida 33405
U.S.A.

Disa Orchid Society of South Africa
c/o The Editor
P.O. Box 507
Rondebosch
7700 Cape Town
South Africa

Orchids Australia
(Journal of Australian Orchid Council)
Don Gallacher, Publications Director
P.O. Box 11
Highbury
South Australia 5089

The Orchid Review
21B Chudleigh Road
Kingsteignton
Devon TQ12 3JT
U.K.

South African Orchid Council
P.O. Box 81
Constantia 7848
South Africa

Biological Control

Defenders Ltd.
P.O. Box 131
Wye, Ashford
Kent TN25 5TQ
U.K.

Dr. M. J. W. Copland
Department of Biological Sciences
University of London
Wye, Ashford
Kent TN25 5AH
U.K.

Green Gardener
41 Strumpshaw Road
Brundall, Norfolk NR13 5PG
U.K.

Scarletts Plant Centre
Dept. RH, West Bergholt
Colchester CO6 3DH
U.K.

CITES Certificates and Information

in the U.K.:

Wildlife Trade Licencing Branch
Department of the Environment
Tollgate House
Houlton Street
Bristol BS2 9DJ
U.K.
Telephone: 0117 9878469

in the U.S.A.:

Permit Unit
Plant Protection & Quarantine
Animal and Plant Inspection Service
U.S. Department of Agriculture
638 Federal Building
Hyattsville, Maryland 20782
U.S.A

in all other countries:

CITES Secretariat
15 Chemin des Anemones
C.P. 456
1219 Chatelaine
Geneva, Switzerland

Phytosanitary Certificates

in England & Wales: Ministry of Agriculture, Fisheries & Food
Plant Health Division
Foss House, 1/2 Peasholme Green
Kings Pool
York YO1 2PX
U.K.
Telephone: 01904 455191

in Scotland: Department of Agriculture & Fisheries for Scotland
Pentland House
47 Robbs Loan
Edinburgh EH14 1TW
Scotland
Telephone: 0131 244 6354

Nurseries that Stock African Orchids

Adelaide Orchids International
Australian Orchid Link
16 Pine Road
Woodcroft 5162
S. Australia
Telephone: 61 8 381-2011

Akerne Orchids
Laarsebeekdreef 4
B-2900 Schoten
Belgium

The Angraecum House
10385 East Drive
Grass Valley, California 95945
U.S.A.

Clemson Orchids
3637 Pleasant Road
Ft. Mill, South Carolina 29715
U.S.A.
Telephone: (803) 548-1682

De Wilg
Bermweg 16B
Nieuwerkerk aan den IJssel
Holland

Duckitt Nurseries (Pty.) Ltd.
Oudepost Farm
P.O. Box 14
Darling 7345
South Africa

Hoosier Orchid Company
8440 W. 82nd Street
Indianapolis, Indiana 46278
U.S.A.
Telephone: (708) 668-4588

B. Junginger
D-72229 Rohrdorf
Reuteweg 18
Germany

Marcel Lecoufle
5, rue de Paris
94470 Boissy-Saint-Leger
France

MCM Orchids (Michael C. Morgan)
P.O. Box 4626
Wheaton, Illinois
U.S.A.
Telephone: (9708) 668-4588

Mecca's Orchids (Joanne Lalli)
1268 Eppinger Drive
Port Charlotte, Florida 33953
U.S.A.
Telephone: (941) 625-0162

Nooitgedag Disa Nursery
7 Sunnybrae Road
Rondebosch
Cape Town 7700
South Africa

Orchideeen Wubben
Tolakkerweg 162
3739 JT Holl. Rading
Holland

Plested Orchids
38 Florence Road
College Town, Camberley
Surrey GU15 4QD
U.K.
Telephone: 01276 32947

Uzumara Orchids
9 Port Henderson
Gairloch
Ross-shire IV21 2AS
U.K.
Telephone: 01445 741228

Whitmoor House Orchid Nursery
Ashill, Cullompton
Devon EX15 3NP
U.K.
Telephone: 01884 840145
(no mail order)

Appendix 2

African Orchid Genera Not in Cultivation

Most of the African orchids not at present in cultivation have rather dull white or greenish flowers. The number of species given below refer to African species only (see Chapter 4 for the total number of species in each genus).

Acrolophia Pfitzer
   Terrestrial. Nine species, very close to *Eulophia,* most from Cape Province, South Africa, but with a few in tropical Africa.

Auxopus Schlechter
   Terrestrial. Two species of leafless saprophytes in tropical Africa.

Bartholina R. Brown
   Terrestrial. Two species endemic to Cape Province, South Africa.

Brownleea Lindley
   Terrestrial, but two species sometimes epiphytic. Six species in tropical Africa and South Africa.

Cardiochilos Cribb
   Epiphytic. One species, related to *Tridactyle,* from northern Malawi and southern Tanzania.

Centrostigma Schlechter
Terrestrial. Three species closely related to *Habenaria.*

Ceratandra Lindley
Terrestrial. Three species endemic to Cape Province, South Africa.

Chaseella Summerhayes
Epiphytic. One small species, related to *Bulbophyllum,* known from Kenya and Zimbabwe.

Chauliodon Summerhayes
Epiphytic. One leafless species from West Africa.

Cheirostylis Blume
Terrestrial. Three species, forest-dwelling, from tropical Africa.

Corycium Swartz
Terrestrial. About 14 species, most in South Africa but with 2 extending into eastern tropical Africa.

Corymborkis Thouars
Terrestrial. Two species, forest-dwelling; one widespread in tropical Africa, the other confined to Mt. Cameroon.

Diceratostele Summerhayes
Terrestrial. One species, *Diceratostele gabonensis,* forest-dwelling, from West Africa.

Didymoplexis Griffith
Terrestrial. Two species of leafless saprophytes, one in tropical Africa and one in South Africa.

Dinklageella Mansfeld
Epiphytic. Two long-stemmed species from West Africa.

Distylodon Summerhayes
Epiphytic. One species from Uganda, known only from the type collection.

Dracomonticola H. P. Linder & Kurzweil
Terrestrial. One species from South Africa, previously known as *Neobolusia virginea.*

Epipactis Zinn
Terrestrial. Three species in tropical Africa.

Epipogium R. Brown
   Terrestrial. One species of leafless saprophyte in tropical Africa.

Evotella Kurzweil, Linder & Chesselet
   Terrestrial. One species in South Africa.

Hetaeria Blume
   Terrestrial. Five species, closely related to *Zeuxine,* in tropical Africa.

Holothrix Lindley
   Terrestrial. About 55 species, mostly in South Africa, but with several in tropical Africa. Most species have the floral parts much divided, and those with larger flowers are very beautiful.

Huttonaea Harvey
   Terrestrial. Five species from South Africa.

Malaxis Swartz
   Terrestrial. Seven species, closely related to *Liparis,* in tropical Africa.

Manniella Reichenbach f.
   Terrestrial. One species, *Manniella gustavi,* found in forests in West and Central Africa. The species often has attractively mottled leaves and might be worth growing for its foliage.

Monadenia Lindley
   Terrestrial. Sixteen species, one in tropical Africa, the rest in South Africa.

Neobolusia Schlechter
   Terrestrial. Three species in tropical Africa and South Africa.

Nervilia Gaudichaud
   Terrestrial. About 13 species, most in tropical Africa but with a few extending into South Africa.

Oligophyton Linder & Williamson
   Terrestrial. One species with tiny flowers, in Zimbabwe.

Orestias Ridley
   Terrestrial. Three species, forest-dwelling, in tropical Africa.

Pachites Lindley
   Terrestrial. Two species, endemic to the Western Cape, South Africa.

Phaius Loureiro
Terrestrial. Two species in tropical Africa, not, alas, showy like the Asiatic and Madagascan species.

Platycoryne Reichenbach f.
Terrestrial. Seventeen species in tropical Africa, many with bright orange flowers. Many would be well worth growing, but are reputedly difficult.

Platylepis Lindley
Terrestrial. One species, forest-dwelling, widespread in Africa.

Pteroglossaspis Reichenbach f.
Terrestrial. Three species, very close to *Eulophia,* in tropical Africa.

Rhaesteria Summerhayes
Epiphytic. One species from Uganda, known only from the type collection.

Roeperocharis Reichenbach f.
Terrestrial. Five species in eastern tropical Africa.

Satyridium Lindley
Terrestrial. One species, endemic to the Western Cape Province, South Africa.

Schizochilus Sonder
Terrestrial. Ten species, mostly in South Africa but with a few in eastern tropical Africa.

Schizodium Lindley
Terrestrial. Six species from Cape Province, South Africa.

Schwartzkopffia Kränzlin.
Terrestrial. Two species of leafless saprophytes in tropical Africa, very closely related to *Brachycorythis.*

Taeniophyllum Blume
Epiphytic. One small, leafless species, with tiny flowers, in tropical Africa.

Taeniorrhiza Summerhayes
Epiphytic. One species of leafless orchid from Gabon and Zaire.

Thulinia Cribb
Terrestrial. One species (only described in 1985), endemic to the Nguru Mountains of Tanzania.

Triceratorhynchus Summerhayes
     Epiphytic. One species from Uganda and Kenya.

Zeuxine Lindley
     Terrestrial. Four species, forest-dwelling, from tropical Africa and South Africa.

Glossary

Acuminate: tapering to a point

Angraecoid: an orchid belonging to the genus *Angraecum* or closely related to it

Apiculate: having a short, sharp point

Apicule: a short, sharp point

Auriculate: having an earlike outgrowth at the base of a leaf or floral part

Auricle: an earlike outgrowth at the base of a leaf or floral part

Axil: the angle between a leaf and a stem

Axillary inflorescence: one arising in the axil of a leaf or leaf base, as opposed to a terminal inflorescence, which comes from the end of a stem

Bifid: divided into two at the tip

Bract: a small leaf at the base of a flowerstalk or an inflorescence

Bullate: with the surface raised between the veins

Caespitose: forming mats or tufts

Capitate: in a compact cluster (referring to an inflorescence)

Caudicle: the lower, stalklike part of a pollinium which attaches the pollen mass to the viscidium

Ciliate: fringed with fine hairs

Clavate: club-shaped, or thickened at the end

Column: in an orchid, the organ formed by the fusion of stamens, style, and stigma

Conduplicate: folded in bud

Cordate: heart-shaped at the base

Coriaceous: tough and leathery

Cryptic: well camouflaged

Distichous: arranged in two opposite rows

Epichile: the apical part of a lip

Epiphyte: a plant that grows on another plant, but without obtaining nourishment from it (that is, not a parasite)

Epiphytic: growing on another plant without being a parasite

Erose: uneven

Falcate: curved like a scythe

Fimbriate: having the margin fringed with long, slender processes (usually referring to a petal)

Fynbos: the characteristic vegetation of the Cape Region of South Africa, usually shrub-land with many small-leaved, bushy plants

Geniculate: bent like a knee

Glabrous: hairless

Glaucous: pale blue-green or grayish-green

Hypochile: the basal part of a lip

Imbricate: overlapping

Inflorescence: flower and flowerstalk together

Instar: an insect stage between molts

Internode: the part of a stem between two nodes

Lamina: the blade of a leaf

Ligulate: strap-shaped

Ligule: a thin, membranous appendage at the apex of a leaf sheath

Lip: the unpaired petal of an orchid

Lithophyte: a plant that grows on rock

Lithophytic: growing on rock

Mentum: a chinlike projection formed by the united bases of the lateral sepals and an extended column foot (for example, in *Polystachya*)

Mycorrhiza: fungi that live in a symbiotic relationship with a plant, usually in the roots

Node: the place where a leaf joins a stem

Nonresupinate: with the lip at the top and the median sepal below (referring to an orchid flower)

Obovate: wider near the apex than the base

Ovary: the part of a flower that contains the ovules and eventually becomes the fruit containing seed; in orchids, the ovary is inferior, lying below the sepals and petals

Papillae: small projections

Papillose: covered with small projections

Parasite: an organism that obtains its food wholly or partly from another living organism

Pedicel: the stalk of each individual flower in an inflorescence

Peduncle: the stalk of an inflorescence

Petiole: a leaf stalk

Pilose: with rather long hairs

Plicate: folded in pleats

Pollinarium: the male reproductive part of an orchid flower, consisting of the pollinia from an anther with the associated parts, the viscidium (or viscidia), and stipes (or stipites)

Pollinium (pl. pollinia): pollen grains cohering into a mass

Pseudobulb: a swollen, bulblike structure at the base of a stem

Pubescent: covered with short, fine hairs

Pycnidium (pl. pycnidia): a spore-producing body in certain fungi

Rachis: in orchids, the main axis of an inflorescence above the peduncle, to which the flowers are attached

Resupinate: with the lip at the bottom and the median sepal at the top (referring to an orchid flower)

Reticulate: net-veined

Rhizome: a stem on or below the ground with roots growing down from it and flowering shoots up

Rostellum: a projection of the stigma of an orchid separating the fertile part of the stigma from the anther

Rugose: wrinkled

Saccate: pouched

Saprophyte: a plant, usually without chlorophyll, that obtains its food by the breakdown of dead organic matter in the soil

Saprophytic: obtaining food by the breakdown of dead organic matter in the soil

Scabrous: rough to the touch

Scandent: climbing

Secund: facing in one direction

Sessile: without a stalk

Sheath: the lower part of a leaf clasping a stem

Spathulate: spoon-shaped

Spur: a slender, usually hollow, extension of part of a flower, usually the lip but in *Disa,* formed from the dorsal sepal

Staminode: an infertile or rudimentary stamen

Stigma: the part of the column that receives pollen

Stipe or stipes (pl. stipites): a stalk joining the pollinium to the viscidium

Stolon: a running stem that forms roots

Terete: cylindrical; circular in cross-section

Truncate: ending abruptly as if chopped off

Tuberculate: covered with small, wartlike protuberances

Umbellate: forming an umbel

Verrucose: warty

Villous: covered with long, weak hairs

Viscidium (pl. viscidia): a sticky disc attached to a pollinium

Bibliography

Adams, P. B., ed. 1988. *Reproductive Biology of Species Orchids.* Orchid Species Society of Victoria & School of Botany, University of Melbourne, Australia.

Aiton, W. T. 1810–1813. *Hortus Kewensis.* 2nd ed. London.

American Orchid Society. 1995. *Handbook on Orchid Pests and Diseases.* Rev. ed. American Orchid Society, Palm Beach, Florida.

Arditti, J. 1994a. Lewis Knudson: plant physiologist and orchidologist. *Proceedings of the 14th World Orchid Conference,* 361–367.

_____, ed. 1994b. *Orchid Biology: Reviews and Perspectives, VI.* John Wiley, New York.

Arends, J. C., and J. Stewart. 1989. *Aerangis gracillima:* A definitive account of a rare African orchid of Cameroon and Gabon. *Lindleyana* 4(1): 23–29.

Ball, J. S. 1978. *Southern African Epiphytic Orchids.* Conservation Press, Johannesburg.

Bechtel, H., P. J. Cribb, and E. Launert. 1992. *Manual of Cultivated Orchid Species.* 3rd ed. Blandford Press, London.

Chapman, J. D., and F. White. 1970. *The Evergreen Forests of Malawi.* Commonwealth Forestry Institute, Oxford.

Christensen. 1994. In *Orchid Biology: Reviews and Perspectives, VI,* ed. J. Arditti. John Wiley, New York.

Compton, R. H. 1976. The flora of Swaziland. *Journal of South African Botany,* supplementary volume 11: 1–684.

Cribb, P. J. 1978. Studies in the genus *Polystachya* (Orchidaceae) in Africa. *Kew Bulletin* 32: 743–766.

_____. 1984. Orchidaceae. In *Flora of East Tropical Africa,* vol. 2. Balkema, Rotterdam.

_____. 1989. Orchidaceae. In *Flora of East Tropical Africa,* part 3. Balkema, Rotterdam.

_____. 1997. Orchidaceae. In *Flora of Ethiopia.*

Cribb, P. J., and J. M. Fay. 1987. Orchids of the Central African Republic—a provisional checklist. *Kew Bulletin* 42(3): 711–737.

Cribb, P. J., and F. Perez-Vera. 1975. A contribution to the study of the *Orchidaceae* of the Cote d'Ivoire. *Adansonia,* ser. 2, 15(2): 199–214.

Cribb, P. J., and J. Stewart. 1985. Additions to the orchid flora of tropical Africa. *Kew Bulletin* 40(2): 399–419.

Cywes, S. 1994. The latest in *Disa* breeding. *Proceedings of the 14th World Orchid Conference,* 337–341.

Cywes, S., and M. Cywes. 1992. Disas—a hundred years of hybridising. *Orchid Review* 100: 113–118.

Dowsett, R. J., and F. Dowsett-Lemaire. 1991. *Flore et Faune du Bassin du Kouilou (Congo) et leur Exploitation.* Tauraco Research Report No. 4, Belgium.

Dressler, R. L. 1981. *The Orchids: Natural History and Classification.* Harvard University Press, Cambridge, Massachusetts. 2nd ed., 1990.

_____. 1993. *Phylogeny and Classification of the Orchid Family.* Dioscorides Press, Portland, Oregon.

Exell, A. W. 1944. *Catalogue of the Vascular Plants of São Tomé.* British Museum.

Fay, M. F. 1994. The scientific basis of orchid culture media and new developments in the field. *Proceedings of the 14th World Orchid Conference,* 368–372.

Frosch, W. 1994. Asymbiotic propagation of European orchids. *Proceedings of the 14th World Orchid Conference,* 334–336.

Garay, L. A. 1973. Systematics of the genus *Angraecum* (Orchidaceae). *Kew Bulletin* 28: 495–516.

Garay, L. A., F. Hamer, and E. S. Siegerist. 1994. The genus *Cirrhopetalum* and the genera of the *Bulbophyllum* alliance. *Nordic Journal of Botany* 14: 609–646.

Garay, L. A., and R. Sweet. 1974. *Orquideologia* 9:206.

Garay, L. A., and P. Taylor. 1976. The genus *Oeceoclades. Botanical Museum Leaflets, Harvard University* 24: 249–274.

Geerinck, D. 1984, 1992. *Flore d'Afrique Centrale, Orchidaceae.* 2 vols. Belgium.

Hall, A. V. 1982. A revision of the southern African species of *Satyrium. Contributions from the Bolus Herbarium* 10: 1–142.

Harrison, E. R. 1981. *Epiphytic Orchids of Southern Africa.* 2nd ed. Natal Branch of the Wildlife Protection and Conservation Society of South Africa, Durban.

Hillerman, F. E. 1990. *A Culture Manual for Aerangis Orchid Growers.* Hillerman, California.

_____.1992. *A Culture Manual for Angraecoid Orchid Growers.* Hillerman, California.

_____.1994. Hybridizing angraecoids. *American Orchid Society Bulletin* 63 (8): 890–895.

Hillerman, F. E., and A. W. Holst. 1986. *An Introduction to the Cultivated Angraecoid Orchids of Madagascar.* Timber Press, Portland, Oregon.

Hooker, J. D. 1886. *Disa atropurpurea. Curtis's Botanical Magazine,* t. 6891.

_____. 1989. *Disa lacera. Curtis's Botanical Magazine,* t. 7066.

Jones, K. 1967. The chromosomes of orchids, 2. *Vandae* Lindl. *Kew Bulletin* 21: 151–156.

_____. 1974. Cytology and the study of orchids. In *The Orchids: Scientific Studies,* ed. C. L. Withner. John Wiley, New York. 383–408.

Jonsson, L. 1981. A monograph of the genus *Microcoelia* (Orchidaceae). *Symbolae Botanicae Upsaliensis* 23(4).

Kemp, E. S. 1983. *A Flora Checklist for Swaziland.* Swaziland National Trust Commission.

Kurzweil, H. 1994. The unusual seeds of the *Disa uniflora* group, with notes on their dispersal. *Proceedings of the 14th World Orchid Conference,* 397–399.

la Croix, I. F., and P. J. Cribb. 1995. *Flora Zambesiaca.* Orchidaceae, part 1.

_____. In press. *Flora Zambesiaca.* Orchidaceae, part 2.

la Croix, I. F., E. A. S. la Croix, and T. M. la Croix. 1991. *Orchids of Malawi.* Balkema, Rotterdam.

la Croix, I. F., E. A. S. la Croix, T. M. la Croix, J. A. Hutson, and N. G. B. Johnston-Stewart. 1983. *Orchids of Malawi,* Vol. 1, *Epiphytes.* NFPS, Blantyre, Malawi.

Linder, H. P. 1981a. Taxonomic studies on the Disinae: 1. A revision of the genus *Brownleea* Lindley. *Journal of South African Botany* 47(1): 13–48.

_____. 1981b. Taxonomic studies on the Disinae: 3. A revision of *Disa* Bergius excluding section *Micranthae* Lindley. *Contributions from the Bolus Herbarium* 9: 1–370.

_____. 1981c. Taxonomic studies on the Disinae: 4. A revision of *Disa* Bergius section *Micranthae* Lindley. *Bulletin du Jardin Botanique National de Belgique* 51: 255–346.

_____. 1981d. Taxonomic studies on the Disinae: 6. A revision of the genus *Herschelia* Lindley. *Bothalia* 13: 365–368.

_____. 1989. Notes on southern African angraecoid orchids. *Kew Bulletin* 44(2): 31–319.

Linder, H. P., and H. Kurzweil. 1995. Taxonomic notes on the African *Orchidoideae* (Orchidaceae): a new genus and combination. *Willdenowia* 25: 229–234.

Mabberley, D. J. 1987. *The Plant-Book.* Cambridge University Press, Oxford.

McDonald, G. 1995. The genus *Stenoglottis* in South Africa. *South African Orchid Journal* 26(4): 115–119.

McGough, N. 1993. The application of CITES to orchid trade. *Orchid Review* 101: 156–157.

Moriarty, A. 1975. *Wild Flowers of Malawi.* Purnell, Cape Town, South Africa.

Morris, B. 1970. *The Epiphytic Orchids of Malawi.* The Society of Malawi, Blantyre.

Morton, J. K. 1961. *West African Lilies and Orchids.* Longman, London.

Northen, R. 1975. *Orchids as House Plants.* Rev. ed. Dover Publication, New York.

_____. 1990. *Home Orchid Growing.* 4th ed. Prentice Hall Press, New York.

Pettersson, B. 1985. The etymology of the generic name *Disa* Bergius (Orchidaceae). *Taxon* 34(3): 457–461.

Piers, F. 1968. *Orchids of East Africa.* J. Cramer, Lehre.

Podzorski, A. C., and P. J. Cribb. 1979. A revision of *Polystachya* section *Cultriformes* (Orchidaceae). *Kew Bulletin* 34: 147–186.

Ramsay, M., J. Stewart, and G. Prendergast. 1994. Conserving endangered British orchids. *Proceedings of the 14th World Orchid Conference,* 176–179.

Robbins, S. 1990. *Bonatea steudneri,* a new record of an orchid in Saudi Arabia. *Orchid Review* 9(98): 298–300.

Roberts, A. 1986a. Hybridizing and making a glove box. *American Orchid Society Bulletin* 55(8): 820–821.

_____. 1986b. Making a clean air station. *American Orchid Society Bulletin* 55(9): 924–925.

Rolfe, R. A. 1897–1898. Orchidaceae. In *Flora of Tropical Africa,* vol 7. Ed. W. T. Thistleton-Dyer. London.

_____. 1912. The evolution of the Orchidaceae. *Orchid Review* 17–20.

Schelpe, E. A. 1966. *An Introduction to the South African Orchids.* MacDonald, London.

Segerbäck, L. B. 1983. *Orchids of Nigeria.* Balkema, Rotterdam.

Senghas, K. 1986. In *Die Orchideen,* Schlechter. 3rd ed. 1:110.

Stewart, J. 1979. A revision of the African species of *Aerangis* (Orchidaceae). *Kew Bulletin* 32: 239–319.

_____. 1989. The genus *Stenoglottis. Kew Magazine* 6(1): 9–22.

Stewart, J., and B. Campbell. 1970. *Orchids of Tropical Africa.* W. H. Allen, London.

_____. 1996. *Orchids of Kenya.* Timber Press, Portland, Oregon.

Stewart, J., and E. F. Hennessy. 1981. *Orchids of Africa.* Macmillan, Johannesburg, South Africa.

Stewart, J., and I. F. la Croix. 1987. Notes on the orchids of southern tropical Africa 3: *Aerangis. Kew Bulletin* 42: 215–219.

Stewart, J., H. P. Linder, E. A. Schelpe, and A. V. Hall. 1982. *Wild Orchids of Southern Africa.* Macmillan, Johannesburg.

Summerhayes, V. S. 1943. A revision of *Microcoelia* Lindley. African Orchids 13. *Botanical Museum Leaflets,* Harvard University, 11(5): 137–170.

_____. 1944. *Ancistrorhynchus* Finet. *Botanical Museum Leaflets,* Harvard University.

_____. 1948. *Tridactyle* Schltr. *Kew Bulletin* 2: 281–301.

_____. 1949. African orchids 19. *Kew Bulletin* 4: 427–443.

_____. 1960a. *Diaphananthe* Schltr. and *Rhipidoglossum* Schltr. *Kew Bulletin* 14: 139–143.

_____. 1960b. *Cyrtorchis* Schltr. *Kew Bulletin* 14: 143–156.

_____. 1968a. Orchidaceae. In *Flora of West Tropical Africa,* vol. 2. Ed. F. N. Hepper. Crown Agents, London.

_____. 1968b. Orchidaceae. In *Flora of East Tropical Africa,* vol. 1. Eds. E. Milne-Redhead and R. M. Polhill. Crown Agents, London.

Thompson, P. A. 1977. *Orchids from Seed.* Royal Botanic Gardens, Kew.

Townsend, D. A. 1995. An introduction to *Polystachya,* species, hybridisation to date, and culture. *South African Orchid Journal* 26(3): 101–104.

van der Laan, F. M., and P. J. Cribb. 1986. *Ossiculum* (Orchidaceae), a new genus from Cameroon. *Kew Bulletin* 41(4): 823–832.

Vermeulen, J. J. 1987. A taxonomic revision of the continental African Bulbophyllinae. *Orchid Monographs* 2: 1–300. E. J. Brill, Leiden.

Vogelpoel, L. 1985. *Disa uniflora, Its Propagation and Cultivation.* Disa Orchid Society of South Africa, Cape Town.

————. 1987–1989. New horizons in *Disa* breeding. *Orchid Review* 95 (June, July, August); 96 (January, February, April, May, August); 97 (April, June, July).

————. 1991–1992. *Disa* hybridization in the western Cape—current status and future prospects. Parts 1–5. *South African Orchid Journal* 22 (December); 23 (March, June, September, December).

————. 1993a. A cultural calendar for disas. *South African Orchid Journal* 24: 37–40.

————. 1993b. The blue disas. Part I, blue *Disa* species. *South African Orchid Journal* 24(3): 67–68

————. 1993c. The blue disas. Part II, the blue *Herschelianthes. South African Orchid Journal* 24(4): 101.

————. 1994a. *Meneris tulbaghia*—the exclusive pollinator and breeder of *Disa uniflora* and *Disa ferruginea. South African Orchid Journal* 25(3): 85–90.

————. 1994b. Growing *Herschelianthes. South African Orchid Journal* 25(2): 62–65.

————, ed. 1995. *Disa Awards.* Disa Orchid Society of South Africa, Cape Town.

Walter, H., and H. Lieth. 1960–1967. *Klimadiagramm-Weltatlas.* Jena, Fischer.

Warren, R. 1991. Aseptic seed collection. *Orchid Review* 99: 28–32.

White, F. 1983. *The Vegetation of Africa.* UNESCO, Paris.

Williamson, G. 1977. *The Orchids of South Central Africa.* J. M. Dent.

Withner, C. L., ed. 1974. *The Orchids: Scientific Studies.* John Wiley, New York.

Index of Plant Names